PENGUIN BOOKS

CONVERSATIONS WITH MANI RATNAM

Baradwaj Rangan is a National Award–winning film critic, and currently deputy editor at *The Hindu*. His writings on cinema, music, art, books, travel and humour have been published in various national magazines like *Open*, *Tehelka*, *Biblio*, *Outlook* and *Caravan*. He has co-written the screenplay for the Tamil romcom, *Kadhal 2 Kalyanam*. He teaches a course on cinema at the Asian College of Journalism in Chennai.

PRAISE FOR THE BOOK

'In a country where a century of cinematic riches is compromised by the poverty of its archives, *Conversations* feels path-breaking'—*The Financial Express*

'A masterclass in film and who better than Mani Ratnam to take you through the processes of film-making?'—*DNA*

'One of the finest books on Indian cinema ever . . . Rangan's questions are as delightful as Mani Ratnam's answers, given that they are incredibly informed and analytical'—*Outlook*

'A big boon for aspiring actors and screenwriters . . . Amazing insights on how to make the vital connection between the pen and the screen'—*The Hindu*

'A wonderful book . . . The interviews touch on [Ratnam's] experience of growing up in a film family, his influences and then settle down to a fireside chat about his films'—*Hindustan Times*

Conversations with
MANI RATNAM

With a Foreword by
A.R. Rahman

Baradwaj Rangan

PENGUIN BOOKS
An imprint of Penguin Random House

PENGUIN BOOKS

USA | Canada | UK | Ireland | Australia
New Zealand | India | South Africa | China | Singapore

Penguin Books is part of the Penguin Random House group of companies whose addresses can be found at global.penguinrandomhouse.com

Published by Penguin Random House India Pvt. Ltd
4th Floor, Capital Tower 1, MG Road,
Gurugram 122 002, Haryana, India

Penguin Random House India

First published in Viking by Penguin Books India 2012
Published in Penguin Books 2013

Copyright © Baradwaj Rangan 2012, 2013
Foreword copyright © A.R. Rahman 2012
'A Note' copyright © Mani Ratnam
The copyright for the photographs vests with the respective directors or producers of the films.
Page 321 is an extension of the copyright page.

All rights reserved

15 14 13 12

ISBN 9780143421108

Designed by Marina Bang
Printed at Replika Press Pvt. Ltd, India

This book is sold subject to the condition that it shall not, by way of trade or otherwise, be lent, resold, hired out, or otherwise circulated without the publisher's prior consent in any form of binding or cover other than that in which it is published and without a similar condition including this condition being imposed on the subsequent purchaser.

www.penguin.co.in

To Latha, who's surely someplace with
a luminous beach and litres of
dishwashing liquid

Contents

Foreword—A.R. Rahman viii
A Note—Mani Ratnam x
Introduction—Baradwaj Rangan xi
1. *Pallavi Anupallavi, Unaru, Pagal Nilavu, Idhayakoyil* 1
2. *Mouna Raagam* 30
3. *Nayakan* 43
4. *Agni Natchatiram* 67
5. *Geetanjali* 80
6. *Anjali* 89
7. *Thalapathy* 103
8. *Roja* 119
9. *Thiruda Thiruda* 135
10. *Bombay* 144
11. *Iruvar* 161
12. *Dil Se* 181
13. *Alaipaayuthey* 195
14. *Kannathil Muthamittal* 208
15. *Aayidha Ezhuthu/Yuva* 229
16. *Guru* 246
17. *Raavan/Raavanan* 267
18. *Kadal* 288
Filmography and Awards 311
Acknowledgements 319
Copyright Acknowledgements 321
Index 323

Foreword

IN MY TEENS, in the 1980s, I grew up in awe of Hollywood. David Lean, Steven Spielberg, Ridley Scott and film-makers like them. But when I started watching Mani Ratnam's films, my loyalty changed. I saw that this man directed moving and sensitive films that were rooted in my own culture, and they had an almost unreal quality, which made me feel good. What better thing could happen in my life than if this same film-maker, whom I admired from a distance, came asking me to compose music for his next film? I never thought that this would happen.

I met Mani Ratnam while he was planning *Roja*. At that time, I was discovering my Sufi zone and, in many ways, didn't care about failure or success. I was happy and sad, all at the same time. So when he came to me in my modest studio, back in 1990, I didn't want to feel overjoyed, because if he didn't like what I had done, he could throw the music at my face and leave. I was prepared for anything, but things worked out. We worked together closely and made the *Roja* soundtrack with a kind of unique creative energy.

Mani Ratnam, whom we all call 'Mani Sir', became a great friend. He carefully selected the pearls in me and made a garland of them. Until three or four years ago, I would send him every album, like a student seeking his guru's approval. I used to call him and ask him what he thought about almost every song that I composed, whether they were for him or another director. Sometimes he would say, jokingly, 'It's fantastic. Why don't you give it to me?' At other times, he'd say, 'No, it could be better. You could try this, you could try that.'

As the years passed, I realized that he is one of the key people in my life to have triggered my imagination. Gaining knowledge is easy. You can read books. You can learn by working with someone and observing what he does. But very few people push you and say, 'This is not good enough; you can go much further.' His advice never made you feel like a subordinate but sounded more like encouragement from a friend. That's a great quality in him. He's not like a teacher, but like a co-worker and co-creator—someone exploring ideas with you. As we worked together over the years, we discovered many things. We knew, for example, that we needed a track like *Humma humma* in order to include a song like *Kehna hi kya*, because a film's soundtrack cannot sell on melody alone. That's something we came to understand—the mixed moods that an album has to offer.

When you're in the movies, people respect you so much. Even your family can start regarding you differently. You can get it all, and you could lose it. Suddenly the ground beneath your feet could disappear and you could fall, and people could move away. Very few people value the real you. Most people value a side of you, which is more or less false. With Mani Sir, even if you fall out of favour with the box office, he sees you for what and who you are, and respects you in much the same way that he always had. He has the same attitude towards actors, cameramen and all the people he works with. That's a great quality, and in my experience, few have this quality.

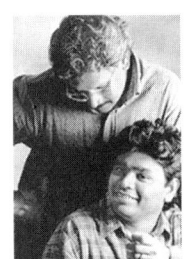

In the journey of exploring art, allowing one to make mistakes in one's work is very important. It makes one grow creatively. It needs courage. Some directors are very successful making the same kind of film, but in the long run we do not respect them as much. Here's a man who wanted his style of stories to have commercial success, yet unafraid to sometimes fail. And because of that, he has kept growing from film to film.

Though a lot has changed now, people here in India had a different mentality from those in the West those days. Not many people here wanted to push themselves in order to excel at something. They were satisfied with okay stuff. So I really, really respect people like Mani Sir who had raised the bar here, in those conditions with our limited resources and technological talent.

I think it's great that Mani Ratnam has spoken to Baradwaj Rangan about his work and in so much detail. One of my friends has taught me an Italian word, *sprezzatura*, which refers to making the most complex thing look simple and easily doable. While other creators make a big show of their art, Mani Sir makes it look as if anyone can do what he does. Though it's really not that simple. There's so much thinking, craft and sensitivity that goes into his work. I am still seduced by portions of his work in *Iruvar, Nayakan, Dil Se, Guru, Bombay* and his latest offering *Kadal*.

I try to be a man of faith. And here is a man who's an atheist by choice. We coexist as opposites. When I have a problem, I think that tomorrow will be better; that's because of my faith in spirituality. But what does he do? I wonder about this. But what connects us is the humanity in him and his movies. Personal tragedies in the past had demotivated him a little and slowed him down. But he was strong enough to survive it. It is difficult for me to say whether I admire him more as a film-maker or as a person.

A.R. RAHMAN

A Note

THERE ARE TWO THINGS that bother a film-maker. One, when he is offered a lifetime achievement award. The second is when he is asked to do a book on his films. Both invariably mean that the sell-by date is round the corner, or worse, that it has passed. While I have tried avoiding both sincerely, at some point you have to stop and turn and face it squarely.

A book on his work gives the film-maker a chance to intellectualize what was once an instinctive decision. You rationalize, make it look more profound, argue your case and sometimes answer a few critics who anyway were not interested in your side of the case. So it becomes a bit of offence and a bit of defence, the intellectual dressing of babies—finding a possible, probable, or hopeful reason for the action/decision. Maybe it is true, maybe not so true.

It is also a chance to be brutally honest, to be yourself and let your films remain what they are. To try and relive and share the process as much as memories allow you to. Memories are not totally trustworthy. They tend to colour things favourably.

I often find it very difficult to watch my own films. Five minutes in, and I start seeing only mistakes, and I desperately wish that I can correct them somehow. Reliving all my films in this book, from the earliest to the most recent, coming face to face with each one, back to back, was a bit like going to the psychiatrist for therapy.

As I sit down to write this note, even as I struggle to get ready for my next shoot, I realize that, at the beginning, when I started my first film, if someone had offered me these twenty-odd films as my body of work up to this point, I would have accepted them happily. But now that I have struggled and toiled my way here, when I look back, I tend to take the good parts for granted, and look at the rest of it and wonder: if only . . .

MANI RATNAM

Introduction

SOME MONTHS AFTER I began working on this book, after the initially awkward and nervous meetings with Mani Ratnam had steadied into reasonably confident conversations, I ran into the director Gautham Vasudev Menon. We talked about this and that, the generalities that unite two professionals plying their trades at opposing ends of the cinematic spectrum—him the maker, me the masticator—and then, for some reason, I told him about the book and about meeting Mani Ratnam for the first time in his office at Madras Talkies, where he spoke to me and I spoke to the table in front of him. Instantly—and if only for that instant—Menon and I were bonded in a secret brotherhood. He laughed and said he wasn't surprised. He had done the same thing when a hero he'd sought out for a project had dispatched him to Mani Ratnam's office to narrate the screenplay. 'I couldn't look at him,' Menon said. 'I mean, how *can* you? He's the man who made *Nayakan*.'

PERHAPS ACKNOWLEDGING THE POWERFUL SEDUCTIONS of the cinema, almost every city, at some point, has had a movie hall named Eros. The one in Madras was on LB Road, on a plot that, today, houses a shiny showroom for the kind of foreign car that people those days could drive only in their dreams. But even in the early nineteen-eighties, when pachydermal Ambassadors lumbered down roads too tiny to contain them, Eros was crumbling. A faded art-deco façade opened out to an absurd excuse for a snack counter, with pre-sealed packs of popcorn and cloudy glass jars stocked with palm-sized packets of roasted gram speckled with an evil-looking spice. Inside, where air conditioning would have necessitated a drastic revision of the ticket price of two-something rupees, the task of circulation was entrusted to fans, drooping from the ceiling on long stems and pressed reluctantly into service, like a napping child roused and ordered to fetch a bunch of bananas from the stall down the street.

I bring these things up not to wade in nostalgia for an India that bears little resemblance to the country today, whose cities boast the biggest of buildings with the finest of facilities. I bring this up because–despite the stale snacks, despite the strangulating heat, despite handed-down prints that flickered as if possessed by the ghosts of a thousand previous projectors—this long-dead theatre will never die in my memories. This is where, in 1985, I saw my first Mani Ratnam movie. It was *Idhayakoyil*, the director's fourth film, and the one that he considers his worst. I saw it three times.

I wish I could say that I recognized, before anyone else, a titanic talent submerged under the wreck of this melodrama about thwarted eros, with a singer pining for a long-dead love (who will never die in his memories) and spurning the young woman who falls for him. But the reasons for my repeat viewings were probably the presence of Ilaiyaraaja's marvellous music and the absence of 24-hour TV, which meant that instead of flipping through channels and landing on a movie we felt like watching, we went to the theatres next door and saw the movies that were showing, like *Pagal Nilavu*, which Mani Ratnam had made earlier. This time, too, the earth didn't move. But the release of *Mouna Raagam*, the next year, brought to Madras some mild tremors, which, by the director's next movie, *Nayakan*, intensified into a full-blown quake that reshaped the landscape of Tamil cinema.

Even today, twenty-five years after the release of *Nayakan*, some of us remember our experience of the film as if we'd unknowingly stepped into the competition ring at a village fair and ended up flattened by the local wrestler. We couldn't move, we couldn't speak—during the film and even afterwards, as we lurched back home in a late-evening bus, too stunned to slip into the genial ritual of post-movie analysis, too numbed by the serendipitous shock of stumbling into a moment that would forever alter our expectations of Tamil cinema. We knew we could no longer resign ourselves to perfunctory cinematography and tinsel-strewn sets and an incestuous ethos birthed from Tamil films over the years. We knew, now, that we could not only dream about international standards of filmic achievement but also attain them. Today, a quarter of a century older, I realize that we may have overestimated Mani Ratnam and undervalued the impact of the pioneers before him on Tamil cinema, but such is the impetuousness of adolescence. The body blow dealt by the film drove out reasoning and rationality. What was left was pure physical sensation.

AT THIS POINT, I suppose, I should define 'we'. I refer to people like me, born in Madras in the nineteen-seventies and ripening into cinematic awareness in the decade that followed, in Mani Ratnam's decade. We are possibly the most qualified to write about Mani Ratnam. We might also be the least qualified. Others, born in earlier and later decades, did not feel his impact the way we did, but they, shorn of our hyperbolic adoration, are probably better equipped to pin down his place in the

Tamil-cinema continuum. We couldn't—because to us he wasn't just a film-maker, and he didn't just make films. *Mouna Raagam* onwards (and with the grand exceptions of *Nayakan* and *Thalapathy*, which wove riffs around the adult experience), he was a zeitgeist-defining showman who propped up in front of us mirrors into our selves—our young, urban selves. No one, just no one, had put on screen what we thought, what we felt, what we dreamed the way Mani Ratnam did.

Mani Ratnam was certainly not the first film-maker who animated his films with the lifeblood of the young. During the course of these conversations, he revealed that he grew up in thrall to the taboo-splintering dramas of K. Balachander, so attuned to the rebellions of youth, and before KB, there were directors like Sridhar who, in the nineteen-sixties, bequeathed a youthful exuberance to films like *Kaadhalikka Neramillai*, a two-and-a-half-hour romantic romp, which belied a title that sighed that there was no time for love. But, among other things, the girls in Sridhar's movie threatened to burst out of salwar kameezes glued to their zaftig frames. This enslavement to voluptuousness was our parents' youth, not ours. Our fantasies were forged over visions of a sylphlike Amala in a pink sleeveless top, swaying to music from her Walkman, as the backlighting bestowed on her an entirely warranted urban-goddess aura—and if there's another artifact of pop culture that hotwired itself into the very being of the Tamil youth the way *Agni Natchatiram* did, I'm not aware of it. Call it solipsism, call it tunnel vision—I call it the unvarnished truth.

The sun that you saw in the opening credits of that film, scudding through clouds into a clear sky and blinding the screen with its brilliance—there was no better visual metaphor for the Mani Ratnam of the era. He was dazzling us with the trail he was blazing, and we were the first to see the light. Just as words bind themselves better to pristine parchment than to palimpsests, his images sank into our souls. (The older generation, having watched a lot more cinema, and having weathered a lot more trailblazing in the movies, was more guarded about welcoming Mani Ratnam, as if to embrace him would be to wallow in the shallow pools of youthful faddishness. It was a while before they realized that Mani Ratnam was no fad, that he was here to stay, and that he would go on, after *Roja*, to make the kind of movies that *they* wanted him to make, and that, in a sense, he'd become *them*.) Hence my claim that no one knows—or feels about—Mani Ratnam the way we do.

THAT SCENE IN *Agni Natchatiram* where Harold Faltermeyer's theme for *Beverly Hills Cop* bounces off the walls as Amala and her girlfriends anticipate their first taste of nicotine with stolen cigarettes—that was us. That was the garish synth music that blared from our two-in-ones. That was the forbidden-forest fascination that cigarettes held for us. Mani Ratnam didn't judge smoking—and if this made him irresponsible in the eyes of the grown-ups, it only made him cooler to us. Most film-makers, then, were adults who'd left their youth far behind, and their portrayals of the young harked back to their times. Mani Ratnam, on the other hand, seemed to be one of *us*, someone who, in front of his parents, would pore over cyclostyled sheets from Brilliant Tutorials over late-night cups of tea from a thermos—only, hidden in those impenetrable thickets of IIT problems would be a comic book or a much-thumbed copy of *Debonair* magazine. With his depiction of the youngsters in *Agni Natchatiram* and the films that followed, he seemed to completely *get* us.

He seemed to get that school isn't all that it's cracked up to be when the youngest sister in *Mouna Raagam* wanted Revathy to get married on a weekday so she could bunk classes. He seemed to get that virginity isn't all that it's cracked up to be when he unleashed a waggish scene in *Agni Natchatiram* with an unmarried Nirosha walking into Karthik's house and confessing, in the presence of his comically horrified family, to being pregnant. He seemed to get that respecting elders isn't all that it's cracked up to be when the little girl in *Anjali*, in the midst of a heated family argument on the building's staircase, urges her father to shout back and silence the bald neighbour asking them to take their dirty laundry indoors. (A mere translation does little justice to the level of disrespect in her choice of phrase: '*Saridhaan poda, sotta thalayaa.*' Get lost, baldie!) He seemed to get that happily-ever-after isn't all that it's cracked up to be when he had Nirosha reveal, in *Agni Natchatiram*, that the older man she was dining with wasn't her father but her mother's second husband, while her biological father lived someplace else with his second wife. He seemed to get that idealism isn't all that it's cracked up to be when, again in *Agni Natchatiram*, Karthik, desperate to locate Nirosha's address using the numbers on the licence plate of her car, qualmlessly bribes a clerk at the transport office.

But it wasn't just the subversive excitement of raising the middle finger to the establishment. Mani Ratnam's early cinema, simultaneously, had its feet planted on the unshakeable ground of that very establishment. Prabhu, in *Agni Natchatiram*, was an Assistant Commissioner of Police. We were being told that it could be a nice thing, a *cool* thing even (with those Aviator sunglasses), to serve the government—that it wasn't just about becoming an engineer or a doctor or a chartered accountant, which is what our parents, mired in middle-class mores, wanted for us. In the same film, Mani Ratnam had Vijayakumar, the IAS officer, in a dhoti all through, and showed us, long before P. Chidambaram began dropping into our living rooms on national television, that you could make a quiet statement with four yards of crisp, starched cotton—that it wasn't always about slacks and shirts and a tie dropping from the collar. He had Revathy travel in a local bus in *Anjali* and he made the youngsters take local trains in *Agni Natchatiram* and showed us that public transport wasn't beneath our dignity—that you didn't become any less because you didn't zip around town on a moped or in a car like the rich kids.

AND AS IF UNDERSTANDING that lessons secreted into entertainment are more likely to animate those of us in schools and colleges than well-meaning words of wisdom from tired teachers, Mani Ratnam had Kiran Vairale in *Pallavi Anupallavi* migrate to the US to pursue an MS in Biochemistry (a first in Indian cinema, perhaps), and showed us that you needed to chase your dreams—that it didn't matter if you had a girlfriend or boyfriend back home. Unlike what our parents kept telling us, settling down could wait. This, incidentally, was Mani Ratnam's first film, and it's remarkable how it contains hints of all the themes and tropes we associate with the director today. The protagonist leaving his comfort zone and accosting an alien reality. The woman's plight after marriage. The child with a single parent. The knottiness inherent in urban relationships. The rebelliousness and also the touching confusion of the youth. The mastery over the emotional canvas of the middle class. The daughter's backslapping equation with her father. Expertly directed child actors with formidable lung power. The girlfriend's wisecracking rapport with the boyfriend that's founded on an utter disdain for conventional mawkishness, cute but never cloying. Heroines without heavy make-up. A predilection for earth colours and ethnic Indian design. *Pallavi Anupallavi* has it all.

Above all these things, it was just this feel for middle-class Madras life—beyond travel-story-ready clichés like filter coffee and idlis and Kanjeevaram saris and peanut vendors at the Marina—that Mani Ratnam displayed in his early films. (That is surely why these films flopped when transported to generic anycities in their Hindi remakes.) If Bharathiraja carried Tamil cinema out of the studios and planted it amidst the paddy fields of the rural South, Mani Ratnam steered it back to the streets of Madras. He told us, in *Agni Natchatiram*, that if you visited the Egmore railway station at night, you could run into pretty girls exiting the train compartments in midis and shorts. He knew that Adyar was a tonier neighbourhood and West Mambalam more middle class, so when Vijayakumar's wife from Adyar signs her name on a bail application form at the police station, it's in English, while the other wife, the one from West Mambalam, the middle-class wife, writes out her name in painstaking Tamil.

That's why, to those of us who grew up in the nineteen-eighties, *Agni Natchatiram* isn't just a silly—though supremely well executed—masala movie, but the quintessential

Madras Movie. Because if you look at the big picture, it certainly doesn't say anything *important*—except, perhaps, that Amala could really carry off a leotard. And it certainly doesn't feature those other things—invisible craftsmanship, soul-rattling performances—that are widely regarded as imperatives for great cinema. But the film belonged to us in a way no other film had until then, in a way no other film has until now. It was the ultimate hanging-out movie, the equivalent of an inconsequential couple of hours spent with buddies—your Tamil-speaking buddies, who uncomplainingly sat beside you in theatres like Eros. It left you with the satisfaction that life's all good, as did *Geetanjali*, which came next. So it didn't matter that Mani Ratnam went ahead and cast a non-star named Raghuvaran as the protagonist in *Anjali*. Because for us, the real hero was the director. It was Mani Ratnam.

THIS WAS HOW WE anticipated *Roja*. We—the audience that grew up on Mani Ratnam, who came of cinematic age with his films—smiled as Arvind Swamy reduced his unsuspecting villager-bride to a coughing wreck by sticking a cigarette between her lips. We smiled when he said he wasn't all that bad a person, that there was some good in him as well, and that she should give him a chance. Then they made up and went to Kashmir—husband and wife—and we laughed when she broke open a coconut in the temple and the pistol-crack attracted a few alarmed soldiers. (What a wonderfully offhand, almost *casual*, nod to the tension in the region.) Then Arvind Swamy got kidnapped, and the film morphed into something we weren't expecting. Hitherto unseen shades of the Mani Ratnam protagonist—young, urban, reasonably privileged; in short, like us, and probably like Mani Ratnam himself—were beginning to emerge. For instance, an engagement with national sentiment (as opposed to matters of Madras), while A.R. Rahman's chorus from *Thamizha Thamizha* thundered on the soundtrack, like the urgent voice of Mother India herself.

Arvind Swamy *looked* like the Mani Ratnam heroes from earlier, but something was changing in him, as probably in Mani Ratnam himself. Both appeared to have broken out of the Madras Movies ghetto. And at least in the first viewing, this sense of *betrayal* was a little difficult to digest. Mani Ratnam, who seemed to have been put on this planet to make movies for us, now seemed to be making a movie for grown-ups, whom we saw as fundamentally joyless creatures lashed to joyless routines, beginning with coffee and headlines from *The Hindu*. Today, as one of those grown-ups, I think I know why we flinched so melodramatically when we saw *Roja*, why the film seemed like a personal affront. *Mouna Raagam* onwards, Mani Ratnam's cinema was either married faithfully to our young, urban, Madras ethos, or else, like *Nayakan* and *Thalapathy*, completely divorced from it. Even if the characters left Madras for other cities, like Revathy in *Mouna Raagam*, they never lost their youthfulness, their urbanity, their innate Madras-ness. (Even the dubbed-from-Telugu version of *Geetanjali*, which came to our theatres as *Idhayathai Thirudaathey*, was essentially a Madras Movie.)

And here, in *Roja*, we were promised a Madras Movie at the beginning, with all the coolness and the irreverence, the lightness of touch that deflated heavy-weather situations to tempests in tea cups, and a protagonist who, like some of us, cracked crosswords in the bathroom. But midway, we were left stranded in an alien land as bewildering to us as Bombay was to Kamal Haasan in *Nayakan*, and Delhi was to Revathy in *Mouna Raagam*. Some sort of cosmic joke was being perpetrated. We, so adoring of Mani Ratnam, had finally found ourselves in our own Mani Ratnam movie, and it was far from the answer to fervent prayers. The exaggerated sense of betrayal, I now realize, stemmed from our selfish desire for Mani Ratnam to keep making Madras Movies—because no one else was capable of making them, and if he stopped, what would we do, whom would we worship?

ROJA MARKED THE END of the Madras Movie phase that began with *Mouna Raagam* (which makes it somewhat ironic, in our eyes, that Mani Ratnam's production house, today, bears the name Madras Talkies), the end of making specifically urban-looking, urban-feeling, urban-voiced movies for urban Tamils. The Mani Ratnam hero, like us, could no longer afford to keep looking inwards—and as we grew up and assumed responsibilities, so did he. In *Bombay*, as in *Roja*, he set out to work in a faraway state and saw what the rest of the country was like. He got married in *Alaipaayuthey* and *Kannathil Muthamittal*, and discovered what life was like at the other end of the light-hearted romantic tracks of *Agni Natchatiram* and *Geetanjali*. He plunged into politics in *Iruvar*. He was trapped by a terrorist in *Dil Se*. He worried about where the nation was going in *Aayidha Ezhuthu/Yuva*. Even the movies set in Madras, after *Roja*, radiated outwards, circling areas of ever-larger interests. The duo in *Iruvar* looked towards ruling the state. The couple in *Kannathil Muthamittal* looked even farther, to another land of Tamils.

Post-*Roja*, Mani Ratnam did cook up locally flavoured movies for Tamil audiences, like *Thiruda Thiruda*. But a thrilling vastness had invaded his vision. The Mani Ratnam of the Madras Movies phase may have made an *Alaipaayuthey*, but he may not have conceived an *Iruvar*, a *Kannathil Muthamittal*, whose narratives flow freely between the personal and the political. So while some of us, from Madras, saw Tamil cinema as pre-*Nayakan* and post-*Nayakan*, Mani Ratnam's career is one that pivots around *Roja*. Pre-*Roja*, he spoke to us. Post-*Roja*, he speaks to us and to everyone else. He speaks, in *Dil Se* and *Bombay*, about the rents in our national fabric. He speaks about (and to) the youth of the nation in *Aayidha Ezhuthu/Yuva*. He speaks, in *Guru*, not so much about a man who lived, as a nation that was. He speaks of marginalized peoples in *Raavan(an)*. An interesting thought experiment with the latter, derived from the Ramayana, would be a contrast with *Thalapathy*, drawn from the Mahabharata during the Madras Movies days. *Thalapathy* exists in a world of golden sunsets, unclouded by political climate. *Raavan(an)*, on the other hand, unfolds in the midst of disillusioned tribals prone to making points through kidnappings ripped from our headlines.

The last two films from the post-Madras Movies phase—*Guru* and *Raavan(an)*—aren't my favourite Mani Ratnam movies, but they're still worthwhile instances of how to graft extremely personal concerns into extravagantly commercial films. Mani Ratnam is a flamboyant film-maker whose films, too often, are accused of being nothing but strung-together pretty pictures, or worse, extended ad films, as if to employ and exploit the full scope of a visual medium were some sort of mortal sin, and the only true cinema is one that's shot on shabby sets with the cast shivering in a single set of clothes. That is surely the aspect that sets Mani Ratnam apart from most other auteurs, who either forsake songs and dances and entertainment altogether in their telling of stark stories, or lock themselves into ivory-tower visions rewarding only to the truly devoted.

Mani Ratnam is one of the few mainstream film-makers from India—and I refer to those with a wholesome *Indian* sensibility, harking back to *Indian* directors from earlier decades—who has not made a mockery of the middle path, which, as with Buddhism, is a path of moderation, between the extremes of moviemaking solely for pleasure and moviemaking as penance. Even those who dislike Mani Ratnam's films will concede that these are not failures of vision or ambition, that they begin to falter (if at all) only when marketplace compromises reveal themselves. At least on a screenplay level, these films are textbook-ready examples of how to marry what you want to do with what the audience may be willing to accept. Would Mani Ratnam be a better film-maker if he ignored the market altogether, if he renounced commercial compulsions and began to pursue an austere cinema? The question, to me, is redundant, because Mani Ratnam does not *want* to go there. He wants to make movies that great numbers of people can enjoy, without besmirching entertainment with the taint of pandering. Sometimes he wins. Sometimes he loses.

WITH *RAAVAN*, HE LOST BADLY. The film opened to hysterical reviews up north, some of which suggested, condescendingly, that he return to making films in Tamil. (In other words, it was just us, earlier, who wanted Mani Ratnam back so he could continue making Madras Movies, and now *they* were saying the same thing.) The box-office business wasn't heartening either. And yet, it's *Raavan* that made this book possible—rather, my considered review that proffered the positives alongside the negatives. Suddenly my publishers, who had been talking to me for years (despite my swatting aside, like irksome mosquitoes, every idea they came up with), had a proposal I could not say no to. And I said yes for two reasons, first as a man of science, then as a man of faith. I wanted to embalm in amber the fingerprints of a film-maker who is, in a sense, a dinosaur, one of the last of a dying breed in India: the mainstream auteur. Secondly, I was intrigued by the opportunity to record the deliverances of a film-maker who was, at some point to some of us, a golden god.

Appropriately enough, the office that Mani Ratnam occupies is situated in the highest floor of Madras Talkies. There is no elevator. Like any true believer, anywhere else, you have to climb flights of stairs to reach the sanctum sanctorum. I was there to tell him I was going to write a book about his films. We live in the same city, after all. It was just basic courtesy. I got his email address from one of his assistants and shot him a note about wanting to meet. Almost instantly, I received in my inbox a response as laconic as the dialogue in his Madras Movies. He said: 'Hello, Would Monday noon at my office suit you?' At that point, my book was going to go through each of his films, one per chapter, a mass of analysis and deconstruction like what Donald Spoto wrote about the films of Alfred Hitchcock, which was one of the first books on cinema I read. I am, by nature, more interested in tales than their tellers. I was not interested in writing a biography.

Inside his office, I outlined my plan to his desk—I still wonder what Mani Ratnam must have thought, sitting across someone who refused to meet his eyes—and he didn't seem very impressed. A mild panic began to churn inside me. I knew I wanted to write about him, and I couldn't think of any other approach that would interest me as well as my publishers. Then he said something I never expected to hear in a million years. 'You like cinema. I like cinema. Let's talk and see what happens.' I was a devotee standing on one leg on an anthill, and here was god before me bestowing the rarest of boons. But after the first flush of exhilaration, I had doubts about how

Introduction xix

this was going to turn out, as we didn't really know each other and both of us are fairly introverted and reclusive people. Could two negatives combine into a positive? But I said yes—simply because I couldn't say no. How do you say no to the man who made *Nayakan*?

AND SO WE BEGAN TO TALK. It was slow going at first. I was skirting around him, his films, leaving a wide swath, wanting to convince him that I was hungering for a serious discussion about the evolution of his work and not juicy morsels of making-of moments. I was not interested in personal details—only as much of a man as can be revealed from his work, and perhaps a little more to set up context. And he, I think, was trying to make sure that I was not going to waste his time with trivialities, that I knew his work in itself and as part of the Tamil-cinema continuum. We talked about films from before he made his first movie. We traded a lot of movie memories. We became comfortable around one another to the extent that two people in a professional context warm up for a collaboration. And gradually, he began to talk without being conscious of the recording devices I placed in front of him. I could feel the conversations beginning to flow.

Though we talked about the films in series, I was not aiming for a definitive discussion about each film. (You can manufacture an entire book out of a *Nayakan* or an *Iruvar*.) I wanted to wing it, set the pitch, so to speak, for a jam session between two musicians, where we improvised riffs about, as well as around, a theme (in this case, the movie under discussion). Sometimes, I had a fair idea about how he'd play, but I'd throw a cue at him all the same, hoping for a surprise, a contrapuntal note. I learnt when to stop, when to recognize I had reached a wall and couldn't push any further. Other times I learnt to be grateful that a man so private was sharing so much, confessing so much, revealing so much. After going through my rough notes of the first few sessions, he mailed me this bit of self-appraisal: 'In the initial section my answers seem a bit unsure, but I seem to get better as it goes on.' I can only hope, in my efforts here, that I was as hard on myself as he was—and always *is*, apparently—on himself.

I also learnt to let go. While discussing one film, I ventured that the actors hadn't quite done their jobs, that a better cast would have really lifted the film. He agreed. But later, he asked that this portion be struck out, as it was his fault that the actors hadn't done well. 'No point blaming them for my mistakes.' There was another time he spoke of a senior film-maker a little more expansively, with nothing but respect, but eventually he felt uncomfortable with the passage and out it went. Most times, I followed his lead when it came to people, though I stubbornly called the tune when it came to the content of the films and the processes that created them. And I learnt to overcome my diffidence about expressing my reservations about his work, which made him react defensively a few times—but mostly he sought not to change *my* opinion but to explain his stand, where he was coming from. Even if we agreed to disagree, the arguments were always rewarding.

I LEARNT TO RESPECT his fundamental discomfort with what he calls 'intellectualization.' I don't consider myself an intellectual at all, and I'd simply be trotting out a *maybe* theory about his films or his process, but he'd come down hard. Looking at his explanations about the swing in *Guru* or the pigeons in *Nayakan*, he is clearly a film-maker who thinks beyond the text, but he seems to chafe when someone else mines his work for subtext. In this aspect, and in some others, this book is almost an autobiography. I wrestled, at first, with the impulse to massage his responses into uninterrupted prose, but after a while, it began to sound like just my voice, with little indication of his commitment to this project. That's why I opted, finally, for the conversational format. After all, a sustained duet cannot be billed with just one performer. Also, this is the first time he is talking to someone so extensively and it made sense to retain his voice, even if the first take was often discarded and we'd go back and forth until both of us were happy with the session.

Thus the Donald Spoto approach gave way to the François Truffaut model. The format of this book is something of a homage to *Hitchcock/Truffaut*. The title, on the other hand, is a tribute to Michael Ondaatje's profoundly spiritual *The Conversations: Walter Murch and the Art of Editing Film*. It is these two books that hovered over me as guiding spirits during my conversations with Mani Ratnam. If I have managed to capture the smallest fraction of the insights into a creator's cinema as Truffaut did, along with Ondaatje's lavish love for the medium, I will consider myself successful. That judgement, of course, rests with the reader. But in one respect, there is already a sense of succeeding beyond my wildest expectations. Me sitting across the director who defined and dominated my generation, poking him, prodding him, leaning in and listening to him, sharing a conspiratorial chuckle, arguing for my beliefs and watching him argue for his, being a gushing fan one minute and retreating to a critical distance the next, and learning, always learning, first-hand from a master—who would have believed this day would come? Certainly not that boy slouched at those matinee screenings at Eros.

1
'I remember telling Balu Mahendra, I want to run'

Pallavi Anupallavi (1983)

Vijay (Anil Kapoor) loves Madhu (Kiran Vairale). She's smart, pretty, age-appropriate. But she isn't Anu (Lakshmi), a mature, middle-aged woman (separated from her cheating husband) whose indulgent friendship leaves Vijay confused about the nature of his feelings for Madhu. A regular romantic movie would pivot on the question: Whom will he choose? The issue here, however, is: Who is he?

Unaru (1984)

Peter (Ratheesh) heads a group of fishermen seeking restitution for a livelihood devastated by the construction of a port. They form a union, whose leader Janardhanan (Sukumaran) acquires increasingly self-serving motives, and whose unwitting right-hand man is Peter's friend Ramu (Mohanlal). When Peter dies, protesting the exploitation by the unions, Ramu rises in revolt.

Pagal Nilavu (1985)

An unsuspecting Selvam (Murali) works as a hired hand of the unscrupulous village elder Devarajan (Sathyaraj), whose illegal ways come under the scanner of Inspector Peter (Sharath Babu). To Peter's disgust, his sister Jyoti (Revathy) falls in love with Selvam, who now has to choose between a life with Jyoti and his loyalty to Devarajan. The choice, inevitably, comes at a high price.

Idhayakoyil (1985)

Surya (Radha) falls for Shankar (Mohan), a celebrated singer still grieving the death of Gauri (Ambika), his love from his village. Surya rehabilitates the alcoholic and reclusive Shankar, but his present is too entwined with his past for him to reciprocate her love. He advises her to marry someone else—but when have romantic heroines heeded sane words of advice?

BARADWAJ RANGAN: Inevitable first question. Do you remember the first film you saw?

MANI RATNAM: I can't say for sure. Films were taboo at home. It was a big joint family, with my two brothers, a sister, cousins, aunts, uncles, and none of the younger lot was particularly encouraged to watch films, except those made by the family. My uncle, 'Venus' Krishnamurthy, was a producer. (It's just a coincidence that the name was the same; otherwise we had no connection to Venus Studios.) My father, S.G. Rathnam, was a film distributor all his life. The first film Venus Pictures made, I think, was *Amaradeepam*. They remade it in Hindi. Then they made *Uthamaputhiran*, *Kalyana Parisu*, *Pattanathil Bootham*, and Hindi films like *Suraj* and *Apna Desh*.

We kids were allowed to tag along whenever they went to watch bits and pieces of films they were making—the rushes, basically. If they were going to a preview, they might take us if there was enough space in the car. Otherwise we were out. I remember *Uthamaputhiran* very clearly, though that's also because I must have seen it again much later. But going to a theatre and watching a film was almost like playing cards—it was out of bounds. If there was a film my uncle was going to produce, he would take the family to the beach and narrate the story. That's one of the memories I have. Food was taken to Marina Beach and he would ask us—only the elders, the kids would just hang around—what they thought of the story. I don't know if he actually took anything away from what they said.

RANGAN: That sounds like an early version of an audience preview. At what point did you begin watching movies regularly?

RATNAM: It was in middle school, at the hostel, to be precise. I was reasonably interested in movies by then. You don't realize it at the time, but later you find you had an opinion about films. I don't know if every kid has an opinion and remembers that opinion, but I remember liking certain films and not liking certain films. When you're a kid, you actually like all films. But there are some that you like particularly. And whenever we came back after watching a film, there was always this question in the car from my uncle: 'How was the film?' And in a family that thrived on films, it was a more loaded and relevant question. Surprisingly—in one form or the other—I always had something to say about a film, not just that it was good or indifferent. I didn't know anything about the aspects of film-making. I'd casually seen bits of shooting here and there, but I'd always been very bored with it. In the summer holidays, whenever there was a film shooting—even if it was outside Madras—they would take us along, and it would be the most boring thing on earth. They would shoot the same thing over and over again. We couldn't understand why they were doing this. We found it ridiculous. It really surprises me that I ended up in film-making, considering that I didn't enjoy watching film shoots at all.

If I have to consciously make an effort to remember, the first film that I liked very much was *Hatari* [the Howard Hawks film starring John Wayne]. Our neighbour, a friend's mother, took us kids. I was fascinated by it. That was probably the first film that I saw without the family. I came back and insisted that my folks see it. I must have persuaded them enough, because they took me again when they went to see it. They came back and I got a shelling from my father. 'What kind of film did you take us to?' So obviously we never saw eye to eye on films after that. And before that, there was a film I remember—*Jungle Cat*, I think it was called. There was this theatre called Elphinstone. I don't remember much about the film, but I remember that there used to be an ice cream parlour there. It was supposed to be the best in town, and we had ice creams there.

I actively started seeing films when I was at the hostel in Besant Theosophical School, which was inside the Kalakshetra campus. Next door, at a walking distance, there was a touring cinema with a thatched roof. They would screen two films at night for one rupee, which was the highest-priced ticket. They'd screen an English film and then they'd screen a Tamil film. They had a single projector, which meant that after twenty minutes they had to stop and change the reel. That's when I started seeing a lot of films. We used to sneak out at night through the fence, in our lungi and banian, as if we were going to take a leak.

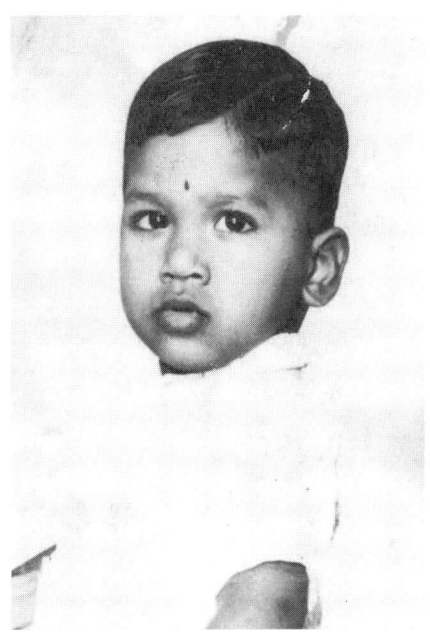

'It was a big joint family, and none of the younger lot was particularly encouraged to watch films, except those made by the family.'

And sometimes, we'd see our house master there. We'd ignore him and he'd ignore us and pretend it never happened.

RANGAN: That's hilarious. That's a scene right out of [Vikramaditya Motwane's] *Udaan*.

RATNAM: Is that so? They'd change the English film once in three days, whereas the Tamil film would play for a week. The first things you tend to like as a kid are the actors. When I was in seventh standard, when I was around ten or twelve, I must have started becoming a big Sivaji Ganesan and Nagesh fan. I watched most of their films. And sometime later you realize there's a brain behind it, and then you start noticing it's the director, and then you go back and realize that a lot of the films you like have been made by the same man, and you start following that director. I think all those transitions started happening in middle and high school. Between thirteen and fifteen, I found K. Balachander. In the touring cinema—Jayanthi, it was called—I found Laurel and Hardy. I've seen films there that I could not possibly have seen elsewhere. I found this series of films that were called Ken Clark films. I've never seen these films in the main theatres, but they would be screened there and we'd all go and watch them.

RANGAN: So you never saw films at an actual theatre in the city?

RATNAM: Oh, I did, when we had four or five days off and I came home from the hostel. That was the time I started seeing movies avidly. I remember there was one particular holiday—about seven or eight days—and I got to see ten films. Then you start watching the Deepavali releases on the day of release, with a bunch of people of the same age group, and it becomes an easy habit to get into. I think that's the phase when I seriously began liking and watching cinema.

RANGAN: After watching these films, would you discuss them with these same-age-group friends?

RATNAM: Films were meant for watching. I don't know if I thought there was something to discuss. So I never really discussed films till much later, till I was doing my undergrad at Vivekananda College, and later in Bombay, during my MBA at Jamnalal Bajaj Institute of Management Studies. (I specialized in Finance. None of my producers believed me whenever I went overbudget.) Taste or preference in films is something that evolves without your being aware of it. It's like liking a cricketer or a tennis champ. It's like liking Rod Laver. If you liked somebody, you watched him play or listened to the commentary, keeping the transistor close to your ears. It becomes very important for you when he's playing. It's the same with cinema. When you like a director or you like an actor, they matter to you and you seek out their films.

RANGAN: When you were in Bombay, did you continue to watch films? Work must have come in the way.

RATNAM: I think those two years of management studies were kind of hectic. But we would watch films at night once in a while. But not as much as here [in Chennai], where the four years after school—one year of pre-university and three years of BCom—were a licence to watch films. There was nothing really to keep me away. Academics didn't really demand much. There was a lot of free time, so it was sport and films that really kept me going.

'*When I saw* Udhiri Pookkal, *I was probably just starting work on my first film. I thought it was brilliant.*'

RANGAN: Did studies come easily to you?

RATNAM: I would like to say that I topped the class right through, but that wouldn't be true. Or I would like to say that I was at the bottom of the heap, but that's not true either. Unlike my films, my academic life was not dramatic. Middling would be more or less right.

RANGAN: What got you out of your MBA mould and into the movies?

RATNAM: It was an accident. I was interested in cinema only as a viewer. I never thought I'd take it up as a career. I never thought I would be in a creative field, that I would sit and write and actually direct films. I was in management consultancy, but to be honest I was not too happy with my job—consultancy as a service, which was just studies and reports; in some way, an extension of academic life—and I was trying to move away into actual production activities in the mainstream industry, in the marketing or manufacturing companies that used to hire me as a consultant. A friend of mine, Ravi Shankar [the son of the celebrated director B.R. Panthulu], was about to make his first film in Kannada, *Bangarutha Ghani*. So Ravi and I started working on a script, with another friend Raman [son of the Carnatic veena maestro S. Balachander].

Every evening, after my office hours, we used to meet at Ravi's house and argue vehemently over the script, about what would be good and what wouldn't. None of us had any idea how a film was written or made. We were just confident that we could do it—a confidence that stemmed from ignorance. We fought and disagreed at every step. Up to that point in my life, except for writing a few letters occasionally to my father from the hostel asking for money, I had not done any form of creative writing. In these mad, late-evening sittings of three amateurs, I discovered that conceiving a scene or a set of sequences could be exhilarating. When a thought or an idea comes up from nowhere and you are able to see it bloom even as you are explaining the idea to two argumentative friends, it gives you a high, an intoxication, an immense joy. That's when the bug bites you. That moment was my baby step into films.

By the time we finished the script in some form (though in English), I decided to shift from being a management consultant to an executive in one of the big corporate firms. Before I shifted jobs, I thought I would take a small break for three months—a kind of sabbatical—to see what it would be like to be part of a shoot. The film was to be shot in the Kolar goldfields. Ravi had started the shoot earlier with a miniature set erected in the driveway of his house. The film started with a special-effects shoot (in 1979, when special effects were very rare in India) by one first-time director and two know-it-all friends. Our only source of knowledge was *American Cinematographer* magazine. When the shoot shifted to Kolar, I quit my job and went along.

At Kolar, my job was to sit with the Kannada dialogue writer, Udaya Sankar, and explain what we had written in English and get the dialogues as close as possible in Kannada. The cast included Vishnuvardhan, Srinath, Ambareesh, Lakshmi and Roja Ramani. Unfortunately, the film was not completed and our maiden attempt did not hit the screens. But by the end of the first schedule, I had decided that this is what I wanted to do. I can't put a finger exactly on when I made the decision but somehow it had been made. I wanted to direct films. That is what I wanted to do for the rest of my life.

I don't know if my new love for film writing brought about my disillusionment with management consultancy or vice versa. But both happened together. So that stint of scriptwriting was a career-changing few months. That's when I thought I'd write a script, sell it to a director, work alongside and learn everything about direction, and then I thought I would be ready for a full-fledged career in films. In the worst-case scenario, I could go back and get a job. But that was just insurance. Once you get bitten by this bug, you remain seriously bitten. But when I wrote [my first film] *Pallavi Anupallavi*, I thought I could give it a shot myself. The thought of selling it to a director disappeared quickly. No. Actually it disappeared so slowly that I could never put my finger on when I started thinking of directing it myself.

'Bharathiraja came in around the mid-seventies . . . I was stunned to see 16 Vayadhinile.*' Kamal Haasan and Rajinikanth before they were megastars.*

RANGAN: You don't seem to be one of those people who saw a particular movie as a child and knew that very day that they wanted to become a film-maker.

RATNAM: I wish I was. Then I wouldn't have wasted too much time on other things. But jokes apart, even now, I feel that if there were enough good Tamil films being made, I wouldn't have become a film-maker. If you looked back seriously, there was Balachander. He was brilliant. And then Bharathiraja and Mahendran came in around the mid-'70s, the time I was just finishing my education. I was stunned to see [Bharathiraja's] *16 Vayadhinile* and [Mahendran's] *Udhiri Pookkal*.

When I saw *Udhiri Pookkal*, I was probably just starting work on my first film. I thought it was brilliant. It's still one of the best Tamil films I've seen. The standard was right up there. You never thought he had any hesitation doing the film. But the rest of the films, predominantly, were still not good. Tamil cinema had stagnated. The films were so, so ordinary and without any flair that you felt you could do better even if you didn't know anything about cinema. And I'm not just talking about a particular year or two. Right from my college years, it had been pretty ordinary. There was nothing you could take back home. If there were many more Balachanders and Mahendrans, maybe I would have been happy just watching Tamil films instead of wanting to make them.

RANGAN: It's a form of making your decision sound rational. As in: 'I can go do this *because . . .*'

RATNAM: Maybe it's a rationalizing statement, but that's what I felt. It's like I'm going to play a match, a tennis match, with some player I don't know. So you practise a bit before the match, and somewhere you start realizing that, yeah, you can take this person on and it's not going to be difficult. You know what you can do, and you see the other person and you are able to judge the situation. Maybe you're wrong, but most of the time that is what you say to yourself: 'I should be able to take this match easily.' It's that kind of thing.

RANGAN: Roughly which year(s) did all this occur?

RATNAM: I finished my education in 1977. I worked for a year and a half, till the end of '78. So mid-'79 onwards I started looking at cinema as an option. I started writing *Pallavi Anupallavi* (in English) in 1980. That took a month. From then on, till the film was released, around '83 January, it was a tough time. I used to hang out with a group of people getting into films at that point, like (cinematographers) P.C. Sreeram and Suresh, and (the directors) Bharathi–Vasu, and Kutty Prakash, who runs a sounds studio today. Bharathi–Vasu got their break the same time I did. By the time I returned from my first schedule, they'd finished *Panneer Pushpangal*. All of us were convinced that we were the best things around, and yet the industry was blind to us. We used to hang out every day at Woodlands Drive-in. Coffee was all we could have and we didn't know who had the money to pay the bill. If we ran out of money, we would sit there and wait for somebody else to come by and buy another round of coffee for everybody.

RANGAN: What was the reaction at home when you said you were quitting your job and getting into films?

RATNAM: My mother panicked. She wanted a secure career for me. She'd lived her entire life on the fringes of the film industry and seen too many ups and downs, and she didn't particularly want her children in it. She wasn't sure what I wanted to do. She couldn't understand why I got myself educated and got a good job and then suddenly quit to go away for a shoot. She was pretty worried. My father was fairly okay with it.

RANGAN: Was there a point where you sat your father down and said, '*Appa*, this is what I want to do?'

RATNAM: I didn't have to tell them anything. There are different ways of communication, and my father and I were never two people who would sit and talk about things. I just quit and started work on the film, and they understood that this is what I wanted to do. They knew they had to feed me for a little while longer.

RANGAN: Considering that you ended up a film-maker, have you ever wished you'd gone to film school or wondered what it would have been like?

RATNAM: I think it would have been good. I would have seen a lot of films that I still probably haven't seen. There's nothing comparable to the experience of sitting with a group of thirty or forty people who are all watching cinema and breathing cinema. It's a huge formative thing. In my case, I was on my own, trying to learn things. I have no regrets about this, but that would have been a great experience. If I had known this is what I would do for a career, then perhaps that should have been the right way to go about it.

RANGAN: As the son of a film producer, was it easier to make your first film?

RATNAM: Though I'm from a film family, the people I knew were mostly those I met while carrying my scripts around. I had a friend, Kitty [the actor and director Raja Krishnamurthy], who was two years my senior [at Jamnalal Bajaj]. When I started my film career, he was working at [the hotel] Chola Sheraton. He used to write short stories and he knew people in the Tamil literary circles. So I used to sit with him and work, having coffee at Chola. He knew Kamal Haasan, and I used to tag along with him whenever he went over. I met Kamal with the *Pallavi Anupallavi* script, for the role eventually played by Anil Kapoor. I told him the story and he told me five stories in return.

But he got hold of his brother Charuhasan and asked him to take me to [his friend, the director] Mahendran. Charuhasan did take me to meet Mahendran, but Mahendran had just returned from a shoot at the Chennai port. He had come back with a crate of beer, and after a brief hello to me, the two of them got talking over beer. I was forgotten. I didn't want to work as an assistant director, because that was a long-drawn career path involving a number of years and a number of films. I wanted to make a film quickly. However, if I were to assist someone, Mahendran was a fantastic option. But he was not interested. He was busy chatting with Charuhasan. Years later, I reminded him about this incident, and he smiled and said, 'Be happy that I ignored you then, so that you could make it to the top on your own.'

'[My first film] centres not on the young couple but the older woman [Lakshmi] whose husband has betrayed her.'

Like I said, my idea was to get a producer, or else, to sell the script to a celebrity director so that I could work along with him and learn all about film-making. I chose three directors to get in touch with—Balachander, Bharathiraja and Mahendran. I tried my luck with Balachander first. His production company, Kalakendra, was run by Durai, a client of my brother G. Venkateswaran, who was a chartered accountant. I gave my script to Mr Durai and asked him if he could hand it over to Balachander. The script never reached Balachander. I waited patiently for a month before taking it back. Then the Mahendran encounter happened.

My last option was meeting Bharathiraja. I met him at his office. He asked me to come the next day, perhaps hoping that I would not turn up. But being a corporate man, I took this appointment seriously and presented myself at his office punctually. He was possibly more impressed with the neat spiral-bound script I was holding than my animated narration in English. Years later, he told me that he did not understand much of my narration as I was huffing and puffing away in English. He had to make up his own story from what I had narrated. He was doing *Nizhalgal* and so he said he may not be able to do my script. However, he was emphatic that we would meet again soon. This was the first encouraging remark I got after taking my plunge into films. I can never thank him enough for that.

Then I turned to producers.

P.C. Sreeram and I would hop on a two-wheeler, his Lambretta or my Yezdi, and visit the offices of producer after producer. I met Raj Kannu [who produced *16 Vayadhinile*], Gowri Shankar of Devi Films, and some twenty others. The idea was to convince the producer to finance the script, to let me direct and to have PC photograph it. But it took me two years and three films before I could convince a producer to do *Mouna Raagam*, which was where PC and I first worked together. I had come from the organized sector and hence my visits to these producers were meticulous and well planned. I used to maintain a chart of people to meet, the first meeting, the first follow-up, the next follow-up and so on till they got struck out from the chart. There was always the famous answer: 'Come back next week.' If it was a clear no, it would have been easy to take, but week after week of listening to 'come back next week' was rather painful.

RANGAN: I'm wondering why you didn't just ask your brother, G. Venkateswaran, for financing. After all, he did produce *Mouna Raagam* later.

RATNAM: He was in films, yes, but if he'd wanted me, he would have asked me. Even *Mouna Raagam* went to two or three other people before GV Films [then Sujatha Productions] came in. These other producers would say they'd make it and they'd go ask GV for funds. So he decided to produce it himself. At the time, GV Films weren't into production at all. They were essentially funding and distributing films. The first production they got into was *Mouna Raagam*, which meant that I had to start taking care of the production in addition to direction. But then, I ended up doing a lot of that even in my first film. The trouble with this is that someone trusts you and lets you do your own thing. It's not your money. It may be your brother, but it's still somebody else's money and therefore you have to make doubly sure that you stay within budget and so on. There's that extra burden. Whereas now, when I produce my own films, it's my call.

RANGAN: By the time you made *Pallavi Anupallavi*, mainstream films like *Udhiri Pookkal* had already depicted subtle relationships and succeeded. The audience, it appeared, was ready for the kind of film you were trying to make.

RATNAM: When I was making my first film, I thought I was making a mainstream film. I did not think of it as experimentation. In my mind, I had no doubts about it at all. It was a simple story, narrated in an entertaining manner. There's just a conflict and the growth of a person. The film deals with a man–woman relationship, and it starts with a guy who thinks he knows everything there is to know about relationships and what he wants, and the film ends when he realizes that he doesn't know very much, that life is not as straightforward as he thought it was. It's more about discovering yourself. It's a transition that I think most of us go through at that age. We are all like that. Relationships are really society-driven. You might be in a relationship, but you're still just yourself. A man remains a man. At some point, you grow up and realize that there are flaws within you. I was just trying to get that aspect in.

RANGAN: *Pallavi Anupallavi* is a slightly heavy love story for a first-time film-maker working in a commercial/mainstream format. (In your case, the lighter love stories like *Geetanjali* came much later.) It centres not on the young couple (Anil Kapoor and Kiran Vairale) but the older woman (Lakshmi) whose husband has betrayed her. This is a rare instance of a director's preoccupations—for instance, the plight of the married woman in a crisis, which you later pursued in *Mouna Raagam* and *Alaipaayuthey*—crystallizing in his very first film.

RATNAM: When you're outside seeing the films being made, especially the love stories that glorify relationships, you find them false. I was trying to say that it is not as simple as they say it is. It's not always a Laila–Majnu story. The love stories say that you'll die without this particular person, and you know that's not how it is. You don't die, you just carry on. You may be hurt, emotionally broken, but you get back on your feet. Life goes on. You assume that you meet a girl and that's going to be it for life, and then you realize you're not

'*It's not always a Laila–Majnu story. The love stories say that you'll die without this particular person and you know that's not how it is.*' Anil Kapoor and Kiran Vairale in Pallavi Anupallavi.

exactly like that, that you could be attracted to or be involved or interacting with other women at the same time. You reveal a layer of yourself which surprises you, that nature has made you this way. It is this realization that's the crux of the film.

It was not only a reaction to the films around me but also a reaction to what was happening to the people around me. You discover a lot about yourself when you're getting into an independent zone. When you've just gone through your post-graduation, you come to question certain beliefs—how you deal with truth, how you deal with crisis, how you deal with the opposite sex, and what your stance is versus your behaviour. There are a lot of times I may have a certain stance but I might behave in a different way. It's the first time this is happening, and there's a voice inside you asking you, 'Buddy, what are you up to?' So the film was trying to capture that part of relationships, which I thought was real. At the first-film stage, you are, in a way, naïve. You think that you can be true to this aspect of life and that it will stand out. I was trying to say that the rest of it is bullshit and this is the truth.

RANGAN: Perhaps the naïveté of the protagonist, a first-timer to life's complexities, is in some way a parallel to the inevitable naïveté of the first-time director.

RATNAM: Maybe the first-time director was much more naive than the character in the film. But I've gone through the naïveté and come out of it, and I still stand by the film. Sometimes the truth sounds naive, or you might have to be naive to speak the truth. But during the first public screening, you understand everything that you did not understand during the making of the film. It is not just what you say; it is also how you say it. That is equally important and sometimes more so. You learn that while talking to people, you have to talk in a language that they understand. There's no point talking in English to someone who speaks only in Kannada or Tamil. You can say what you wish to say, but you have to say it in a way that they comprehend. Otherwise, they're just going to shrug their shoulders and go away. *Pallavi Anupallavi* taught me this.

RANGAN: *Pallavi Anupallavi* is a very tight little film—the way the shots are, the ins and outs of the scenes. Did you discover along the way, that you had this innate flair that many other directors didn't?

RATNAM: At some point, you realize that you care about some things a little more than the next guy. When you watch a film, you know the way the shot was taken or the way the narrative was constructed. [Mahendran's] *Mullum Malarum*, for instance, was so startlingly different from anything that had come before in Tamil cinema. It really stood out. You need not know exactly what it is that stands out, but it would stand out for you. That is the beginning. There was something really special about the direction,

Balu Mahendra's cinematography, the characterizations, the costumes, the compositions, the colours, the light, the way it was cut and, of course, the music. The sheer restraint in it is really remarkable. I think the real starting point is the script—the content and the narrative. The way a scene starts, the way it finishes—most of it gets played out there. And then, it's just a question of being able to translate it well onto film.

The most important aspects at this stage are the performances you can extract from the actors to make the scenes come alive. When somebody sees a film, they see the film. It doesn't matter if it's your first or hundredth. You can't go to the person in the theatre and say, 'I'm sorry. This is my first film. I still have a lot to learn.' There are no excuses. You have to deliver. I still remember the introduction I wrote for my first consultancy report, where I'd said, 'The attempt of this exercise …' My boss told me that attempts finish with college. 'We are here and someone is paying money for this report. So you can't attempt. You have to clearly deliver.' With films, this is all the more true. A film has to be produced well. And after being part of the audience for too long and being too critical of several films being made, you want to make sure you reach the levels of something you appreciated. In some fashion or the other, everything that you liked goes into your film—your taste, your aesthetic, your restraint. You bare yourself.

'If they'd asked me to do [my first film] in Konkani, I wouldn't have hesitated.' *The first-time director with crew and cast.*

RANGAN: The collaborators you surrounded yourself with were also unusually simpatico. Even with the costumes, say, you don't have those shiny nylex saris or the big-buckle belts that were seen in Tamil cinema at the time.

RATNAM: You've grown up in a city and you're making a film about people of a similar background. So it's very easy for you to decide the kind of look that's there. At that point, even the good directors would not pay attention to these aspects. Costumes were somebody else's job, and unless the cameraman was very particular, the colours were never seriously looked into. In your first film, you're particular about everything. Also, in a first film, there aren't that many people around. You'll have to do everything yourself—whether it's picking up the clothes or buying the specific kind of coffee mug or making sure that the envelope from an American college has the university's name correct and the correct American stamp on it.

Pallavi Anupallavi, Unaru, Pagal Nilavu, Idhayakoyil

That's very important, and you can't delegate it. You've grown up that way. You've been exposed to these things. Those were not the difficult things. If you know what you want, it makes it easier for the others to go with you. It's only when you don't know what you want that their choices come into play. This is a medium where you can take a call on the final product. Whether it's a tune or the way the film is cut or the way someone is dressed, you can take a call and say if it works or not. You can point your collaborators in the direction you want to go, and they'll hopefully go your way. If not, you've got to convince them or let yourself be convinced after a good fight. So I had Lenin [editing], Balu Mahendra [cinematography], Thotta Tharrani [production design] and Ilaiyaraaja [music]—possibly the four top technicians in each of their fields.

RANGAN: How did a first-time film-maker manage this?

RATNAM: You just have to meet them, tell them your story, and ask them if they will be a part of it. At the most, they're going to say no. I didn't have anything to lose. I wanted to work with Balu Mahendra. I was fascinated by the way his films were shot, especially *Mullum Malarum*, which was really an eye-opener. You come into a Tamil film and you're seeing a format which is new, wider, shot in 35mm but with a mask, like a rectangle. And then he had this way with natural light and baby zooms—tiny zooms that were not the kind of zoom shots that were being used. There are two people and one of them moves out of the frame, and he tightens out slightly to the other person and goes away. There is this very small movement of zoom, but more to balance out the composition.

It's the kind of thing we'd not seen in Tamil cinema before. Our zooms were either a pull-back from somebody or a full-on charge into their face. Here it was really delicate, like a caress, and with the background music it turned into something poetic. It was wonderful to watch. I did not have Balu's contact information. I found his number and went and met him when he was at [Hotel] Palmgrove, in some discussion. He was about to do the cinematography for Peter Selvakumar's film. He asked me to come the next day and tell him the story. I went to his house the next day on my bike. Sitting on his terrace, I told him the story. And he agreed to do the film. It was really nice of him. This was my first film and I wanted to make sure that the technical aspects were good. I wanted a good product.

RANGAN: And this aspect of baby zooms was something you were able to single out by just viewing the film as a member of the audience.

RATNAM: But when *Mullum Malarum* came, I'd already decided to move into films. So I was watching films much more carefully. I was reading books like *Hitchcock/Truffaut* and anything I could lay my hands on. At that time, there was hardly any literature on cinema. You couldn't get a book on films—Indian, foreign, whatever—in India at all. Even the number of films you got to see in Madras was very limited. Whatever films and books you could get your hands on, those were your inputs. My first film took nearly two years to make, and I had a lot of time on hand. I studied films mainly from the books at the USIS and the British Council.

RANGAN: One would have thought you'd have gone with P.C. Sreeram from your Woodlands gang.

RATNAM: PC was a friend, but the producer did not want a new director as well as a new cameraman. They wanted somebody established. So I had a choice between Ashok Kumar and Balu Mahendra. The two of them were really doing something special, and I didn't have any issues about asking them. But Ashok Kumar was busy with a few other things.

RANGAN: What about Lenin?

RATNAM: He was a neighbour. He still lives opposite my house. I knew him but not all that well. The first time I met him was after I saw *Udhiri Pookkal*. I liked the film. I had no clue what editing was and what role Lenin played in it, but I knew that the film was brilliant and I wanted to meet anybody who was associated with it. I spent quite a bit of time with him. We'd sit and talk. When I started *Pallavi Anupallavi*, he was the first person I met. I told him I'd gotten this break and wanted him to edit my film, and he said yes. Even when I sat in on the post-production, I didn't know how it would be edited. He had to explain what each mark meant and how he would be going about it. Music, cinematography, editing—my knowledge about all these aspects was strictly limited to the books that I could lay my hands on.

RANGAN: And next, you met Ilaiyaraaja—the beginning of an extraordinary partnership.

RATNAM: I actually met Tharrani first. Right behind my house, in Venus Studios, they were shooting [Singeetham Srinivasa Rao's] *Rajaparvai*. Tharrani had done a set for the house where Kamal Haasan's character stayed, so we—the jobless Woodlands gang, P.C. Sreeram and me—went to see it. There was this friend of ours who was working on the film—on the sound, I think; so we had that access, and when they were not shooting, we went to see the set. It was constructed on the first floor and the way Tharrani had improvised a set on a real location was beautiful. It was real and still effective and dramatic, something that they were not doing at that point of time. So I met Tharrani afterwards and interacted with him a couple of times. He was the next person I asked for my film.

And then Ilaiyaraaja, who was huge. He was a huge star. His music was phenomenal. I don't know if I should say this, but we'd booked a Kannada music director for the film. I can't tell you his name, but I'd met

'[The film] was about the new blood looking for opportunities, and the older generation that wanted to continue in the same old fashion.' Mohanlal in Unaru.

him and I'd given him an advance. And then I happened to see a Kannada film that had his music. I heard the background score and I panicked. I didn't want my film to have that kind of score. It is not that the score was not good—just that it was old-school. I decided to move on without actually having the courage to tell him, 'I'm sorry, this is not working for me.'

I asked Balu Mahendra whether he could put me on to Ilaiyaraaja, and he introduced me to Raja. I said I was doing a Kannada film with a very small budget but I wanted him to do the music. I told him I couldn't afford to pay his market price. He didn't bat an eyelid. For probably one-fourth or one-fifth the amount he was getting at the time, he agreed to do the film. We just met. I told him what the outline was. He smiled and said we'd work on the composing. That was it. But whenever I entered his studio, I was mortally scared that I would run into the other music director and not know what to say. It took me a year to convince myself that maybe he would have forgotten my face. But this is what I mean. You also come to know what you are willing to do for your film. I was willing to do something I feel miserable about even after all these years.

RANGAN: I look at it differently, that even at that point you were very clear about what you wanted. You were not willing to compromise.

RATNAM: Maybe. But it also shows that you'll do quite a few things that you didn't know you'd end up doing. But Ilaiyaraaja was amazing. This was a Kannada film, a small film by an unknown. And he was a star, an unbelievable talent. Music would just pour out of him. He was so quick that you had to quickly decide whether the tune was absolutely right for you, and if it wasn't, you had to quickly think of some other direction from which to prod him and get a different tune. And he was really sporting. He would do that. The range of films that he was doing, that he could discover himself in each and every form—that was quite amazing.

RANGAN: Even in front of the camera, you managed to get a big star, Lakshmi. And then you had two little-known Bombay-based performers in Anil Kapoor and Kiran Vairale.

RATNAM: Lakshmi was in my friend Ravi Shankar's film, whose script I'd worked on. She was impressed with the story outline and said she would do it, probably assuming that I already had a producer. I went to my uncle 'Venus' Krishnamurthy and told him that Lakshmi would act in it; this was even before she had said yes to the script. That's how my first film got the green light. My uncle now heard my script and said that he would produce it, provided I did it in Kannada, with a small budget. They had a distribution office in Bangalore and therefore a Kannada film made sense. At that stage, I would have grabbed any opportunity, agreed to any condition. A first film is a first film. I'd written the film in English. I could have translated it into any language. If they'd asked me to do it in Konkani, I wouldn't have hesitated.

The project fell into place. I didn't know Kannada, but it is a south Indian language and they're not too different from one another. We shot it in Coorg and Bangalore. In April 1980, I had seen the Telugu movie *Vamsa Vriksham* by Bapu. Anil Kapoor was the hero. I got his number and called him up. He turned out to be a producer's son. He was going to Kerala for a fashion show. He stopped here on the way and that's how he came aboard. Hasini [Suhasini] was already popular through [Mahendran's] *Nenjathai Killadhey*. She flatly refused the female lead role when I offered it to her. (Years later, though, I made her another offer that she could not refuse.) Anil then brought Kiran into the film. For the child character, I chose Rohit Srinath, whose father Srinath was in Ravi Shankar's Kannada film. It was a pleasure working with Rohit and I still cherish the experience. He did a few more films and also played the rich kid's character in *Malgudi Days* [based on R.K. Narayan's stories] on TV. He became an engineer eventually. My first shot for the film was with Rohit. I started my career with a good actor.

RANGAN: What was that first scene?

RATNAM: It was a scene between mother and son, during the song *Nagu endide*. I remember the child's expression. He's angry with his mother and he's sitting with his legs inside a swimming pool. Then he thaws and there's a rapport that comes about. That was the first scene we shot. The boy was scared of being pushed into the water. But we had to do it. If you can push an actor into deep waters, you should do it—literally or otherwise. It works for the film.

RANGAN: Anil and Kiran were as new to the language as you were. Did you have somebody on set guiding you about inflections in the dialogues and things like that?

RATNAM: I had an associate who had worked with Balu on his Kannada film *Kokila*, a wonderful person named Shivanand. His father was a well-known theatre person, so he had grown up with Kannada theatre and then come into films. I had him and his assistant helping me with the dialogues. But he could only tell you what the lines meant in Kannada. You still had to get the performance. That's your job. You have to make it work. He would make sure that the Kannada was correct. He would sit with the actors and teach them patiently and then he'd monitor their dialogue delivery. Kiran had a flair for languages. She had a smaller role and could learn the lines. Anil had to work really hard. But he looked right for the part. He looked young; he looked like today's generation—so he fell into place. And he did work very, very hard. Every night he would sit with the dialogues and learn them by heart. It was tough, but none of us had anything else going on and we were willing to give everything to this film. We wanted to do films and that's what we ended up doing.

RANGAN: Your very first film, then, gave you the kind of exposure that must have helped while making films in Malayalam, Telugu, and later in Hindi. The latter, again, is a language you've said you don't know very well.

RATNAM: You're confident enough because you've done it before. You did your first film in an unfamiliar language and that didn't inhibit you. You could get in and find your rhythm and manage—because, in terms of emphases and pauses and how something is said genuinely, the south Indian languages are not very different from one another. The really difficult thing is not the language but making the film, making the scene work, keeping it real and yet making it pacy and entertaining. Achieving that balance is such a tricky art. Compared to that, language is a lesser burden. You have to cross that bridge, you can't think about it too much.

RANGAN: Did *Pallavi Anupallavi* pan out the way you wanted, in terms of the shooting?

RATNAM: I've not been trained in film-making. All my knowledge was bookish and inferential. I had to learn everything on the job. Everything was new. I could not afford to share this truth with anybody on the set. I had to pretend on several fronts, making people believe that I knew the craft. The result was drastic. I had a huge advantage that my first day of shooting was with Rohit, who was brilliant. The kid made that part of it very easy and smooth. So the problem, mainly, was trying to come to terms with myself. When you conceive a scene at the writing table, it is just you and your imagination. On paper, the characters were a name, a notion, an abstract image in the mind—now, on location, those

'[The film] was so startlingly different from anything that had come before in Tamil cinema.' Rajinikanth and Shobha in Mullum Malarum.

abstractions were going away and becoming specifics with a face, with a preset body language, and sometimes with very clichéd reactions. You're seeing somebody very specific, walking in a particular fashion, possibly wearing something you don't like, and the scene is taking place now in this corridor—there's a certain harsh reality about a frame, about cinema, whereas on paper, in writing, it is still just an image of the character and not the face of the character.

So you sometimes start thinking that all the people around, playing the different characters, are being themselves. You feel that everyone is messing the entire thing up, tearing apart the mental graph that you had carried from the time you started the script. Then there is the geography. There is a camera and there are actors. There is the sun playing hide-and-seek.

There are so many options and variables. Each element brings its own presence to the party. This shift from paper to film, this metamorphosis, is the chemistry that makes or mars a director. That was the first day, and by the third or fourth day I remember telling Balu Mahendra, 'I want to run.' And he said, 'Don't worry. I felt it the first day when I started directing a film.' He said that the disillusionment would pass soon, and he was right—in the sense that you slowly start learning that this transition from paper, from the abstract to reality, is your coming to terms with a different medium, that you have to rediscover everything in this medium. You actually reinvent your ideas on film.

There has to be a leap from paper to screen. That's the job of a director—to elevate what's in the script to the next plane. You have to put in an effort to bring in other elements to make it alive. That is the key—to make it alive, to make it magical. You have to take the elements around you and invest them in that scene. You have to be able to draw the actor into that particular moment, so that he will bring something of himself into the character he is playing. It's like shedding one skin and taking on another. The most difficult thing in the first phase was this transition. And then you discover that there are some things that you cannot write and can only capture. Whatever you write, there is the magic of actually capturing a moment, a face, an expression, a bit of light, a movement—and you really discover that while making films. You discover that those are the things that really elevate a scene on the page to the next level. I'd never assisted anybody before, so I wanted to be sure that what I did was grammatically correct. I wanted to be accepted or rejected for the content and not for the spelling and grammatical errors.

Also, we had no budget. To complete the last three days of shooting, we had to wait for a year and nine months. We ran into call-sheet problems. Each day was a mini battle. You'd go on a fifteen-day schedule, and for ten days there'd be no generator van, no lights, no support. You'd just go with the camera and the reflector, and you'd shoot. It took me about five years to get a crane as part of the standard equipment, and my first high-speed shot was in my fifth film, *Mouna Raagam*, when Divya and her sisters pour a sheet of water from the terrace on their romancing brother below. I could not afford it till then. But you learned to work with what you had or what you could afford. After fifteen days of shooting, we saw the rushes. I was relieved, to say the least. Not because it was great, but because it had transformed from paper to film. The second schedule was relatively easier because I was ready for the chaos. After all these years of film-making, whenever I stand behind the camera, I still have the same feeling as I did on the first day. Every film still seems like the first film.

RANGAN: What were the reactions when you first showed *Pallavi Anupallavi* around?

RATNAM: After seeing the first copy, my father did not say if it was good or bad, or if he liked it or not. He told me, in no uncertain terms, that this film, at best, would fare well in the A centres, but fail at the B and C centres. He was right eventually—it was an average success. It got the Karnataka State Award for Best Screenplay. It would have been nice to get a pat on the back instead of an accurate prediction. V.S. Laxman of Ananda Pictures, who was a family friend and a big distributor, was more generous. He said that this was the best first film since Sridhar's. That was the best compliment I got for *Pallavi Anupallavi*.

On the day of release, I was at the theatre in [Bangalore's] Kempegowda Circle. The show was not full. Many people were passing by and I would tell myself that

'She flatly refused the female lead role [in Pallavi Anupallavi*] when I offered it to her.'* Suhasini with Mohan and Prathap Pothen in Nenjathai Killadhey.

this man here and that man there will walk into the theatre. But they didn't. It was a heart-wrenching experience. Watching the film with the audience was unadulterated torture. You want the film to move faster and arrive at the best shot and dialogues (at least, as per your judgement) and the humorous parts as quickly as possible. You want to run into the projection room and turn the reels faster. There was always a second's delay before the reaction could be heard or felt. That second was quite unbearable.

RANGAN: After making a film, did you finally understand what the director's job entails? You said that it is to elevate what's in the script to the next plane. Is there anything else?

RATNAM: In the studio system in the West, I think they slot you. From whatever little I've seen over there, the director is primarily required to deal with the talent, with the actors. But here, they give you enough freedom. Your role is not predefined. They let you breathe a little. No one tells you what to shoot, and whether you can shoot more or whether you need to shoot less. They just want you to deliver a good product. As long as you are willing to put your neck on the line, they trust you and they let you do what you want.

The director's role is much larger here. Anybody can take a scene that's been constructed, finished, finalized, and shoot it. That's just an execution job. If you have good actors, you just need to take care of the rough edges and you're okay. But if you're looking at ways to take the script to the next level, looking for something extra within the scene—the way it's shot, the way it's performed—then that becomes the real job of the director. What I try to

Pallavi Anupallavi, Unaru, Pagal Nilavu, Idhayakoyil

do today is search for that way to add value to what's on paper. Sometimes you get it, and sometimes you don't—but you have the opportunity to push for more.

RANGAN: Your second film, *Unaru*, was in Malayalam.

RATNAM: That was where I got a break. The only person who saw my Kannada film and asked me to do a film was N.G. John, a producer from the Malayalam film industry. His last two films, *Eenadu* and *Iniyengilum*, with director I.V. Sasi, were huge hits. And his next film was mine. I went through a real struggle there. The last schedule of *Pallavi Anupallavi* was stretched inordinately to a whole year, so I started working on my next script, named *Divya*, along with another script which I never ended up directing. (Though at one point, while considering a Telugu film, I flirted with that other script. I ended up making *Geetanjali* instead). *Divya* eventually became *Mouna Raagam*, my fifth film and my first hit. This time I wrote in Tamil. I realized that it's stupid to write in English and then try to translate it because the rhythms in English are very different. The humour is very different, and with *Pallavi Anupallavi*, it took us more time to translate than to write the original script. Anyway, I couldn't convince a producer about either of these new scripts. And then the offer for the Malayalam film came my way.

RANGAN: And you zeroed in on the subject of labour relations, which seems a very

'I narrated the script for Mouna Raagam, and the producer said it wouldn't work ... He was in a political zone.' Mammootty (right) in Iniyengilum.

drastic departure for you—then as now.

RATNAM: I narrated the script for *Mouna Raagam*, and the producer said it wouldn't work. After *Eenadu* and *Iniyengilum*, he was in a political zone. *Iniyengilum* was about a group that went to Japan and came back to India and tried to bring about Japanese discipline here. *Unaru* was about corruption in the labour movement. (They still have these strong unions which control everything.) *Unaru* was about the new blood looking for opportunities, and the older generation that wanted to continue in the same old fashion. It was about the corruption that seeps into union politics. It was a film I had a tough time on because the producer was also part-scriptwriter. We had a writer, a wonderful man named Damodaran Master. He was a physical instructor in a school and a football umpire, but he was also a prolific screenwriter. The three of us would sit on the script and it would be a battle. I think it was basically because the schools we came from were very different.

RANGAN: They were more old-school.

RATNAM: They had given two huge hits, and I made sure that their new film was not a hit. So they were from the right school, probably. But I don't know why they chose me. Sometimes, they think a director's job is to take shots, whereas I feel that a director's job is to tell a story and get performances. That was possibly a point of conflict. Actually, the next three films—after *Pallavi Anupallavi*—were very difficult for me. It was a struggle that made me question if this was what I really wanted to do. *Pallavi Anupallavi* had money issues, but everything else was what I wanted to do. Nobody asked me to do things differently. Whereas here, there was a lot of interference. I would fight with them all night long about some scenes that I really hated. And the next day, along with lunch, those scenes would come back for me to shoot. It was tough to find space within something that was so restrictive and still hold on and leave my stamp.

The film possibly suffers because there were two people—actually three—pulling it in different directions. The film is in-between, neither theirs nor mine. It was lost in the middle. I'm not a big fan of *Eenadu* and *Iniyengilum*. But for me *Unaru* was an opportunity to do another film, which is all I wanted to do. So I was ready to go in and see if I could convert *Unaru* into something I would like. There are moments and shots and flavours in the film that are mine—there are kids and old women, conflicts and relationship issues, all in a film based on the union movement. But there are also very conventional elements like someone becoming a prostitute because of poverty. And to get that into your school of thought becomes a bit difficult. I used to curse my luck all the time.

But those were learning curves, learning about the kinds of problems on sets and how to handle them. *Pallavi Anupallavi* had three or four characters in a frame. In *Unaru*, every frame had a minimum of ten characters. I didn't know how to shoot ten people and get a scene working. I had to learn that very fast. For me, the details in a scene were very important. They had a conventional way of taking a master shot and using a few inserts. I was trying to choreograph it a bit, getting the movement to flow and have other business along with it to make it look like it's really happening. So the film was a struggle in more than one way. But the rest of the team was very good. Ramachandra Babu was the cameraman. Ilaiyaraaja did the music. And Lenin cut the film. The film was shot in one stretch. We started shooting on February 1, and the film was released on April 14.

RANGAN: Now that you mentioned it, what is the reason for the continued presence of kids and old women in your films?

RATNAM: India's like that. We have big families, closely knit families, and there's really very little interaction that does not involve different generations. It's just a reflection of that Indianness.

RANGAN: And then we come to *Pagal Nilavu*. Your first film in Tamil already shows your fascination with the *nallavana–kettavana* [are you a good man or a bad man?] question you later posed explicitly in *Nayakan*.

RATNAM: Maybe I still haven't gotten over it. Maybe there is no clear answer to that question. Anyway, the producer, 'Sathya Jothi' Thyagarajan, was a friend. We'd grown up together. His father and my uncle were partners. He became a producer and knew that I'd become a director. Even before I started my first film, I used to meet him. Once again, I tried to pitch *Divya*, but he wanted something with action, in the commercial mould. When you meet a producer, you can't have just one idea. I had the germ of this idea, and we did this story.

RANGAN: In Sathyaraj, you got hold of an actor who was getting to be quite popular.

RATNAM: He was on the rise as a bad man. I'd never seen a film of his at that point. The producer suggested his name. I met him and asked him if he'd act with his current hairstyle, which was near-bald. He said he had no problem. And then we had Murali and Revathy playing the lead.

RANGAN: I remember an interview of Murali, where he said he was constantly being pressured from two sides—because he was dark-skinned, his father wanted him to use make-up, but Revathy kept insisting that he looked best without make-up.

RATNAM: I don't think he had a choice. We were very clear that we wanted no make-up. I don't think Revathy would have interfered with that. He was darker than the other actors, so he was more self-conscious. But ultimately, he had no issues. Maybe he had conflicts in his mind, but they never came out at all. No one wore make-up in the film. The cinematographers I've worked with are very good, and they all prefer a clean face, without make-up.

RANGAN: The lead-in to the fight between Sharath Babu (a cop) and the punk-youngster Murali has the same dynamics as the relationship between cop Prabhu and punk-youngster Karthik in *Agni Natchatiram*. You seemed fond, at that point, of depicting that aggressive side of youth.

RATNAM: It's there in each one of us in some fashion or the other. At that age, at that time, you are a little brash. But every character that you write need not be something that you are. Anil Kapoor, in *Pallavi Anupallavi*, was also in the same age bracket, but he was from a richer background. So, to an extent, he was a little more sober and sophisticated. Sometimes, you just put yourself in someone else's shoes.

RANGAN: Early on, Revathy is always seen

'At that age, at that time, you are a little brash.'
Murali (left) and Sharath Babu in Pagal Nilavu.

with a camera around her neck, an incidental detail that, without spelling it out, tells us something about her. You managed to bring some understated shading even into what you call a commercial-mould film.

RATNAM: I don't think this was a huge step in that sense. This cop [Sharath Babu] has just been transferred to a smaller town. He comes with his young daughter and his sister [Revathy], who's finished her education. What would she do? That's what the photography is about. It's still just at the surface level and not as detailed as I'd have liked it to be. We still have no clue what she's interested in, what she wants to be. Ideally, it should be much more etched out. When you're working in the mainstream format, you know that if you can reach this level, you can push it further.

RANGAN: There's one scene that's better than I remembered, and I bring it up because it belongs to an older school of film-making. Sharath Babu comes to Radhika, the local dance teacher, to enrol his daughter and sister in classes. As he's about to leave, his shirt gets caught on her anklet bells. That's shorthand that he's going to become romantically involved with her. And when Radhika learns that the daughter had learnt dance from her mother till the latter died, she says she'll continue the lessons, thus signalling that she's ready to take over as mother and wife. This sort of melodramatic symbolism isn't your type of filmmaking at all.

RATNAM: We all grew up admiring film-makers like K. Balachander; so maybe these are just things that you have to do at some point and get them out of your system. You're still trying out what works for you and what doesn't. Later, you try not to make your handwriting so visible. But this was an early time and I wasn't so inhibited about being flashy. As you go along, you realize that you can do the same things without giving out signals that this is what is happening.

RANGAN: The character played by Sathyaraj, Periyavar, is a don-type figure like the ones you later created in *Nayakan* and *Thalapathy*, but unlike those films, there's no attempt to make Periyavar a sympathetic figure—except in the late scene where he reveals to his granddaughter, at the dinner table, that he had an impoverished upbringing.

RATNAM: The film is from Murali's point of view. He works under this man, believing that this man is good, and slowly he realizes that his employer is not as clean as he appears to be. Instead of being an author on the outside—stating that this character is good and this one is bad—I tried to reveal Periyavar through Murali's journey. When he realizes the truth about Periyavar, we also realize the truth. In *Nayakan* and *Thalapathy*, the stories are told through the viewpoints of the gangsters, so we get to know about them right from the beginning.

RANGAN: Didn't you want to write your own dialogues in your first film in Tamil?

RATNAM: We were trying to make a mainstream commercial film. The producer knew the sensibility of what he wanted. A.L. Narayanan wrote the dialogues—but not all of it. We used what we wanted, and the rest was done with someone else or by me. It didn't matter to me who was credited because it'd still be you. Because even if someone else writes the dialogues, you're still making sure that he's writing something close to what you want, close to the way you think your characters would speak. So it was not really an issue. But yes, the film was based in a smaller town, and it needed someone who could get that flavour right, someone who could put himself in those shoes and speak that language.

RANGAN: *Pagal Nilavu* was where you first used songs in the commercial format—the hero-introduction song (*Maina maina*), the hero-heroine-teasing-one-another song fashioned along the lines of older songs

'The film was based in a smaller town, and needed [a writer] . . . who could put himself in those shoes and speak that language.' Radhika (left) and Sathyaraj (far right) in Pagal Nilavu.

where two people in the same vicinity would pretend to be unaware of each other's presence (*Vaaraayo vaanmathi*), the yearning-for-a-man song (*Vaidehi Raman*), and so on. Your earlier films used songs mostly in the background.

RATNAM: More than the songs, this was the first time I shot a dance sequence—and that was new. I didn't have a clue how to shoot a dance. Both in *Pallavi Anupallavi* and *Unaru*, the songs were a part of the narrative. They weren't different visually, as the characters didn't really sing or dance. So this was a leap. You're shooting drama at one stretch. Then you break away to shoot songs. Then you get back to drama. These are two different mindsets. With songs, there's a certain amount of abstraction, a certain amount of flamboyance. It's like a film within a film, and it has its own graph, with its own peak and so on.

Even today, after so many films, the first day of shooting songs is really the most difficult. Because you have a concept for a song but you don't know how to convert this concept into action. Unless the song involves no choreography (like *Vaaraayo vaanmathi*), you have to be in sync with the choreographer, have a rapport, and you have to push them in a direction where they get to break new ground. We were shooting *Maina maina* and *Nee appodhu paatha pulla* together, in the sense that we finished the first and shot the next. I had to learn very quickly. In a way, it's like learning film-making. It's a new game within a game. You have to learn the rules and be able to play with them, and when needed, bend these rules. There have been masters in song picturization like Guru Dutt and Vijay Anand and Sridhar, and you treat them as benchmarks. You try to reach that level. You battle with it and try to come out on the other side.

RANGAN: I thought shooting songs would be easier (from your perspective) because the bulk of the work is taken care of by the choreographer.

RATNAM: A choreographer comes in after doing another song in another film. When he or she comes to your set, they are just listening to the song and its rhythm. They really do not remember what the character is at the point, or where the song appears in the film, or where it should be emotionally, or how you've been shooting the rest of the film, all of which dictate the kind of shots and the cutting points you require. So you've got to bring them into your zone. It's a two-way interaction. It's like working with a cameraman. You have to get him around to your way of thinking. You have to land on a concept for the song. And then you try and find a way of executing this concept.

RANGAN: In the film's comedy track about a husband whose wife refuses to sleep with him, Goundamani plays a Malayali named George Kutty. Is this a remnant from your *Unaru* experience?

RATNAM: This was something written by

the people who did the comedy track, Livingston [the actor] and Kumar. The fact that Goundamani was in the film made it a mainstream comedy track, where they're used to a certain style. And here, if you ask them to play it naturally, they're not comfortable. This particular track was shot on sets. I didn't have the clout to get it shot in more realistic locations. That's the thing with early films. Till you have your say, you have to battle with these issues. The comedy track in my next film, *Idhayakoyil*, was done by Veerappan, who was a part of the producer's set-up and who'd written a lot of tracks for Goundamani. That comedy track worked much better, to be honest.

RANGAN: Your earlier films have this parallel-running comedy track, but your later films incorporate comic elements much more subtly, without a separate 'track' as such.

RATNAM: I think it started with *Pagal Nilavu* and *Idhayakoyil* having comedy. *Pallavi Anupallavi* had no comedy track. In *Mouna Raagam*, too, it wasn't written as a comedy track. The part about the lively Sardarji was there even when the script was called *Divya*. It's part of the narrative about a girl who goes to an alien place and doesn't know the language. *Mouna Raagam* did well, but not everywhere, and when we made *Agni Natchatiram*, we wanted it to succeed even in the areas where *Mouna Raagam* could not. And therefore, we thought we'd put in a comedy track. The style of the film was very flippant and it could take the comedy track; whereas with *Geetanjali*, I felt it was a compromise that wasn't helping me at all. With *Agni Natchatiram*, I didn't feel it was wrong. I enjoyed it to an extent. But with *Geetanjali*, it just didn't feel right. I don't mind having comedy in a film, but it should be in the same vein as the rest of the film.

RANGAN: *Idhayakoyil* was your first excursion into a rustic setting. Were there apprehensions about shooting in an unfamiliar milieu?

RATNAM: There were much bigger problems to worry about. This was, I think, the most important film of my life. It was such a big compromise. I've never felt so miserable during any shooting. But it gave me clarity. That's when I looked back on why I came into this business—it was not to make movies like *Idhayakoyil*. And I decided that if I did compromise henceforth and made commercial films, they would be my own compromises and not the ones thrust on me by somebody else. I sat back and made a list of film-makers who had survived. Whether it's a Balachander or a Bhimsingh, they've done their films the way they wanted to all along. That's the only way to really play the long game. That's why I made *Mouna Raagam* next.

RANGAN: How did you end up making the film in the first place?

RATNAM: The producer [Kovaithambi, of Motherland Pictures] had the dates of both top heroines, Ambika and Radha. He also had a story ready. Someone suggested my name. He had no clue who I was. He had not seen any films I'd done. He sent over the story on a cassette. I put it on and I went to sleep. It was not my kind of film at all. I was into *Pagal Nilavu*, which was not yet released. So I went to tell him that I had a film underway, and till it was out, I could not do another film because that was the way I worked. In front of me, he called up the managers of both heroines. He cancelled the dates that he had and postponed the shooting. He told me to finish *Pagal Nilavu* and come back to him.

I was stuck. I should have just told him that I didn't want to do the film. Now I had to do the film. But then they were very successful producers and I thought I could go in and convince them with different ideas. I narrated the story of *Divya* to his writer. He said it wasn't their kind of story. I tried working out a few options. But they had a story and a very simplistic way of looking at it: 'At the interval point, one heroine dies. At the climax, the second heroine dies. The film is a hit.' I thought I could get into it and make something out of this film. I wrote an entirely new screenplay based on the concept they had, going closer towards the [Charlie Chaplin's] *Limelight* kind of storytelling, about a huge star. The film is like that, about a singer and a new girl who's coming up. The producer listened to it and said it was not young, not modern. He said, 'You just take the shots. We'll look after everything else.'

RANGAN: I suppose the one significant aspect of this film, apart from the songs by Ilaiyaraaja, is that it presages the love-and-death angle you later explored in *Geetanjali* in a much lighter vein. This is more melodramatic.

RATNAM: I didn't think of *Idhayakoyil* while writing *Geetanjali*. Except for Ilaiyaraaja's music, there was nothing much I cared to remember about the film. The music was brilliant. That was the saving grace. There were a couple of songs that I really enjoyed working on, because I could do them the way I wanted to. *Naan paadum mouna raagam* was my homage to *Pyaasa*, a lost poet alone in an auditorium, with only his poetry and his past.

RANGAN: Did that song give you the title for your next film, which finally made you famous?

RATNAM: Yes.

Pallavi Anupallavi, Unaru, Pagal Nilavu, Idhayakoyil

2

'The film came out of this first-night scene'

Mouna Raagam (1986)

Divya (Revathy) is wrenched from a carefree existence when she's married off to Chandrakumar (Mohan), an eminently decent man who's puzzled by his new wife's insistent aloofness. Divya's sullen conduct is due to Manohar (Karthik), a high-spirited fellow she had once loved, and she has to decide between clinging to a long-dead past and capitulating to a most agreeable present.

BARADWAJ RANGAN: So you finally got to make Divya into a film.

MANI RATNAM: Yeah, it was practically like a second film. After *Pallavi Anupallavi*, this was completely my film, done the way I wanted it to be done, the way I thought it should be done. I cast Mohan, whom I'd worked with in *Idhayakoyil*. I tried working with PC [Sreeram] on *Idhayakoyil*, but that fell through. This was the first time we were able to work together. The rest of the collaborators were from my older films.

RANGAN: And you had Revathy, whom you'd worked with in *Pagal Nilavu*.

RATNAM: Yeah. She was very good even in her first film [Bharathiraja's *Mann Vaasanai*]. She came in as a talent. And by the time *Mouna Raagam* happened, we had a rapport. But she was not who I was thinking of while writing *Mouna Raagam*. I was still doing my first film then, and I thought I'd end up doing this too in Kannada. I had someone like Anant Nag and Supriya Pathak in mind when I finished writing it. But it took quite a few years before I could finally make the film, and by then Revathy came into the picture.

RANGAN: Considering that this was the first time you were doing your own thing, so to speak, was it an easy shoot?

RATNAM: It was a lot of fun—it's just that we had to look after the production also. The only thing that changed between *Divya* and *Mouna Raagam* was the Karthik portion, which was not there in the earlier screenplay. In *Divya*, the girl's past was not there. It was just the story of how a girl settles into an arranged marriage. But by the time I'd done a few films, I realized that this was not enough to make the story reach across to a larger audience. There are still a lot of women who walk around trees in prayer to get married, who don't eat on certain days of the week so that they'll get married—and here, there's a girl who's refusing to get married.

So I decided that if I needed to make this accessible, I had to give the audience something that wouldn't make them question the character, but they'd accept that as a plot point. And then the film can deal with the concept of an arranged marriage—two strangers suddenly thrown together, and how they find a way to adjust. That's how her past with Karthik came in. As a film, it would have probably been better had it remained true to the original concept. It was something I resisted at first. But having made this decision of giving an easier reason for her resistance to the arranged marriage, we thought we'd make the flashback portion light and breezy.

RANGAN: It's hard to believe that Karthik's character [in the flashback] was an afterthought, because he's so identified with this film. I've always felt you could

'It took quite a few years before I could finally make the film, and by then Revathy came into the picture.'

---

have had a song in the Karthik portions. They were so alive. It must have seemed like a natural choice to have an exuberant duet there.

RATNAM: When something in a set of sequences is in itself elevating, you don't need a song to elevate it further. When the scenes are doing the job, you don't need a song.

RANGAN: With the Karthik character, the film comes to bear a resemblance to [Mahendran's] *Nenjathai Killadhey*, which is also about a woman torn between the man she loved and the man she married. Your treatment, of course, is very different, but while making a film, do you worry that a subject you get into has been touched upon earlier?

RATNAM: You should be confident that you're not just telling a common story but trying to attack it from a specific direction. But that's a chance you take at any point of time. And we in India generally tend to believe that we are not as good as the westerners. Anything that you do in India, if somebody in the West has done something similar, you think that is where it has come from. You never ever think that something can be created over here. In [Lars von Trier's] *Dancer in the Dark*, there is a beautiful piece of choreography on a moving train. The film was made after *Dil Se* and *Chhaiya chhaiya*. If it had been made before, we in India would have said that *Chhaiya chhaiya* was copied from that. But one has to go with the belief that you have a strong and unique enough take on a subject. To me, it was very clear that *Mouna Raagam* was about this relationship within an arranged marriage. I just needed to rationalize the heroine's behaviour, and Karthik was the rationalization. If I'd done the film ten years later, I'd have left out the Karthik character. But at that point of time, we did something that was entertaining and would reach a wider audience. I was not worried about *Nenjathai Killadhey*.

RANGAN: Karthik is something of an anarchist, but that background isn't really explored in detail. You get glimpses—like a poster of [the Taviani brothers' wartime fantasy] *The Night of San Lorenzo*. *Unaru* apart, have you ever thought of making a full-fledged political film?

RATNAM: To an extent, I think *Aayidha Ezhuthu* [*Yuva*] was a political film. It dealt with student politics. Here, in *Mouna Raagam*, we're telling the story of this girl. At first, we see Karthik's other side only when she sees him beating people up or at the police station. And then she sees him with his friends, planning something she's not sure she wants to be a part of. She's not even into finding out why he's doing this. His motivation is not important to her and therefore not important to us. So, what we're seeing of him is what we're seeing through her. That is all that was required.

RANGAN: I think Karthik's was the first character in Tamil cinema to ask a girl out for 'a cup of coffee'. It was like a date, and no one spoke like that in the mid-1980s. In fact, in young-love stories like [E.M. Ibrahim's] *Oru Thalai Raagam*, they hardly spoke at all.

RATNAM: To date, there's still a huge segment of the population where there's hardly any communication between a young man and a young woman. There's no space where they can interact—so the situation of *Oru Thalai Raagam* is very real. But in one section of the urban population of that time, there was the possibility of interaction. There was the possibility of not being shy and the girl not turning around and walking away when somebody spoke to her. That was

---

'If I'd done the film ten years later, I'd have left out the Karthik character.'

the section I was dealing with in *Mouna Raagam*. Guys in real life said things like, 'Let's go out for a cup of coffee.' These were guys who grew up with *The Doors* and *The Beatles* and things like that. So asking a girl if she'd like to have a cup of coffee was not a big thing. It just wasn't reflected in Tamil mainstream cinema at that point. That's all.

RANGAN: When Mohan says that he learnt to cook *kaiya-suttu-kaala-suttu* [by clumsily burning his hands and feet], is that line autobiographical? Is that how you learnt to cook?

RATNAM: I still haven't learnt cooking. But if I do, that is how I will learn.

RANGAN: In general, how autobiographical are your films? How much of your persona is revealed through your films? We spoke about this a bit while discussing *Pagal Nilavu*.

RATNAM: I don't know if there's anything explicitly autobiographical, but you do invest shades of yourself in everything you write. Even if you're writing someone like the villain in *Agni Natchatiram*, you enjoy being him during that period; so there's a bit of you in him. That's the huge advantage of being a writer or a film-maker. You can live the lives of several kinds of people at the same time. You have the liberty of going away from who you are and put yourself in someone else's shoes and think from that standpoint. That's another form of putting yourself into your movies, existing as someone who's not from your world. If I were directing someone else's script, the characters would be a combination of that writer's mind and my mind, and the actor's of course. You'll find all of us in there. But if it's my script, then it's me and the actor.

RANGAN: What about the Tamilian characters who struggle with non-Tamil languages—Roja in *Roja*, Divya in *Mouna Raagam*, Velu in *Nayakan*? Is there an element of autobiography in them? You said you didn't know Hindi when you were in Bombay.

RATNAM: I still feel the same way when I go to Bombay. I still don't know Hindi. I still struggle if I have to speak to somebody who speaks only Hindi. So it's there, probably to a greater extent in *Mouna Raagam* than in *Roja*. Quite a few of my stories have taken place outside Tamil-speaking places. This also brings about a certain amount of restriction, because the communication needs to be in Tamil [for the sake of the audience] and yet the story is taking place outside, so we have to find ways and means of making it real, making it look like it's happening, and have just a few characters who would know the language. In *Roja*, we had to find a character who spoke Tamil, the Janakaraj character in the temple, to help me understand what was going on in Roja's mind. Her conflict, her desire, her anguish, her fight—she needed somebody to bounce those thoughts off and

'To date, there's still a huge segment of the population where there's hardly any communication between a young man and a young woman.'

help her communicate with the officials. So in Kashmir we had to create a character from Tamil Nadu.

But I had a huge problem with the Pankaj Kapur character. He is a Kashmiri militant. He has to speak and I have to understand him. It's a battle, in the sense that you push yourself into a corner because of the language. But in *Bombay* that was not the case—Tamil people do live in Bombay. They interact and there is Tamil spoken. So you try to use it to your advantage instead of it becoming a burden. That's the beauty of India. The real communication is in different forms, and you can position each one in a way that suits you and find a reasonable logic for it to be correct. With different films, you have to do this differently. It cannot become a conventional pattern. It becomes a gimmick after a while, and it gets tougher if you do films set outside Tamil Nadu all the time.

RANGAN: Hollywood's World War films solved this problem by having the Germans speak English with a German accent, the Italians with an Italian accent. In a sense, this is what actors like Mehmood did, when speaking Hindi with a thick 'Tamil' accent.

RATNAM: I think it sounds very odd. I think we've gotten used to fifty or sixty years of World War films to accept English with a German accent. It's taken quite a bit of time, but I don't think it will sound right with anything else. I don't think that, in a French film, a German can speak French with a German accent and get away with it. And I don't think that's really the right solution. It's better to have the person

Mouna Raagam 35

speak in Hindi and still find ways to communicate. In our films, we still need logic or we will not be able to accept it. So we have to come up with means and ways in which to place those stories, and after some time you run out of tricks.

RANGAN: What do you do then?

RATNAM: I started making films in Hindi when I ran out of tricks.

RANGAN: Ah, so *that's* why you started making Hindi films. Jokes aside, the Karthik portion, with its casual youthfulness, came to identify you. But then a lot of what came to be identified with your films was first seen in *Mouna Raagam*—the dramatic shiny-dark cinematography, the boho-chic sets . . .

RATNAM: The story is about a person who goes to a strange place where she doesn't know the language, where it's colder. She's an alien, and then she starts belonging to that place. That's why it was set in Delhi. This was an indoor film and both PC and I were ready to experiment. We didn't want it to be claustrophobic. We wanted the indoors to look as lively as the outdoors—because there weren't too many characters, and we didn't want it to look like a play. So PC came up with this idea of backlighting inside a house. It was wild and brilliant. [Thotta] Tharrani found us this house right in Chennai which had a lot of sunlight coming in and which was so different that it could be convincing as a Delhi house, and give PC all the freedom to light the inside like the outdoors.

RANGAN: This was also the first time people noticed the kind of stylish, almost-staccato dialogues that became your trademark.

RATNAM: It's not stylized for the sake of stylizing. The film is based in a city, and this is the way educated and Anglicized (to an extent; in thought) city folks speak. My first film was also written like that, because that, again, was city-based. It just wasn't talked about because it was in Kannada. Balu Mahendra used to write dialogues that sounded less like 'dialogue'. I was particular that my conversations should not sound like 'dialogue'. I didn't want lines that sounded as if they were thought and written for a situation. They should resemble conversation. So it was an attempt at making it as easy as possible, and I tried to use dialogue only to get across what needed to get across. There were other things being conveyed through visuals, through performances, through the mood. So the dialogue was just to capture the way people react or behave in these situations.

RANGAN: Was *Mouna Raagam* the first time you got involved in the consolidated aspect of film-making? There was unison in everything, from the title design to the fonts to the stills. Those days, even the big production houses were very indifferent about the marketing and advertising aspects of their films. This is probably a result of your management background.

RATNAM: It has less to do with my management background than the probability that I'm a control freak. My first film *Pallavi Anupallavi* also had it. It has to do with the way you want to present your film. Every aspect that you present to the public should be in sync with the film's vision, so you make sure that all outputs—whether a still or a blow-up or a font or a design—represent something about the film. It is a way of knowing what the film is all about. It's a slice of the whole product. That's the only way you can have a cohesive product. If you are a film viewer, the first thing you notice is the title and the next thing is the first visual that you see. Whether or not you consciously observe the titles and the designs and the font, it makes an impact. That's why some posters become classics. It's very important to get it right, and it involves a lot of work. I would spend a month or two trying out various options with the person in charge of stills and blow-ups. It's always been like that. The only difference is that those days it used to be an individual, whereas today you deal with a production house.

RANGAN: One of my favourite scenes from the film is when Divya is sitting by the *tulasi* plant—that dramatic top-angle shot—and her sister-in-law (the only one

---

'Every aspect that you present to the public should be in sync with the film's vision, so you make sure that all outputs—whether a still or a blow-up or a font or a design—represent something about the film.'

who understands what Divya is going through, for she too has recently faced this situation) comes to take her in for her wedding night. Divya pleads to be left alone, wondering how she can be expected to do something like that with a man she doesn't know. I'm probably generalizing, but this level of inquiry into a woman's psyche is not something you'd expect to find in a young male director.

RATNAM: The basis for the entire film was just that one thought. *Divya* was first written as a short story, in pathetically poor Brahmin-Tamil. (I was writing in Tamil for the first time after school, so I was rusty. You can't read it now. My wife laughs at it.) In our society, we bring up girls with all possible restrictions—with regard to clothes, with regard to talking with boys—and then suddenly, one day, we push them into a room with a strange man and ask them to start living with him. We educate these girls, expose them to the world, and yet, we expect them to toe the line in this matter. And however understanding the man is, the fact remains that he just wants to get his hands on her. So it is a huge process for a woman who's able to think for herself. The film came out of this first-night scene, and the short story is only about this first night. All the things she says later—*kambilipoochi maadhiri* [that his touch feels creepy], and all that—are actually about this night.

RANGAN: So in the short story, the man has his way with her that night (unlike in the film, where Mohan waits patiently for Revathy to come around).

RATNAM: Yeah, the short story was only that. It was not planned as a film at that point. Only after I wrote the story did I realize I could base a film on it. So I took a month off between the long schedule gaps of *Pallavi Anupallavi*, when I had nothing else to do, and wrote the script of *Divya*.

RANGAN: When her husband is hospitalized, Revathy does something unusual for a Mani Ratnam protagonist. She prays before a huge statue of Ganesha. Your characters, especially your leads, aren't typically shown as religious.

RATNAM: Either way—whether a character is a believer or not—it becomes interesting. Either way, it gives a shade to the character. There is this girl who's a bit of a rebel. She talks of progressiveness and is ready to fight when asked to settle for a conventional marriage. But when she's pushed, when her husband is fighting for his life, there is this traditional quality that surfaces, and she prays. It's a natural instinct to want to lean back on a higher power at that moment. So despite all her other strong qualities, there is that vulnerability in her. It makes her more

---

'She gets married, goes to somebody else's house (which is completely strange), and the strange land accentuates this struggle.'

human, and this shot conveys that with very little effort.

RANGAN: The protagonist of *Nayakan* undergoes a similar trajectory. When younger and at the peak of his power, he isn't especially pious when his wife, after prayers, waylays him with the *aarti* paraphernalia. (His lips seem to straighten out in an indication of impatience.) But after losing her, he performs rites for her departed soul. Much later, when his daughter asks him if he thinks he's God, he touches the *rudraksham* he wears around his neck.

RATNAM: He is probably a little more religious than Divya. Any religious person would do something like that. But it's not in your face. It's the quality of the actor that brings genuineness to this sort of thing.

RANGAN: Divya's plight is exquisitely brought out by Ilaiyaraaja's background score. What is your involvement with this process? Do you sit with your composers for each scene and tell them what you want?

RATNAM: It's your film. You have to be with them—otherwise, how do you let them know what you have in mind? Ilaiyaraaja is amazing with background scores. He is so good, so fantastic. He sees the movie once, then puts the reel on while he's scoring, and as the reel is playing, he jots down a word here and a word there that are cues for him. And when the reel is over, he sits and writes his score. That's it. He knows where the music should come, where it should finish, and what kind of score it should be, and as he finishes writing, his musicians are already copying their parts of the score and are ready to perform. He works at that speed. So if you want to say something, you have to say it.

For example, when Karthik makes his entry, the shots are bleached. The camera is hand-held—PC was lying low on a bedsheet to get the low-angle walking-in shot and the rest of us were pulling the sheet, PC and the camera. The scene has a Spanish feel to it, like a Western. That's all you need to whisper into Ilaiyaraaja's ear, and he would give it that kind of colour. He would convert it into that kind of tone. And then, when he finishes writing and plays it for the first time, when he conducts the score with the reel playing, you see the marriage between the music and the scene, and invariably it's fantastic. But if there's something specific that you want to say, you have to tell him right then, as he is watching the reel. Otherwise it's gone. By the time you say Jack Robinson, it's over. The scoring is over. It's too expensive to go back and correct it. But he's so good. He knows precisely what the soul of the scene is, and he is able to support it.

RANGAN: Do you have a similarly collaborative equation with Rahman?

RATNAM: With Rahman, the score is an

ongoing process. It's not like 'we have a recording today from 9 a.m. to 9 p.m.', and that is when the music will be scored. He does pieces and sits with you and we look at the score. Or you tell him this is how you look at the score. Sometimes you put temp music and show it to him and tell him about the pacing and where you want the score, and if he differs, he'll work on it and show it to you. It's a two-way street. Rahman is really a very, very director-friendly composer in that sense. He's willing to go in whatever direction you want to, but within that he'll find something that's very much his own. So it's always been a process of discovery, of finding things.

There are two things when we do the score. It should take the story to the people. It should be a link and do what it's meant to do. And—equally important—it should keep pushing the envelope as much as possible. However much you want to reach people, it doesn't mean you have to reach them through clichés. Sometimes you have to change completely, do something unconventional. There are certain standard and clichéd background-score cues that are very easy to fall into and which will work very well, but the idea is to make the score kind of lateral, instead of just supportive. Then it gives another dimension to the film.

The easiest example I can think of is from *Bombay*. The violence was not scored with rhythmic violin pieces, like it was war, but instead like agony, like a wail. While the action is ferocious, the background score is a scream of pain, an aching melody, shouting for it to stop. It's completely against

---

'There is this girl who's a bit of a rebel. She ... is ready to fight when asked to settle for a conventional marriage.' Revathy and Mohan in Mouna Raagam.

the grain of the visual. It could very easily have gone the conventional way of doing action like action, making the score big and dramatic, whereas we could go this way and tell another story, adding another layer which is like a subtext to the entire thing. We've done this in a lot of films, not doing something necessarily the way it's always been done. If I sit with you on those films, I can take you through each decision.

RANGAN: *Mouna Raagam* was the first of your films to feature a Tamilian leaving his/her home and facing struggles in an alien land with an alien language and culture. This trope has been constant throughout—in *Roja*, in *Bombay*, in *Nayakan*, even in *Guru* (where the Gujarati son-of-the-soil finds himself unwelcome in Bombay). This appears to be a reflection of your own experiences as an 'alien' in Bombay, while doing your MBA.

RATNAM: I think it really is an externalization of what the girl goes through. She gets married, goes to somebody else's house (which is completely strange), and the strange land accentuates this struggle. The language and the culture are not familiar, and the only person she is familiar with is the person she has a problem with. It was completely a dramatic decision. We were doing the film here in Madras. We shot the Delhi scenes here. We went to Delhi for two days and to Agra for a day. Budget-wise, it would have been easier for me to send her to Bangalore. But I thought that it would help to know that she's far away and that she can't just come back home.

RANGAN: And in your next film, *Nayakan*, you have this same conflict but on a grander scale. The protagonist not only goes to an alien place with an alien language, he's also required to fight alien forces and rise to the top.

RATNAM: That was the story of [the Bombay don] Varadaraja Mudaliar. Sometime after *Pagal Nilavu*, R.C. Prakash, the producer of [Bharathiraja's] *Tik Tik Tik*, wanted to do a film with Sathyaraj. I told him this outline—not really an outline but just an idea for a film. It was a project that was thought of vaguely at that time, but nothing happened until after *Mouna Raagam*. Just in terms of writing, *Nayakan* was so different from whatever I'd done before. *Mouna Raagam* was about a girl who didn't want to get married. She got married and she settled down eventually. When the thought of the film came to me, the finish came along with it. *Nayakan* was sort of biographical. I just knew about the rise of the man. Where does the story go after that? How does it finish? I had no idea how to get a hold of it. I had to do it bit by bit. By the time the shoot began, I had the complete first half of the script. I had a rough idea about the second half, but I didn't have an end.

3

'Two films at the same time —it was a roller coaster'

Nayakan (1987)

Sakthivelu (Kamal Haasan) is raised by a kindly Muslim in the slums of Dharavi. He realizes, soon, that rather than pleading with those in positions of power, as the poor are wont to, he'd rather be those men. His rise as a don, flouting black-and-white notions of morality, is followed by his fall in the eyes of his very moral daughter Charu (Karthika), who marries a police inspector (Nasser) to absolve herself of her father's sins.

BARADWAJ RANGAN: After your unsuccessful attempt to work with Kamal Haasan in *Pallavi Anupallavi*, you finally roped him in.

MANI RATNAM: Kamal had sent over a producer, 'Muktha' Srinivasan, when I was working on the script of *Agni Natchatiram*. *Agni* was the film I wanted to do after *Mouna Raagam*. I was trying to reach the markets I could not with *Mouna Raagam*, by making a film that was younger and more commercial. So 'Muktha' Srinivasan came home and said, dramatically, '*Kizhakku endha pakkam?*' [Which way is east?] He made me stand in that direction and gave me an envelope. I thought it was money—an advance maybe—but it was actually a video cassette of a Hindi film. He said Kamal wanted me to see the film. I was not interested in a remake but the producer insisted that I see the film. Though a cheque would have been more appreciated than a cassette, I said I'd see it. I put the tape in. It was about Shammi Kapoor in a nuthouse [*Pagla Kahin Ka*]. I couldn't bear it. I was very sure I wasn't interested.

So when he returned the next day, I told him I had always felt I was not good for remakes. It was better to get someone efficient, someone who'd do things quickly and get the film out as soon as possible. He wasn't flustered. He asked me to get into the car and go with him to AVM Studios, where Kamal was shooting, and tell Kamal what I'd told him. I realized that, as much as I didn't want to do this remake, he didn't want me for his film either. I met Kamal during his lunch break and told him that *Pagla Kahin Ka* was not my type of film and I wouldn't be able to do it. Kamal then asked me what kind of film I would prefer to make. He said that the tape was just to start a conversation. I went to say no, but now I had a chance to make a film with Kamal and he was asking me what kind of film I'd do with him. I said there were two possibilities. One was a very sleek, city-based action film, a *Dirty Harry* or a *Beverly Hills Cop* or a Bond-ish film, the kind of thing that had not been done much in Tamil cinema. It still hasn't been done. I am a big fan of sleek action films. I've always wanted to do something like that. The second possibility was the life of Varadaraja Mudaliar.

RANGAN: What intrigued you about his story?

RATNAM: The two years I studied in Bombay (1975–77), he was at his peak. People in the Matunga belt thought he was God. I used to wonder how anyone could treat a fellow human as God. I never understood why they would do this. It fascinated me. It was such a dramatic story, this man going from Tamil Nadu to Bombay and ruling the city. I outlined this thought to Kamal and he said fine. That's it. It was done. Decided. *Mouna Raagam* took five years to get approved. *Nayakan* got cleared in ten minutes. It was September, I think. He said he'd given 'Muktha' Srinivasan dates

'Apart from his ability to emote so well, Kamal is a master of technique.'

in December and we could start shooting. Meanwhile, I was getting ready for *Agni* and I'd fixed a schedule for January. I hardly had any time now because Kamal had committed too. Two films at the same time—it was a roller coaster.

We had scheduled three days of shooting in December, and I told Kamal I wouldn't be ready with the script. He said something that surprised me. He said that I could treat the three days as test shoots, with three get-ups for the three ages of the character. And we did just that. That is the kind of luxury I'd never had. The producer had no clue that we were shooting three scenes that were tests and may not make it to the final cut. They didn't, though they were nice scenes. But the test shoot helped to get Velu Nayakan's look right, and we also got the other details (art, props, shooting style, costumes) right.

The first real schedule of *Nayakan* took place in January. We finished fifteen days of shooting in the Dharavi set. After a two-day gap, we started work on *Agni*—the *Ninnukori* song and some early Amala–Prabhu sequences. It shows. Till today, PC and I feel we did not do justice to *Ninnukori*. But after that back-to-back schedule of two films, I realized that I could not work on both at the same time. So we stopped working on *Agni* for a year, till we released *Nayakan*, and then we started again. It was a good thing that my brother's company was producing *Agni*. I could tell him I'd do it later. Otherwise I'd have been in trouble.

RANGAN: So the film that really, really put you on the map was a complete accident.

RATNAM: Yeah. I think Kamal too didn't expect much from the film—at least not at the start and not what it became.

RANGAN: Looking at Kamal's performance or anything else, did you have an inkling that *Nayakan* would become what it became?

RATNAM: With the time and effort you invest in each project, you expect that each one will work. It's not that in *Nayakan* I was going out of the way and doing something extraordinary. It's just that it's such a pleasure when there's an actor who delivers more than you can imagine. It takes a weight off your shoulders, because you no longer have to carry the scene by yourself. I realized that I didn't have to stage a scene to prop up the actor. It was enough if the camera caught him. He brings credibility to the lines and makes it so effortless. He adds to the entire picture.

Apart from his ability to emote so well, he's a master of technique. He did quite a bit of the make-up for the other actors in the film. If I had someone with a wound that didn't look right, I'd go to him and ask him to fix it. He'd sit with the actor and get it done, and by that time I'd have finished all the other shots I had to do. He was really a part of the team that way. We could ask him for anything we wanted for anybody else and he would do it. He was the one who convinced Janakaraj and Delhi Ganesh to cut their hair and grow convincingly old along with Velu Nayakan. He would bring his own gun for a shot, and save us the trouble of using a terrible dummy. He had this bottle made of sugar glass, which he had brought from US, and he used it in the fight with the cop. He made sure that the scene played out real. It is a big boon to have an extra mind on the set.

RANGAN: Kamal had done a gamut of make-up-oriented roles earlier, many of which (like *Sagara Sangamam*) involved grey-haired wigs—but the level of authenticity of his old-age make-up here was astounding, right down from his bald spot.

RATNAM: We've seen him in all these roles before, and we know what we like and don't like about that kind of make-up. I was very clear that I wanted a clean-shaven old man. There's something very proper about Velu Nayakan, and I wanted him to look like you'd see him in real life—with a neat *veshti*, a nice shirt, and no beard. Kamal was a little apprehensive because he felt that the exposed jaw line would give away the fact that this was a young person. He felt that a beard would cover this problem. But I was very sure that I didn't want it to look like *Sagara Sangamam*. I wanted something clean.

And because we imposed that restriction [of the character being clean-shaven], we were pushed into doing something more. We were shooting the film mostly as the story unfolded. We'd almost finished everything before we got around to shooting the old-age portions. Luckily at the time, he had finished *Pushpak*, and he'd started doing one film at a time. So he could afford to cut his hair in the middle and make that bald spot. When he finished the film, he took his hair off completely

'There's something very proper about Velu Nayakan, and I wanted him with a neat veshti, a nice shirt, and no beard.'

and waited for it to grow back for his next film [*Sathya*]. He was willing to go that extra mile. My decision was only that I didn't want him to look like he'd looked in other films—because I've seen it, and it's always bothered me. So I said we would not do that. The rest of it was all him. He was so good with make-up.

RANGAN: What about his weight?

RATNAM: That was padded on. It wasn't a Robert De Niro kind of thing where he actually put on weight. He had dentures done to add some weight around the jaw. We didn't want to do too much; otherwise it might have become another Marlon Brando [in *The Godfather*]. It was done subtly.

RANGAN: Just about everything about the character felt right, down to the fly on his arm when he drops dead.

RATNAM: That's a very Sergio Leone-ish touch. The props people know how to do this, by adding sugar and stuff. The fly makes the corpse look real. You can do it only when you have an actor who can remain absolutely dead even with a fly buzzing around him.

RANGAN: I remember an interview with Kamal where he said he'd initially been unsure of you as a director. But during the shooting of the *Naan sirithaal Deepavali* song sequence, you corrected an expression of his, and that moment on he knew he was in good hands.

RATNAM: When he's seated at the brothel and when Janakaraj does some buffoonery and goes away with a girl, he had a look that said, 'Oh shit!' You could read 'English' in his reaction. I told him about this and we quickly went for one more take. After the shot he came up and said, '*Thamizh ketta vaarthai-la thittitten.*' [I swore in Tamil.] That's what it took. He has this ability to convert thought into action in an amazing fashion.

There's a sequence where Kamal discovers that his father is hanging dead in a cell. We'd taken half the shots before he came that morning. Now there was the scene of him coming and seeing his father. There were two cops who were pushing the surrounding crowd away. Kamal gave very specific instructions to one of those cops to push him hard on the right shoulder while he was peering into the cell. So when the scene unfolds, Kamal is doing nothing. The cop hits him so hard on the right shoulder that Kamal gets a wobble in the face, without having to do anything himself. He got the other guy to do the hard work for him. Though the actor playing the cop was very hesitant to push this huge star in a rough fashion, Kamal forcefully convinced him and we ended up with a great shot.

There are so many scenes in *Nayakan* where he's done such things. In the scene where he comes to the whorehouse for the first time, he sees this girl—Saranya—who says she has a maths exam. He asks her to study and she slowly goes away from the bed. He's taken his shirt off. He doesn't know if he should get into bed or sit in the chair. With his actions, it's so mesmeric—you can actually see the mind oscillating, to wait for her in bed or to sit in the chair till it is time to leave. But I had to tell him that this is possibly the moment where the theme music would begin to play and I wanted him to do nothing. I did not want this oscillation. I just wanted him to look at the girl. I just wanted the two dolly shots of him watching her and her walking away.

So you have to be careful with him. He has so many ideas, and you could easily fall for the way he executes these ideas. You have to be careful about which ones you want to keep and which ones you don't. There's a sequence where his son is dead, down below in the house. We took the first take, a top-angle shot where Kamal folds his dhoti and walks down. I felt he was too much in control. He's seen a body from upstairs, and he suspects it's his son and he can't believe it. He needed to be less in control. All you need is to tell him this, and he will convert this instruction into action so effortlessly. His range is unbelievable. I learnt quite a bit about what an actor can do from him.

RANGAN: In this sequence that you just spoke about, the one where he discovers

---

'We built the entire Dharavi-slum set in Venus Studios, and Tharrani gives you these wonderful frames.'

49

his son is dead, I'm curious about the emotional logic behind Velu putting on his glasses and becoming especially determined to see his son's charred corpse—after being advised against it. Before he's told not to see it, he's just distraught, but afterwards, he's like a man on a mission.

RATNAM: He doesn't look at it as seeing his son's charred body. He just looks at it as seeing his son's body. He still thinks he's going to see his son. He's probably not registering what the people around him are saying. Also, Velu Nayakan has seen too many hard realities in his life, and I can't see him turning away from this one.

RANGAN: But in that scene when he enters Saranya's room, there's no hesitation at all. When he entered Sridevi's room in a similar situation in *Moondram Pirai* [*Sadma*], there was fumbling, there was embarrassment. Here, he unbuttons his shirt and looks around, like he's been to these places before.

RATNAM: Maybe he has. But no. If you look at the song [*Naan sirithaal Deepavali*], there's a woman who puts a foot up and blocks his way. Janakaraj has to clear the way. That establishes who among the two has been here before and who hasn't. But given the fact that he's here, he's come for a focused purpose—that's all there is to it. And I do think the character in

'Right from the beginning, we had only a new face in mind, because we felt the character would come through much stronger with a new actor.' Kamal Haasan with the 'new face', Saranya.

Nayakan is vastly different from the one in *Moondram Pirai*. You can't obviously play it the same way.

RANGAN: One of my favourite expressions of Kamal comes when he marries Saranya in the temple, and Janakaraj, behind him, gets all emotional. Kamal shoots him a look as if to say, 'Dude, I can see why she's crying, but what's up with *you*?' It's hilarious. The scene is essentially emotional, but this reaction makes it quite funny too.

RATNAM: It was Kamal's idea. That entire bit was between Kamal and Janakaraj—they worked it out between them. The brief was for Jana to be moved and happy. But by becoming so overcome with emotion, he made the scene alive. That's a nice pitch to have. In a serious, emotional stretch, it's good to have something that makes you smile. It makes it beautiful and it takes away the drama of Kamal marrying a prostitute like that in a place like that. All that melodrama is taken away by this one gesture. That reaction is the chemistry between two good actors. And when something magical like this happens, you make sure you shoot it. Your job becomes simpler.

RANGAN: Did you ever think of this scene from a feminist point of view? He's marrying her without asking her permission or if there's someone else in her life.

RATNAM: Oh, come on—I don't think you have to look at it that way. I can't see him going down on his knees and proposing to her and her accepting it. The positions of dependence and independence of these two characters are so drastically different that I don't think this is an issue of feminism. The situation is so drastic that the man–woman issue is not very important. If there's a male who's a bonded slave, for instance, no one is going to ask him before freeing him.

RANGAN: When the cop drops Kamal off at the slum and leaves, there's a very instinctive thing Kamal does, when the residents of the slum gather around him. He sprinkles his blood on the kids and makes them giggle.

RATNAM: He did it. I just said 'Action'. The rest was all Kamal.

RANGAN: Saranya brought to the part a fragility that an established actor couldn't have. She was effectively your first big 'discovery', cast opposite Kamal, one of the biggest stars around. At that early stage in your career, was it difficult convincing people about this casting?

RATNAM: Right from the beginning, we had only a new face in mind, because we felt the character would come through much stronger with a new actor. It would be more real. I had no problems convincing people. If you're successful, they give you a longer rope. *Mouna Raagam* had done well. Also, [the producers] Muktha Films were breaking away from what they'd done in the past. They were working with an outside director for the first time. They were making a film on a much larger scale than they were used to. So they did not really question my casting. For most of the film I had complete freedom. We were looking for someone and this photograph came to us. Looks-wise, she was more or less what we wanted. We called her in for a test. I think we shot the test at the wedding hall owned by the producer, and we were convinced that we could get what we wanted out of her. She was the first and only person we saw for the role.

RANGAN: Conversely, in *Mouna Raagam*, you cast Kanchana, who had practically retired by that time, in a small part as a lawyer. You've done this in other films too, using almost-forgotten former stars like Jayachitra, Sumitra and Jayasudha.

RATNAM: When you have a smaller role—very less in terms of screen time but crucial to the narrative of the film—and when you don't have film-time to establish the character, a certain amount of star quality helps. You have a presence that is pre-established, and it helps to make the character memorable. The character becomes a consolidated impression of what Kanchana is, and her screen history gives it a certain weight and strength.

RANGAN: The scene where Saranya is introduced is underscored by an exquisite theme. In Hollywood, this would have been marketed as part of a separate soundtrack. How did you brief Ilaiyaraaja with respect to the background score, which has become a classic?

RATNAM: You don't have to tell him it's a love scene. It's that, obviously. It's just that when you are doing the songs, sometimes, you need to say that these instrumental passages can work as a theme. You need to remind him of those things. He's doing so many films that you have to remind him that we thought we'd do it this way. He may not even remember that these songs are meant for this film. He'll say, 'Oh, *adhu indha padathula irukkaa. Naan* Rama Naidu *padam-nu nenachen.*' [I thought this song was meant for that Rama Naidu production.]

RANGAN: Regarding instrumental passages in songs being used as themes, I have this question. We have five or six songs per film that define the predominant emotions. Why can't the instrumental versions (or the interludes) of these songs be used as background score instead of developing brand new themes for each of these emotions? As much as I love these themes as stand-alone music, I think, sometimes, that our films end up with too many musical cues.

RATNAM: The interludes in songs try to help you with what you're going to shoot within the songs. If you have a clear idea, then you say, 'This is what I am planning to do. This is what I want in the first interlude, the second interlude,' and so on. So they write it that way. Otherwise, they do what is musically right and you interpret it your way. That is done to kind of support the song, to pep it up and get the mood, and not all this music can be taken and put into scenes. A scene has a different rhythm, a different tempo, so it will require support which is unique to that. But it can lean and borrow from the themes we have developed in the songs. It can—and it does.

But the thing is that we in India use songs outside the film so much—on radio, on television, in every form—that it looks stale if you use only songs as your background score. It's exhausting. People have been listening to an Ilaiyaraaja song for three months, four months before the film's release. They know the song thoroughly. So when they come to the film and if the background score is only those songs, it may not serve the purpose you want. You should use the score in such a way that it brings in something more, some freshness or a variation of the tune already used in the song.

RANGAN: The theme song, which Ilaiyaraaja sings over the titles, is rawer (he uses the more colloquial '*yaar adichaaro*'), whereas the version that comes later, sung by Kamal, is more polished ('*yaar adithaaro*'), as if suggesting the eventual refinement of Velu Nayakan.

RATNAM: We recorded Raja's version first. It was the first sitting during composing. I'd just narrated the story to Raja and this is the first thing he played after that. It was amazing. It's a lullaby and we had this key refrain—*yaar adithaaro* [who beat you, little one?]. That was the only thought we had in mind. When we went for recording, before Kamal came in, we had this rustic version, which doesn't have a score behind it in a full-fledged form. It has this folkish quality. And because it was going to get repeated through the film, we also wanted a more orchestral version, and in this version the language became a little more sophisticated.

If you do a variation on a piece of music, there will be a part with the flute, one with strings, and so on. It's like that. We had versions of the same lullaby done in different styles so that it's the same theme but with a certain amount of variation, which gives us richness. The latter version is a more evolved version, recalling a time that has gone by. So it's a rustic song that, over time, becomes refined and polished. It's not necessarily the man who's become sophisticated.

RANGAN: When you sat down for composing, you knew that you wanted a theme song (that would be repeated)—as opposed to just a one-time song.

RATNAM: I didn't know how many times I'd use it in the film, but I knew it would be repeated and become an underlining factor in this man's life.

RANGAN: This was the first time you were

using something like this. All your earlier songs were one-time-use numbers.

RATNAM: Because it was a short song. Also, this was the first time I was doing a film that wasn't a 'story' kind of film but more of a biopic in nature. It brings with it certain other tools that you might have to tie together. Even for my first film, *Pallavi Anupallavi*, we had recorded a full instrumental piece, a three-minute version of a song, without words, which served as a theme through the film. So this wasn't the first time Ilaiyaraaja did a theme song for me.

RANGAN: The location for the *Naan sirithaal Deepavali* song is fantastic, with that huge tree bursting through the middle of the house.

RATNAM: It was an abandoned house, or maybe a club, and it doubled as Kamal's house too (after he moved away from the slum). You'll see the same tree from inside the house, when people come to meet him—the drawing room is lit by the light coming through the tree. This building used to be where the new [hotel] Taj Mount Road is today. It was called 'Indian Express building' in the film industry, and it was right next to the old Express offices. It was where they used to shoot rape sequences and climax fights. It was a brilliant location, and [Thotta] Tharrani converted the exterior into the whorehouse and used the other side for Kamal's house. They were breaking it down at that point.

They waited for us to finish the film. By the time Feroz Khan did [the Hindi remake] *Dayavan*, the building was no longer there.

RANGAN: Did you think of having this Bombay-based song in Hindi, like *Tu hai raja* in [K. Balachander's Delhi-based] *Varumayin Niram Sivappu*?

RATNAM: No. I just wanted a Tamil song.

RANGAN: In the montage-based *Nee oru kaadhal sangeetham* song sequence, there's a stretch where Velu and his wife sit down for a meal. There's an argument about who eats first and then he shakes her hand in mock-disgust and mimes that she's so skinny. When you have 'dialogue scenes' like this within a song, do you write out the lines, even though these lines are eventually going to be drowned out by the music?

RATNAM: Yes. Because if you think there should be dialogue and they don't move their lips but start miming instead, it looks ridiculous. Even now I see it in films. Why would they not say something? Because they know the soundtrack will cover up their lines? You have to be careful about this. It has to be real. The idea of putting a stretch like this in a song is to make the song a little more believable. So you definitely think about what's going to be said. As you write down the things you're going to shoot in the song, you know what needs to be said in such places. And with an actor like Kamal it is easy to improvise the lines.

RANGAN: There's a kernel of philosophy embedded in the *Andhi mazhai megam* song sequence, in the lyrics, about the irrepressible spirit of the downtrodden ('*Desam ennum solayin vergal naangale*'). You do this in *Raavan* too, in *Thok de killi* ('*Kelon ko khaate gaye, hum ko pehenke chilka chilka*'). In films like *Kannathil Muthamittal*, however, the philosophy is more 'audible' because it unfolds as a stretch of dialogue [between Madhavan and Prakash Raj, as they discuss the troubles in Sri Lanka]. If you want to say something about an issue, aren't you better off with the latter approach? Many people switch off during songs and don't get around to listening to the lyrics.

RATNAM: If you want to underline this more, it shouldn't be done through throwaway lines. It should be a part of the narration, a part of the script, the way the screenplay unfolds, which means that the film will take a political stance upfront and not just in the layer below. In *Raavan*, for instance, the story is about the human relationship and the political stance is in the layer below. We wanted to keep it that way. On the surface, it's still a human drama that's set in a place, in a period where the equations are different and have other political undertones.

'Some films require a style. You can't go away from that style for that film.'

RANGAN: But you could call *Dil Se* a human drama too. Yet there you have an explicit dialogue stretch where the insurgent leader, interviewed by the protagonist, talks about being sidelined by the powers at the centre.

RATNAM: *Dil Se* is a little different because you travel with the girl a lot more, and the girl is a little more extreme. And as we see from her flashback, it is a more issue-based film. You could get into politics because the film itself had that as a base. In the fiftieth year of Independence, it was looking at a dramatically violent activity that was being planned. There the human drama was not the base.

RANGAN: You're saying that it's okay, in some films, if the audience doesn't get these undertones (when they are embedded in songs).

RATNAM: No, it's not that they don't get it. It's just that it's not underlined. I'm sure that there are enough hints to point the audience in that direction, as to who these tribals are in *Raavan*, what they are fighting for. In fact, the sequence where the Hanuman character comes to talk to Beera took a more overtly political stance than what is there in the final film. But I felt I didn't need to get into this in just one scene and try to balance things out. It is enough to give a few indications and get on with it.

RANGAN: What about films like *Roja*, where there's a hint of an ideological discussion when the protagonist talks to his captors, like the similar walk-and-talk in *Kannathil Muthamittal*? You touch upon the issue and return to the main story. At these points, have you felt like putting across your views on these hot topics in greater detail?

RATNAM: You probably write a lot more, shoot a little less, and keep only what the film can take. The first draft, you write really fully, with all that you want to say about the issue. Then you kind of fine-tune it, and a couple of scenes that are just about the issue will go away. And you keep what is really the essence, which is true of every film. Because you're telling a story. It's not a platform on which you debate an ideological issue beyond a point, beyond what the characters can realistically say. Most issues can be looked at from two different points of view and there is a stance. If that comes through clearly, then the further points in the discussion are just more steps in the same direction. If you've set the platform and if you are willing to clearly say that the two views are there—two distinct views that they can debate about—then I think the story is doing what it's meant to do. You don't have to say Point 1, 2, 3, 4, 5. If you lay out Point 1 and Point 2, the rest of it can be extrapolated.

RANGAN: *Nayakan* was where the somewhat sarcastic legend began, that a Mani Ratnam film will be filled with darkness.

The cinematography is one of the most remarkable aspects of the film.

RATNAM: You don't start by saying 'I want to make the film dark'. We try to make it real while keeping it as visually interesting as possible. In the initial stages, I don't think this aspect was commented upon very much. But critics like to slot things in convenient categories. It's very easy to put a tag on to something, and these tags are made up by people who don't understand fully what we are trying to do.

RANGAN: P.C. Sreeram's cinematography is not just simple sepia. He livens up this sepia with bursts of silvery, concentrated light, like in the scene where Velu kills Inspector Kelkar with a sledgehammer.

RATNAM: We did some tests. Some of it was conventional, the way period films typically look, in a sepia-ish tone. Also, I had to make a decision whether to go with Cinemascope or 35mm. We did a test for that too. And then it was a call that we took. The sepia looked too convenient—too many films have been done this way before. We wanted to evoke the period indirectly, without going with the obvious cliché. We said that we would be more colourful, and within that we would get into the drama that the film naturally required. There was always light and darkness in the central character, so we shot in interiors that had that kind of quality. To bring across the period in another fashion [than sepia], we had to take the effort of registering the time passing, which meant that art and costumes became very crucial.

Also, when we started shooting *Nayakan*, we were trying to do *Agni Natchatiram* alongside. The first schedule of *Nayakan* was followed—after a gap of two or three days—by the first schedule of *Agni*. And *Agni* was the opposite of *Nayakan*. It was not a period film. It was trying to be a little futuristic, a little hip and stylish. The making was entirely different, and I guess somewhere along the line, as we kept pushing ourselves in two extremes, a bit of one rubbed off on the other. So wherever we thought we could get away with it, where we felt it added something and made the period look slightly unpredictable, we used some *Agni* techniques in *Nayakan*, things like the bursts of light you mentioned. It came about because we were doing two films that were in two extremes. It helps to have someone like PC as your DoP.

RANGAN: I guess that's why even the bad prints on DVD look so dynamic, so fresh, unlike other films whose cinematography has deteriorated with the degradation of the print.

RATNAM: But why do you see a bad DVD print? See the original. It's a film of extreme contrasts between light and shade. The contrast is very deliberate, very strong. So even with generation loss in prints, the contrast still remains dramatic enough.

RANGAN: Do you take these things into

account while you discuss a film with your cinematographer?

RATNAM: No. You just want the film to look correct. You don't think about what happens afterwards. If it is good enough, it will survive.

RANGAN: Many scenes contain a frame within a frame, with the centre of the action shot from outside an arch or a doorway. It gives the impression of the protagonist being an outsider, observed from a distance.

RATNAM: We weren't trying to do that exactly. It was a style that evolved from the time we started the film. The story took place in a lot of cramped places, and we had to capture the activity in a way that would highlight this. Even the scene between Velu and his sister, outside the police station (after his foster father is found hanging), is shot from between two huge pillars. They are in that small gap, as if they are crushed in. It wasn't an intellectual decision. It was just our way of picturizing the film in the most effective manner.

RANGAN: Did this motif evolve as you were doing those cinematographic tests?

RATNAM: We just did a few tests at the beach and the seashore. Nothing much. The frame-within-the-frame came in automatically much later. This is the first film for which I used sets. We built the entire Dharavi-slum set in Venus Studios, and Tharrani gives you these wonderful frames. When you use sets you can add in things that will make the shooting and staging exciting. The hut where the foster father lived has this ventilator on top and the door below. We could capture—with the crane—Velu coming into the slum through the ventilator and move down to the foster father who is praying. That gave us the first frame-within-the-frame, if I remember right. And then the house we talked about. The house was very dark. The light from outside is cut away by the tree. And that gave us all the elements we required. Like a note you pick for a particular piece, it was a pitch we picked for the visuals.

RANGAN: And once it became a part of one or two scenes, it became logical to extend this leitmotif.

RATNAM: I don't know when it became a conscious part of the narrative, but it did. It becomes a style. Some films require a style. You can't go away from that style for that film. For example, when we were shooting *Iruvar*, we went literally with direct light. We avoided conventional backlighting and the glossy look. And once you get used to that style, you're unable to shoot something that's pretty, with backlighting. Once you hit a pitch for a particular film, anything else stands out glaringly.

RANGAN: Several shots are framed with pigeons, even the terrace of Velu's home.

RATNAM: We had to bring the pigeons in even as the sets were being constructed, and breed them for a while. The film is based in Bombay and was shot mostly in Chennai. We shot all the iconic places in Bombay. We shot the streets and what we needed to establish that it's Bombay. Once the audience was drawn into the story, we could get away with recreating Bombay in Chennai. We wanted to create the ambience of Bombay without unnecessarily underlining it. The pigeons brought about the feel of a place that was not very well off, but where the people were alive and feeding off each other and sharing things, which was the reason for the place's existence. Like pigeons, the people in the slum arrive and scatter around a hub. The pigeons represented Velu Nayakan's background in one frame—they bring in a sense of Bombay, and they bring in a sense of a group living together in close proximity.

RANGAN: Velu Nayakan is the Mani Ratnam protagonist most famously identified with *nallavana–kettavana*, because he actually faces this question at the end. Is he good or bad?

RATNAM: I'm not here to have a take on the character. My opinion would be mine alone. What you try to do through a film is share a story. If you go to a city like that and if you came across someone like that—someone you think is on the other side of the law, but to a group of people he is the nearest thing to God—it really intrigues you, fascinates you, scares you. What is right for that group of people is wrong for a whole lot of other people. There are many ways of looking at it, which makes all the difference. All the film is trying to do is look at his story, from his perspective. Did he know what he was doing and did he have a reason for it? If I can put the viewer in his position and see that there may have been a reason he was pushed into that zone, then maybe it is possible to understand him better and deal with him better.

RANGAN: Are you saying that when you make a film, you're a detached third-person narrator, that your viewpoints don't cloud the characters?

RATNAM: I'm not saying that. But I'm also not interested in putting forward or thrusting my point of view at any cost. If I say something in a film, it doesn't mean that that's me. It just means that I have put myself in the character's position and that the character is saying those things. That's all. My stance could be entirely different. I could do a film about something that's the exact opposite of what I believe in. That's the most liberating thing about being a creator, whether you write or make films. You can be what you're not.

RANGAN: When Velu, as a boy, runs to his father and unwittingly leads the cops to him, he's wearing an oversized shirt. It looks like his father's shirt. There's something very poignant about this little boy in a grown-up's clothes.

RATNAM: It's his father's shirt. It looked right, didn't it? If it did not look right, we wouldn't have gone with it. That's what it's about. It's not a special occasion. He doesn't need to be all dressed up. He's just wearing something he's used to going around in. You're constantly looking for these kinds of things that ring true. It could be something that you've seen before in real life, and while shooting it just falls into place. There is no intellectualization of the boy aspiring to be like his father, etc. It's just something that evokes real life.

RANGAN: This isn't about intellectualization. I thought maybe you shot some childhood scenes that were later deleted.

RATNAM: No. The entire childhood portion was shot in a day and a half, on the Mahabalipuram Road, except the Bombay shots that were done earlier along with the Bombay schedule. It was the last part of the film, and we had three days to finish all the patchwork.

RANGAN: When you wrote *Raavan*, in the scene where Raagini unwittingly leads Dev and his troops to Beera, did you think back to this scene where Velu leads the cops to his father?

RATNAM: Not till you brought it up.

RANGAN: When young, we see Velu doing these violent things, like killing the cops who killed his father and his foster father. But as he grows older, he seems to become a more benevolent character, though he still deals with violence. He's either delegating these tasks or he's mellowed with age.

RATNAM: If you see the early life of Velu Nayakan, he's silent. He hardly speaks. He's a closed-in child who's been hurt and who turns violent when he has to. Even when he has small kids, he has some restraint. But as he becomes older—middle-aged and beyond—he begins to open out. He's a little more gregarious, flamboyant, opened-out, animated, verbal—he's somebody who's grown into his skin, gotten used it. He becomes more expressive. You can see what he's thinking and feeling, whereas the younger version would have been a lot colder. And in that kind of world, you don't keep doing violent things all through.

He has a team working for him, a dedicated team that thinks he's close to God. It's always like that in real life. After a while, it becomes about administration and decisions more than actual execution. In fact, we shouldn't have had the character doing that bit of violence after his wife is killed. He actually goes out and shoots an enemy through the peephole in a door. That, I think, is an overstep. He wouldn't have done that. It doesn't make any sense for him to do it on his own, but we wanted the emotion of his anger and his revenge

'The act of violence by Kelkar probably pushed him over the brink but it's Velu's upbringing that made him what he turned out to be.'

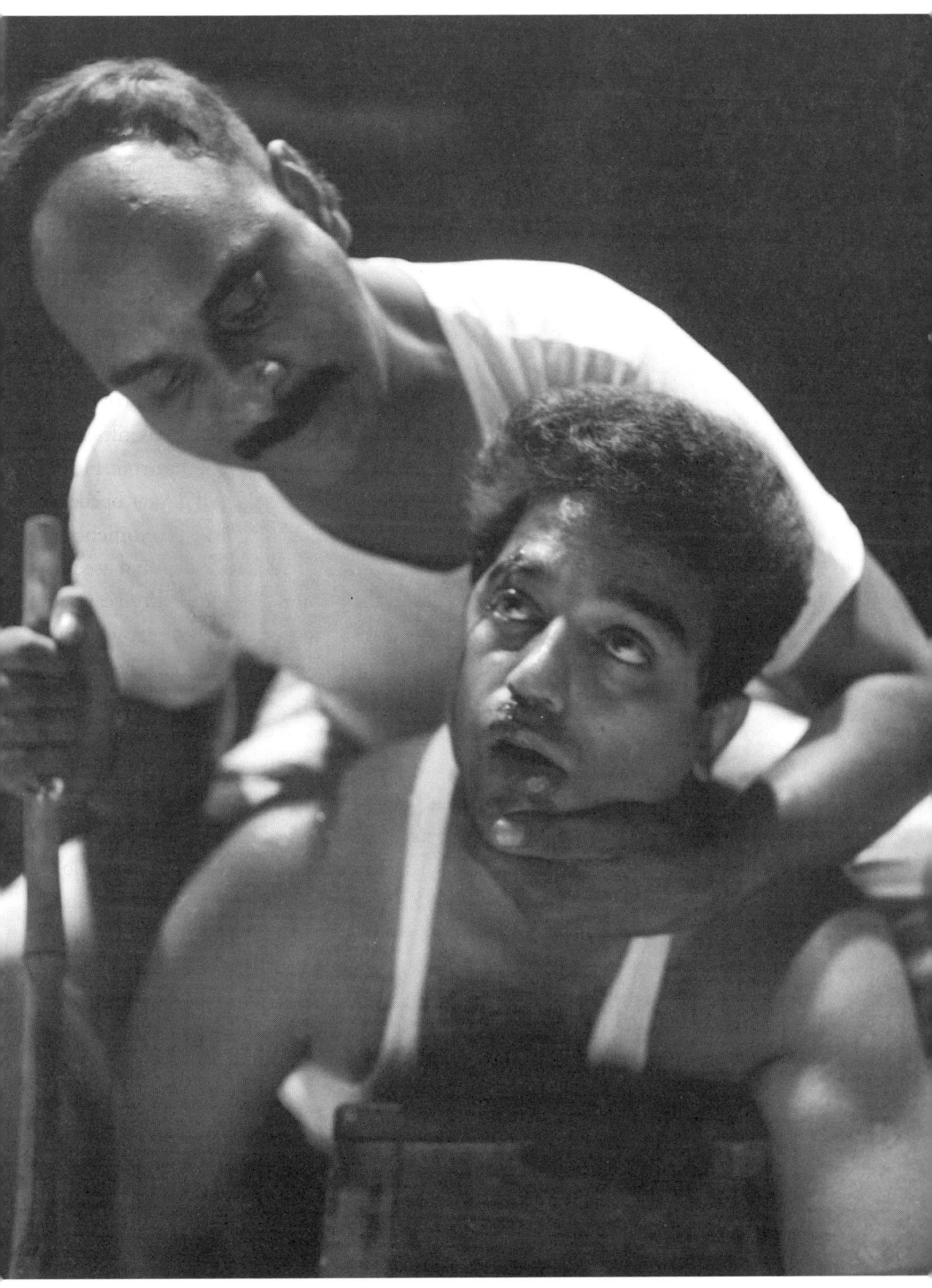

to be connected, so we took the liberty of making him do that. We had to take that extra step to connect the two different phases of his life.

RANGAN: From the scenes where Velu is shown committing violent acts, we know that he is indirectly responsible for the death of his father and his foster father. Does this inform what he does later?

RATNAM: Whatever he became eventually, this was his formative period, in terms of what he learnt, what he did not learn, who to trust, who not to trust, the fact that he's willing to carry this cross, the fact that there's only one door open and he's going through that. After this formative period, there's no explanation about why he's like this—only questions. All this is what cumulatively makes him—guilt, anger (or a combination of both), the need to survive, and the need to rebel against the establishment. All this is there in him. We're not saying that this behaviour is because of this happening—but it's all there.

RANGAN: The first time Velu assumes his foster father's responsibilities—that is, stepping on to the other side of the law, in order to help someone in need—is after he's been beaten up by Inspector Kelkar.

RATNAM: Someone who's grown up under the care of an old man like that, I think, would not be blind to what's happening. He's aware of what's happening. He knows it's not supposed to be done, but he also knows that there's some logic to it. He sees the old man living the way he has lived, going out of his way to help people. The act of violence by Kelkar probably pushed him over the brink, but it's Velu's upbringing that made him what he turned out to be. He's a natural extension of what the old man was.

RANGAN: The reason I ask is that you don't always explain everything in your films. The audience is expected to tide over these ellipses and figure out for themselves why someone is doing something. Even in *Raavan*, the attraction that Beera feels for Raagini doesn't really come with a 'because'.

RATNAM: It's the way you tell a story. You don't have to explain everything, assuming that the audience needs all this information. Besides, not everything can be explained. Even if I go out of my way to explain why I feel a particular way about somebody, I may not be able to do so. You can reason that you've seen something similar in another film and therefore this is equal to that. If the sense comes through, it is enough for you to move on with the emotion. You're not trying to explain or rationalize every step. You're just trying to depict.

RANGAN: I guess that extends to the sense of the period too. At no point in *Nayakan* is there an overt statement of the year in question. It's set in a generic past, where a factory costs a mere ten lakh rupees to build. Even in *Raavan*, the walkie-talkies gave an indication of the time, but there was no caption about the exact year.

RATNAM: Sometimes, it helps to have the time spelt out. If the film is very metric, or if it's in a thriller mode, cleanly divided by lines, then it helps the tempo. But if the story flows and if what you want to say comes through in other forms, you don't have to spell it out in so many words.

RANGAN: How detailed are you when briefing the supporting actors? For instance, when Kamal hands over money to Kelkar's widow for the first time, there's an extra in the scene who gets up. The scene would have still worked had she not been there, but because she gets up, it's like a mark of respect that highlights what's happening in the foreground.

RATNAM: You try to make a scene alive by having something like this, not necessarily connected to the drama but something that can happen around it. And it becomes very crucial when you're shooting a wedding or a death scene, for instance. There has to be something happening that's out of context, like a telephone that goes off in the middle, which makes the scene look real by breaking into the event.

RANGAN: I like the shyness in 'Nizhalgal' Ravi when he looks away after accepting the paan that his father offers him.

RATNAM: It's a handing-over-the-baton kind of thing. He recognizes it. And it's the first time the father calls him '*nayakan*' and gives him something, shares something with him. This is an obedient son who's a little hesitant to take that extra step, so he's very awkward about it. This paan incident is again an improvisation by Kamal, I think.

RANGAN: Then there's the daughter (Karthika). When Tinnu Anand shows up at the spot Velu is performing rites for his departed wife, you cut away pointedly to the daughter's reactions. It's like she's seeing Tinnu Anand for the first time, and therefore seeing, for the first time, a part of her father's life she knows nothing about.

RATNAM: I should see it again. I remember the wide shots and the detailing, but not this. If I remember this scene right, this is when she really sees her father and what he is, the larger world he belongs to. She has been away, probably studying somewhere else, and has seen him only in brief periods as a kid. Now, as a grown-up, she starts noticing things about him. The true picture starts to emerge in her mind. Till then, she only knows the man she used to have fun with in a car on the beach.

RANGAN: The daughter marries a Maharashtrian named Patil. Is that just something that happens because she's in Bombay? Because he talks in Tamil most of the time.

RATNAM: It would be too convenient if

everybody is a Tamilian. He speaks Tamil for you and me to understand. If he spoke in Hindi or Marathi, I will not know when to say 'okay' and 'cut'.

RANGAN: This was a big breakthrough for Nasser. He's terrific as Kamal's opponent. Even his wiry frame is in sharp contrast to Kamal's girth.

RATNAM: We were searching for someone for this rather huge part. I think Kamal was the one who suggested Nasser when we were thinking of actors like Raghuvaran. We called Nasser in and made him try on the costumes. He had to put in a lot of effort. I think it turned out really well.

RANGAN: Karthika accuses Kamal of being evil, but he never really comes across that way. Similarly, in *Guru*, whose protagonist is a lot like Velu Nayakan, Madhavan calls Abhishek Bachchan a *beemari*, a sickness of society, and you think that this moral judgement will begin to colour Abhishek's character. But that doesn't happen. Abhishek comes across more like a lovable crook than a cause of society's rot. Our sympathies are with Kamal and Abhishek. Even though these characters are being indicted by Madhavan and Karthika, they are not being indicted by the movies themselves (and by extension, by the audience). What purpose, then, does this opposing point of view (put into the mouths of major supporting characters) serve?

RATNAM: Like I said before, a director tries his best not to put words into a character's mouth. We try to develop characters who can think and act for themselves. What a Karthika or Nasser feels is what the character thinks. He or she is not bothered if Baradwaj Rangan thinks Velu Nayakan is lovable or not. If that character has a point of view, he will say it when he thinks he should say it. And if a counterpoint has to be made, it has to be made very strongly. The whole film is telling one story, and if somebody is going to make a dent in it, he should not throw a weak punch. He has to hit out. He should feel strongly about it. He should not be a pushover. That's what the film is trying to say, that there is another point of view however much you rationalize, however many reasons you have for becoming Velu Nayakan. Everyone has reasons, but you cannot use that as a blanket statement for the entire society. There will be people who point fingers. There will be people who won't be scared of your power or money, and who'll keep raising this statement against you that you are taking us in a direction we shouldn't be going.

RANGAN: That's true, but do you think it's enough that these opponents raise these points at just one or two places in the movie, which is still largely a positive portrait of the protagonist?

RATNAM: We can harp on it if that is the story. If the story or the film is just a debate, then yes, we will do it this way.

'She has been away . . . and has seen him only in brief periods as a kid. Now, as a grown-up, she starts noticing things about him.' Kamal Haasan flanked by Karthika and 'Nizhalgal' Ravi.

But the film is about a life, about a person with his positives and negatives, about his emotions, his relationships, his moral conflicts. The debate on the moral issue is just one aspect of a wider picture.

RANGAN: From a cinematic (or dramatic) viewpoint, do you think a story could be told with equal amounts of sympathy and empathy about Madhavan or Karthika?

RATNAM: Yeah. But I don't think it will be a biopic. Or it can be a biopic, but the whole thing will assume a Biblical form, like a Cain and Abel story. It is a conventional storytelling format. It has been done a lot of times.

RANGAN: I might be able to take something like *The Ten Commandments*, where Moses is so far-removed from my own period. But in a modern-day movie, I'd find it easier to identify with flawed human beings like Guru or Velu Nayakan. Madhavan or Karthika might make for a story that's a little too idealistic and goody-goody.

RATNAM: I think goodness is a very strong trait. If showcased well, it makes for powerful films that will move people and leave a lasting impact. It will not be boring or goody-goody. Ninety per cent of the films we see and like are films about the good ones. There is a basic desire that the good one should win; this is the dominant feeling that's reflected most in cinema. We still see *Gandhi*, a classic. Every Western, every classic that you write about is invariably about good winning over evil. Every Rajinikanth movie is about that. Maybe the good is coloured in different shades, but at a bare-bones level it is still the same. Some films search for the good in the badness.

RANGAN: You mean bad in the goodness.

RATNAM: Both. I mean, if you look at the Mahabharata, it deals with both sides. Rightfully, the Kauravas are the ones who should claim the kingdom. There's nothing that's not right about it. If you take that stance and if you don't tell it totally from the point of view of the Pandavas, which is what is usually done, if you try to look at it equally from both sides, then it could be a different story. So I'm not saying that that's not possible at all. I just think that this is easier. It is more attractive, more seductive to take a darker, greyer character and have him flourish. The other one is slightly more difficult to do. I think Ram is more difficult to do than Raavan, basically because his story has been told too many times.

RANGAN: Did the decision to bring the curtain down on Velu's life with a montage of earlier scenes happen on paper or later, while editing?

RATNAM: It was not on paper. The death is probably a better place to finish, but we felt the film needed to unwind for the music to flow before the credits came on.

RANGAN: You wanted him dead on the spot. No last words, no last looks. He drops—that's it.

RATNAM: He had two-plus hours to say whatever he wanted to say. What is left for him to say after he's been shot, in those last moments?

RANGAN: Have you thought of making a sequel to this film, something like *The Godfather Part II*? There seems to be so much material in the protagonist's life that's not in the film.

RATNAM: Never. When you finish a film, you're glad to be rid of it. You're happy you don't have to go back to that script again. Been there, done that.

RANGAN: When was the last time you saw *Nayakan*?

RATNAM: Probably at the time of release. I've seen bits and pieces of it afterwards, but I see only the flaws in it. Why go through that? I don't see any of my films after they are released. I can't bear them for more than five minutes. Honestly, I can't. For those five minutes, I'll think, 'Hey, this isn't so bad.' But the sixth minute, I'll see something that will make me turn it off. At the Venice film festival, I was trapped into watching *Raavan*. Otherwise, I watch my films so many times while making them that I don't want anything to do with them afterwards. That's why I sometimes can't remember the things that you are talking about. It's the edit stage that I remember, and while you're editing, there are scenes that don't make it to the final cut. I see more of the body of work as it is being formed, while you see only the finished product.

4

'We were able to do some very fancy things'

Agni Natchatiram (1988)

The two wives of Vishwanath (Vijayakumar) have accepted each other grudgingly. But his two sons—Gautam (Prabhu), Ashok (Karthik)—detest the very sight of one another. Their games of one-upmanship, however, will have to end if they are to save their father from the murderous Chidambaram (Umapathy), whose illegal activities Vishwanath has been appointed to probe into.

BARADWAJ RANGAN: Whether it's the masala-movie heroes in *Agni Natchatiram* or the more seriously dramatic ones in *Nayakan* or *Thalapathy*, your characters remain life-sized. They're heroic—yet their flaws make them human.

MANI RATNAM: In *Nayakan*, we're just trying to look at what has been classified, very broadly, as bad, and trying to see if there's anything inside it, and we're trying to do this by exploring the life of the character. It is more difficult to make a movie about a pure hero—someone who is all white. That is unreal. That is a statue, an icon, and not a character. I think there are flaws in everybody, including the audience, and if you have a character that is flawed, there is something you identify with. He looks real because he has elements which are not perfect, and that's true of 99 per cent of the people who live in this world. These characters don't come from a comic book, someplace where people are only good and always do extraordinary things. Character flaws make a person more believable. When you say a person is bad, what is good in the bad person becomes the story. 'He is a good guy, but . . .' The *but* is the story. Without the *but*, we really have nothing. In films like *Roja* or *Bombay* or *Mouna Raagam* or *Agni Natchatiram*, you deal with an ordinary person, an average guy. The characters in these films are ordinary people, the kind we meet day in and day out, with all their flaws and merits.

RANGAN: I don't know if I'd consider *Agni Natchatiram* an 'ordinary' film. It operates in a fairly heightened masala mould. That's why it's interesting that even in a realm typically filled with archetypal 'good' and 'bad' characters, you focus on a flawed man who fails to be a good father to his sons, a good husband to his wives.

RATNAM: I am talking about the characters being ordinary everyday people, and not the film. Those distinctions, of conventional good and evil guys, are no longer valid. There have been other film-makers who've broken such conventions to pieces. They've cleared a path for you and shown that the Tamil cinema audience can accept realistic characters. You're coming after *16 Vayadhinile* has been made and has become a huge success—or even *Mullum Malarum*, where a mainstream hero is shown to be a flawed person.

RANGAN: But those aren't exactly masala movies, like *Agni Natchatiram*.

RATNAM: Is masala a bad word? It's just a pitch, a flavour. You can pitch your film high or low, but that doesn't mean the rest of the dynamics should change. The reality of the story and the characters is still the same. A film does not have to be unrealistic to be entertaining. *Agni* aimed to be a fun film, to tell a story in a different tone, but the characters are real. I think the emotion and the conflict in *Agni* are very genuine and earthy. There is nothing masala about the core. It is the garb, the exterior that is flashy, which makes it easy

'*Agni aimed to be a fun film, to tell a story in a different tone, but the characters are real.*' Karthik (left) and Prabhu.

for you to classify it as masala. It has the look and feel of a fun film, but there is an honesty at the core which is as valid as *Mouna Raagam* or *Nayakan*.

RANGAN: Come to think of it, the only films you pitched at this level appear to be *Agni Natchatiram* and *Thiruda Thiruda*.

RATNAM: Well, to an extent, *Geetanjali* too. In fact, more so—because its core is more unreal and superficial than *Agni*. *Agni* and *Geetanjali* were masala movies, in the sense mainstream masala is accepted in India. *Thiruda Thiruda*, while being a masala film, is not the kind of film that's done in India. It's probably a westernized first cousin of *Agni* and *Geetanjali*. You don't see many caper films being made here.

RANGAN: What is your reaction when people say Indian audiences like to keep their stories and their heroes uncomplicated?

RATNAM: I don't think this is true. I think we like to coin theories and create concepts that sound global. The audience likes to watch films. They've always watched films of various shades. They like to watch simple, clear, unsophisticated films, and at the same time, they like to watch something like [V. Shantaram's] *Do Ankhen Barah Haath*, which was pretty unusual for its time. They did not say no to it. So it depends on how convincingly you are able to tell your story. You should be convinced first that this film can be made, that it can work, and you should be able to tell it in a way in which you can engage your audience right through. If you're making a mainstream movie, then you're communicating constantly, making sure that you reach across to them and that they're able to understand what you're trying to say. As long as you do that, it's fine. You shouldn't be talking in Sanskrit to someone who does not understand it. He will switch off in no time.

RANGAN: After *Nayakan*, *Agni Natchatiram*

comes as a completely different kind of film—in terms of period, in terms of energy, in terms of mood.

RATNAM: We began shooting *Agni* again after *Nayakan* was released in Diwali 1987. *Agni* was out the following April, on Tamil New Year's day. We were doing 'look tests' for both films simultaneously, and they were defined in two extremes. With Ilaiyaraaja, we used to record in the mornings for *Nayakan*, and in the afternoons for *Agni*. In the morning sessions, the studio would be filled with period instruments and the orchestra, and in the afternoons, there'd just be electronic equipment. After *Nayakan*, *Agni* was liberating. We were able to do some very fancy things. It was fun.

RANGAN: *Agni* was a very defining film for the youth of the 1980s, what [Sridhar's] *Kaadhalikka Neramillai* was to young audience of the 1960s. But there's a difference. There are these two young couples, but the driving force of the film is this principled bigamist.

RATNAM: That's the film. The rest of it is just costume. It was a far easier script to write than my earlier films because the basic premise was so dramatic, and yet, it had all these fun elements. Every time the heroes met, it became a conflict point.

RANGAN: And despite so much conflict strewn throughout the film, any of which could cross over into a physical realm, there was just one major action sequence—towards the end, with the horses loping around the heroes.

RATNAM: But that's narrative. That's what you learn when you start writing scripts. It is not the number that counts—it's the intensity. When you saw *Jaws* for the first time, you just saw the tail fin. You never saw the shark till the end. What gave you a high while watching were the music and the shark's fin, and with just these elements, a director could create a pop sensation across the world. The more he held back, the better it was. It is basically storytelling. That's what it is in this case too. It would have had much less impact if they'd been fighting throughout the film. Action is just gratification. The promise of action is much more potent. The fact that you and I can get into a conflict is much more powerful than you and I actually fighting it out, in which case it's just about who wins or whether it's a draw. But this promises me that every time they meet, there is a tension that keeps building.

RANGAN: But in general, you don't seem to be a big fan of action sequences. Or at least your films don't accommodate too many. Even in *Nayakan*, there is just one action sequence—early on, when Kamal kills the inspector.

'*I felt we'd never made a good James Bond film in India. I always wished we could do action better . . . now things have changed.*'

'Action is just gratification. The promise of action is much more potent.'

RATNAM: Oh, I love action. But only when it's well-made. I don't like action just for the sake of action. The fight at the fish market in *Pagal Nilavu* was the first action sequence I shot. I was shooting with a stunt master, and the challenge was to get him to come around to my way of thinking, to make him choreograph the sequence the way I like to see action—without dupes and long shots. I think the big screen is meant for action. You've grown up watching [John Sturges'] *The Great Escape* and things like that, and when done well, it's really poetry. Songs and action are two beautiful tools that you have. You shouldn't use them left, right and centre, but with style.

RANGAN: Among the two scripts you narrated to Kamal Haasan, one became *Nayakan* and the other one was for a sleek action film. You still haven't made that action film. Is it because you've become known as a 'relationships director' and hence people don't expect you to make an action film?

RATNAM: I have tried my best not to get classified into 'a kind of director'. I have tried to move from *Mouna Raagam* to *Nayakan*, from *Roja* to *Thiruda Thiruda*, basically keep all options open and not get bracketed into one genre. And here you have classified me as a 'relationships director'. I haven't heard of that classification before. But let me tell you—even in action films you have to make relationships work. And 'relationship films' could also have action. If you are talking of a full-fledged action film, then *Thiruda Thiruda* was the closest I came to it. It's not about what people want. It's what I want. I was ready to do one flippant, fun, rollercoaster after *Roja*. During the pre-*Agni* time, I felt we'd never made a good James Bond film in India. I always wished we could do action better, because only a few films like [Ramesh Sippy's] *Sholay* had superb action sequences. But now, a lot of directors like Ram Gopal Varma do action brilliantly. People have started caring about the presentation of action sequences because they love action. The scene has changed drastically.

RANGAN: In *Agni Natchatiram*, there's a scene where Karthik is almost run over by a car, whose driver calls him a bastard. This, of course, upsets him, because his mother isn't legally married to his father. In that sense, he *is* a bastard. But in this moment of rage, I found it odd that he thinks logically enough to protect himself by wrapping a handkerchief around his hand before smashing the car window.

RATNAM: He's someone who's been in such situations and fights before and he knows what it's like. Perhaps it's just a natural instinct.

RANGAN: The title sequence starts with low-key sounds of nature, and then it

'Even in the younger generation, there were a lot of purists who objected to the things I'd done.'

becomes more aggressive, with sounds of traffic and so forth, until, finally, a boom is heard and the sun explodes in your face.

RATNAM: It's the onset of *agni natchatiram* [the height of summer]. It starts slowly and reaches a peak with the sun, and then it cools down. The visual seems very simple because it's just the sun coming out, but we actually had to time it and measure the length of the shot. We went one day, P.C. Sreeram and I, with a stopwatch. Unlike now, when we ramp the shot to the length we need, we had to shoot it to the length that we required, and we had to ensure that the start-to-finish had that escalation.

RANGAN: You have a similar kind of title sequence in *Roja*. There, over a black screen, you have sounds of fighter jets and nature and parade commands and gunshots and birdcalls. It's an early indication that this story is a mix of war and peace.

RATNAM: I told the sound engineer, A.S. Lakshminarayanan, that he had to tell the story of what was happening in Kashmir simply in terms of sound, over a black screen. The main element, the visual, was taken out and we tried to prepare the audience for the film with just the sound. It's just below the surface. The visuals kicked in later—after the title. We tried to convey what we could without being upfront about it.

RANGAN: What makes you decide whether you want to go for an abstract 'story' during the opening titles—like in *Roja* and *Agni Natchatiram*—or have the titles come on while a scene is playing, like in *Thalapathy*?

RATNAM: It depends on where the titles come in the screenplay. If there's a prelude which lands on a note, and if that note needs it, then we tell a story. If the beginning is dramatic enough, like in *Geetanjali*, then you don't need a story. The impact of the prelude is enough. Or if the titles are right on top, then you may tell a story very simply. Sometimes you tell the story in one layer, like in *Roja*, with only the sound and not the visual. Basically, you don't want the titles to be too much of a distraction. They should just help you get into a particular mood. Sometimes, being quieter and simpler is a better way of doing it.

RANGAN: What about the titles in something like *Aayidha Ezhuthu/Yuva*, which rush past with great speed, like the vehicles on the bridge at the end of the film. They seem indicative of the energy, the drive of youth.

RATNAM: I think it's also momentum. That scene on the bridge is what the film is pivoted around—the accident, and what happens before and after. So the titles kind of give a sense of being on the street and being on the move. It's not static. It's progressive in one direction or the other.

RANGAN: In *Agni*, the plot point that

brings about the villain, all that stuff about explosives being manufactured in Sivakasi, doesn't rear its head until about forty-five minutes into the film. That's a long time to wait to hint at this development.

RATNAM: The film kicks off with whatever's emotionally right for the story, which is the conflict between the two families. To be very honest, I wanted to do this film without a negative character—because he really is not part of the story. He's just an extra element, like Karthik in *Mouna Raagam*. It's just a convenient way to bring about conflict. I tried a few times to write the film without this character, but the narrative became too complex. Ideally, if I was not trying to reach every segment of the audience, I would have gone with something like that. But as this film was designed to reach the places *Mouna Raagam* didn't reach, we tried to use certain conventional elements and still have a stylization. And having gone for the character, we tried to make him as dramatic and exciting as possible.

RANGAN: It's easy to see why you and P.C. Sreeram shot *Nayakan* in that sepia-yet-not-quite-sepia style, which suggests a long-ago period. But the science fiction-style lighting in *Agni* is completely unexpected in the context of a domestic drama.

RATNAM: When you're younger, you want to try different things. In *Agni*, it started right from the titles, with the sun flaring away. And every time the heroes meet,

---

'Character flaws make a person more believable. When you say a person is bad, what is good in the bad person becomes the story.' Prabhu and Amala.

there's electricity. This was the first film where we spent time and effort to get the effects—it was very effects-oriented in terms of sound. Even the music is electronic, with very few live instruments. We wanted to push the envelope in terms of style.

When we were doing the background score, there was a music director present, one of Ilaiyaraaja's friends. He came and told me, 'Please re-shoot this climax. Don't release it like this. People will complain of eye problems.' [The entire climax was shot with strobe-light effects.] And he promised me that he'd change his name if *Agni* became successful. He said, 'You're making a mistake. I've been in this industry for so long.' He was just a well-meaning, old-fashioned thinker not willing to change, but even in the younger generation, there were a lot of purists who objected to the things I'd done. I normally don't show a film to too many people before its release, but after release, a lot of people asked me why I was doing this. People said things like, 'I thought he had good taste'. But there's nothing that says that films have to be made a certain way. I've always felt that different stories can take different styles.

RANGAN: This is possibly the most burning question of this session, one that's been eating me up. The name of the character played by Nirosha is never revealed in the film. Did she have a name in the screenplay?

RATNAM: Are you sure? I haven't looked at the film in a long time. No, she did have a name. It doesn't come up early because Karthik sees her as a mystery woman. But it must be there in the script. Maybe you should ask Nirosha. Maybe she'll remember.

'I've always felt that different stories can take different styles.'

RANGAN: *Agni* was your biggest hit up to that point.

RATNAM: *Nayakan* did make an impact. But yes, *Agni* was made on a smaller budget and therefore the return on investment was much more.

RANGAN: Those days, there were no multiplexes and you were forced to address all kinds of audience. But today, are you tempted to make niche films courting a smaller sliver of the audience?

RATNAM: I think a film has to be good, regardless of how it is made. Just because something is personal and caters to a niche, it doesn't become a good film. A lot of mediocre films get made under the name of art cinema. If you're not trying to communicate to a large number of people, that's fine. But the ones made for the niche audience should still hold water. The content and form should be good enough. If I get a story that I want to tell and if it demands that kind of niche treatment, then I would do it.

But I feel that if you want to share an idea or an issue that's probably relevant, probably serious, there's more reason for it to reach more people. The mainstream approach, sharing it with as many people as possible, will serve it more. That's the path I have chosen. I am a product of mainstream cinema. I've liked mainstream cinema all my life.

And I don't think mainstream cinema needs to be stupid. I think it can have the sensibility of the so-called serious cinema and still remain connected to a large audience. It doesn't have to be abstract for the sake of abstraction. It doesn't have to be intellectualized for the sake of intellectualization. It can just be a sharing, a communication, a conversation with a large group of people.

RANGAN: Then again, at one time, something like [K. Balachander's] *Aboorva Raagangal* used to be mainstream cinema. Today, it would be considered niche, almost art cinema, because the audience that patronized these films don't go to theatres any more. What the so-called 'youth audience' wants is the only definition of mainstream cinema.

RATNAM: Yeah, that's sad. And the bandwidth within which you get to play becomes narrower and narrower. Even in the time of *Aboorva Raagangal* the bandwidth was narrow. Now it's become even more so. The distance between what you want to do and what you know will work, what might be acceptable, is greater. The demographic has changed and it's a big problem. It stops you from pursuing certain things.

RANGAN: I sense this with film-makers I speak to. They say things like, 'You can

do this, but you also need a *kuthu paattu* [item song] . . .'

RATNAM: Putting in a kuthu paattu is not going to save a bad film that's not working at all. That's a distributor kind of mindset. What really matters are two things. One, the concept of your film. What are you trying to say? That should be something that the audiences going to theatres today are able to relate to. And two, the way in which you say it. How is your narrative going to hold them, connect with them? How is the penny going to drop? Beyond that, the levels are not really an issue. It can be different grades, different shades—it doesn't really matter. I think there will be an audience for each one of them. If the content is something they are able to connect to, and if the form is something that helps this communication, then I think it should be okay.

RANGAN: You're saying that if *Aboorva Raagangal* was made in a form suitable to today's theatre-going demographic, it would still work.

RATNAM: No. That is only the second part. What pushes *Aboorva Raagangal* slightly out today is that the content goes beyond the bandwidth. Even then, it was not exactly mainstream, but the audience bandwidth was bigger,

Mani Ratnam (left) and K. Balachander (right) at the silver jubilee celebrations.

so it could easily ride along the edge. Whereas today, it seems to lie completely outside. If you're going to do something like that today, between you and me, perhaps it should be about a different stratum of society. If the same story about relationships that criss-cross is set in a stratum of society that is much lower, and if the presentation is rawer and harsher, maybe it will still connect. Because the upper-middle-class set is not coming to the theatres today. I think the same ideas can be expressed in different ways to make the connection to today's theatre-going audience.

'[Nirosha's character] did have a name. It doesn't come up early because Karthik sees her as a mystery woman.'

5

'It's like taking a cliché and doubling it'

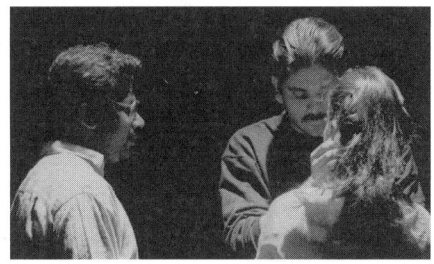

Geetanjali (1989)

Prakash (Nagarjuna) leaves home, seeking solitude in Ooty, when he realizes that he doesn't have long to live. His gloom, there, is dispelled by Geetanjali (Girija), a spirited local who appears to embody the very essence of life. And then, just when he falls in love, just when he begins to live again, he's told that her days are numbered too.

BARADWAJ RANGAN: After three hits in Tamil, you took an unexpected detour, making *Geetanjali* in Telugu.

MANI RATNAM: After *Nayakan* was over, I sat down to write the remainder of *Agni*. I finished it two or three days ahead of the time I had allotted. I still had some time left before shooting, and I sketched the flow of *Geetanjali*. It's like taking a cliché and doubling it. If I'd said I wanted to make a film about a young man who thought he was dying, it would have been a cliché, because it was constantly being done at that time. So I decided to double it—with the girl also dying—and treat it very positively. It was really only one line that drove the film, of one character wanting to say—in a film of that sort—'I want to live. I don't want to die.' The sheer joy of life is what the film was trying to capture. I didn't intend to do this film immediately. It was just an idea that came, and I penned it down. There was another script that I'd completed and was planning to do in Telugu. That was also a love story, but it was a kind of road movie. I never made that film.

RANGAN: Regardless of which script it was going to be, you knew that your next film was in Telugu with Nagarjuna.

RATNAM: I'd agreed to do a film with the producers. Nagarjuna came in much later. It was a young story. I met a few young stars and settled on Nagarjuna. The more important collaborator I met while doing *Geetanjali* is Pani Sir. We needed an associate director to take care of the Telugu dialogues. He'd directed a couple of films before. He'd worked with Jandhyala. He's somebody who's come up from being a boom person, in the sound department. He's been with us since then, a huge asset who takes care of everything methodically. He takes care of anything that's specific or technical, when a camera has to be serviced or maintained, when film festivals have to be coordinated with, when older films have to be restored—everything. We gave him a big farewell party a few years ago. We said he'd been working too much, taking on too much responsibility. Two days later, he was back in the office. He's still here.

RANGAN: *Geetanjali* begins with the hero in a hospital, due to an accident after his graduation ceremony. But instead of beginning at college and ending at the hospital, linearly, you begin the story at the hospital, go into a mini-flashback with the college, and return to the hospital. Why was it important to incorporate this flashback right at the beginning?

RATNAM: It's just a dramatic way of starting a film, by getting into something that hints at what's to come. If you begin happily and then stage the accident, it looks like a U-turn five minutes into the film. It's too dramatic a turn for that point in the film. Whereas this way, you say that this is about this guy who is being taken into a hospital, and the reason he is being taken in is this. The accident is a red herring. It reveals to us something more about the hero's condition. So if I had had the graduation and then had the accident, there would be too many things that stand out right next to each other—the accident, and then the fact that the hero has a fatal condition. It will look forced. But if you take away the impact of the accident earlier, the plate is cleared, and the story kicks in when he finds he has another problem. I wanted to separate these two things cleanly.

RANGAN: By this time, the Mani Ratnam–Ilaiyaraaja combination had really become something to look forward to. Even while writing, did you envision *Geetanjali* as such a huge musical? It has seven songs.

RATNAM: It was a very small film, with a very short running time (for a film of that time). The idea was to celebrate the joy of living with a love story, with songs. The *Vaarayo vaanmathi* song sequence in *Pagal Nilavu* had the hero enacting a drunk-Devdas kind of scenario, in a shawl and with a dog beside him. That was the first song Ilaiyaraaja was composing for that film. He'd given me time to compose only one song, which had to be shot in the first schedule. At that time, he played me another tune.

He said he'd composed it for a Devdas film in Tamil. I asked him to give it to me. He said he'd give it to me if I made a Devdas film. It was like seeing someone really beautiful and not being able to even say hello.

Music was just flowing out of him that day. He composed *Vaarayo vaanmathi* for me and my quota was over. I was listening to these brilliant tunes going to others, to films like [Rajasekhar's] *Kakki Chattai* and to other producers. When we sat down for *Geetanjali*, some five or six years after that day, I reminded him of the Devdas tune that he said he'd give me if I made a Devdas kind of film. I said this was a Devdas kind of film. He fiddled about with his harmonium and recalled the tune in a flash. That became the first song we finalized for *Geetanjali*. It was *O paapa laali*. And when the first tune you have is at that level, it only keeps getting better and better.

RANGAN: In many ways, the *O Priya Priya* song sequence seems to be a dress rehearsal for the *Sundari* song sequence in *Thalapathy*. In *Geetanjali*, the lovers are kept apart by a fatal illness, and this is mirrored expressionistically in the song—they are kept apart by armies and quicksand.

RATNAM: First of all, we wanted a visual contrast. The story is about two people coming together in a cold place, and therefore it was good to have them

82   *Conversations with Mani Ratnam*

drawn apart in dry land, a desert. The lovers were coming together physically towards three-fourths of the film. If you are going to have a song at this juncture, it should add another layer to the story. And if it can be grander, if it can add a visual contrast, then it can be something more than just a song, something you can carry back home. It's almost like a ballet. Like an alter-ego, it counters whatever's happening in the story. It adds another text to it. It becomes exciting to tell a story in two different forms—one in the bigger version through the narrative, and one in a nutshell through a song. Even the music has been conceived and coded for a visual of this sort.

RANGAN: When you sit down with your music director to compose songs, do you already have very specific ideas about how you want to shoot them?

RATNAM: For some songs I have very clear ideas. Otherwise we will not get what we want. The music will not help you reach the point you want if you don't brief the composer fully. If I have to make something like this believable in the narrative, then the music should play a major part. If I suddenly bring

'When the first tune you have is at that level, it only keeps getting better and better.' Mani Ratnam directs Nagarjuna for the O paapa laali *song sequence.*

in camels and quicksand and the music doesn't have the same tone, if it is just a romantic melody, then it just won't work. So if you want this kind of song sequence, you need to plan ahead, while selecting the tune. The music director has to know that the song is going to be shot like this and the score has to be a little more dramatic—drums and chorus and orchestra—to go with the dramatic visuals.

RANGAN: The all-enveloping mist is one of the film's most dramatic visuals. Was the mist part of the screenplay, or was it one of those serendipitous on-set discoveries?

RATNAM: It was part of the screenplay. We waited for winter to set in and we shot the film in November and December, in Ooty. About ninety per cent of the mist is real. The interior scenes were done with dry ice, but for the exteriors, we shot at places where there would be mist. It is basically a love story, and I wanted to show something blooming in a stark atmosphere, like the last poetry that comes out when life is fading away. The misty setting lends an air of poignancy to a tale of this sort. It makes it that much more delicate and poetic.

RANGAN: The 'I love you' moment occurs only in the second half. He falls in love with her only after realising that she's like him, and they seal the deal with a kiss in the *Om namaha* song sequence.

Till then, the film is filled with games of one-upmanship. There's not the slightest bit of romantic flirtation. That's unusual for a love story.

RATNAM: The initial portions are about two people who are flirting, but not in the conventional way. It's a flippant film. It's fun. And within that, you're trying to hit a few chords that are genuine. That's all.

RANGAN: But that's what is so interesting about your early films. On the one hand, they are, as you say, flippant. But unlike the regular, anonymous masala movies, they are also very personal films.

RATNAM: I didn't come in to make the conventional masala films. If I was doing masala, it would be something that I would want to do. These two films especially—*Agni Natchatiram* and *Geetanjali*—were made along those lines. It was a fun phase.

RANGAN: The big break-up, here, happens at a railway station. Trains are a presence in all your films, except maybe *Anjali*. I thought there were no trains in *Kannathil Muthamittal*, but I watched it again recently and saw that the child, after she runs away, is found in a railway station. What do trains mean to you?

RATNAM: I can't figure this out myself. I guess a train gives me a nice way to tell a story, like a journey. There is this professor, a friend, Lalitha Gopalan, who's written a book. She teaches film studies in Georgetown University. She has a similar theory that I have a thing for cars because they're there in every film of mine. She had a list of films—*Bombay*, *Nayakan*—where there were cars, and she believes that they really mean something. To me, they mean nothing more than what they are. In *Nayakan*, for instance, they're just an easy way to indicate the transition of time. It's this period, so he's in this car. It's that period, so he's in that car. That's all. But she was trying to trace the cars through the films and say something. After the book was released, she called up one day and said that she saw my last film—I don't remember which one—and it didn't have any cars. She sounded disappointed.

RANGAN: I guess there is some validity to her observation because you may like some images and be drawn to them unconsciously. Again in *Raavan*, the scene where the Ram character pretends to doubt Sita (so that she will lead him to Raavan) is set in a train.

RATNAM: In this case, the train very easily conveys that their story is on a path, a journey that can be traced, but you don't know what's going to come later. At that point in *Raavan*, you think they are back together, you think things are normal, and then it is pushed to the lie-detector bit and the story just turns around. If

'I wanted to show something blooming in a stark atmosphere, like the last poetry that comes out when life is fading away.'

this had occurred in their house, in a room, or in the camp, the scene wouldn't be the same. On a train, it's conveyed much better that they are on a journey towards normalcy, and he's willing to put one more hurdle in that.

RANGAN: Basically, the train suggests that their journey has not ended.

RATNAM: It looks like it has. It looks like they are heading home. But then the train stops, and there's a question mark about where next.

RANGAN: Another recurring visual motif in your films is a scene featuring a mirror—in *Guru*, the protagonist compares his paunch with his wife's pregnant belly, or in *Alaipaayuthey*, the sisters undress for the night while discussing the events of the day.

RATNAM: I like mirrors because they are a beautiful device through which I can visually present the scene. They give the feeling of talking to yourself, like that scene in *Bombay* where the heroine talks to herself in the mirror. The mirror helps you do what in literature a paragraph or a monologue can do. It gives a sense of introspection. I've used mirrors in all my films and I try to use them differently.

One sequence I'm really happy about is in *Iruvar*. It's a fairly significant scene. It's when Anandan, the actor, returns to shooting after being shot. The scene starts on a hilltop, and then something comes up in the foreground. It is the mirror of a make-up box as it is opened. From the visual of the hill, we suddenly move to a face in a make-up-box mirror. It is Anandan, starting his make-up. He hears a voice and he brings down the mirror. There is this girl where his reflection was. She's with a mirror, getting herself ready. She's asking about his first wife. He answers her. She asks him more questions. He puts his mirror back up, covering her face with his own reflection in the mirror, and continues answering her. The next time the mirror goes down, she's right up in front of him. It's a single shot, but goes in and out of various faces, between the past and the present, and because of the mirrors, we're able to capture it all in a simple and striking fashion that's aesthetically pleasing. It's the scene where he changes and gets drawn to the girl.

RANGAN: I like scenes with mirrors because they lend a slightly surreal touch by doubling the number of characters. There are two people on screen, but actually there are four. It changes the visual dynamics. What about rain, which again is a very prominent motif in your films? In the break-up scene at the railway station in *Geetanjali*, for instance, it's raining. Are these motifs—rain, mirrors—written into the script or are they sometimes spot decisions?

RATNAM: Most of it is written. Some of

'It was really only one line that drove the film, of one character wanting to say—in a film of that sort—"I want to live. I don't want to die."' Nagarjuna and Girija.

the shots with mirrors have been spot decisions. When I wrote that *Iruvar* scene, a mirror was nowhere in the picture. These things typically come up the day before, when you are thinking how you're going to shoot the next day's scenes. Then you go to the shooting spot, see whether it is practical, whether it will work. You may be very excited about it the previous night, but the next day it may not work. But sometimes it works. But rains are not like that. You need to plan ahead because you need to get the rain machine—though there are times we've called for it overnight.

For the scenes with rains, I think Kurosawa is to blame, not me. His films are filled with the elements. On the big screen, the fact that you feel you can smell the earth in the outdoors—you can get that across with rain. Rain helps to add a certain emotional dynamic to the situation, apart from what's being done by the characters. It adds to the drama. It accentuates the emotion between the characters. Nature is a huge device—whether it is the sun or the wind or rain or the sea or the barrenness of landscape. Its presence adds so much to a scene. It's just that rain is so visible and so noisy that it tends to stand out and you look at it in isolation. But film-makers, in general, try to use all the elements.

RANGAN: The heroine's father, in

Geetanjali, is a widower. In *Yuva*, too, the urban character has a single mother. In *Roja*, the hero is shown only with his mother. In contrast, Roja's family has a gaggle of relatives. Is this something that signals the kind of background, rural or urban, the character comes from?

RATNAM: Not really. *Mouna Raagam* has plenty of characters around Revathy, and she's an urban character. It's not an urban versus rural thing. In the case of *Roja*, I think the educated urbanite is slowly getting into smaller families. It's reflective of a particular stratum where the size of the family is getting smaller and smaller. Restriction of space and westernization could be the cause. Whereas the middle class, the lower-middle class and rural households still tend to have larger, extended families staying together. It's just a reflection of what's happening around.

RANGAN: Even with six songs and the works, *Geetanjali* and *Agni Natchatiram* clock in at an economical two hours and fifteen minutes, when the trend of the time was the 16-reel film, which ran about two hours and forty minutes.

RATNAM: I think my shortest film (compared to the Indian standard) would have been *Geetanjali*, because the screenplay was very simple. *Agni Natchatiram*, too, was of less than average length. But films like *Nayakan* and *Thalapathy* did run on a little longer.

My films have been on either side of par.

RANGAN: And by the time we get to *Raavan*, we are looking at two hours and ten minutes running time.

RATNAM: I think it also depends on the kind of film and the pace of the film. If the story needs to unwind leisurely, then you take more time. But a film like *Raavan* starts on a high note, with an abduction. So you have to go with that kind of a rhythm. Your narrative has to necessarily be short. At least that's the way I see it.

RANGAN: Like Karthik in *Agni Natchatiram*, Nagarjuna smokes in *Geetanjali*, as does Madhavan in *Alaipaayuthey*, Arvind Swamy in *Roja*. Are you a former smoker who's reliving the rush through his protagonists?

RATNAM: I've never smoked in my life, but I guess I have too many friends who are smokers. All my cameramen are smokers. The guys in my unit are smokers. When you grow up in a hostel, there are always guys trying to sneak a cigarette in. It's a part of growing up—especially at that time, when it was prohibited for youngsters. People used to go to night shows so that they could smoke. They were not interested in the film, while I was interested only in the film. Today, people are much more casual about their vices. Back then, it was a big thing.

6

'Even Revathy's costumes are all in pastel shades'

Anjali (1990)

While Chitra (Revathy) believes that her daughter Anjali (Shamili) died at birth, her husband Shekhar (Raghuvaran) has been tending to the girl, who is developmentally challenged. Chitra stumbles on the truth and brings the child home, but she's unprepared for the reaction of her other children—a boy and a girl—and rejection from Anjali.

BARADWAJ RANGAN: Your films are populated with very vibrant children. In an early film like *Idhayakoyil*, they are just children, like that servant girl Silukku. She's a typical 'child character' as used in the movies, for a bit of comic relief and a bit of sentiment. But the children of *Nayakan* and *Anjali* and *Kannathil Muthamittal* shoulder the burdens of adulthood. In *Nayakan*, for instance, the daughter is troubled by rumours that her mother died because of her father. They're mini-adults in a way.

MANI RATNAM: With the kind of joint families that we live in, children are invariably a party to life that goes on around them, and they have their own ways of dealing with events. I had a friend who passed away, and his child—who must have been ten or eleven at the time—would not accept this. She just wanted to go to school and be with her friends on the day of his funeral. She wore her uniform and went to school. That's the only way she could deal with it. When life is taking a major turn, children have their own ways of assimilating it and reacting to it. They're sturdier, probably, than we give them credit for. So this will be reflected in our films. If children are put in dramatic situations, they will have their unique views. It often gives you an unusual angle to look from.

RANGAN: The comment often heard about the children in your films is that they're excessively precocious (though the Tamil word *adhigaprasangi* is probably more precise) and act like adults. The truth is that they're simply facing adult situations.

RATNAM: Did people really say that? Then they are probably not listening to children and are caught up with themselves. It is silly to be bothered about these kinds of comments from people who want only stereotypical moulds. I've seen films where kids tend to act out too much. That is not what I seek. What I try to portray are kids I know, kids who are unique and not cute the way adults see them. Some orthodox viewers are not willing to accept that kids can be smart, and some others are too used to seeing grown-up lines spouted by kids. The people who make these comments have just their adult perceptions of what a child should say. They don't observe children and they've never put themselves in a child's shoes. We don't give enough credit to a child's intelligence. If you take the time to observe children, you'll see that their minds are always active and working at a rate much faster than yours. The children in my films are real. They're based on kids I've seen around me. It's something I'm very confident about.

RANGAN: Even in *Geetanjali*, the kids seem to have completely accepted the heroine's heart condition. They rattle off specific scientific details to the hero.

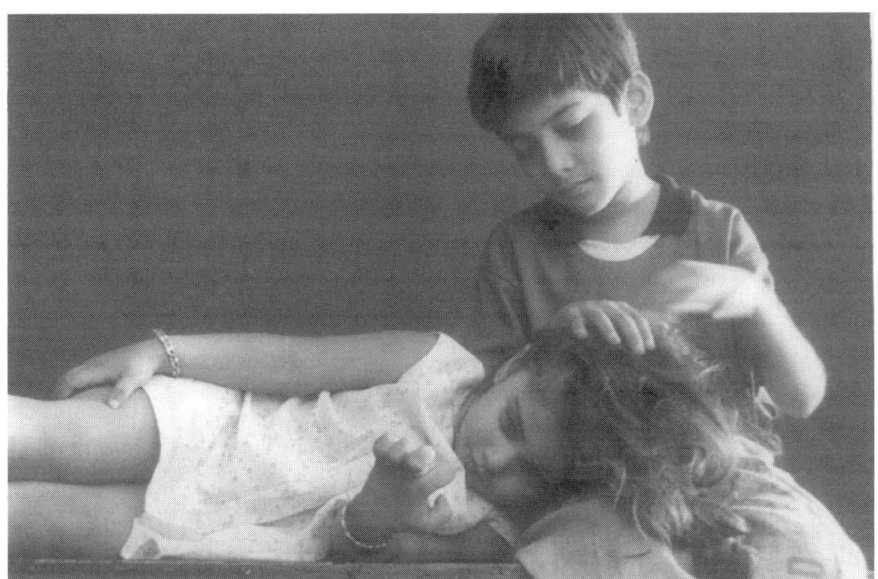

'Shamili was healthy, cheerful and so beautiful. It was very difficult to look at her and feel that there was a problem with her.'

RATNAM: In *Geetanjali*, they are three sisters growing up together. The elder one could have a strong influence on the other two. If the youngest one has heard the elder one giving a wild answer to an often-asked question or remark, she could easily repeat that answer without fully understanding the meaning. That was what you saw. It is not her own answer. It just shows that the question has been put to the sisters several times before.

RANGAN: Do you find it difficult or easy working with children? Do you chance upon these actors, or do you audition a lot?

RATNAM: We audition. But I've also been

very lucky. From my first film, I've mostly had very good child actors. It's such a treat to work with them. I think kids are wonderful, and as actors, they're either very good or very bad. It's an instinct that makes them do something in an uninhibited fashion. It's very easy for them to be real. The best thing about them is that they don't imitate some other actor.

Right or wrong, we all get influenced not only by life but by other actors. Something that Brando did or Sivaji Ganesan or Kamal Haasan did will stick around somewhere in the mind and influence you. But kids are without those burdens. They are just themselves. If they are angry, they're angry like they would be angry. Sometimes you get stuck with a child who's not good or not interested in acting, and it becomes very difficult. Because they can't fake it. They're more interested in Sachin Tendulkar than in their character and scene, and you can't do anything because they're being honest. You have to figure out how to get around this. But if they're good, they can really make a scene. It's such a pleasure to watch them perform.

RANGAN: We talked about ellipses in *Nayakan*. In *Anjali*, a child is born in the first few scenes, and then two years elapse before the family moves into a new flat. You don't tell us what happened during this time or what prompted this move. Why didn't you, for instance, have this family in this new apartment complex right from the beginning?

RATNAM: The opening is like a prologue, a set-up—it's like a short story, really. The first six scenes were written like a short film. It begins with two kids trying to stop a cab to take their pregnant mother to the hospital. Then there's a mini-climax and this short story comes to an end, and we move on to the titles. Then they come into this place which has all these kids—it's like the start of something new. It seems pleasant. They establish a rapport with everyone. Everything seems settled. And then the storm comes.

RANGAN: You make it sound like a horror film, where a family moves into a house and all's calm until the ghosts crawl out of the woodwork. Actually, you do have ghosts here, those zombie-like creatures in the sci-fi landscape of the *Raathiri nerathu* song sequence.

RATNAM: A ghost story? I hope we are talking about the same film. No, I am not telling it like a ghost story. There is a prologue about the birth of Anjali and then this story starts. What is missing is a title card saying, 'A Few Years Later'. If that card had been there, I don't think you would have raised this question, and if I had known that Baradwaj Rangan would raise this question, I would have placed that card.

If you look at the kids in this film, they represent the next generation of Indians that was making its presence felt. That was the time Michael Jackson was becoming a big name in India. Kids were into that westernizing mode. All the kids in the film were very fashion conscious. They would be this small, and they'd already be into things like sunglasses. You could see that this is where urban, upper-middle-class kids were heading. You're just trying to get into their world and look at life and the dreams in that world. That's how that song came about.

RANGAN: How did the idea for the film come about?

RATNAM: The idea for *Anjali* was in my mind by the time I was finishing *Nayakan*, while we were doing the mixing. I vaguely remember talking about the subject with my sound recordist. I had even named the film *Anjali*, which is why we were hesitant to call the Telugu film *Geetanjali*. Both Geetanjali and Anjali were the names of the girls in the films, but Anjali was a more relevant name in the context of the film. With Geetanjali, it was just a Tagore-ist connection, to his poems—that was the starting point of the name. Also, it was the name of a sixteen-year-old girl who died of cancer, Geetanjali Ghei. She was a poet, somebody who looked at life from a different perspective.

I actually wanted a name like *Ninnukori*... for the Telugu film because I wanted the title to sound incomplete. *Ninnukori* means something along the

'The father [Raghuvaran] appears stronger because one thinks it is more difficult for the mother to accept such a situation.'

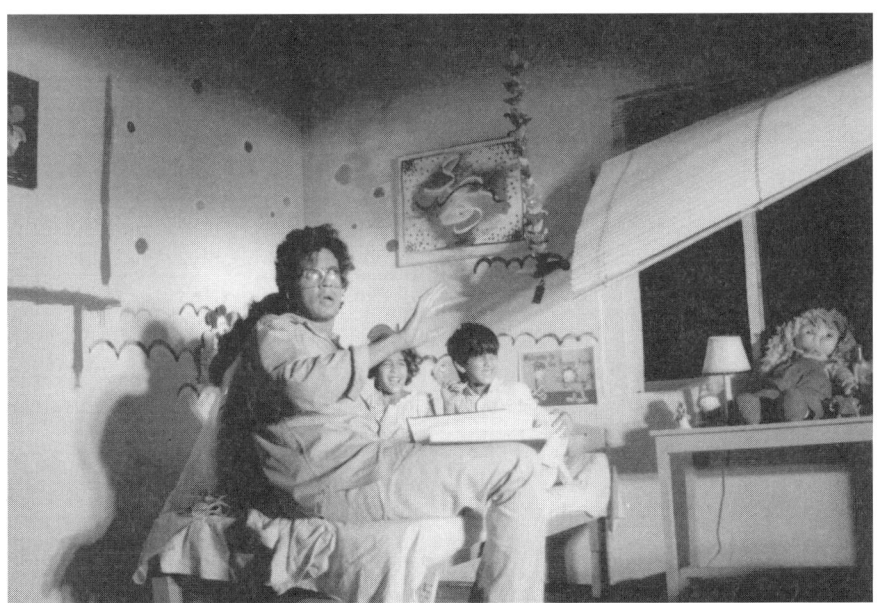

lines of 'when I call for you' or 'when I want you'. It's not necessary that the thought should be completed in the title. But the producers and the Telugu writer didn't like it. Their first objection was that it's an incomplete title and it wouldn't sound right. I didn't know Telugu when I was making *Geetanjali*, and if you don't know the language, you can't argue that it's okay. In Tamil, even if the title sounds incomplete, like *Kannathil Muthamittal*, you can say that it's okay because you're sure of it. But with Telugu, I was dependent on others, and they were not too sure the title worked. Maybe they were right. We tried a few options and then we had to land back on *Geetanjali*.

Anjali is about your own resistance to seeing something that's happening around you. I don't know if I'd like this revealed in a book, but I had a close neighbour who had a child with a small problem. For years, I could not look the child in the eye. It's something that bothers you. You don't do it, and the fact that you are trying to avoid it is always there at the back of your mind. I think those feelings came together in this story, trying to understand why we try to hide from such a person and then, when we cross that mental barrier, how we build a rapport with that person.

RANGAN: So you had this core in mind, and then for dramatic purposes you kept the child hidden for half the film.

RATNAM: Yes, that was for dramatic effect. When we did the film, we wanted to base it on children around us. We—Pani Sir and I—went around Chennai looking at various schools for special children. We sat down and spent time at each of these schools, and we found that not a single school had such kids between the ages of one and five. All children with problems were brought in at a much later age, when they were seven or eight. Finally, we found a school in Anna Nagar. It was called Ashirwad, I think, and it was run by a couple. The man was a doctor who'd given up his practice to set up this school. They were doing an amazing job. We spent quite a bit of time there, and a lot of *Anjali* came out of what we observed in those sittings. Ashirwad was the place *Anjali* was born.

RANGAN: Did that doctor influence the character of the father, who is strong and sacrificing and makes the decision to care for the child and yet keep her away from his wife?

RATNAM: I think that was just a dramatic decision. It's probably the weakest part of the film, and the only thing that doesn't age well. You can see that it's a card being played by the director. It does not flow naturally with respect to the rest of the film. But we did this because we were trying to make the film in a mainstream format, and we were trying to make things dramatically interesting for the normal audience here.

The doctor in Ashirwad was not too aware of what we were going to do, because at that point, the script was at an exploratory stage. If you are trying to do a film on a mentally challenged person, it's not as though you are completely ready with what you are going to portray. You want to get into that world and see if you can get it into your head and then start to build around it. So while you work on the script at one end, you try to explore the actual background and do a little bit of research, so that both go hand in hand. It's not that you conceive something totally different and fit reality into that. You take it in. You see how it is, what it means, and then you see if you'll be able to convert it into a film.

But they had a poster on the door that spoke about the concept of a special child, and that formed the basis for the sequence where the daughter asks her father why Anjali was born in their house, and why not at a neighbour's house. And he explains that Anjali is a special child, and that God gave her to them so that they would be able to take care of her. That was really the concept behind Ashirwad. That poster really struck a chord, and that message became the heart of *Anjali*. It led to the way the father looked at the situation, and the way he would get his children to look at the situation. Another reason the father appears stronger is that one thinks it is more difficult for the mother to accept such a situation and then go about setting things right. I think the two parents deal with the problem in

'All songs were conceived and composed with a children's choir in mind.'

two distinctly different ways. We talked to Mohan for the role, but it didn't work out. Raghuvaran was excellent as the father.

RANGAN: You seem to be saying that the father would be less emotional and more practical about the situation.

RATNAM: Probably, yes. If we had to generalize, I think he would be a little more rational and not impulsive. The mother would be too close to the child to be rational about how best to bring up such a child. Maybe I'm talking about this particular father and this particular mother.

RANGAN: If you were to make *Anjali* today, how would you modify what you call the weakest part of the film—the mother being kept in the dark and the whole 'oh my husband is cheating on me' red herring?

RATNAM: I don't know, but I'm sure it can be done. There were two elements that brought this subject of an unusual, mentally challenged child into a mainstream format. One is the fact that it is wrapped inside the story of the mother not being aware—thanks to the father—that the child was still alive and being cared for somewhere else, by a doctor. The other is the fact that the events are set in a colony with all these children, these modern-day children who pushed the story into a musical format. These two aspects were the front for a subject that was slightly out of the mainstream, and it's with these two feet that we tried to move the project forward. They were used as a vehicle through which to tell the story of this child, and make the audience look at the child the way the other two children [her brother and sister] look at the child.

RANGAN: The second half of *Anjali* has a terrific emotional hook—the question about when the child will learn to love her mother the way she loves her father. The father dominates the first half and the mother the second half. There's a nice balance to the film.

RATNAM: When you form an outline for a film, when you structure the plot, it needs to have these things worked out. The plot was devised along the lines of the father, at first, not revealing that the child is alive and later revealing this fact. Beyond this, the only story threads possible are that of the other two children and the society outside accepting the child, and finally the child accepting the mother. It's really a two-way thing, two opposites—the child reaching out to the others (her siblings and the society outside), and the mother reaching out to the child. That's what keeps the second half alive. In the first case, the child is the outsider seeking love and acceptance. In the second case, the mother is the outsider seeking love and acceptance. It would become very monotonous if everything is from the point of view of the child.

RANGAN: The inclusion of children in the colony infuses a lot of energy into an otherwise low-key story. Also, it's something very fresh in a mainstream film. This 'volume' of children (both in the sense of numbers as well as noisiness) had never been seen before.

RATNAM: Those were the days—the seventies and the eighties—the cities were seeing more and more apartments coming up, and there were enough numbers of people who grew up in colonies that had these big groups of children. Instead of hanging out with the children from the adjacent street, you could hang out with children from the same building. This gave the film a platform that was realistic and, at the same time, light-hearted and lively.

RANGAN: Did you always want all the songs to be sung by children? Even *Motta maadi*, a song about an adult couple in love, is sung by these kids.

RATNAM: Absolutely. In *Motta maadi*, the guy and girl are not the story. The story is that the kids are seeing this happen, like they see everything else. The film is seen through their eyes. They are the ones propelling the film, taking it forward. All the songs were conceived and composed like that, with a children's choir in mind.

Till then, invariably, all songs for children were sung by S. Janaki in a false voice, and they were mostly one-offs. The songs in this film were entirely sung by a chorus. The other day, I was talking to the son of Gangai Amaran [Ilaiyaraaja's brother], and I was remembering how all the kids in Ilaiyaraaja's family—Karthik Raja, Yuvan Shankar Raja, Bhavatharini—used to be present during the recording sessions for *Anjali*, singing the songs. They used to come from school. Sometimes they even used to bunk school.

RANGAN: Do you remember the initial reactions you got when the audio cassettes were released? I was quite taken aback when I slipped the cassette in for the first time and heard an entire album without a single adult voice. It was a very unexpected Ilaiyaraaja–Mani Ratnam collaboration.

RATNAM: I don't particularly remember, because when you're making the film, you take this aspect for granted. You know that that's how the songs have been conceived. It's not something you're surprised by. We tried to project this aspect—that it was a bunch of kids—through every visual form. Even the album cover had a little girl on it. In fact, what we were worried about was that people would think that it was a fun film about children—which it is, but it's also an emotional story. We were trying to tell a tragic story through this bunch of exuberant kids. There was a

Anjali 97

serious layer underneath all the fun, and we didn't want people to mistake it for a *My Dear Kuttichathan* kind of joyride. It was important to get that across.

RANGAN: By this time, your films had acquired a signature cinematographic style. P.C. Sreeram was largely responsible for developing that style. For *Anjali*, though, you went with a different cinematographer, Madhu Ambat.

RATNAM: PC and I have grown together. We never take each other for granted. At the beginning of each film, we'd check with each other if we wanted to work together on it. We were always pushing each other, and we were scared that we would get into a position where we'd fall back on things we'd tried before and not press forward in new directions. So we decided we'd work separately for a while—take a break and go different ways and grow a little more. We were very sure that we'd do films together again.

When it came to choosing a new cinematographer, I didn't think of it as a major exercise. It's just that you have to strike a rapport and then work together well for the end result. If you like a cinematographer's work, you meet him in person and sit and chat. If you are on a common wavelength, if you like similar things, if you hate similar things, there's a good chance you'll get along well and be able to do something together. If that person is as interested or as enthusiastic about taking that extra step and pushing the envelope, then it's very good. It was a big help that, visually, what I'd done with PC had made a mark, so the next person could come along and look at that as a benchmark and see if he could do something different—not just another version of it, but something entirely different.

RANGAN: Was it a conscious decision to keep the character played by Prabhu in the dark all the time? He's a bit of a shadow figure, and his scenes unfold at night. It's only towards the end that he's seen in bright light.

RATNAM: We tried to look at him the way the kids would see him. This is one person in the apartment complex who doesn't come out much, and as a kid, this makes you curious. And if a story floats around about him, you believe it, and though you know that it's dangerous and prohibited, you're tempted to dig into it. So the character was really shown the way the kids were seeing him. We tried to explore something that looked larger than life, something scary and dangerous—and then you see a human being behind it all.

RANGAN: This film has very strong backlighting, with huge shafts of light bathing the characters and the interiors. As in *Agni Natchatiram*, this was an unusual lighting scheme for a largely domestic film.

RATNAM: Almost 90 per cent of the film

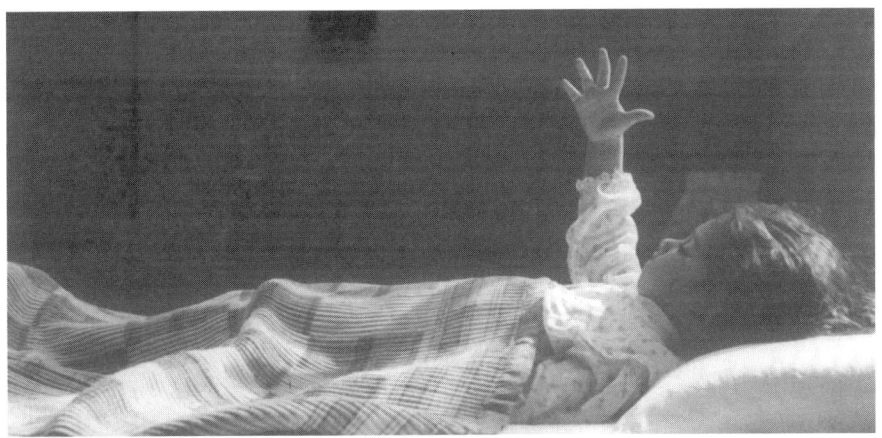

'It's really a two-way thing, two opposites—the child reaching out to the others . . . and the mother reaching out to the child.'

was shot in Venus Studios. The flats were erected there, and the indoor scenes were shot on those floors. This was the first time I was working on a film where the indoors were completely shot on a floor. I wanted a visual style which was like those kids, modern and upbeat. So the colours are not earthy and Indian, but more whites and blues. Even Revathy's costumes are all in pastel shades—white and off-white and beige. Also, the child who comes in, Anjali, is someone we see very slowly through the course of the film. The first time we see her, she's a mystery. She's just a figure in a backlit frame. And, gradually, as the kids interact with her, she is revealed in her entirety. We see more and more of the child. We can't switch to that kind of lighting suddenly when the child comes in. We had to set it up right from the beginning. That's why this lighting happened—firstly to bring about an urban, upper-middle-class look, and secondly, to highlight the narrative arc of Anjali.

RANGAN: To my eyes, this lighting lent an ethereal dimension to the child. She's like an 'alien' amidst these normal kids, almost a visitor from another planet. Even her father describes her as someone the angels from heaven dropped into the family.

RATNAM: Before we began the film, we did a test with Shamili. I don't remember if PC shot it or Madhu did—no, actually Madhu shot it. Shamili was two-and-a-half or three at the time, a nice, robust child—healthy, cheerful and so beautiful. It was very difficult to look at her and feel that there was a problem with her. So we had to make dentures that made her look less of an angel, which gave a hint about her condition without being obvious. But how do we get such a young child to act like a mentally handicapped person? That's what we were trying to see.

We were shooting on video in a small house. We shot for half a day, then we had lunch and started shooting again. Towards the end of the day, I'd almost given up. I thought I wouldn't do this project. The things that we did looked false. It looked like it had been done before. Finally, only when we took away the physical independence of the child, when we made her more dependent and uncoordinated, did we get hold of how she should act and behave. We made sure that she was not so perfectly coordinated that she could stand up and run. She leans on a parent or a wall or some support, that she requires a little more than a typical three-year-old would require.

The test was not for her. It was more for us to figure out a way to get hold of Anjali as a character. We needed somebody who could perform and still look a certain way. With an adult, this is possible, but with a child, I didn't know how to get at that. It was a struggle to find a process through which we could deal with this aspect of the character. If we had not found a solution that day, I don't know if the project would have come through at that point.

But after this test, things went smoothly. Earlier, we'd made a test of a special child named Esther, from that school in Anna Nagar. We had shot Esther at home, Esther when she was smiling, Esther when she was crying, Esther when she was angry—two or three days of her life we'd captured on film. We just had to tell Shamili that she had to smile the way Esther was smiling, and that's what she would do. So we really had to find a way to tell a small child how to behave in a particular fashion. Her father took a lot of effort. He would make her watch the tape every day, and by the time we came in, she would be ready to do what we wanted. But it would all be in relation to what Esther would do. That's how we really got a hold on the character of Anjali.

RANGAN: And once Shamili saw these videos, there were no problems.

RATNAM: Yeah. She was fantastic. She'd seen her elder sister, Shalini, act and there was no inhibition at all. She was at an age where we could sit down and communicate with her and do whatever we wanted to do to get through a scene. And she would do it—except that when we had a lunch break, she would have a substantial lunch, after which she needed an hour of sleep. She needed that rest, and then she'd be okay to shoot in the afternoon. We had to plan the shoot in such a way that we gave her that time. She was the central figure not only in the film but also in the shoot.

RANGAN: What is your philosophy when it comes to actors? Obviously, different actors need different levels of inputs, but in general, do you hand over a scene and look for what they bring to it, or do you control certain aspects of the

'I've seen films where kids tend to act out too much. That is not what I seek.'

performance according to the way you see it in your head?

RATNAM: My philosophy is not to have a philosophy. An actor makes a scene alive. My job is to get them to be as real as they possibly can be. If the actor brings in a certain amount, then you provide the rest. If he doesn't bring in anything, then you push him all the way. So it could vary any which way. Also, from the time you start the film to the time you finish, the actor will change. He will know more about the character. He will grow in confidence. He will understand and anticipate what you like and what you don't like. It's a kind of rapport that you develop.

Of course, in some cases you are very unlucky and get stuck with somebody who cannot do what you want and is not interested either. Then you might have to scream and shout and threaten them and promise that you're going to push them down a staircase and kill them. I don't mind doing anything so that there is some magic that happens. So there's no single theory that you stick to with actors. But as far as possible, I'd like the actor to put something of himself into his performance. I don't want it to be just a reflection of what I am saying. We choose this person because he is close to the character and is able to represent it. And I want the person who's putting his face on screen to put his mind also on screen.

RANGAN: Do you believe in rehearsals? Some directors feel that it takes away from the spontaneity of what happens in front of the camera. Then again, film-making is expensive, and time spent in rehearsals is time saved during shooting.

RATNAM: I believe in rehearsals, but I don't believe in over-rehearsing. I sit and chat with the actor over several sessions. But it's not like a play. I don't do too much reading and correction. To a large extent, because I've learnt film-making in an unstructured manner, I cannot divide my shots and pre-visualize them and do a storyboard and go execute them at the shooting spot. I conceive a scene on paper, on the table, and then, when I shoot, I put the actors in position and chalk it out. That's when things fall into place. I like to keep a bit of it alive for this point, where you try to see if you can take it to the next level, beyond what is there on paper. That effort is fairly important.

I don't like long, stretched-out shoots. If somebody delays things, it should be me and not anyone else. We generally tend to shoot very fast, especially because we are so dependent on good light, and good light in a tropical country occurs in such a small window in the morning and late afternoon that we are used to a panic situation. So you have to strike a rapport with the actors and be able to work something out that gives them confidence. It's a three-way thing. It's between you, your cinematographer (who understands what the scene is, why we are doing it, why the rush) and your actors (who understand where we are shooting, why we want to shoot it in this light). Each one has to understand the others, and then it becomes easier.

RANGAN: You said you're not much of a storyboarder or pre-visualizer. But considering how elaborate some of your scenes are, wouldn't it help?

RATNAM: I storyboard only when I have an elaborate action sequence, like the climax of *Thiruda Thiruda* that involved a train. That required a storyboard so that we'd be able to execute it—not literally in the storyboard sense but so that the action could be planned along the lines of what would happen in tunnels and what would happen on top of the train. The logistics became very important in this case, as with the songs that required special-effects shots in *Anjali*. It's only if something requires special effects that I tend to storyboard. Otherwise I don't.

RANGAN: So you're not like Hitchcock, in the sense of storyboarding even camera movements.

RATNAM: I wish I was, but I'm not.

7

'That's just my fascination with Kurosawa'

Thalapathy (1991)

Surya (Rajinikanth), the abandoned child of an unwed mother, finds a friend in Devarajan (Mammootty), a local gangster. Surya's rise through Deva's ranks endows him with power and privilege, but he still yearns for love—from Subbulakshmi (Shobana), but more importantly, from his mother Kalyani (Srividya), whose son Arjun (Arvind Swamy), the district collector, is on a mission to rid the town of gangs.

BARADWAJ RANGAN: It's surprising that you didn't turn to the story of Karna earlier, because he's a classic embodiment of *nallavana-kettavana*. Perhaps the difference from *Nayakan*, this time around, is that even amidst the gangster goings-on, there's a strong mother–son story.

MANI RATNAM: I think the gangster milieu is a readily identifiable extension of the wrong side, which is what the Kauravas were. The other film that was based on the epic was [Shyam Benegal's] *Kalyug*. That was set against a completely industrialized backdrop, with two warring families that formed a close parallel to the two warring kingdoms in the epic. Benegal's film was about the Mahabharata, where Karna was one among many players, whereas my film was specifically about Karna. My story seemed to flow very easily into a small-town underworld set-up, in which right and wrong didn't need to be explained in great detail but were there in an apparent sense.

The basic premise of Karna's plight is so dramatic that the milieu becomes secondary. When we wrote the script, this was one of the few instances where anything we touched became a dramatic scene—when he meets Duryodhana, when he meets Arjuna, when he falls in love with the girl who gets married to Arjuna, when he meets his mother, when he meets her husband. So I looked at this as an emotional story that just happens to be set against a gangster background. It didn't bother me at all that I'd made a film earlier in the same genre, because otherwise you're saying you can't make more than one film with the same backdrop. That logic doesn't hold water. You can find different shades within the same milieu—and it wasn't just the mother–son relationship. It was always about Karna, about his relationship with Duryodhana, the fact that he finds his own family and still has to hold back.

RANGAN: There's still a hint that this is as much the mother's story as the son's. The prologue features these *Bhogi* [the day before Pongal] revellers in the foreground, and in the distant background, on top of a hill, there's a speck of a bullock cart carrying the mother. She's beginning her journey.

RATNAM: It is still her story. But we didn't want to get into the who, what and why of her story. That's what I said. You take any part of the Mahabharata and you instinctively find a film within that. Here, the focus at the beginning was always about the child that was born. We see an underage girl who delivers her baby and leaves it in a bogie. We tried to make the train take a curved route, almost like a river. We had to search a lot in order to find a railway path that gave the feeling of the child being carried along in the water.

RANGAN: Why did you decide to shoot the beginning in black and white?

RATNAM: It's a very brief portion that brings us to the child, to the point of him being adopted. Black and white gives the

'Karna comes dramatically into the Mahabharata in the sequence where Arjuna is performing with his bow and arrow. So an action scene is not out of place.'

sense of this being a prologue without us having to define it as a prologue.

RANGAN: You make very specific use of the sun in your framing because Karna is the sun god's son. Did you have a backstory about who the sun god equivalent was in your retelling? Who impregnated Kunti?

RATNAM: You're getting into gossip-column territory now. The film consciously avoids the who and the how of the underage girl's first love. It was the child, the son of Surya, who formed the story. The Karna character is called Surya to maintain the link to Suryavamsam. The first time colour seeps into the film is when the child is held up against the sun, and that becomes a motif right through the film. It's a very strong reference to where he came from, and it links this story to the epic. We had to shoot around the times the sun was at a point we wanted. For instance, in the sequence where Surya's mother comes into his hut, later in the film, we wanted to make sure we had a huge sun bleaching the frame right behind her. We wanted the sun present when the mother and son met. So we had to erect the set in such a way that it would catch the morning sun. We would get there at five o'clock, rehearse and be ready so that we could do this major shot with that background.

Similarly, when the child is found and picked up from the water, we had to look for a place where we'd get a flowing stream with the sun in the background. And the scene where the father meets Surya was a single shot against the setting sun. It was

Thalapathy 105

a big scene. We were shooting in Mysore, at the edge of a dam. We had to get there by lunchtime so that we could set it up, have a couple of hours for rehearsal, and do the scene by around 4.30 p.m. or so. We were ready, but just before the shot, Rajinikanth said that he wanted to do it the next day. He said that he was still not ready. So we shot it the next day. We did it in almost one uninterrupted take. We just shot a few inserts later, for cutaways.

RANGAN: Your location was Mysore (even though the story takes place in an unnamed location) and your characters are Tamilian. How important is geographical correctness to a film, especially considering the importance you give to visuals and backgrounds?

RATNAM: First of all, when you are shooting with a big star like Rajinikanth, and most of the shoot is outside the studios, in actual locations, it is easier to shoot outside Tamil Nadu. Otherwise, the crowds that come to watch Rajinikanth would be a very big problem.

Secondly, where a film is shot is an artistic, economic and logistical decision. Do you think all World War films set in Germany are shot in Germany? It has to evoke Germany. It is like saying that the camera in a fight scene should be placed exactly where the punches land on the opponent. Geographical correctness on film is not equal to where you shoot but what you shoot. If what's on screen looks correct, if it evokes the place and the period, it does not matter if it was shot on the floor or in Timbuktu. What's important is emotional integrity. It has to be plausible. It has to make people believe that it really happened, and the background should enhance and not distract from the story you're telling. It should not intrude and tell the audience that it's the wrong place.

Otherwise, a location is just a tool to tell a story. I've shot *Bombay* and *Nayakan*—both of which were set in Bombay—here in Chennai for the most part. You have to have the confidence that you can do it where it is logistically easier and budget-wise easier to execute your film. This film was set in a small town in Tamil Nadu. We needed a town that had a specific type of character, a definition, a specific look. We looked around and landed on Mysore. It gave us everything we were looking for—a waterfront, a river—and it became a very big part of the film. The slum, of course, was a set erected by [Thotta] Tharrani in Chennai.

RANGAN: Having made a landmark film with Kamal Haasan, did *Thalapathy* come about because you wanted to do something with Rajinikanth?

RATNAM: Rajinikanth was a friend of my brother GV, and they were talking about a film together. I'd met him a couple of times because he'd expressed an interest to work together. But I didn't have anything for him then. I didn't want to make a conventional film with him. He was a huge superstar. I needed something that

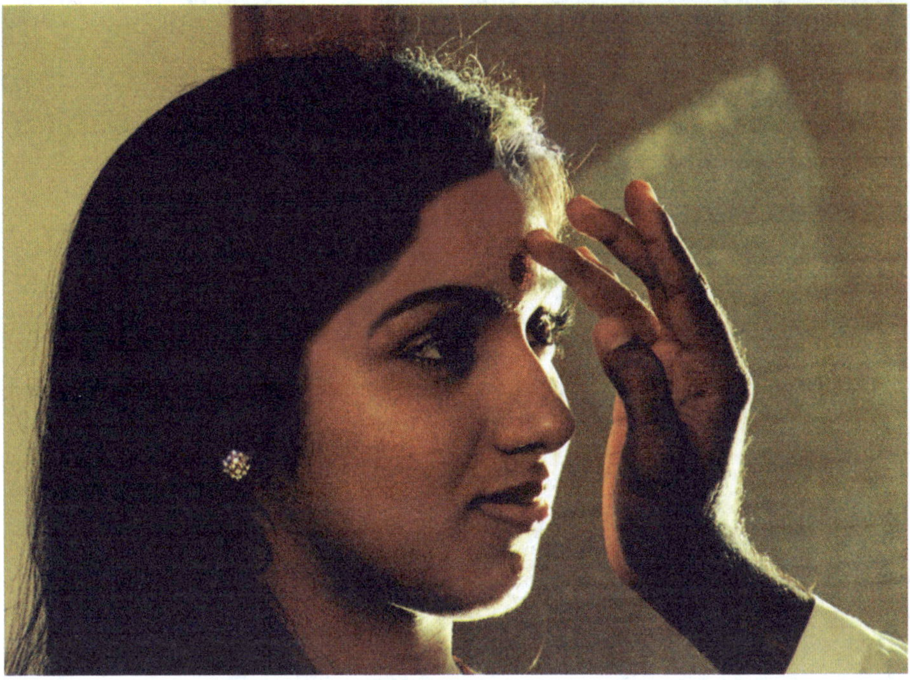

(Previous page) Velu and his wife just after marriage, in Nayakan.
(Above and facing page) The many faces of Revathy in Mouna Raagam, *as she settles down in an arranged marriage.*

(Previous page, above and facing page) **Agni Natchatiram**, *a masala movie packed with songs, action, drama and romance.*

(Above) The many shades of love in Alaipaayuthey.

'When we cast Bhanupriya, I specifically told her that there wouldn't be any songs for her.'

would have scope for his stardom but yet remain my film. I wanted something that would be right for both of us. I wanted something he could not say no to and something that I really wanted to do.

And then this concept came up, which is basically Karna's story. This is one of the best characters in the Mahabharata, completely backed by and loved by the author. It was a new terrain for me—*Geetanjali* and *Anjali* were in a different genre altogether. I was coming off a film with a lot of kids. This was the other end of the spectrum. This was very dramatic material, and we had the chance to reinterpret an epic. We had a way of looking at it through modern eyes, yet bringing in a lot of things that were there in the original, without keeping them upfront. That kind of fascinated me and I started working on that. I thought Rajinikanth would be good for this story.

I went with GV to meet him. He was very keen. That's how it started.

RANGAN: It's interesting that he didn't have any reservations about this project, because it has a sort of parallel hero in Mammooty. Rajinikanth didn't—and still doesn't—usually share screen space with another male star to this extent.

RATNAM: Rajini was very clear right from the beginning that if Karna's story had to be told Duryodhana had to be important, and it was important to cast him correctly. So before, during or after, he had no issues on these grounds. He was so confident of himself as a star. As long as the subject appealed to him and he could see the character straightaway, there were no problems.

RANGAN: Whenever directors take on a star,

a mass-hero of Rajinikanth's magnitude, they begin to think along the lines of 'these are the things I can do, these are the things I cannot do'. Did that figure in your writing? In the end, for instance, the character does not die, like Karna in the epic.

RATNAM: I think you have to be aware that you've got a huge star with a huge following. You are in the market after all; you're aware of these things. But you don't have to be bound by them. Because if that's what you're doing, then you're just making another Rajinikanth film. In my mind, I kept telling myself that *Mullum Malarum* was the benchmark in terms of his performance. It is mainstream Tamil cinema, not parallel cinema. But it was very realistic, and was performed very, very realistically. The dialogues were real. It probably was his best performance. He was absolutely casual, without any of the 'style' traps he fell into, though he did that [the stylistic elements] before *Mullum Malarum* and even afterwards. So I knew that there was something in him that would make a character ring absolutely true, without pulling the star element into it or resorting to other things like a cigarette going up and coming down. He could carry the character by himself, on his shoulders, and still be real and effective.

So I had no issues, no doubts. I wanted something that would give him the chance to go close to his performance in *Mullum Malarum*. That was all. Other than that, even though he's a star, I knew that the character of Karna was large enough that I didn't have to worry about 'feeding' his

'It wasn't just the mother–son relationship.' (From left) Jaishankar, Srividya and Arvind Swamy.

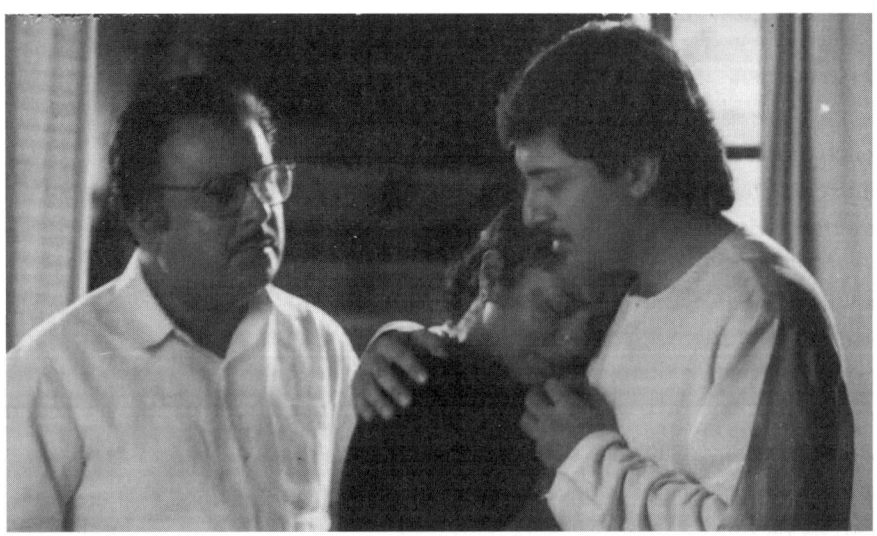

fans and things like that. We just went with the script, whatever shape it took. Even the finish of the film, where our Karna character lives on, was because I've always wished that he lived on. So much has gone wrong. There's so much stacked against him. Maybe there's a bit of hope, a bit of optimism in this, but I felt that his death would look too doomed, too tragic. It was how I saw the character. I didn't even consider the original option, where Karna dies. It was thought of this way from the beginning.

RANGAN: This film has what is possibly your most masala-moment ever—the 'hero introduction scene' for Rajinikanth with a slow-motion fight sequence.

RATNAM: You seem to be caught up with masala a bit too much. I did not think of it then or now as masala. It was more of me, my sensibilities, than Rajini. It's not conventional masala.

RANGAN: I don't mean masala in a derogatory sense. I love that pitch. It's just that it's a pitch your films aren't often set in, so it's interesting to explore the reasons you opt for this pitch.

RATNAM: Karna was the only one who could match and surpass Arjuna. He was a great warrior. He comes dramatically into the Mahabharata in the sequence where Arjuna is performing with his bow and arrow. So when you come to a modern-day Surya, an action scene is not out of

'That line wasn't meant to be taken literally, as referring to someone who was fair-skinned. It just meant someone who could speak English, somebody who is sophisticated.'

place. We are telling this story of a child that was abandoned at birth and left on a train and found by a bunch of kids and then picked up by someone. These seven to eight minutes of build-up lead to this particular moment, which should reveal what everything so far has resulted in. So it was important that the way the hero comes in has a dramatic impact. It is the culmination of the introductory sequences and the start of his story. It was not a conventional Rajinikanth scene. We plunge right into the middle of the action, without establishing the characters or the reason. It was stylized, in high speed (almost like the rain song in *Geetanjali*), filmed in slush and muck, and even the way we edited it was very different from what we'd done till then.

RANGAN: With *Raavan(an)*, the title gave away the fact that it was based on an epic. But no one knew what *Thalapathy* was about while it was being made, and only after the film's release did people start talking about parallels. In hindsight, do you think *Raavan(an)* would have fared better had you called it, say, *Beera* [the name of the Raavan-equivalent character], and not drawn attention to the epic?

RATNAM: Even today, a lot of people do not know that *Thalapathy* was based on the Mahabharata. The parallels are hidden sufficiently inside the story to make it work. That is the way I wanted it—at a layer below and not crying out loud. But because we had done *Thalapathy* that way, we decided to have the epic element of *Raavanan* upfront, so that it's not like we're playing the same card twice. I don't know if it would have fared better as *Beera*. It's a hypothetical situation. But possibly the prejudices wouldn't have been there. They wouldn't have taken it so personally. They would have seen it as just a story. But I felt confident enough that I could reveal the source and still be able to tell a story.

RANGAN: When you make films based on a familiar arc, does it free you up to do some things because the audience already knows? For instance, Surya becomes Deva's trusted lieutenant very quickly, and we accept this because we already know that this is what happens in the Mahabharata. There's no need for a protracted detailing of his rise through the ranks.

RATNAM: Godard did a great favour to all film-makers by destroying this need for a step-by-step narration. If a man has to go from point A to point B, it is no longer necessary to show him getting out from point A, getting into a car, and driving and reaching point B. He taught us to cut straight in. He gave the audience the credit of putting the obvious together.

The basic premise in this stretch of *Thalapathy* is that Surya's rise should connect and make sense to someone who will not make the link to the original. There's a musical montage that details this. It sets the tone for what he does in Deva's organization. Emotionally, all that's important is the fact that this man has gone against him, and Surya still does him good. Deva admits that he was wrong and takes him in without batting an eyelid. This is something Surya has never faced, so for him it's a special kind of bonding. And there is a constant parallel to the epic. So whether you're conscious of it or not, you are able to understand the bond between the two. That's all you need to say. Beyond that, there's no story. There's only explanation. And explanations remain explanations. People understand these things emotionally, and if something works emotionally it doesn't have to be mathematically explained.

RANGAN: In the scene where Shobana, the Draupadi character, sees Rajinikanth beating up a man on the street, she appears to be repulsed and yet strangely attracted.

RATNAM: I didn't see this scene of action as the start of an attraction. She sees a different side, the different world that he's in, and, more than anything, it scares her. It jolts her out of her world, and this jolting is what makes you open up or shut down. Being scared becomes her way of opening up.

RANGAN: What is the point of origin of his attraction to her?

RATNAM: I think it's a result of what he saw when he saw her first, which is shown in a song. There is a certain amount of art in her world; there is a certain amount of music that's completely alien to him. When he goes to meet her, she's with children and she's teaching them classical music and dance. It's a different world, and there's some kind of fascination or attraction because of that.

RANGAN: Why did you choose to introduce the Draupadi character not through a scene but in the song *Raakkamma kaiya thattu* (in the *Kunitha puruvamum* portion towards the end)?

RATNAM: The song was conceived and composed with her introduction in mind. It was about two different strata, two different kinds of people who come across each other, about blending two worlds and merging them in a particular fashion. It's about an attraction towards what you are not. Two contrasting people become simultaneously aware of each other, and we were able to do it easily in a song that isn't just an item. It has a story to say. It starts a relationship between two characters. We were able to get across something that is really sociological into a musical bit. Sometimes, it starts with just a glance.

RANGAN: And this contrast is manifest in the pagan celebrations of Surya and company versus the explicitly religious tone of these latter portions. You even have tridents and such signifiers as shadowy foregrounds.

RATNAM: In a festival, there are different kinds of things that blend in together. These things are treated differently by different strata. And yet, it's a common melting pot. In a temple festival, for example, there is a definite element of religiousness to it, but at the same time, there is also an element of entertainment and joy and celebration. It's there all over India. There is a contrast between the two and yet there is also a link.

RANGAN: There's a beautiful uninterrupted shot where you start from the river and keep pulling back to reveal various aspects of Shobana's world and then you stop at Rajinikanth standing at a corner—at the edge of her world and at the beginning of his. Was this the first time you used a Steadicam?

RATNAM: No, the first time I used a Steadicam was in *Roja*, in the shot that introduces us to the terrorists' hideout. This scene in *Thalapathy* was done the old-fashioned way, using a crane and trolley, and it was the very first thing we shot in the film. This was the first film where I was going with stereophonic music, and this scene was conceived to highlight this. Earlier, songs used to be recorded in stereo. Audio cassettes used to be in stereo and could be listened to on a stereophonic music system. But the mix for the movies was done on an optical mono track. 70mm films always had stereophonic sound. [Jijo Punnoose's] *Padayottam* was done in 70mm and had DTR [Discrete Track Recording]. [K. Balachander's] *Ek Duuje Ke Liye* was mixed in 70mm. But this was the first time I had the luxury of stereophonic prints and this shot was really an indulgence.

We have the sounds of water, birds, then the sounds of prayer and the music class and finally the sound of the dance class, with the teacher and the girls—and even while shooting, we were thinking about which sound would come from the left speaker and go all the way to the right and so on. Even the songs were recorded in Bombay because we knew that the music would be in stereo on screen. It was a really big leap for me at the time. *Geetanjali* was the first time I used the CinemaScope-anamorphic lens. That was a big thing for us, to move from 35mm to anamorphic widescreen. People had started using anamorphic even earlier. For *Nayakan* and *Agni Natchatiram*, we preferred the traditional square-ish format. With *Geetanjali*, we could afford to experiment because there was an expanse to it. It was an outdoor film. The love story lent itself beautifully to CinemaScope. We could have a wide screen with just two people in one corner. There was a bit of a learning curve. Your throw is off at first, and it took us a few days to get used to it. In *Thalapathy*, we were liberated in terms of sound. We were on the verge of a huge change in the way sound would be designed in Indian cinema. I did not know then that digital sound and the 5.1 soundtrack were around the corner.

RANGAN: Other than this riverside shot, did stereophonic sound influence your filming and shot-taking in any way?

RATNAM: Not really. One thing you learn is never to reduce something to a gimmick. We tend to do that in India when a new toy comes into our hands. There should be some restraint. You should know how to use it so that the audience is not aware and yet it envelops them. So there was no point where we went overboard. But we were conscious of this technology when we were shooting. It gives you a certain amount of freedom. It helps you understand how you want your sound. You don't want to be flashy, but you should be able to get the sound you're looking for.

'A location is just a tool to tell a story.' Shobana and Rajinikanth.

RANGAN: This was your first collaboration with Santosh Sivan.

RATNAM: I'd seen his film—[Aditya Bhattacharya's] *Raakh*. It was quite dramatic, quite stunning visually. After *Anjali*, we were looking at a film that had action, which had dramatic elements, and I was keen to meet him and see if he'd be interested in working with me. So he came down, and obviously he wanted to assess me as much as I wanted to assess him. When we met we got along very well and it became very easy to do the film together. Santosh is a great guy to have in your team.

RANGAN: We talked a little about the *Sundari* song sequence when we discussed the *O Priya Priya* number in *Geetanjali*. There's an interesting Samurai angle here.

RATNAM: That's just my fascination with Kurosawa. For quite some time, I'd wanted to make [a film version of Kalki Krishnamurthy's novel] *Ponniyin Selvan*, so I think there was some hangover from there too. We had to do a love song, and we were constantly looking at ways to elevate the song to another plane, to give it a more operatic quality. This was about two different kinds of people and their emotions. He was really like a warrior. The film was called *Thalapathy*. He lent himself to a guy who leads an army. And she was the classical dancer, the one who was waiting. So instead of just shooting a love song, we shot it in a way that visually hinted at what was going to come later. There was that element of flirting with danger. Every time he went out, there was a chance he might not come back to her. She had to wait and it was a relief to find that he was back. The life of a warrior has a kind of parallel to the life of an underworld person. The song touched on the life they would lead if they lived together.

RANGAN: Even the way the song comes in is a bit of a counterpoint, because she tells him that she likes him, and you expect a 'happy' song. But we get this expanse of troubled togetherness. Later, she goes on to marry the character played by Arvind Swamy. Did you cast Arvind because you wanted someone fair-complexioned, to contrast with Rajinikanth? He even tells her as much. ['*Unakku enna venum? Vellayaa oru thol . . .*']

RATNAM: When we shot that scene, we hadn't cast the part yet. We couldn't find anybody right. That line wasn't meant to be taken literally, as referring to someone who was fair-skinned. It just meant someone who could speak English, somebody who was sophisticated, educated, somebody not like Surya. That's all. That's the kind of person we were looking for. The search had been going on for a while and we were lucky we found somebody who was more or less absolutely right for the part. Even Rajini asked me later if that was why I wrote that line.

RANGAN: I thought you'd wait for everything to come together before you start shooting. Because the Arjuna character is very important to this film.

RATNAM: Sometimes you don't want to compromise. You don't want to do something for the sake of doing it. You're still pushing the edge and you're confident you can get someone good. You have a backup—even if it's not someone specific. And if you search for something more while you have a backup, then you may land on the right one.

RANGAN: While scripting, did you have a larger Rajinikanth–Bhanupriya track, for which the song *Putham pudhu poo* was composed? In the film, they hardly have any scenes together. Even the song plays only in the background, in an instrumental version.

RATNAM: When we cast her—I remember, she'd come home—I specifically told her that there wouldn't be any songs for her. I was very clear about that because the role was like that. He was in an awkward situation while getting married to this woman with a child. He was the cause of her husband's death. So it can't be the start of a new romantic track. The *Putham pudhu* song was recorded more like their theme music. When we started composing, the first track that we got for the film was *Chinna thaayaval*, which becomes a theme for the loneliness of

---

'When we wrote the script, this was one of the few instances where anything we touched became a dramatic scene.'

Karna. We wanted a composition that would have this image of a Karna who is standing alone, brooding, and who is doomed to be a loner from birth, when he was abandoned.

Putham pudhu was a tune Ilaiyaraaja had given me much earlier. Each time we sat down for composing, I used to take home a cassette of the session so that I could listen to it several times. This song was there in one of the earlier tapes—I don't remember which film's composing session it was. We finished composing for *Thalapathy* and I was telling him that there was this one tune that kept coming back to my mind. I liked the track and we recorded one more number for the film. I knew I could use it somewhere in the background.

If something brilliant had happened, perhaps I'd have integrated the song into the film a little more, but we didn't shoot too much around the couple—only what's there in the film. And sometimes—I've told you this before—when the screen time is short for a character, you need a bigger actor, with stature and star quality, to be able to get the character across. The casting of Bhanupriya showed that there was some weight to the character, and you don't have to invest in terms of songs and things like that. Her very presence makes the character strong. That gets your story across as much as a backstory does.

RANGAN: One of the best-picturized songs in all your films, in my opinion,

'Rajini was very clear right from the beginning that if Karna's story had to be told Duryodhana had to be important.' Rajinikanth and Mammootty.

is the version of *Chinna thaayaval* that unfolds in a temple, with mother and son meeting and yet not meeting in the midst of swirling crowds. It's shot like scenes and then cut according to the song's rhythm.

RATNAM: You don't have to cut it completely according to the music, but you have in mind that it's a song and that it's not exactly in sync. A mother and a son reaching out to each other is a bit of a cliché in Indian cinema. We had to find a way to make it a little more poetic, a little more lyrical, and have another way of getting across the search and the accidental coming together, with one seeking and the other one not knowing about it. The song was shot to get that impact. We had to get the people, the junior artists, to move and to look natural and still give a sense of searching.

RANGAN: The songs here have a stronger sense of being tied to the emotional core of the narrative, as opposed to something like *Anjali*, where the songs were show-stopping set pieces.

RATNAM: In *Anjali*, the songs were set pieces, like in *Thiruda Thiruda*. The songs were my front. They were my defence, my platform, to take the story of that child into the mainstream. So I was not ashamed to just leave the songs there and go to the next scene. But here, the story is so Indian and so dramatic and so known that I could have just gone bare. I didn't really need the songs to entertain, because the drama was doing that for me. The songs had to help me in a different fashion—to get across the mood or the celebration of an emotion. So they became an integral part of the narrative and not just a prop.

RANGAN: Yes, they seem to belong to the characters, in the sense that *Chinna thaayaval* marks the mother, *Yamunai aatrile* marks the lover, and so on.

RATNAM: Like I told you, *Chinna thaayaval* was conceived more as a song for Rajini. It's about his loneliness, his seeking the person he's never met. So it was like a lullaby that was never sung. But yes, *Yamunai aatrile* was about a stratum that was above his reach. So it kind of represented his lover's entire character.

RANGAN: I can't help noticing that you've been clutching a bunch of pencils through this entire session.

RATNAM: Are you trying to find meaning in the pencils too? That's the trouble with critics, reading into things that are not there. Well, I write with pencils. I use my laptop as long as I'm writing in English, till I get to the dialogue stage. And if it's a Hindi film, I write the dialogues too in English. But when I write in Tamil, I prefer writing in longhand, with pencils. I can't key in Tamil at a decent speed.

RANGAN: Well, critics do tend look beyond the film-maker's professed intentions.

I prefer to trust the tale rather than the teller. But more importantly, while speaking to reticent film-makers, you have to be shameless and ask all kinds of questions, in the hope that at least some of the answers will yield gold.

RATNAM: Hah. The price of gold is coming down.

RANGAN: At this point when *Thalapathy* happened, had you thought about making a Hindi film?

RATNAM: No. I was not fascinated with doing Hindi films. I had been asked enough times. Ramu [Ram Gopal Varma] had already gone there, but I was not keen.

RANGAN: *Mouna Raagam, Nayakan, Agni Natchatiram* and *Geetanjali* were all remade in Hindi, but they vanished without a trace, while their originals are pop-culture milestones. What do you think got lost in the translation?

RATNAM: Those films were made indifferently. If somebody had made them with a little bit of care and sensitivity, they may have worked, like *Alaipaayuthey* did [as *Saathiya*]. These are not films that work on dramatic terms alone. It's more about the way they are executed, the emotions they carry and the performances, and if you take away these things and just put the bare-bones together, it may not hold.

RANGAN: Also the casting, I'd assume. I landed on *Vansh*, the remake of *Agni Natchatiram*, while flipping channels and saw that the father was being played by Anupam Kher. In Tamil, you presented Vijayakumar in a white dhoti and with that strange hair parting. It was like seeing a brand new actor. Whereas with Anupam Kher, you just roll your eyes because he's played this part 75,000 times.

RATNAM: I saw a bit of *Dayavan* [the *Nayakan* remake]. I didn't get past the childhood portions. I think it was the point where the kid was trapped into betraying his father; I'm not sure, but if I see the film again, I can point it out. They didn't get the point at all. Feroz Khan came here before he was to do the film, and I felt I had to tell him how I would go about it and then leave it to him. To me, *Nayakan* is the story of a man going to an alien zone and establishing roots and becoming somebody in that territory. It is really an underdog's conquest in an alien zone. So for the Hindi version to root the story in Bombay was itself odd. I said I would have either set it in Calcutta, or even in London. He had a different perspective. He felt that the identification with Varadaraja Mudaliar was the key to the entire thing, whereas I thought the key, the story, was really about the alien man making it. That was the emotional chord. We differed, so I said fine, and we left it at that.

8

'He's not pure . . . he's a hip idealist'

Roja (1992)

Roja (Madhubala), a young girl from a Tamil Nadu village, finds herself unexpectedly married to the ultra-urban Rishi (Arvind Swamy), a cryptologist. Just as they ease out their differences, he is kidnapped, in Kashmir, by militants who demand, in exchange, the freedom of their jailed colleague. Roja, trapped between an unfamiliar culture and an unyielding establishment, may be Rishi's only hope.

BARADWAJ RANGAN: *Roja*, for me, is a very personal film, even though it's not a favourite. My friends and I had adopted you as one of us, someone who held the same brash, irreverent world view. You showed us—in *Agni Natchatiram*, for instance—that it was cool to bribe the clerk at the motor vehicles department in order to get the address of a hot chick. And then we saw *Roja*, and the first feeling was that of betrayal. This was a responsible film, a shockingly patriotic film. You'd forsaken us and become one of *them*.

MANI RATNAM: Just after the film's release, P.C. Sreeram called me—he was in Pollachi, I think, shooting [Bharathan's] *Thevar Magan*—and said, 'I told you that at the end of the film everyone should stand up and clap. Why haven't you done that?' He sounded very angry even though he hadn't seen the film. Only his unit had. PC is like that. He'll say something like, 'At this moment, everybody should get up and clap.' That's it. How you do it is your problem. He just wants the result. He did the test shoot for *Roja*. So he was aware of the story and he was with us when we were casting. He was very disappointed that I hadn't done it. So, that was one reaction I got. And then Ram Gopal Varma called from Hyderabad. He saw the movie there and he walked out of the film. He said he couldn't take it. These were the first two reactions I got for *Roja*. And now, yours. So I am kind of used to varied reactions.

I think that even a 'cool' guy, when cornered, does have strong reactions. I think it was as 'cool'—if that's the term you want to use—as my other films were. It still had a lot of earthy elements, like the city guy going to a village and getting down from the car and smoking a cigarette in front of his mother. These were still things that were not done in films at that point because it was not the correct thing to show. *Roja* dealt with something that was happening around us. It was about a politically important issue, and the weight of the issue had a bearing on the overall tone of the film. But the characters were still normal people. The girl was someone who believed in herself, who'd do what she thought was right. And the male character was a guy who was educated and urban and had all the qualities you can easily identify with if you're from the city. So I don't think it was as drastic a departure as *Iruvar*. That's where I felt I took a couple of steps forward. *Roja* was just an extension of what I had done till then.

RANGAN: The way the marriage happened, the subsequent S-O-R-R-Y sequence—all of that was what we knew, the familiar style we loved. I think what bothered me was this: in your films until then, your heroes—with the exception of, say, Mohan in *Mouna Raagam*—had been, to some extent, an embodiment of *nallavana-kettavana*. They were like us, with bad traits and good traits. But here was Arvind Swamy, who appeared supernaturally good. There's that '*Jai Hind*' bit, for instance . . .

RATNAM: I don't think he's very different

'Maybe it was just time Rahman came.'

from any of the urban, educated people who we've known or grown up with, except that he is at a different place at a different time. That's all. He is the classic ordinary man in an extraordinary situation. And when he's put into a dramatic situation like this, kidnapped by extremists, he fights back in the only way he knows. When they come to record him as proof that he's alive, he says *'Jai Hind'*, which is a very patriotic thing, but in that situation for the terrorist it is like a swear word. He's smart enough to know what can get under their skin. Obviously, the intention is not just that he's proclaiming his patriotism, but telling the other guy what he can do with himself. It is like telling them to go to hell in not-so-mild terms. He says what will hurt them the most, and the way he says it is with a certain arrogance.

It is no different from an expletive, knowing that the other guy is going to react. The situation brings something unexpected out of a cryptologist. He's pushed into a corner and he's not going to back off any more. He is going to lash out. That is all. He's not a superhero. He doesn't take on all the terrorists. But he's not a coward either, who will shut up and be quiet. If, for example, [the novelist and screenwriter] Sujatha Sir had been in that situation, he'd tell his captor a few things that that man would not forget till the end of his life. Rishi is that kind of person. He's fighting with his hands tied. He can hurt with words, if not with arms. He is in a different place and using a different tool to counter his enemies and state his point of view. He's saying, 'I'm not going to be a pushover.'

RANGAN: He's not hesitant about going to Kashmir because it's a part of India. He's so inflamed by the sight of the burning flag that he falls on it to put out the fire. He's a 'hero'—if not in the conventional heroic sense, then certainly in a moral sense. At any point, did you consider that the character might work better if he was shown to be a bit afraid in the situation he's trapped in?

RATNAM: I thought there was a certain arrogance in the character, which is why he says that thing about '*Indhiya thimiru*' [the arrogance of an Indian]. When he says that Kashmir is a part of India, it's not a statement made in innocence. It's a statement that comes from arrogance. He tells his much-older boss, 'Maybe you're scared but I'm not scared.' There is a difference in the way the two of them look at it—maybe it's an age thing, maybe it's just the way he is. I think there is a certain amount of moral arrogance in the honest middle class. And some of them, even when pushed into a corner, retain this arrogance. You can see it on different planes, in different situations. The character of Rishi came in those shades. In a way, he is a little romantic—a guy who wants to get married to a village girl. Why does he want to get married to a village girl? But there are people like that, and it works in a particular fashion. They tend to have an attitude.

RANGAN: That is true. What I am talking about is whether you, during the writing, thought about putting this character in a grey area, given your penchant for *nallavana–kettavana*.

RATNAM: To me, *this* is the grey area.

'In a film, when a narrative takes a sudden turn, it should not look like it's forced, showing the hand of the writer.'

He is somebody who uses swear words in a different form. He's arrogant. He tells his boss, 'You are a coward. I am not a coward.' He tells these things in a polite, civilized way, but the attitude is there all the same. He feels that he has to get married to a village girl, not wanting to know if that girl wants to get married to a city guy. So he is grey to me. He's not pure. He's not a perfect idealist in that sense. He's a hip idealist.

RANGAN: Were you ever apprehensive of crossing the line from patriotism to jingoism? Because right from the [Krishnan–Panchu's] *Parasakthi* days, and probably even before, Tamil cinema has had a strong tradition of jingoism, which suited the rhetoric-driven films of the time.

RATNAM: I wasn't too worried about it. Ram Gopal Varma still feels it's jingoism. But sometimes emotional honesty is what matters. About the flag-burning sequence, whether you or I would do what he did is probably a question, but there's no question that we'd want to do it. Because it is as much about the national flag as it is about an actual fight, with each side trying to send a strong hook across. If you're going down, you will go down fighting. That is how I looked at the character. When he said *Jai Hind*, when he fell on the flag, it was done with anger. It's not just patriotism. He's pushed and it's a kind of rebellion. He's arrogant. He is not going to give in. He's not practical. He's willing to be a little more romantic and violent.

RANGAN: So by falling on the flag, he's basically saying, 'Fuck you.'

RATNAM: It's done and played with that exact attitude.

RANGAN: The way you explain this makes me think of the point in *Aboorva Raagangal* where Kamal Haasan calls a bunch of people, '*thevidiya pasangala*' [bastards] and gets beaten up.

RATNAM: Yes, that's how he gets beaten up. So, really, it's Balachander's fault, not mine.

RANGAN: Your movies never have expletives though. I can't recall any offhand.

RATNAM: Perhaps I save them for real life.

RANGAN: Was this a film K. Balachander approached you to do? Or did you approach him with a story in hand?

RATNAM: He approached me. He was my inspiration in Tamil films. He was one of the reasons I took up film-making. So when he asked me to make a film for his banner, I wanted it to be one of the best films they have produced. It needed to be of KB's standard. I was working on something for my own production house when he called. You always have one or two ideas in your mind. I went over the next day and told him the *Roja* outline. He was okay with it, but he didn't like the title. He said:

'*Roja . . . paakku thool maadhiri irukku.*' ['Roja' is a local brand of crushed betel nut.] I was amazed. I thought the title represented Kashmir because the rose is something beautiful but with thorns. The contrast between harshness and tenderness is built into it. But he said, '*Paakku thool maadhiri irukku.*' Trust a pure Tamilian to come up with something like that.

RANGAN: Don't you consider yourself a pure Tamilian?

RATNAM: I mean, he thinks in those terms straightaway. He was not thinking of imagery. Anyway, Tamil medium-*la padichaa dhaan* pure Tamilian. English-*la yosicha Thamizhan illa. Adhaan* problem. [You're a Tamilian only if you are educated in a Tamil-medium school. You're not a Tamilian if you think in English.] So the next day I went and told him another title. *Irudhi Varai* [Till the End]. It is Tamil, proper. But they have this grammatical concept of *arai-chol*, so *irudhi* was not acceptable. He said he preferred *Roja*. Finally, I used *Irudhi Varai* as the title of the book that gets published in *Kannathil Muthamittal*.

RANGAN: I vaguely remember a half-page ad in a Tamil paper—*Dinathanthi*, I think. There was a long stem, capped by a rose with Madhubala's face; though I don't think I recognized her. She'd done [K. Balachander's] *Azhagan* . . .

RATNAM: No, not *Azhagan*. She'd done [K. Balachander's] *Vaaname Ellai*. The *Dinathanthi* ad was not the picture of a rose but a rough sketch of straight lines drawn with a pen to represent a flower with a long stem. The image was carried through the entire promotion of the film.

RANGAN: With your earlier films, it appeared that the characters came first and then you spun a story around them. But in *Roja*, it looks like you decided to do something 'Indian', and then worked around that.

RATNAM: I didn't think it was an Indian platform. We thought it was a Tamil film. Something similar happened in real life. An engineer was kidnapped when he'd gone on a project to Srinagar, and his wife was fighting for his release. She had written an open letter to the terrorist which says, to a large extent, what Roja says when she goes to meet Wasim Khan [the terrorist] in jail. The content of the scene is exactly what the content of the woman's letter was. It struck a chord. From her point of view, her husband had done no harm to anyone. He was a good man. And her appeal was to the goodness of the terrorist. It is her plight that the film is based on. It really came out of the character, not the plot. There isn't a very big plot in that sense. The rest of it is just building up towards this jail scene. This is the crux of the film. And it came from that open letter.

RANGAN: Is there a reason Rishi was an ordinary professional and not a cop or a young minister or somebody 'worthy' of being kidnapped?

'When he says that Kashmir is a part of India, it's not a statement made in innocence. It's a statement that comes from arrogance.'

RATNAM: But that was what was happening in Kashmir at the time. This isn't something that we imagined very creatively. It was an engineer who'd gone on that assignment. He had nothing to do with the government, and he was kidnapped. These people were caught in the middle of a fight they were not even a part of. *Roja* came out of that.

RANGAN: All these years later, it's strange to see the media had such a low-key presence in such a sensational story.

RATNAM: The time the film was released, there was no 24x7 media. The lady who wrote the letter was not hounded—though today she would be.

RANGAN: The film is a departure from your family-oriented films. The family is now placed in the context of the nation. Roja is fighting for her husband, which is the kind of domestic situation we're used to in your films, but the fight is taking place on a national platform.

RATNAM: We were producing *Dasarathan*, with Sharath Kumar, for our company, Aalayam. A friend of mine, Kitty, was directing it. Even before *Dasarathan*, I'd told him the outline of *Roja*. I was caught up with *Anjali* or something, so I said, 'Why don't you do this?' He thought about it, but he said, 'No, I want to do something of my own.' That was fine. But as I was telling him the outline, it became more crystallized. When he didn't pick it up and when KB asked me, I told him the outline. All the developments happened after that. It was a classical Indian story—about a woman who would fight death—placed in very contemporary terms. There is always an appeal about it.

RANGAN: Did you have in mind, specifically, the Satyavan–Savitri legend? That would make this, like *Thalapathy*, a contemporary reworking of an epic theme.

RATNAM: Absolutely. You know that emotionally it's a chord you can relate to, and when set in today's context, it blends in to become something fresh.

RANGAN: What is the advantage in beginning the movie with the capture of Wasim Khan? If you'd begun with Roja, for instance, the situation she's getting into would have remained largely unknown till the point of the kidnap.

RATNAM: I think it's one of those things that fell into place very nicely. In a film, when a narrative takes a sudden turn, it should not look like it's forced. It should not look like a deliberate twist in the tale, showing the hand of the writer. If you say that this is where it is heading, right on top, it's like [David Lean's] *Lawrence of Arabia* opening with the accident and the death of Lawrence. It presages what's going to come. In that fashion, this opening is a little classical in its form. It says that this is where the story is headed, and that it's set in two different worlds. This simple device ties the two worlds together. Otherwise, they look like two clearly different entities, and we can get there only after Rishi and Roja get to Kashmir. Because getting kidnapped is such an outlandish thing for a normal person who's grown up in Tirunelveli, the prelude makes it easier for us to take that sharp turn.

RANGAN: And if you'd decided to go that way, Wasim Khan's capture might have made for an equally dramatic 'interval twist', which is now the point of the kidnap of the protagonist.

RATNAM: Rishi getting captured is a very dramatic point. That's when the story turns on its head. That can never be diluted. Whatever you do before, this will still be a shockingly dramatic element in the story. The choice was whether to bring in Wasim Khan at the beginning, or take that bit off completely. The rest would have been the same. Having the Wasim Khan segment helps to ease the blow of Rishi's kidnap, which comes when the audience doesn't expect it. Otherwise, it might look totally out of place—it might take a little while for me to understand who these extremists are, what they are doing in this love story, and why they are kidnapping Rishi. Now, I've opened with Wasim Khan's arrest, and I am stating that this is my terrain—*thamizh-la sollara maadhiri, 'idhu dhaan kalam'* [this is where it's going to happen]. There is extremist activity. There is violence. There is a search. And there is a conflict. Into that war zone, we are taking our ordinary characters. So the audience is prepared for the situation. The ground is laid out for that.

RANGAN: Usually, the tendency is to chain-link the various events in a screenplay. So, after Wasim Khan's capture, we might have had a shot of Roja's father reading a newspaper with the headline, 'Wasim Khan captured'. But you have the capture as a separate block, and you don't refer to it at all until after Rishi is kidnapped. Instead, we cut to a peaceful village and the heroine-introduction song.

RATNAM: I think the opening block does the same thing that you say, but in a different way. There, with the newspaper headlines like you said, you are linking things by a direct visual or content reference. Here, you are linking by contrasting. It is still a link which says that that is Kashmir and this is Tirunelveli—that is troubled and this is serene. And that is why the story can take that song on top. There is so much drama in the opening, and this serene quality is set against all that drama. There is a part of India, deep down south, totally unaware of the troubles in the northern extreme. So it brings two corners of the country right next to each other.

RANGAN: There is a rather annoying cultural tradition of people from the north referring to anyone south of the Vindhyas as a 'Madrasi'. When Roja runs into the army camp after the kidnap and talks in Tamil, an officer asks if anyone there knows 'Madrasi'—not 'Tamil'. Even in *Bombay*, there's this line about wanting to know if the couple is 'Madrasi'. Have you ever felt like educating people about this, through your films, given your experiences in Bombay?

RATNAM: If that is how someone refers to us, then the best way to deal with it is to ignore it, I feel. If it hasn't been learnt in all these years, there's no point in explaining it now. Let the learning happen when it needs to happen. But we don't have to feel insecure about it. I don't feel the need to educate anyone on geography while making *Roja*. I just make the film.

RANGAN: Just before the kidnap, Roja is in a Pillaiyaar temple. It's a strange place, and she doesn't know the language. You don't show how she found her way there.

RATNAM: If the screenplay had asked us to follow the girl, instead of staying with Rishi, we would have easily found a way to tell you that detail. I don't think she'd have done anything dramatically very different from whatever she's doing to find a place of worship in a place where she doesn't know the language. If you'd followed her, it would have been a sequence where she asked someone where the temple was. The other person would not have understood her, so she would have used sign language. She would have made the situation funny and entertaining, and then found the place. Maybe they'd have taken her to a church or something. The scene would have been something of that sort. She would have stood there in the church and said the same things she said to the Pillaiyaar. And it's not a major temple that she goes to—just a small one on the outskirts of the city. She thinks that she has a direct line to the almighty, that she can appeal to God all by herself, and it didn't matter which God it was. It all boils down to the same thing.

RANGAN: I ask this because, as we've discussed earlier, ellipses are a constant in your films. You don't feel the need to connect events that would normally seem to warrant connections; the emotional logic of the transition is enough. You don't go after 'logistical logic'. Even in *Raavan(an)*, we don't see how Raagini, at the end, finds her way back to Beera's hideout after she gets off the train.

RATNAM: There was a logical sequence on paper, and I actually shot a couple of things—like that bus journey. This is what happens: Raagini gets off the train; she gets on the bus; and she gets to the bus terminus. She would have asked for Beera's brother. We had taken that shot where she finds the brother. She speaks to him. And then he brings her to Beera. Only the shot where the brother brings her to Beera remains in the film. The 'logistical logic' is sometimes irrelevant. As a viewer, we've learnt to put pieces together and form a story. We're getting better and better at it, so the less time the director spends trying to link things up, the more time you can spend on saying what you really want to say.

RANGAN: Roja is just eighteen in the film. In villages, of course, people are married off early, but it feels odd that a

'In a way, he is a little romantic—a guy who wants to get married to a village girl.'

guy from the city would be okay with such a young bride.

RATNAM: Look at the engineering colleges, and you'll see many students go back to their villages and get ... When they finish school and get into college, they get married.

RANGAN: Also, I guess the marriage is an accident. You place a number of little obstacles in the way of the couple getting together. He first comes to see her sister and then settles on her, and this rankles her. At one level, this imparts to the story the tragedy of her losing him just as these obstacles are cleared.

RATNAM: It starts and finishes as a personal story of Rishi and Roja set against a larger backdrop. We get involved in their lives and the small problems between a man and a woman who are getting married. It gets us into their world, so when the change comes, you are in their world and you face the kidnap just like they face it. The script pulls us into their lives. It could be any kind of issue, but the audience needs to be neck-deep in their lives. Three days ago, on the front page of the newspaper, there was this item about a marriage that had been fixed. The man who was to get married, a welder, ran away the day before the wedding, even before the reception. They hoped he would come back. But he didn't. So his younger brother, who was twenty-four, got married to the girl the next day. Roja's marriage was something

'You're not too sure if deep down in Tamil Nadu people are aware of the Kashmir problem.' Madhubala and Arvind Swamy.

like this. Twenty years after the film, this still happens around us.

RANGAN: The old women, in your films, usually make a cameo appearance. But here, they're almost like a Greek chorus. They're there when Rishi comes to the village. They're there when the news of the kidnap appears on television. And they're the lead dancers in the *Rukkumani* song sequence.

RATNAM: I get the feeling that you did not like *Roja* at all. Like Ram Gopal Varma. The more I think back about your questions,

Roja 129

the more I feel that I would do most of the film exactly the same way if I were to do it again today. About the old women, you don't see that many old people together in a city or a town. But in villages, you tend to see a lot of them hanging around. Many youngsters go to towns and cities to make a living, leaving the older folks in the villages. So the proportion of older people tends to be higher in villages than in the towns, and it's just more colourful to see these old ladies hanging out together. It becomes a kind of a palette for the scenes. The first half has a sense of light-heartedness because it's just a romantic story. It's also a little plot-heavy. This just makes it a little more entertaining and colourful, easier and more fun.

RANGAN: There is a point where Rishi is in a discussion with his captors and he asks them if they're from the 'neighbouring country'. It's as if you don't want to name the country. But later, a television newsreader says 'Pakistan'. Why didn't you want Rishi to say the P-word?

RATNAM: If you are Rishi, caught there, when you are trying to talk to them or get them to talk about something they don't want to talk about, you push little by little. You're not going to say straightaway that they are being misguided by Pakistan. You tread softly. You test the waters, see how much they are willing to open up and then you take the next step, and then you take the next step. This is the first time he gets to talk to them, when they are on the move, and therefore he is a little guarded. The next time, when they sit and talk around a fire, they spend a little more time—the rapport has developed a little, enough for him to be able to have a discussion with them. So it takes that graph—the first, second and third attempt.

RANGAN: Did you struggle with how to end the film—whether the villain would be vanquished in the Tamil masala tradition, or if Rishi would be allowed to return to his wife after the villain's confession of having become a human being?

RATNAM: You struggle with the mechanics of the end, but not with the concept behind it. He is an engineer, a cryptologist who'd gone there. You can't see him trying to fight this bunch of guys with guns and things like that. So the only way is that they let him go, or make him a scapegoat. On that issue, there were no doubts at all. We had not built a superhero who needs to fight to win. In a way, if he's able to make one of them think and become a little more human, that is his victory. The ending was true to the plane on which the film was playing.

RANGAN: But there is still a bit of an action sequence on the snow-capped mountainside.

RATNAM: I love that. It is not 'superhero' action—just an attempt to escape. He has attempted to escape earlier, and he does it again. It is good to have the

'These people were caught in the middle of a fight they were not even a part of. Roja *came out of that.*'

impact of an action sequence without the protagonist having to beat up several men single-handed. I come from watching *The Great Escape* and films like that. I wanted the film to reach a catharsis and it did require a certain element of adrenalin. He escapes with help from the Kashmiri girl. There is an element of a chase and being in trouble. And you think he has escaped, but he's caught. And the shore is just on the other side. It's that close. And then the captor lets him go. So it actually has all the elements which make mainstream cinema work.

RANGAN: Did you have any idea that the film would become this national phenomenon?

RATNAM: Not at all. You're not too sure if deep down in Tamil Nadu, people are aware of the Kashmir problem and if they'll identify with it. So it was a bit of an experiment. The film was made on a shoestring budget. The technicians worked for less money with the understanding that the film would also be sold for less money, to make sure that we have the chance to make films like this again. It was not thought of as something that would work on a big scale. And it didn't open very well. It had, practically, new faces, a new music director, and it was about Kashmir. Everything was new. So it took a little time to warm up.

In fact, during the first week, we went on a tour by car, from here to NSC [North Arcot, South Arcot, Chengalpet] and right up to Nagercoil and back. At the beginning, when we walked into the theatre—maybe Monday or Tuesday, the fourth or fifth day of release—the front rows were completely empty. I said, 'Oh my God!' I turned around and saw that the back rows were somewhat filled. But by the time I finished the tour, we could see the film growing. It was a very strange sight. Over three or four days, we could see the change happening. The front rows were filled. It was good to see, with your eyes, that the film could connect with people everywhere.

RANGAN: You retained your cinematographer from *Thalapathy*.

RATNAM: I work with people on two or three films, till we think we both need a break from each other. Santosh is a terrific DoP. He makes shooting so effortless. When I finished *Thalapathy* and was about to start this film, I told him about it and he said yes. *Thalapathy* was a really good experience, and practically the entire team came over to *Roja*.

RANGAN: Except the music director. Considering you've changed your other technicians periodically, the change from Ilaiyaraaja to A.R. Rahman came quite late. Why did this come about? One version is that the producers weren't on good terms with Ilaiyaraaja.

RATNAM: There's no particular reason. Maybe it was just time Rahman came. I can't blame the producers. They actually offered that if I wanted Ilaiyaraaja, they could go and ask him—because I'd done all my films with Ilaiyaraaja up to that point. It was not really that. I just feel that the film industry is not dependent on individuals. If I'm not there, there's going to be somebody else. You come into films because you want to make films, because you have a passion for films. There is nobody who is indispensable in this entire field. And it helps you if different inputs come in, a breath of fresh air comes in, different values come in. So I think it just happened. I still think that Raja is amazing. I think he's a genius and he'll always be one. Till today, I think that some of the best music that I've grown up with is Raja's, and till today, there's nothing that moves me as much as his music. I've no issues on that, and I've never had a problem, really speaking, with him. But professionally you keep growing and there's nothing that needs to be stopped.

RANGAN: The success of the songs validated your instincts. There's a mini-story happening in the *Kaadhal rojaave* song sequence. Roses, snow, children . . .

RATNAM: This is a newly married couple and they've been torn apart. He is aware that she is somewhere, not knowing where he is. There is angst, worry, concern that he's pulled this girl from a small town, from somewhere else, and brought her here, and she's now here, fighting—against what or how long or to what end, he doesn't know. And he is all by himself, practically twenty-four hours a day. If he were a

'The girl was someone who believed in herself, who'd do what she thought was right.'

writer, the thought process would have been written in terms of the randomness with which he recalls the ups and downs of what she could be going through. The song tries to capture this. There is longing, angst and the pain that goes with it. In a way, the children are about the innocence from which he's torn her, and now she's just out of his reach. She's elusive. She disappears constantly.

RANGAN: The offer for a Hindi version came after the film became a huge hit in Tamil. It wasn't something that happened just due to the subject matter.

RATNAM: Much after the Tamil version became a hit and the Telugu dubbing became a hit, the producers and the person who got the film dubbed into Telugu said that they wanted to dub it in Hindi too. There was always the problem that the film deals with a heroine not knowing Hindi and finding herself in an alien culture. There was a huge debate on how this should be handled when dubbed into Hindi. But the people who bought the Hindi rights had already done the dubbing. We just made sure that Madhu could dub in her own voice. Arvind's voice is not as correct as it should have been. The film showed the strains of dubbing.

RANGAN: And the problem was never really solved, of the heroine trying to make herself understood to people whose language she doesn't speak.

RATNAM: The choice was to use Kashmiri, to say that she spoke Hindi and the others spoke Kashmiri. But they were not too sure whether it would reach the audience. The eternal insecurity of not being able to communicate to the

Roja 133

'He is the classic ordinary man in an extraordinary situation.'

audience—that was a restriction. They didn't push it, really speaking. It could have just been a dialect, but then she would have to speak the dialect right through, and they were not sure if it would be understood. It was something they easily compromised on. It is still flawed and does not play as effectively as it does in Tamil or Telugu.

RANGAN: There's still a Kashmiri-speaking female character in *Roja*, the girl from the terrorist camp—though in the film she doesn't utter a single word. In a way, *Roja* seems her story as much as Roja's, except that she doesn't have an outlet for her oppression. Roja screams and suffers, while this girl suffers silently.

RATNAM: In the milieu that we are talking about, of those who've moved to extremism, there is still a group of people who are normal and who have family connections and the same kind of values as people from the rest of the country. Beyond the ideological differences, they are still human beings who care for each other and who wouldn't mind reaching out. It is something else that is blocking them. This girl just makes the character of Pankaj Kapur—her brother—a little more rounded, a little more real, a little more rooted. He's not somebody who's sprung up out of the blue. He's connected to others. He is just another guy. He could be a reflection of Rishi on the other side.

9

'The intent was to go where Bharathiraja shoots his films'

Thiruda Thiruda (1992)

A huge sum of money is stolen, from the Indian government, by London-based Vikram (Salim Ghouse). CBI Inspector Lakshminarayanan (S.P. Balasubrahmanyam) has a bare handful of days to crack the crime, by which time the trail has been infiltrated by petty thieves Kadhir (Anand) and Azhagu (Prashanth), runaway bride Raasathi (Heera Rajgopal), and the sultry dancer Chandralekha (Anu Agarwal).

BARADWAJ RANGAN: *Thiruda Thiruda* was your first film for Aalayam, your own production company.

MANI RATNAM: With Sujatha Productions, I wasn't just a film-maker making films for them. I had the additional responsibility of having to take care of production. So when I started my own company, called Aalayam, with my friend and partner Sriram, we wanted to make films that I had in mind that I was not doing and wanted others to direct. Aalayam started with films like [K. Subhash's] *Chatriyan*. I did *Roja* for K. Balachander. And then when *Thiruda Thiruda* came up, we decided we'd do it for Aalayam. We continued Aalayam for a while, and then we went our different ways. Aalayam is still with Sriram. They produced films after I left. I started my own company, named Madras Talkies. *Iruvar* was the first film I made there.

RANGAN: But *Dil Se* was under the banner of India Talkies.

RATNAM: I think that was post-*Bandit Queen*. This was an idea where Shekhar Kapur, Ram Gopal Varma and I thought we'd work together and make one film each for the company. I made my film. They are yet to do theirs.

RANGAN: You share *Thiruda Thiruda*'s story credit with Ram Gopal Varma. How did that come about?

RATNAM: We went on a trip for a week or so. He had a film he was making, *Gaayam*, and I had this film I was making. For three days, we worked on his script, and for three days we worked on my script. And we came back and did our own films. We didn't take much of the other person's sensible suggestions. That is how Ramu's name is in *Thiruda Thiruda* and my name is in *Gaayam*. Earlier, there were two distinct attempts to make a caper film. One was Kamal's *Vikram*. The other one was *Kshana Kshanam*, done by Ramu. Both didn't work in a big way, and I said, 'That's because these guys don't know how to do it. I'll do it.' It's just your confidence that you think the story is not important. You think you can get the screenplay to keep the film moving. And I got nowhere close to even those two films.

RANGAN: But *Thiruda Thiruda* didn't exactly bomb.

RATNAM: It didn't? It was a mainstream commercial film, and it should have done very well commercially. Otherwise it's no good. It probably would have done better with a different name under the director's credit. Maybe it suffered during the first viewing because it came immediately after *Roja*, and the jump was too drastic.

'Rahman and I were getting completely out of the Roja *zone. The songs here were much wilder, much bigger.'*

But that's the way I've been going along so far, jumping from one kind of film to another, and you learn to accept it. The film had big set pieces. All the musical sequences were big pieces. All the action sequences were big pieces. It was really a collection of set pieces. Only, what bound everything together didn't hold. For a caper comedy to really work, you should have all the elements working well. The script, the performances, the execution and the timing should all be perfect. If some of the elements are below par, it looms large as these kinds of films don't have a big story to fall back on. The film took a while. Sometimes you overestimate yourself. Where the film worked best was in Toronto, when it went for the festival. But it was a fun film to make. I have really fond memories of it.

RANGAN: Would you say that *Roja* onwards you entered a peripatetic stage of your career, with films criss-crossing state (for example, *Dil Se*) and country lines (for example, *Guru*)? Even *Thiruda Thiruda* begins at Nashik, touches London and winds up at a village in Tamil Nadu.

RATNAM: This was conceived before *Roja*. And to be honest, *Mouna Raagam* was based in Delhi. *Nayakan* was based in Bombay. You went where the story took you. There was no other restriction. *Thiruda Thiruda* was an outlandish story. After *Roja*, I had the choice of doing an emotional film that I had in mind, which I still haven't done, or this, which was a flippant caper, a completely different kind of film, with music and action, and set in rural Tamil Nadu. I went with the wilder of the two ideas.

And then a strange thing happened. We started with a premise like that of the Harshad Mehta scam [which had just broken out and was all over the news], that there was this huge amount of money that went missing from the system, and you wondered what happened to the money and what would be its journey if it were found. I don't remember how much it was. The amount may look ridiculous today, after so many years. But back then, it was really substantial. What if this notional money from the scam was converted into actual money, and what if it found its way into the countryside? That was the MacGuffin. The starting point was something real, and we wanted to contrast what was happening between the big scamsters (from the city) and the small scamsters (in the village). But halfway through the script, sometime into pre-production, the Harshad Mehta scam was busted. It was solved, sealed and forgotten. My MacGuffin was six feet underground.

The film was always a carefree adventure set in a village, and the journey remains the same, but the source and the plot changed drastically because of how the Harshad Mehta was suddenly resolved. That was one more lesson for me: Don't pick on scams that are still alive, because you don't know which way they will turn. Things might change

'We also had these terrains that were sliding downwards. It's about movement and flow.'

before you are through and make the premise irrelevant. So we quickly had to come up with another plot as to where the money came from [after which it would go missing], and that is where the Nasik printing came in. The film, therefore, had to start where the money was printed. And that was Nasik. We had no choice.

RANGAN: I knew that your films like *Bombay* drew inspiration from real life, but I had no idea that something this frivolous was rooted in reality as well. And I get what you did, but I'm not sure why you did it. Because from the audience's point of view, all that's important is that there's a big chunk of money that gets lost and there are all these people after it. I'm not sure they'd have cared where that big chunk of money came from.

RATNAM: I think that if you specifically refer to something, and if they know, from real life, that what you referred to has been sorted out, then the whole premise is on shaky ground. You give them an opening for doubt. Instead, you might as well go into something completely fictional, which is not questioned. So we had to reconceive the plot. It became a security-related thing, about the way the money is transferred. It came to be about a computer card. The scale changed, the size changed, the trappings changed.

RANGAN: Did you worry that a film you were conceiving as a lark would come too close to real life?

RATNAM: I don't think so. It's a what-if. You can pick anything, as long as the 'what' doesn't change. If that turns around and you realize there are other things involved, politics and things like that, then the complexity of the plot becomes entirely different from what you picked up. If the situation had remained intact and had not changed due to the resolution of the scam, it would have still been a fun

'The kinds of film that I really like are all in here somewhere, but in a completely different background.' Heera and Prashanth.

film. The issue would have been just a trigger. We're assuming that you wonder what happened to that money.

RANGAN: The fun thing about the film, now, is that there's actual physical money. That's the MacGuffin. There's a truck filled with currency notes. But in scams like the one with Harshad Mehta, the money is notional.

RATNAM: When it becomes a scam, when it assumes that scale, there are points at which you cash out, when the money is siphoned out, and somebody else is playing the number games. That's when it becomes a scam, when you put the money in and boost it and then you pull out. So there's real money there too.

RANGAN: You got back with P.C. Sreeram for *Thiruda Thiruda*. The cinematography was a bit outrageous, with flagrant use of colour filters and such.

RATNAM: It was a very stylized film. Nothing was real about it. I've always wanted to do a caper, and I've always believed that you don't need a story to make a film. It can be a set of events, a huge canvas for flowing through a journey with cinema. We were basically having fun with the medium, and we did not shy away from doing things we wouldn't do in a normal film. Usually, it is because we are a little shy that we don't push the colours and things like that. With this film, we had no such inhibitions. It gave us the liberty to be a little experimental, flashy.

In a way, it's a little like a comic book, with exaggerated colours and larger-than-life musical settings. The kinds of films that I really like are all in here somewhere, but in a completely different background. The intent was to go to where Bharathiraja shoots his films and make an exciting action film there, with the kind of chases you see only in movies based in cities, like in the James Bond films. It was two different cultures—an urban kind of cinema, but set in a rural milieu. A crossing of two genres, that's what the film was attempting. The villain and his crew, including the woman who was very fancy, were from the urban side—very metallic and black and sleek. And the good guys were earthy, rustic. The colours came from there.

RANGAN: A lot of *Thiruda Thiruda* is set in and around rivers, waterfalls—water, generally.

RATNAM: Also trains and carts and other vehicles. We also had these terrains that were sliding downwards. It's about movement and flow. The film keeps rushing, from top to bottom. It's really flow that you're looking at. The film was about jumping from one high point to another, between the elaborate music pieces and the elaborate action sequences.

RANGAN: And the connective tissue that binds these set pieces is that everyone is a thief. Kadhir 'stole' Azhagu when the latter was a kid, and then they 'steal' Raasathi . . .

RATNAM: The film is called *Thiruda Thiruda*, after all. This was a film I had to get out of my system. It's an idea that stuck to me. Just the sheer pleasure of doing those action sequences through the countryside, those chases, sitting in a Jeep and going at breakneck speed through narrow lanes, thick forests, having this strange horse-drawn cart run through villages in the middle of women fighting with each other, through all that chaos—it was fun. I enjoyed quite a bit of the shoot.

RANGAN: This was your second film with Rahman, and it was a giant leap from his simple and tuneful score for *Roja*.

RATNAM: Even while we were doing the background score for *Roja*, he'd started composing the music for this film. He'd already worked on the first song—*Kannum kannum*. We were getting completely out of the *Roja* zone. This was much wilder, much bigger. *Veerapandi kottaiyile* went all over the place. The songs were elaborate pieces, and he'd take quite a bit of effort to get each piece done. It was not done in a hurry. It was done to near-perfection. For the *Chandralekha* song, he wanted to record a piece. He said, 'If I play it as a tune, it will be nothing.' We didn't have any lyrics. We wrote some lyrics, then and there, in English, and we got the singer to sing a one-minute version of the song. That became the composition.

Each song was different. In *Raasathi*, he wanted no instruments, only vocals. The more varied it was, the wilder it was; it started fitting into the film—because there was nothing straight about the film. And his background score was outstanding. He really worked on it. It was a big John Williams kind of score. We wanted it mastered in digital, 5.1 and all that, but we were not yet into DTS at that point. That's when technology was changing. When he started doing *Roja*, we still used to record on half-inch tape. For this, maybe we used ADAT, a tape format that could record eight tracks of digital audio simultaneously. So with each film, the technology was jumping by leaps and bounds. And each time, he was there, on the ball, ready, ahead of his time, waiting for the technology to land where he wanted it to. He came in at the right time, when his every wish was coming true. And it's still coming true.

RANGAN: That's interesting, because by introducing Rahman, you too were on the cusp of these technologies. You were probably the first Tamil film director to have recording sessions that did not involve the composer playing out a bare-bones tune on a harmonium, which is how it was from the earliest days of Indian cinema. Did Rahman's approach—making a near-finished product—make it easier for you to evaluate a tune?

RATNAM: In fact, it was the other way around. Right from *Roja*, what he'd give you was a recorded piece, the scratch. But this scratch would be so well-produced that you didn't know whether you were being seduced by the production quality or by the intrinsic tune. I was used to listening to a harmonium and Ilaiyaraaja's voice and seeing whether that works. With Rahman, there's a track laid, and then he's playing magically, and within that we have to find the tune and see whether that works. Just the sound of it is like a finished product. So you have to listen to it a few hundred times more to make sure that it's the soul that you really liked. You have to kind of peel off his dressing. So it took a while. It was not easy to move from the older school to this one. They have two completely different approaches to music and to film. I think both are brilliant, but both are entirely different.

RANGAN: At the heart of an unconventional film that seeks to coast along on the strength of its action and musical set pieces, there's a rather conventional love triangle.

'The intent was to . . . make an exciting action film there, with the kind of chases you see only in movies based in cities.'

RATNAM: I wanted to focus on the fun element of the triangle. The way it finishes, with the two men being chased by the woman, is what I was aiming at. But sometimes you get a little seduced by something that is very beautiful. When we composed the *Raasathi* song, it came out as a really, really emotional piece. I remember saying, 'Let's keep it for our next film.' But both [the lyricist] Vairamuthu and Rahman said, 'We'll find something else for the next film.' They looked at this as an album which needed a soulful number to complete it, but I looked at it as a film. I was scared. If I had to bring this song into the film, I had to bring in that emotion too.

RANGAN: Wasn't this emotion already present in the brief you gave Rahman?

RATNAM: The song was composed for that situation, but its depth was too much for what we wanted. Sometimes you give a wrong brief to the writer, so they don't write for this situation but for a larger issue. It was like that. It was a folk song. It had to look like it had been around for a long time. It was almost a *Devdas* brief—Parvati is going away, married to someone else, and Devdas is singing this song. It went on a very high note emotionally. That, in a way, made the love track heavier. Otherwise, I was aiming at a lighter feel, with each man trying to dump the girl on the other and get away with the money. Somewhere towards the last portion of the film, I wondered whether that was right or wrong.

RANGAN: It brings in a sudden element of seriousness, especially in the scene where they're literally framed like the vertices of a triangle and the camera spins hysterically around them. So after *Raasathi* was composed, you tweaked the screenplay to accommodate the song?

RATNAM: I just beefed up the last section a little more emotionally so that the song wouldn't be flat and stick out like a sore thumb. I should have made the song a little more flippant, like the rest of the film.

RANGAN: In a film of this type, do you think the audience would care that the emotion is too high in a song?

RATNAM: As a maker, you're not doing it only for the audience. And I think it will show. A song has to be balanced by the narration. You might think that the audiences may not care, but I think they do. The film has to ring true.

RANGAN: Even in a film this frivolous, you haven't let go of *nallavana–kettavana*, though it's here in a much lighter vein—in the scene where Chandralekha confesses to Raasathi that she got involved with the villain not knowing if he was a good man or a bad man.

RATNAM: I don't remember this line at all.

10

'They did not want to be painted grey in any way'

Bombay (1995)

In the face of strident opposition, Shekhar (Arvind Swamy) marries Shaila Bano (Manisha Koirala). Husband and wife leave their village for Bombay, in the hope of a happy future in that most cosmopolitan of cities. Unfortunately for them (and their twin boys), Hindus and Muslims begin to lunge at each other's throats. The city burns. The children go missing. An arduous search ensues—
for the boys, and for peace.

BARADWAJ RANGAN: The problems with the censors ended up defining the film for a while. What are your views on censorship?

MANI RATNAM: I think censorship is very old-fashioned. It can't be taken away overnight. I don't think we are responsible enough to take on the burden just now. But I think that's where we should head. What's the practice in other media should come into films too—there should be some kind of self-regulatory mechanism. You can't have acts written long ago by the British stop Indians from making films today. With *Bombay*, it was more a question of not wanting to take responsibility, not wanting to be the one who cleared it. The attitude of the board or the chief officer was, 'Why take a risk?' And the film ran head-on into the Maharashtra elections. Sometimes we get caught with people not willing to take decisions, or you get caught with somebody who is very dogmatic about it, very old-fashioned and thinks there is only one way to do things. Unfortunately, the film faced both attitudes at a time there were elections, and till the elections were over, the film didn't get cleared.

It was not anything to do with the film. It was just that they didn't want to release it at the point elections were round the corner. Every week, we had to fly out to Bombay with a print, screen the film and come back. We had to keep hanging around, waiting for one committee to see it, and then the next committee. And sometimes, it's not just the censor board watching the film, but the secretary, the minister, the minister's relatives. It was really a joke. We didn't know who was censoring whom. It was a very tough phase. A commissioner of police promised me that this film would never see the light of day. You can't tell me that. You're doing your job. I'm doing my job. You can't say that there is only one way of doing things, the police way of ensuring law and order. There is another way of dealing with it, laterally, through cinema, through art, through writing. But there were others who were sensible, and the film was cleared just one week after the Maharashtra elections.

RANGAN: But this was a Tamil film. It should have been cleared by the censor board in Chennai.

RATNAM: The person here didn't want to take the responsibility. They sent it to their head office in Bombay. In Bombay, the head of the censor board did not want to take the decision and so he sent it to the Maharashtra government. And so on and so forth.

RANGAN: After these discussions, how much of the film was actually reshaped?

RATNAM: Overall, the film would have lost a minute, a minute and a half. That's all. It was nothing drastic. It just spoils the rhythm. In the riot scene, there's an accidental gunshot that kills a woman trying to remove clothes from a clothesline in the balcony of a multi-storeyed chawl. You don't even see her. You just see the clothing, which turns red. They wanted to remove this. They didn't want to show a policeman shooting and killing someone, which happened a lot in real life. Each department that saw the picture looked at things that would affect their department. It was not a broad overall view of what was there in the film. From their side, they did not want to be painted grey in any way.

RANGAN: Is that why the Babri Masjid demolition is shown through newspaper headlines and still photographs?

RATNAM: They didn't want the actual destruction to be shown. We'd done it in such a way that it was a cry, an ache—what we were trying to picturize was the agony. The music is a wail. We had created a miniature of the dome of the mosque. We just showed them climbing, not breaking the mosque. The breaking was shown from the inside—it was a dark interior into which debris falls through and light comes in. It was done artistically. It was the saddest moment in the film. But they wouldn't see it that way. They didn't want this to be shown. So we had to replace this with newspaper cuttings. These newspaper cuttings are a harsher reminder of the incident than what we had shot. Our version was much more emotional, a wail more than anything else. This was like a factual statement.

RANGAN: Was *Nayakan* the first time you

'It developed from being a film about the riot, without songs, to a dramatic narrative that saw the riot through the lives of a young couple.'

faced a run-in with the censor board? When Kamal says '*thevidiya pulla*' (bastard) to the cop, the swearing is masked by the sound of a train in the distance.

RATNAM: There were instances even earlier, where they've been ridiculous sometimes. They said *Mouna Raagam* had to be given an 'A' certificate because this girl is asking for a divorce. It came out of the blue. A lady on the board asked me how a housewife could ask for a divorce. After that, I stopped being surprised by anything the censor committee would throw at me.

RANGAN: After the lightness of *Thiruda Thiruda*, you returned to *Roja* territory here—a serious story about relationships in a (literal) war zone.

RATNAM: The riots happened while we were doing the background score of *Thiruda Thiruda*. We thought that Bombay was the most metropolitan, cosmopolitan city in our country. If this can happen there, you fear that it can happen anywhere. I was telling Rahman that we should do something about it, but at first I didn't think I'd be able to come up with a script. I thought of doing it as a very small film in Malayalam. I met M.T. Vasudevan Nair about writing a script about a kid who gets lost in the riots and seeing things from his point of view. But it didn't happen with MT. The script started from a lost kid, which is now in the latter half of the film, and the rest of it—who the kid is, who the parents are—was developed backwards. In any story, you go back a little to know how we came to this point. From the kid, we went back to the girl who lands up in Bombay's VT station, and then we went further back. The moment the producer felt that the budget would be too high for a Malayalam film, especially for a film based on a kid, we said we'd do it in Tamil.

RANGAN: After *Unaru* in 1984, you made films only in Tamil right up to *Dil Se* in 1998. The only exception, in between, was *Geetanjali*, in Telugu.

RATNAM: If I'd done the film in Malayalam, it would have given me the liberty to experiment a little. I felt they were open enough for a songless film, based on this kind of a theme. Also, this producer, Mudra Shashi, is a friend who'd been asking me to make a movie for a long time. You have a subject that you can possibly do quickly in Malayalam and make it work—so the idea sticks with you. And when you convert it to Tamil, it expands in terms of scale. From the story of two kids caught in a riot, it becomes a story about how they came to be in this position, where they came from, who the parents are. It developed from being a film about the riot, without songs, to a dramatic narrative that saw the riot through the lives of a young couple.

RANGAN: You picked up two new collaborators here, Rajiv Menon and Manisha Koirala.

RATNAM: I had a friend, [the composer] Mahesh. We were college mates. Then he went to XLRI [School of Business and Human Resources] and I went to Bajaj. I used to go for tennis at the Mylapore Club. His house was on the way. I used to park my bike there, and sit and chat for a long time. After the game we used to go to a lot of movies, listen to a lot of music, and I used to spend evenings at his house—lots of debauched nights, probably. One evening I went to his house as usual and there was this man, clean-shaven, and in this long kurta. It was Rajiv. I think Mahesh's sister was a friend of his. He'd come to meet her, and I said hello. I remembered him vaguely, but didn't know who he was.

This was just after the release of *Mouna Raagam*. He said that he saw the film and he gave me a big lecture on how the scenes were choreographed and how Shankar Nag had choreographed *Swami and Friends* and how scenes were edited and so on. It was a huge analysis of what was okay by him and what was not okay by him. And all I wanted was to sit with Mahesh and chat and have a good time. That's how I got to know Rajiv. *Bombay* was the first time we worked together. His work is softer, less contrasty, more realistic, more even. He doesn't go into a cosmetic zone. He brought in a certain amount of difference to what I'd done previously. We waited for the monsoon in Kerala, and shot the early portions of the film in a village. Then we came to Bombay. We created Bombay in Chennai—the interiors, the riots. The film had to gradually take on that tone as it progressed. We were trying to take the graph from an almost bluish school to a darker area—with fire and riots and black smoke. That was done very well, I thought. I think *Bombay* is visually one of my best films. Rajiv's work was quite special.

RANGAN: What about your heroine? She was the first Bombay actress you were using after Kiran Vairale in *Pallavi Anupallavi*. There was Anu Agarwal in *Thiruda Thiruda*, but that character was an exotic creature, from the outside, and so she fit in, whereas the character Manisha plays is from interior Tamil Nadu.

RATNAM: I wanted someone delicate, porcelain, who kind of represented the character. If I'd gone for someone big and popular in Tamil films at the time—I don't remember who it was, probably Khushboo or Madhubala—the Tamil audience would have seen it as so-and-so playing this orthodox Muslim girl. We wanted someone relatively unknown who would fit into that mould more clearly, more perfectly. We wanted someone from outside, with no associations, who'd seem more like the character than a star. We were basically looking at a character who is delicate, fragile, and who gets caught in this storm. Manisha fitted that role.

RANGAN: I was talking to a film-maker recently, and he said one of the problems

'I think Bombay *is visually one of my best films.' Mani Ratnam directs Arvind Swamy.*

with Indian actors is that they rarely know how to enter and exit a scene, keeping in mind a future or past event in their character trajectory. He said everything has to be spelt out.

RATNAM: I think the problem is more with the directors. We don't give actors the full script. We don't give them enough time to live with the script. We tell them we'll give them a narration; then we bring them to the set and tell them this is the scene, and then we tell them what happened before and after. It is the way we make films here. In the West, they know the complete script. They come in and do readings. In India, some of them have started doing it just because Hollywood does it. But to be honest, even in the West, there are people who make films with non-professionals, with non-actors, and they have made brilliant films with brilliant performances.

So there's no single method. If Iranian films and some Tamil films can get performances from people picked from the street, if Bharathiraja can make so many fresh faces act, I don't see what difference it makes what method you use—whether they know the entire script or they know only the moment. Because the process is so subjective, so open, people in the West tend to convert it into a system—so that they can do some training. It is good, but it's not the only way. This is a process between you and the actor. As a viewer, I don't care about your process. I only care about the final result on screen.

RANGAN: Manisha Koirala does have that sense about her of being—to borrow your term—'porcelain'. But as viewers, we carry certain associations, certain

Bombay 149

stereotypes. Did it occur to you that this may not be the kind of robust village girl who readily flashes in front of the audience's mind?

RATNAM: It's like being scared whether people will accept it if we shoot *Bombay* in Chennai. It is your confidence that counts. People who come in to see a film don't come in with suspicions that you are cheating them by showing one thing for another. You don't have to be scared of anything as long as you're convinced that you can evoke the time, the place and the character effectively. If you think that this is the correct person, if she looks correct to you and you do a test with her and you think she fits, then you're not worried about it.

Sometimes, it's very good to cast against the grain. If you take somebody who's perceived in a particular fashion and you go with a character that's completely opposite to that perception, it makes the character come alive—like Madhavan in *Kannathil Muthamittal*. I went back to him only because the role *in Kannathil* was so drastically different from that in *Alaipaayuthey*, or anything he was doing after *Alaipaayuthey*. The character was kind of middle-aged, strongly Tamil, not city-urban but a caustic intellectual. This casting takes the attention away from the actor and shifts it to the character. It gives the character a new dimension, freshness, more thrust. Manisha was like that. I don't think you really wonder if somebody will be accepted. If you are willing to accept it, if you think it's right, then go with it. Go with it with all your conviction. If you say something with conviction, it will come through.

RANGAN: How does your input to an actor change when they are, like Manisha, unfamiliar with the language?

RATNAM: You want the person who is acting to invest in the moment as much as you are willing to invest in that moment. It can't be somebody repeating what I'm saying in exactly the same way, in which case it is me doing all the roles. You have to make the actor get into it. The two of us, together, have to find some truth, some honesty in the character and the situations. And you have different ways of doing it with different people. You do it differently with children. With a very good actor, you control the performance differently. And with a not-so-gifted actor, you do it differently. You have to resort to any which way to find that moment of truth. That's your responsibility. That's what makes the scene alive, believable, everything. And with a person not knowing the language, it is just one extra hurdle—more so for the actor. After shooting, they have to sit with a dedicated person, an assistant director, to learn their lines for the next day. The words may be just sounds to them, but if they understand the scene and if they get the feel with which you talk to them, then that's enough. You have to work a little closer to make sure it comes through in that sense.

'We'd done it in such a way that it was a cry, an ache—what we were trying to picturize was the agony.'

RANGAN: Is the assistant director who teaches them the lines also responsible for nuances like which part of the line needs emphasis?

RATNAM: If you leave emphasis to the assistant director, maybe he'll get it all wrong. It's better you deal with that directly. As long as the actors know the lines, you work with them for the feel. Sometimes, you ask them to forget it's in Tamil. You ask them to say it in their language, in Hindi or Kannada, or Tulu in the case of Aishwarya Rai. Once they say it in a language they are familiar with, they get the hang of it. They know where the emphasis is, what you're referring to. Instead of mechanically marking out the emphasis, it's better for them to become confident and know what you're asking for. And they all pick it up very well.

The bigger thing is not the language, but to get the character and the moment right, the body language right. Manisha, for example, might mix up a word or two, but she would not miss the flow. She would go ahead and finish the shot despite making a mistake or two. We might have to go back and redo a bit but she would not deviate from the character. Spelling mistakes are easier to correct than grammatical mistakes and content mistakes. But at the end, if you're not able to make out that it's a language they're unfamiliar with, if they're able to perform convincingly, with feeling, I think it's worth the effort.

RANGAN: Is this something you ensure in

Bombay 151

a screen test, to see if the feel is coming through?

RATNAM: Yeah. If they can't handle languages at all, it becomes very difficult. Some have a flair for languages and some don't. Some of the men have a problem. Women tend to be a lot more focused and willing to put in that extra mechanical effort to learn a new language. Or it might be that I am more patient with women.

RANGAN: In this screen test, do you give them an especially tough line, something jaw-breaking, to see if they can clear the biggest hurdle?

RATNAM: We just do a scene. Scenes are the jaw breakers. The scene should work. Whether they speak the language or not, I would make them do the same scene in the test. If they're able to convincingly portray the scene, then you have enough to judge them by.

RANGAN: Arvind Swamy first sets eyes on Manisha at an elaborate wedding. But their own wedding is a very simple affair. It's a nice contrast, for had they married someone from their own community, that is how their wedding would have been.

RATNAM: The contrast was not deliberate. But that's what makes this a little more real, in the sense that their relationship gets sealed in that simple moment, away from home, away from their roots, in an alien land, with just each other practically. It isolates them in this big city and sends them into a world where they're going to face ups and downs. It's an uprooting, a transportation, the start of something fresh. That's what was intended.

RANGAN: I'm asking if you had Arvind meet Manisha at the big wedding with this later scene in mind. Or was it simply an excuse to stage a colourful song?

RATNAM: That's what I meant. The earlier wedding was not intended as a contrast. They're strangers from two different communities, away from one another, and with that you create a graph of possible sequences. It's a flow of how interactions between these kinds of people can happen, and out of that, you pick a few possibilities that you crystallize into scenes. This wedding was part of that flow. That's all.

RANGAN: Do you believe in the unconscious? Because if a story has permeated through your system so thoroughly, it could be that this contrast between the two weddings welled up from within, even if not intentionally.

RATNAM: Ah, it is very nice for a critic to look at it that way.

RANGAN: In your eyes, then, writing is a completely conscious process.

RATNAM: I think it's mostly a conscious process. It's thought over and mulled over and debated. I'm meeting quite a few writers in Tamil these days, and those who write novels seem to be a lot more free-flowing than those of us who write screenplays. I think the contrast between the two is very distinct. There are a few directors in whose films I can't see a structure. I see an amazing flow, like poetry or painting. The rest of us are, to an extent, planned, deliberate and methodical, and the art is in not making the method or structure obvious, where you don't see the lines and you don't see the craft. That's where the finesse comes in.

RANGAN: You're saying that even in the poetic moments in your films, I can see the scaffolding if I really want to.

RATNAM: Yeah. Absolutely right.

RANGAN: In *Bombay*, the romance begins with a device you appear to be rather fond of—love at first sight, what's described in *The Godfather* as a 'thunderbolt'. Here, the hero sees the heroine's veil fly up. He's instantly impassioned. And the *Uyire* song sequence tells their love story through visuals. It begins with stormy seas and ends with calm waters, her path to him is blocked by a gate that stands for the barriers between them, and so on. You give a sketch of the love story through the dialogue scenes, and detail the rest of the emotion in this song.

RATNAM: Like I told you, we had an idea about a lost kid, and wrote it backwards. In the first draft, we wrote back up to the point where the mother lands up at the railway station in Bombay. This sequence of their romance was: 'Do you remember that day?' These two people who have no one else in Bombay are sitting down and laughing at what had happened to her when she couldn't come to meet him. It was like . . . moments. It was written like fragments of memory. With any good love story, this is all the length you need—it conveys very easily where it is headed. If the song can help you get there effectively, it becomes more than just a song. It becomes a huge storytelling tool. I remember Ramu asking me, 'It's a second-half song. What are you doing with it in the first half?' Sometimes you think you can take that kind of risk and get to the story faster.

RANGAN: It's also the song itself. It's a bolt from the blue because it's a hugely emotional number, and at first you think their love couldn't have reached that level of intensity so quickly. The song isn't just a general song reflecting a previous development, but a continuing part of the story—as in, they truly get together only here, like how Beera and Raagini discover each other during the *Ranjha Ranjha* song sequence in *Raavan*. The seed for that song is in *Uyire* [*Tu Hi Re*]. Why entrust this kind of 'story development' to a song sequence, where our audiences typically switch off?

RATNAM: We've trained them to switch

Bombay 153

'I don't make movies to give messages.'

off. If you give them something good, they'll switch on again. As a film-maker, you can never have that kind of fear. You should know that what you are saying has enough merit to hold the audience. Otherwise, you have no business telling a story. If you're scared, if you don't have the confidence, then don't have songs in your film. You don't have to follow the convenient graph that everybody has been following. If you've got the audience involved emotionally and if you can take them to the next level, you do it. The graphs depend on your overall screenplay. The love story has to peak here emotionally and land on a plateau before going to the next curve of the graph. The dramatic peak is in this song. And the resolution is what happens after that. The opening portion of *Bombay* is like a short story, and this short story should have a finale. This song is that finale.

RANGAN: Did you work with a choreographer for this?

RATNAM: There was no choreographer. This kind of song is difficult to do with a choreographer because it will get into a false, dance-related zone. In fact, when we shot the song, we didn't even have the interludes. We just had a bar count. We had to tell our story within that and get it to flow, and Rahman scored the interludes based on this flow. But for the *Ranjha* number in *Raavan*, we had an action master and a choreographer working in tandem.

RANGAN: Like you did in *Roja*, you opt for a strongly melodramatic style in *Bombay*. If the hero extinguished the burning tricolour there, here he slices his hand and the heroine's hand to show her father that their blood is the same. This was something new in your cinema, the typical 'urban,

Mani Ratnam protagonist' displaying this kind of overt 'heroism'. And the heroes in *Roja* and *Bombay* are reasonably privileged people, unlike those in *Nayakan* and *Thalapathy*, who were strugglers from the lower classes and whose heroics we are more used to. After several films in a gentle urban voice, were you trying to push yourself, for a change, along a direction more common in Tamil cinema?

RATNAM: Like I told you when we talked about *Roja*, I look at this male protagonist as a rebel who says, 'I will do whatever will provoke you the most.' It's the same with his father, who says that this marriage will happen only after he dies, and the son says that he cannot wait that long. He doesn't necessarily mean it, but he knows what will hurt the father the most. It's the kind of thing a young person will do just to tell you that you can't keep calling the shots all the time. He wants to hurt them in a way they don't expect. And what he does with the girl's father is a counter to this, in a way that will hurt him the most.

I don't think my voice changed during this period, at least not consciously—I think it's only in this particular film, with this kind of sensitive issue, which is very dramatic in our milieu. When the film came out, the Chairman of the Censor Board of India asked me, 'How can you show a Hindu and a Muslim marrying

---

'A commissioner of police promised me that this film would never see the light of day. You can't tell me that. You're doing your job. I'm doing my job.'

```
                                                    M-25062
        Endorsement on Certificate No. 91417-U dated the
    01st MARCH, 1995. issued to the film 'BOMBAY'(TAMIL)
 COLOUR - 35mm - CINEMASCOPE.

 Cuts:                                              ft      fr

 General cut:   Delete the words 'Pakistan',
                'Islamic State' and 'Afghanistan'
                wherever it occurs.    Deleted:      Sound
                                                     only
                (Replaced with appd. words)
 1. Reel 5      Delete the visuals of Rathyatra
                alongwith the dialogue 'Babri        Sound
                Masjid thodenge Ram Mandir           only
                bahayenge'.            Deleted:
                (Replaced with appd.dialogues)
 2. Reel 7 (a)  Delete the dialogues and visuals
                starting from 'Ayodiyile irrukkira
                Babar Majeedai idichu Raamar Koyil
                kattap poaram. Ovvur indhu veeti-
                lleyum panamo porulo vasool panroam.
                Masoodiyai idichu raamar koyil       Sound
                katta ungalaala mudincha uthavi      only
                seneheenganna nallayirukkum'.
                                       Deleted:
                (Replaced with appd. dialogues)
         (b)    Delete all visuals of Babri
```

each other? It's never been shown before on film.' I said, 'Isn't this happening every other day? So many of my classmates have gotten married like this. How long do you want to hide things?' That is the level of safe-play we tend to do in cinema. The drama was a function of that, really. Yes, it's a hard way of telling a story. I knew I wouldn't naturally go this way. But because it was a Hindu–Muslim marriage issue in a small village—not in an urban city—it tends to get dramatic. The film can take this style. You can get to an *aruvaa* [sickle] very quickly in the deep south, compared to the city.

RANGAN: There has always been an element of rabble-rousing in the more issue-driven cinema we've had here, because, as you say, these scenarios tend to get dramatic, and this sort of tone can easily rouse the audience to a fever pitch. They become as emotionally charged as the people inside the movie. It's a way of making them feel what the characters are feeling. Is this what you were going for?

RATNAM: It's actually the opposite. You have to take the audience into the situation and make them see the futility of just reacting, then it serves what we set out to achieve. The cry of agony during these emotional peaks was what we were after. It is often considered that there is only one way that a voice can be raised, and that is the anti-establishment voice. This thought came out of the east European bloc in the 1960s, and all films that were anti-establishment were considered revolutionary and very good. You seem to have the same view. Whether it is relevant or not, whether it is genuine or not, whether it is true or not—if it is anti-establishment then it is very good. The rest is rabble-rousing. But I don't think that's valid. In between the anti-establishment films and the propaganda films, there are films which depict the man on the streets. The everyday man who gets caught in the turmoil that life throws at him. He looks at the larger picture through his life and the events that he comes face to face with. It is this voice that I was trying to speak in.

RANGAN: I guess Arvind Swamy's 'everyday man' character here is a lot like the one he played in *Roja*. There he says, 'Kashmir is also part of our country.' Here he says, 'Is a Muslim automatically an enemy?'

RATNAM: He's an urban, educated guy who thinks he's rational and progressive and, in a way, he's probably the voice of today's urban India.

RANGAN: He also seems to be a bit of a flirt. There is this throwaway moment where this girl yells out to him that he'd said he'd marry her.

RATNAM: I think it's more to contrast the relationships in Bombay, in a metro, with those in a small town. In Bombay, the world around you is in this small corridor—men of all ages, women of all ages—and you exist within that. Bombay was so unique at that point of time, so cosmopolitan, with so many people, that it was really a melting pot. This incident is just trying to show Bombay, the metro. There is casual friendship, silent enmity, and casual flirtation that means nothing and is just a joke. To a girl coming from somewhere else, a religious procession is as scary as anything else.

RANGAN: During the riots, one of the children is saved by a transgender. An obvious extrapolation is that this 'minority' person would have more compassion for minorities like these kids, who are partly Hindu, partly Muslim.

RATNAM: This, again, is a feature that represents Bombay and its cosmopolitan nature very clearly. The transgender community is all over the streets there, very aggressive, very friendly, interacting with the commuting public, very much a part of Bombay life. They are not so open here [in Chennai], but in Bombay, they are a strong community, not a rarity. When you go from here, it's something that strikes you. And they are in a kind of no-man's-land, caught between two genders. The twins are practically like that, caught between two communities, not knowing which one they belong to. So in a way, all these people are in a limbo, trying to find their feet.

'I wanted someone delicate, porcelain, who kind of represented the character.'

RANGAN: You seem to have such strong feelings for Bombay. In your first Bombay film, *Nayakan*, a benevolent Muslim elder adopts the Hindu Velu. And now, Hindus and Muslims are at war. Do you think you'd have been able to make *Bombay* had you not spent those few years studying there and being a part of the city?

RATNAM: It just made it easier for me, because there were images of it, there was a sense of it. Maybe that was why the anguish was there, that this happened to Bombay. Maybe that's one reason I took it up so easily.

RANGAN: Did you deliberately cast Nasser as a Hindu and Kitty as a Muslim? That appeared to be a little statement.

RATNAM: Yes.

RANGAN: You have two levels of Hindu–Muslim conflict—one on a local scale, between Kitty and Nasser, and the other on a national scale. Is there anything to this beyond the obvious fact that this conflict is no longer taking place at a central level but also in the country's nooks and corners? You have that scene where Nasser demands from Kitty bricks with 'Ram' inscribed on them.

RATNAM: I think this moment of establishing a divide, done for a political purpose, percolates down. We just need an excuse to have a difference of opinion with somebody else. You like Dravid, I like Tendulkar—that's enough. And if somebody makes that an issue, then I, somewhere down the corner, will pick that up as an issue. So that does come into the picture. But what we really tried to do with the Kitty and Nasser fight, between the two fathers, is to start their relationship on a very intense note. It becomes an emotional confrontation where they pick up an axe and there could be blood. And slowly, it becomes something almost friendly and comical—a contrast to what is happening on the macro level, in the nation. Here the divide is resolved by the next generation making an impact, by taking a bold decision. The episode with the bricks is more to get the other man's goat. And afterwards it becomes even more light-hearted. What's portrayed is the reluctant friendship and bonding between two older men, whereas on the national scale, it gets more and more intense. That was the contrast we planned.

RANGAN: What is your attitude towards messages in movies?

RATNAM: I don't make movies to give messages. Films are about sharing an experience or sharing your angst or your concerns about something with a larger group of people. If the film gives you an experience and if it puts you in another person's shoes, and you become aware of that person or that issue through the film, then I think it's doing its job. It's a convenience to think that your film has a message and that's why people are seeing it. There are so many inputs in life that come from different factions. Films are just one of them. You can't give yourself too much credit saying that films influence people. I think that people are influenced only if they want to be influenced, and more importantly, only if they are already predisposed towards what you're saying. A message can only make a film the flavour of the month. I don't meet people on the road and say, 'I have a message for you.' Why would I do that on film?

RANGAN: I ask this because in films like *Bombay* (the ending, with its message of hope) and *Aayidha Ezhuthu/Yuva*, you get into a bit of a 'messagey' zone.

RATNAM: I think you are wrong. Bombay's hope is my hope, my wish. That is all. The subject in *Bombay* is so dramatic. There is a dark side to people that comes out during chaos. There is also a positive side, where people do amazing things. I think it's really a phase, as in war. Two sides reveal themselves at the same time. In my mind, it was not a message. It was a cry of anguish. The soundtrack has that quality to it. Bombay recovered very quickly, and a human chain was formed hardly a month later. Humanity, as a group, is positive. This has happened and this has shaken us, but the next day is going to be a better day. Life goes on. There is always hope if you look for it. That's all it was. What is the issue in *Yuva*? There's no issue in it.

RANGAN: I was wondering if you were trying to tell the youth of India to go make something of themselves. Because even the wayward youngster (Siddharth/Vivek Oberoi) joins politics by the end.

'The love story has to peak here emotionally ...'

RATNAM: That's not a message. I think this is the way we are today. All the three main characters in the film have grown up in different environments and have strong views. Then there's a point where they come face-to-face and they look at life as more than just what has brought them there so far. They look beyond that. That is all the film was about.

RANGAN: *Roja* and *Bombay* are both set on a national stage, outside Tamil Nadu, but the former ends on a personal note and the latter on a political note. Roja gets her husband back, and that's the end. We don't really see what happens to the terrorists. But even after Shaila Bano gets her children back, there's a larger point in the film about humanity. Would you say that between these two films, you grew up, perhaps became a part of the establishment?

RATNAM: The ending of *Bombay* is still personal. Why can't concern about the people you live amongst be personal? Why do you restrict the personal concern of a man to his wife and kids? Why should any concern about what is happening around be labelled as an 'establishment' way of thinking? I just don't get it. The film ends with her finding the children. The rest is really just a winding up—or a winding down. You can have any kind of shot to wind a film down, but this—because it's so close to the present, so intense, and we've seen it so many times in newspapers and magazines and television—needed to take an extra step. The film could take it, I felt, because it's really not a wound of the past. It's a wound of the present and it was still healing. But the story actually finishes with her and the children, and Bombay gets back to normal. It's just that the way Bombay gets back to normal was depicted like a reaction to a very recent wound. If the film had been made now, it might have ended differently.

RANGAN: 'Part of the establishment' was probably a wrong thing to say. What I was getting at is the fact that—at least to Tamil viewers—you've become a more responsible film-maker after *Roja*, someone who feels he needs to 'say something' and not just make an entertaining movie.

RATNAM: I've always tried not to get into one kind of film so that I have a range, a choice of subjects. Even in that phase, after *Roja*, I made *Thiruda Thiruda*, which was very light. Why do you ignore that and pick only *Bombay*? Does *Thiruda Thiruda* look like a 'say-something' movie? At various ages, at various times in your life, there are different things that hold your interest. The kind of stories that you think can be made into a film, the drama that catches your attention, changes. It can't be the same as it was when you were in your twenties and thirties. I think it's just time. It's old age catching up.

11

'That's the best wedding scene I ever shot'

Iruvar (1997)

Anandan (Mohanlal), a struggling actor, teams up with Thamizhchelvan (Prakash Raj), a struggling writer. The duo makes a splash in the movies, but success begins to fray away their friendship, especially when they join politics and drift into opposite camps. They seek solace in their women (Aishwarya Rai, Tabu, Gauthami, Revathy), but it's these men, always, who are each other's soulmates.

BARADWAJ RANGAN: Are you an avid follower of politics?

MANI RATNAM: Not especially. I follow as much as everybody else. But this particular period, just after Independence, is so fascinating when you've been here all these years. It's a newborn country, and new political parties are getting formed, getting rooted, getting some kind of identity, sorting themselves out from the Independence struggle. And alongside, there's this new language of cinema being discovered. These two, cinema and regional political parties, are growing at the same time, one leaning on the other.

RANGAN: The *iruvar* [duo] of the title could just as easily refer to the twinning of cinema and politics. This is when a Tamil identity was being formed. Till then it was a common Indian identity. And this Tamil identity was formed with Tamil rhetoric.

RATNAM: The Dravidar Kazhagam had dramatists, orators, writers. It had all kinds of literary people—those who were part of stage plays, street plays—and they used the written word and the spoken word to forge themselves into a party. Cinema was one of the new mediums that were emerging, and these two grew together and each used the other to grow. It's a fascinating phenomenon and very unique to Tamil Nadu.

RANGAN: This far, you were averaging a film a year, but there was a two-year gap between *Thiruda Thiruda* and *Bombay*, and again between *Bombay* and *Iruvar*. Were you busy with something else?

RATNAM: I'm not busy with anything other than making films. That's the only thing that occupies me. We got down to writing a script. It evolved, fell into place, and then we started shooting.

RANGAN: I was wondering if the gap had anything to do with the bomb scare in the aftermath of *Bombay*. Film-making is already so stressful. And then you have threats to your life—and later, the heart attack while shooting *Aayidha Ezhuthu/ Yuva*. You might have said, 'I've had enough. Let's get back to management consulting.'

RATNAM: I don't think these things have anything to do with film-making. You're making a film like *Bombay* as a scream against violence, so you can't be scared of an individual's violence against another individual. That's what you're trying to fight against in your film. It's just something you face.

RANGAN: Are you saying you were prepared for it?

RATNAM: No one is ever prepared for something like this. But it didn't deter me in any fashion. It didn't change any decision I made afterwards in my film-making career—at all. A handful of people can't

'It's a fictionalized account. It combines characters. It gives you the liberty to look at the theme.' Tabu and Prakash Raj.

hold back the way you think, the way you react. It just makes you more determined to do what you want to do. And the health problem is just a reminder about certain other things. It has nothing to do with film-making. It's probably genetic. It's probably the fact that you're not keeping yourself fit. No one says that if you don't make films, you'll be fine. No one promises you a rose garden. These things are minor hiccups in your career. That's all.

RANGAN: And you jumped into *Iruvar*, which ended up being as controversial as *Bombay*, though in different ways.

RATNAM: It's something we'd grown up with, something we were very close to when we were students. To have something like the rationalist movement was fantastic—it really stood up for the backward. It opened your mind. It set you thinking in a particular fashion. It kind of helped you determine what you believed in. Two things were very, very important in my formative years—the thinking of the Dravidian movement, which was such a strong movement, and the increased potency of the film medium. It was fascinating. It's fascinating, even now, to see all those men in white dhotis and white shirts and a *thundu*, who, somewhere, were forming the tomorrow of Tamil Nadu. And then there is this glitz and glamour of the film industry which, in a way, is seeding the political movement. If I'd not done the film then, I would do it now.

RANGAN: You're saying that the film, in some ways, is less a biography than an autobiography. The theme came about from your hero-worshipping these real-life people.

RATNAM: You're putting words into my mouth. If I meant that I hero-worshipped these people, I would have said so. All I am saying is that there was a political movement that was happening right in front of your eyes and there was no way anyone could have been unaware of it. It was a part of growing up, like set theory and calculus. This is true of the entire generation of the time. We've grown up with this movement for the last forty years. Whether you're in it, against it, for it, it has been part of Tamil Nadu's life. It formed a lot of us.

The theme actually came from a conversation with M.T. Vasudevan Nair. I had met him a few times. He was adapting *Hamlet* for the Malayalam screen and I was very keen on directing it. But it did not work out. The budget was too big for a Malayalam film, I think. Later, when I was doing *Bombay*, I went to meet him to see if he would write it for me. Like I told you, *Bombay* was first conceived as a Malayalam film. During that meeting, he mentioned this connection between politics and cinema in Tamil. He thought that it would be fascinating and asked me why no one had thought of it as material for a novel or a film in Tamil. That is where the germ of the idea came from. MT prodded me into it in a way.

RANGAN: You know that the audience knows you're talking about real-life persons. But there's also the need to put a legal disclaimer up in front, that this is not a true story. Does this create any kind of conflict?

RATNAM: It is a novelization. The film is not 100 per cent factual. It's a fictionalized account. It combines characters. It gives you the liberty to look at the theme, and not just focus on so-and-so did this to so-and-so. You get away from the minor details of factual things and go only into the titbits that are thematically necessary. It liberates you from 'oh, he was never like this, he was like that'.

RANGAN: Lyrics like *Aayirathil naan oruvan* and the children harking back to the *Chikumangu* song sequence from *Ulagam Suttrum Vaaliban* are explicit MGR-film references. Did you worry that this would pull audiences outside the zone of the story, the film, and make them focus on exactly what you were trying to avoid—namely, 'oh, he was never like this, he was like that'?

RATNAM: If it's not blatant, if it just gives an indication of a few films of his through the length of this film, a few brush strokes, then I think it adds to the flavour of the film. It's only when you start wearing it on your sleeve, converting it into a caricature, that it hurts. When all the elements—the visuals, the audio, the music, the drama—end up completely representing real life, you feel overloaded. But if only one of the elements is fleetingly touching upon a reference and going away, then it just gives a lingering flavour of the period it belongs to. Hopefully it will just evoke a smile, bring a sense of nostalgia to the visual.

RANGAN: After touching upon MGR, I have to ask you about your Sivaji Ganesan fandom, which you talked about in one of our earliest discussions. The younger generation sees his acting as pitched too high. How did you view him while you were growing up?

RATNAM: He was the only person who could act. With good directors, he performed very, very well. He was very much under control. The fact is that he had stuff in him. He set the standard for Tamil cinema in terms of the ability to perform. He was not scared to do the role of an old man when he was twenty-five. He did all kinds of things that heroes wouldn't do. Heroes are still hesitant to do older roles. He loved acting. We could see it in everything.

How much of this acting you are willing to take is your call or the director's call. As an actor, he was fascinating. He was just fascinating. We grew up on that. But as a phenomenon and as a personality, MGR was fantastic. To get the entire state to be in love with you is an amazing feat. And you wonder what makes the man tick. What is the magic? What is behind it?

What is it that really makes you carry this person in your mind even after so many years? He moved from one successful field to another successful field, from cinema to politics, running a state and forming a party that is still very strong. Purely as a dramatic possibility, he is fantastic.

RANGAN: You're saying that it's easier to fictionalize and dramatize the life of MGR compared to Sivaji.

RATNAM: For me, it's got more drama. As a craftsman, as an actor, Sivaji is fantastic. But I don't know if I can find a drama ready to be made out of his life, whereas MGR was fascinating, really fascinating. He was real and still larger than life. The story was crying out to be made.

RANGAN: *Iruvar*, at that point, was your most ambitious film.

RATNAM: I don't think we started by saying that this was particularly ambitious. You start every film with that notion. But this was a new arena. This was something more multilayered, more rooted, and with a connection much closer to real life than to drama. Several steps were fantastic revelations for me. The backdrop was a strange mixture of cinema and politics, and because the story was inspired by several things that had happened, you discover, in a strange fashion, that the drama that real life gives you is so much more refined than the drama you make up in stories. We discovered that it was so much more

Iruvar

'The idea was to give a sense of flow. We tried to stage the story in such a way that it looked like the camera happened to be there and that the events were not staged for static cameras.' Aishwarya Rai-Bachchan.

beautiful to not be just black or white, but travel along shades of grey.

If I'd made a fictional film, it would have been tempting to make the friends bond very well—like youngsters coming together and becoming really thick; and then they break up and it becomes really bitter. This contrast is so beautiful in terms of dramatic possibility. But in real life, there's no clear dividing line, and this opened up a side of me that I thought was very good. Even in the first sequence where the two characters meet, there's a friendship that begins—but there's also mutual suspicion. There's also the assessment of whether the other guy can help me. There's a bit of self along with this bonding, a layer which is very beautiful, very real and lifelike. There is so much of self in each of the characters that you can certainly identify closely with them. That's what I enjoyed most while doing the film. Even when they break up, it's not like 'I will destroy the other person'. There's still a link, a contact, between the two characters though they are on opposite sides, vying for the same power. That was really new and that made the film fascinating for me.

RANGAN: Another fascinating thing is that there's all this naturalistic drama ('real life', as you put it), and yet, the staging is stylized, rooted in artifice.

RATNAM: That's also because it's set in the entertainment industry. It's set in an era that's bygone—it makes you nostalgic—and it's set in a Tamil that's also from the past. And it's about a writer and an actor, two extreme characters who are extroverts in different fashions. There's a constant play of words and there's a sense of innocence.

RANGAN: A lot of the film plays out in vignettes. Did you instinctively feel that this was the way to go, or did you have longer scenes that you later shrank to their essence?

RATNAM: You're covering a span of almost fifty years, very crucial years, so you have to get the essence of it and still not look hurried, not look like you're putting in too much information. The idea is to strike a balance so that it doesn't look rushed and you're still able to travel along with the two characters. That's the way I could compress it into a feature film. But what exactly are you referring to as vignettes?

RANGAN: Well, till this point, you seemed to be a 'scene director'. Your films could be divided into fifty or sixty scenes whose dramatic crux was well defined. But here, there were many fleeting, vignette-like moments—fragments of emotions and character—that gave a sense of what was happening without necessarily manufacturing an event or a scene out of it.

RATNAM: That is well said. Without referring to any specific part, you've managed to define the vignette style. Stylistically, *Iruvar* was a huge deviation from my earlier films. The narration and the emotion within are far less dramatic—though the story itself is very dramatic. The way it's been shot and staged is also very, very different from how I shot, say, *Thalapathy* or *Bombay*. For the first time, scenes were not cut into several pieces of shots. I had these sweeping set-ups, lengthier shots, with one fluid camera movement covering the entire action. The idea was to give a sense of flow. It was like glimpses of their lives, and we tried to stage the story in such a way that it looked like the camera happened to be there and that the events were not necessarily staged for static cameras, with several cuts and close-ups. It has far fewer shots than the earlier forms. It's not just the construction of a scene but also the way it was shot, the way it was edited—everything was different from what I'd done before.

RANGAN: Did the story bring about this change, or did you want to consciously try out something different?

RATNAM: You don't start off saying, 'Let me try something different.' I think it should evolve with the kind of story you are telling. It should flow in a particular fashion, taking shape as it goes along. Because the story covers a certain span, we didn't want a staccato feel. We wanted it to be flowing, and that dictated the scene conception and the shot conception.

RANGAN: The flow of life, in a manner of speaking.

RATNAM: Yeah.

RANGAN: This was your first period film since *Nayakan*. Is it tougher preparing for period films? Because, even if you're telling a 'fictional' story, you still have to be alert to the musical cues of the period, the acting styles and so on.

RATNAM: That is part of the job. That's the craft. I think that's the easier part—getting the period right and being able to reconstruct the details. Also, you have to revisualize it for your fiction. There are modifications you need to make. But you have tangible things, definite references—so it just means that extra effort is required. What is more difficult with this sort of thing is to compress and condense it and get the essence of the story and make it look like one organic piece. It should capture everything in spirit and not in plot. The fact that you are combining character A and character B should not be a bother—it should feel right. Instead of getting into the exercise of constantly relating facts to the story, you should be able to draw audiences into the film and be able to carry them along with you.

RANGAN: In *Nayakan*, the songs were authentically rooted in that era, in terms of the voices and instruments used. Here, the recreations are highly stylized.

RATNAM: If you resort to the same tool every time, it's the easiest way of falling into a cliché. It's not necessary that the period has to be completely authentic in the literal sense. I remember a film that was set in two periods. They shot the past without using a zoom lens and the present only with a zoom because there were no zooms in the past. I thought that was silly. Because you can say that there was no camera in the past in the first place. And the film was not about films either. I believe in evoking period. We have to have the sense of time and place. How we evoke it is just a tool in the hands of the film-maker.

When we did *Nayakan*, we wanted a particular sound because the rest of the world was going in a different way. We attempted something new by bringing in those older voices, older instruments, and by taking electronics out of the entire recording. This brought a tone to it. It was exciting to do. But with Rahman it was possible to try the opposite, to keep it modern in terms of sound but still evoke that feeling instead of having to reproduce it. They are two different approaches, and we tried this approach because the previous one had already been done.

RANGAN: Some musical cues are specifically rooted in the era, like the *Aayirathil naan oruvan* number, evoking MGR. But then in *Vennila* or *Viduthalai*, there's a studio-produced jazz ethos that was not hugely prevalent in the Tamil cinema of the time.

RATNAM: Even with the *Aayirathil naan oruvan* number, the arrangements and the sound had a contemporary quality, set against old-world melody and lyric. And there were enough references to jazz in the songs of that era. We took that and we just pushed it to another level. The stance we took was this: 'If we were there at that time, what would we like to hear?' So it kind of evokes that period of cinema, but also brings the period to today's context, with a modern sensibility. All the songs were made in that fashion. In *Aayirathil naan oruvan*, if we hadn't used that exact phrase—which is what makes it a little more apparent—it would still evoke the period without directly pinning it down.

RANGAN: Even the way you shot these songs was different. Earlier, you set your songs to either choreography or montage, but here you slice them up like scenes and integrate them into the narrative.

RATNAM: It's a big advantage to have the film industry as a backdrop while doing songs, because the songs now come into a realistic zone. The film industry shoots songs, so the song is no longer outside the narrative. It is a very real aspect of life in the industry. So you can blend songs seamlessly into the rest of the happenings. The song has a logical, rightful place in the film and can be used not just as a song but for something else—for character development, or to detail the shooting process. You have tremendous freedom to put other things into the song. We enjoyed shooting each one of them.

RANGAN: The songs are like a documentary of the film industry of that time, running parallel to the main story.

RATNAM: Yeah.

RANGAN: There's a scene where Kalpana is sulking inside, and Anandan asks her if she plans to report for the shooting. These kinds of asides—are they relevant only to the primary narrative, the love story, or do they also constitute the parallel narrative of the film industry of the time?

RATNAM: If I remember the shot right, she's sitting in front of a mirror, swivelling on a chair, and we just hear his voice—we don't even see him. It is where a personal relationship and a professional relationship cross lines. One emotion from real life, from personal life, gets carried over and the manifestation comes here, and the other person may not want this manifestation of personal life to be made public. There is always a conflict. It's very common, very apparent when you work there in that zone. So it kind of represents the two roles they play very clearly.

RANGAN: It seemed to me that this man was beginning to be obsessed with her, with the way she looks (like his dead wife), and so his irritation is a way of making these feelings less obvious.

RATNAM: He is a huge star, feared by everyone around him. And she is this young, very intelligent woman who will not fall in line so easily. He is attracted to her but he also knows that she is an enigma. His conflict stems from that.

RANGAN: The *Vennila* song is shot against the Taj Mahal, like you did the songs in *Anjali*, *Mouna Raagam*. Do you like the location very much?

RATNAM: You hesitate before you go back to any location that you have used before. But it's typical of that period of film-making, that period of song-making—there was Brindavan Gardens, there were these dams, there was Kashmir, and there was the Taj. Any one of these would have served the same purpose. We were looking for something that would connect to that period, that era when budgets became bigger and they could afford to go to north India and shoot. We wanted to bring in that flavour from the earlier days to subsequent times when colour and spectacle came to mainstream cinema.

The Taj is an amazing piece of architecture. It's probably the most photographed thing in India. However many times you have seen the image, it still takes your breath away when you stand in front of it. But at the same time, it's the biggest cliché. I remember the first time we went to shoot the Taj, for *Mouna Raagam*. It worked only because we went to the riverside, at the back of the Taj, which took us away from the front lawn and made the setting a little rustic. This beauty and that rustic quality made it look like a Raghu Rai photograph. It's something that can be photographed a

'To have something like the rationalist movement was fantastic . . . to see all those men in white dhotis and white shirts and a thundu, who, somewhere, were forming the tomorrow of Tamil Nadu.' (From left) Prakash Raj, Nasser and Mohanlal.

million times but if you're able to find a way to avoid resembling the postcards that they sell outside the Taj, then it's always alive. And it kind of symbolizes any love story, and here we were talking about a relationship which was delicate.

RANGAN: Till *Iruvar*, you were working exclusively with Thotta Tharrani. Here you went with a new art director, Samir Chanda. What is your involvement with this aspect of film-making?

RATNAM: With every department you work with, you have to have a definite view. The people I bring in know their work very well. But they are not really married to the subject. They have not lived with the subject for so long. Left to themselves, they would do a particular thing that would be very good, but it will not be very different from what they're doing for any other film. If you want something extra, if you're looking for something more, then you have to search for the defining look for the film in tandem with your production designer/art director.

I work with my art directors very, very closely because they give you the look, the setting, the surface, the ambience, the texture, the angles and the tone while shooting. In this kind of film, they help you transport the story to the past and make it believable. It can restrict you or it can open you up. I try to pull them in as much as I can into every other aspect of the film. And that's what gets them going. Tharrani is fantastic. He's one of the most creative art directors I've worked with. You could push him—you could ask for more and more and more. But he had other commitments. *Iruvar* was a very intensely art-direction-oriented film, and I needed somebody who could be with me right through. It was not just one schedule. It was a longer shoot, and Tharrani didn't have the time.

RANGAN: What about the costumes? There are a couple of instances where the costumes are interesting, but not necessarily from that period of Tamil cinema—like that catsuit kind of tight-fitting black dress in the *Vennila* song sequence.

RATNAM: A lot of effort was taken to make sure that the kind of clothes that were used in films and in public life of that period were maintained. The stitching and the cuts were according to each period. Bhanu Athaiya, who is an Academy Award winner, was just outstanding—really amazing work. She was there for most of the film. She couldn't be there for the last schedule. All through the film, we imagined what it would have been like if we ourselves had been there. Maybe the catsuit was not in there at that period of Tamil cinema, but it was there in Hindi—the Saira Banu period, the Sharmila Tagore period, *An Evening in Paris*. It had percolated down to Tamil too. But we were not trying to recreate one particular actor. If you really look at it, we didn't have Tamil stars that time who were that slim either. They were of a different size altogether. We were trying to evoke the period, but with a certain aesthetic and visual standard that we would have liked had we ourselves been there. We were trying to capture those days with today's sensibilities.

RANGAN: The first shot of the film is that of a boy, the young Anandan, in a train, looking outside at the speeding scenery. The boy is never shown again.

RATNAM: The boy was very good. We had shot a little more with him. We had written stories, scenes and sequences. But we kept only this scene. Sometimes, you write scenes that will help you to get the flow, and then you might lose them—but it's your backstory. It's what helps you set the character up. He's innocent; he's on a journey; there are dreams in his eyes, and these dreams are open, limitless, like the scenery outside. It's the start of a journey. We don't know where it's going to end, but we are all excited. It's really the start of a life, of a career, of a dream, everything.

RANGAN: At what point do you realize that the beginning needs an abstract moment like this, and not something more concrete that contributes tangibly to plot or character, like, say, a shot of a grown-up Anandan acting in front of a mirror?

RATNAM: When you write a film, the beginning is what you've gone over the most number of times. Whenever you start thinking of an idea, whenever you start getting a hold of the structure, you have a sense of the beginning. You polish it a hundred thousand times. Sometimes, when you finish a film and you put the whole thing together, you might lose what you thought was always your beginning, but you try to capture that feeling in a moment, which would form the start. I think every film-maker has a notion as to what kind of pitch the film should start on, because the entire film is going to be based on that pitch. It's an instinct that really sets the tone for the film.

RANGAN: Your next film, *Dil Se*, also opens with an abstract image—the out-of-focus barbed-wire fence.

RATNAM: We were looking at the harsher side of the fiftieth year of Indian Independence. We were talking about boundaries. We were talking about border states. That is where the problems were still unresolved. We tried to show that these areas are divided from the rest of the country by a raw fence, essentially a boundary and a check post.

RANGAN: Were these abstract beginnings written on paper, or did you shoot them and later decide they would make a great beginning?

RATNAM: I don't know whether the beginning of *Iruvar* was absolutely written the way it is on film. Like I said, it had a little more of a lead-in, which we did not use. But this moment captured all that we had written before. It is the story as seen through the eyes of this boy, and

'There's a friendship—but there's also mutual suspicion. There's also the assessment of whether the other guy can help me.'

---

his attempt to seek a new future in a completely new world. That was always the beginning of the film.

RANGAN: Do you think you'll get around to releasing these notes and other unused scenes on DVD?

RATNAM: None of them exist, at least from the earlier films. All the footage is gone.

RANGAN: There are so many shots with trains in this film—probably more than in all your other films put together.

RATNAM: And all were steam engines. We had difficulty getting them and shooting them.

RANGAN: So this film, at least, should have made you wonder what it is that fascinates you so much about trains.

RATNAM: One of the first films ever made had an engine coming towards the audience, so maybe cinema and trains are forever tied together. Here, the trains set up our period very easily, they give you a flavour. This film is really a journey of two characters. Trains are a very easy tool with which to convey this journey. These trains get integrated into various people who come in and go out of their lives. Tabu, for example, walks into Prakash Raj's life halfway through, like a passenger along the way.

RANGAN: It's a bit of a metaphor, then.

Iruvar 173

RATNAM: I guess. And trains were a very significant part of the Dravidian protests of the time. They were used to send messages to Delhi. So they were very much a part of the narrative, of the period, of the story.

RANGAN: When we spoke about Manisha's casting in *Bombay*, you said that you wanted an actress who was unknown to the Tamil audience and who would not bring baggage to the role. Was the same logic at work here, with the unusual female cast of Kalpana Iyer, Tabu, Aishwarya Rai?

RATNAM: I just went for people who fit the role. Though she's done a lot of Hindi films, Kalpana Iyer is a Tamil speaker. We needed someone who looked like the mother of that kind of man. She could have just as easily been someone from the stage—it just happened to be Kalpana Iyer who happened to be from Bombay. It's easy to go the conventional way, with someone who's done that kind of role several times. I try not to do that because it becomes such a cliché and you never get the character across. You just get the actor across. It is important to get somebody who makes the connection happen between the character and the viewer.

For the heroines, we were looking for a new face, someone who could do both roles—this village girl who is intelligent and yet innocent, and this very young star, educated and confident. It was really two extremes. Rajiv [Menon] introduced me to Aishwarya. She came home. I told her that this was not a star-launch vehicle. If that's what she's looking at, then this is not the kind of film she should do. I have two distinct roles in this film and this is what I'd like her to play. Would she be interested? And she was. At that point, I think she was wondering whether she should step into films or not, and she took that step. She came to the office and we did a test. Suresh Balaji shot some stills. We did scenes with dialogue in Tamil, with costumes and everything.

We basically did Pushpa's character. She probably did the first scene in the test, with Mohanlal. Santosh [Sivan] shot the test. She was very good, and she was on. We started the film shoot with the marriage sequence and that scene at night where she speaks to him. She still remembers the dialogues. The first line was '*Enakku pesanum*' [I want to speak]. So even today, when she has something to say, she'll start off with '*Enakku pesanum*'. Throughout the shoot, we were debating which one she really was—Pushpa or Kalpana. Even now I am not sure and we bully her about it.

RANGAN: Aishwarya Rai's double role reminded me of Kim Novak in *Vertigo*, a woman who looks like a dead woman from earlier and becomes the focus of a man's obsession. I was especially intrigued when the second Aishwarya Rai dies and her body is never found, which in some way reflects on her name, Kalpana, as if she's merely a product of the imagination.

RATNAM: When someone marries more

than once, they tend to seek another person who is very similar to the one who was lost. Or it's used as a rationalization that the new woman evoked memories of the first wife, and that is why the new relationship happened. It's something that's used in public life in several forms, in several places. It's that concept that I was trying to expand, to convert, to adapt into this feature film. It may not be the same person, but if that is the impression you get, if that is the reason you tell yourself or the world why you're attracted to somebody (whom you shouldn't be attracted to), even though there are other commitments, it is in a vague fashion an irrefutable explanation. It gives an emotional sanction to the relationship.

And these are two contrasting characters in the film. The first one is Pushpa, who, like her name, is like a flower—pure, clean and fresh, and smart but very rustic. And there's the second one, who is sophisticated, modern and much more exposed to things than Anandan is. She's very, very different, completely impulsive, completely instinctive, and Anandan is attracted to this person too. He thinks it's because she reminds him of the earlier character, but you see that the characters are really poles apart.

RANGAN: I never thought of it that way. But now that you mention it, even when you fall in love, you do so sometimes because certain traits carry over, and they say that you always fall in love with . . .

RATNAM: The same person. Yeah.

RANGAN: *Vennila*, the duet, seems to be from her point of view—because he's not yet said anything about being in love. The line about experiencing first love ('*vandhadhe mudhal kaadhal*') works in two contexts—in the film these actors are acting in, as well as in *Iruvar*, the film that's telling their story.

RATNAM: This song was for a film that they were shooting. We view the song sequence with the knowledge of what is happening emotionally between the two characters in real life, and that is what gives the other layer to the song. That lyric from *Vennila* does not directly refer to his or her mental framework. This is what I meant when I said that the backdrop of cinema gives you the liberty of having songs integrated into the film. It's not imagination, but a part of their profession. It is what they do for a living.

There are dancers, there are lights—only every time, we didn't want to show a camera, a dance master, a reflector light, and show that it is a shooting. You show it the first few times, then you move on because by now, people would have got it and you just have to go with the flow. You don't have to go into the mechanics of it every time. You can show just the result. Even when we get into the *Viduthalai* song, we really don't see it with the camera and the reflectors and things like that. We just get into the song. And that, again, is for a film that they're shooting. He is not really thinking of rebelling like that. It is a part of the film that is going to be released, and which is being objected to.

RANGAN: Thamizhchelvan doesn't get any songs—only the narrative poems.

RATNAM: He's the writer.

RANGAN: So he doesn't deserve songs?

RATNAM: In this film, the songs are not for the characters. There are no songs for *this* film, for *Iruvar*—they're all for different films being shot within this film. In any case, writers sing songs in their mind.

RANGAN: Anandan gets married the traditional way, with religious rites. Thamizhchelvan opts for a civil ceremony completely stripped of religious significance. And yet, it's the latter's wife whose sari catches fire during their wedding night—like a bad omen, like a punishment for not doing things the 'right way'.

RATNAM: The actor gets married traditionally because he is conventional and would go with whatever his mother insisted on. The writer is a rebel at the start of his political career, and he takes a political stance even in his wedding ceremony. Ideology was not just for the stage. It was a part of their lives too. I still think that's the best wedding scene I shot—Thamizhchelvan's *seerthirutha kalyanam* [non-traditional wedding]. Some time back, I attended [the actor] John Vijay's wedding at Anna Arivalayam. It was a *seerthirutha kalyanam*. Everybody was there from the political scene. These two, the bride and the groom, were in a corner. As soon as the chief minister came, he called them over and gave them garlands. They exchanged these garlands. It was over. The rest of it was just speeches about the married couple, about the Dravidian movement and everything.

So in a way it still resonates. It's still prevalent. It was a new kind of system that was part of the Dravidian movement, which was also trying to fight these beliefs and superstitions and Sanskritization. Even with his wife, Thamizhchelvan had to start cleansing her of those kinds of beliefs. The rationalist movement had to start from the ground up. The fire is not a bad omen as you say, but a chance to cleanse this false belief about good and bad omens.

RANGAN: And in the scene, it's a literal cleansing by fire. See, this is how film theories start.

RATNAM: Hah!

RANGAN: Here's another. There's a wonderful meta-moment, early on, when an unsuccessful Anandan is reduced to an extra with a false beard. He's an actor (Mohanlal) playing the part of an actor (Anandan) who's playing the part of some other character. Later, after he succeeds, he's loved by millions but he has no children of his own; Thamizhchelvan, on the other hand, has a big family. Are these just how things are with these two lives, or is there something deeper? One had the love of the masses but an empty family life, while the other led a full life at home.

RATNAM: We're not constantly taking stock of both characters. Both of them are in public life, but there are things that happen around them personally. You carry the film along with the people around them, with the ups and downs that happen in each one's life. Sometimes it's truncated. Sometimes two or three characters get merged into one. But their personal life follows them as their public life moves along. It's not a balancing act. It's just narrated in parallel, like parallel lines going across, and not like a compare-and-contrast exercise.

RANGAN: The parallels, of course, are deliberate. They get married at the same time. They get their 'other woman' at the same time. And so forth.

RATNAM: It was called *Iruvar*. The duality was constantly there. And it was about their personal and their political/public life. Both were public figures as characters, passionate in different forms. They grew together and they differed together. It's like classmates. Invariably, life events happen at similar points.

RANGAN: Did you find yourself empathetic towards Anandan and Thamizhchelvan in equal measure? Towards the end, when Anandan's advisers badmouth Thamizhchelvan, he's loyal to his former friend. He orders them to step down from the car, on the bridge, and drives away. But Thamizhchelvan allows his

'With Rahman it was possible to keep [the songs] modern in terms of sound but still evoke that old-time feeling instead of having to reproduce it.'

ears to be poisoned. You get the feeling that Anandan is the 'better' friend, the 'better' person.

RATNAM: I think it's the way people operate at different points of time. If you take me and you, for example, if I'm in a position of comfort, confident of where I stand or the way I play a game, then I can afford to be a little generous. But when I'm battling for a position, when I'm still struggling to reach there, that becomes my priority. I may not make time for these interviews. So it depends on which part of their life you make the judgement on. If you take Thamizhchelvan a little later, it could be a different call; whereas if you take Anandan a little earlier, it could be a different call. And it's really about when you are taking that call.

I think it's about positions and battles. Some people have an uphill task right through. Some people move from plateau to plateau, higher up or lower down, whichever way. It could change. So the film is not trying to be judgemental—just emotionally correct. If you really look at what Thamizhchelvan has to say at the end of the film, it's probably much more honest than what Anandan did on the bridge. But he's able to say it only after he's lost his friend. Only then does it all pour out. But in a way, we're still saying that behind this power struggle and this conflict of egos, there is still a human being left, which is how they both were in the beginning.

RANGAN: There's a lot of melodrama in this film that's purely at a visual level, like in the scene where Anandan, still luckless, is on the ground while Thamizhchelvan, having risen, speaks to him from a great height.

RATNAM: The drama comes out of the scale. The drama comes out of several faces with dark glasses crammed into one frame, these dark men in white clothes forming a new party and being passionate about it.

This romantic notion of a political party to change lives and to change the way people think—to see it blossom and grow in front of you and become big and powerful—is the drama that's there in every frame, right through the film.

RANGAN: There are two scenes where the dialogue is cut off and replaced with background score. One is when Thamizhchelvan and his mistress—in other words, his conscience—are on the beach. And then there's Anandan's speech after his leader's death. We hear the beginning and the end, but the middle is drowned out. Was this a conscious design?

RATNAM: To be honest, we had censor problems. They wanted the dialogues removed, and we had two ways of doing it—either cutting that portion out altogether or giving it a stylized treatment by removing just the dialogues and bringing the music in. To me, this is not about fact-finding or drawing an exact parallel to real-life events. The idea is to evoke an emotion. It could be said with words. It could be said with

'For the heroines, we were looking for a new face, someone who could do both roles—this village girl who is intelligent and yet innocent and this very young star, educated and confident.'

music. I think the way it's performed and staged gets across the story that I was trying to tell. We chose to go the stylized way instead of amputating the film as such.

RANGAN: There's another stylization, when you use white-outs when Anandan talks to Kalpana [about Pushpa].

RATNAM: I think it's a Kieślowski thing. It is a beautiful device.

RANGAN: In his room at the hospital, Anandan goes to the window and clasps his hands in a gesture of greeting the crowd outside. The iron bars of the window make it look like he's locked up in prison. Is there a political backstory to this?

RATNAM: There is no backstory. He is inside the hospital and the crowd has been waiting for him outside for days. And the image is so much stronger with the bars in front. We have a similar scene earlier at Thamizhchelvan's house, where they raise their hands to the crowd below. From that moment to this, there has been a huge change. From an innocent, idealistic dream it is turning into reality. They have won the election, come to power and are locked behind all that goes with power. This is where the shift starts.

RANGAN: And Anandan is always the consummate actor. When he falls after being shot at on a shooting spot, there's a series of images from his point of view—he sees Kalpana, the waiting masses, the nurses at the hospital, then Ramani. He's still aware of an 'audience'.

RATNAM: And the camera is also falling with him as he collapses. These are moments before what he thinks could be death. In his mind, those are the glimpses he saw. Those are the faces he wanted to see, those are the faces that got registered as they went past. What we were trying to present, more or less, is the feeling of being in his shoes—somebody who's at the top of his game, and who's suddenly faced with an incident of this nature, when a bullet hits him. He registers these small pieces and the rest are slowly blanked out till everything becomes one big blank thing.

RANGAN: Even at the end, in death, Anandan seems to be preparing for an audience. His arc in the film begins and ends with make-up being applied on his face. And Thamizhchelvan's trajectory begins and ends with an oration. They end up pretty much where they started.

RATNAM: And something that they've done is carried forward even at the end. I'm not saying that they came full circle. But the actor, even after he's dead, has to be presented. There's still an exterior that's very important to him. That's the face he has to put forward. And the writer relies on his words to present his face and what he has inside. It's not the action he does but the hidden words that define him. That's what the film is trying to convey at the end.

12

'The more elusive something is, the more you want it'

Dil Se (1998)

Amar (Shah Rukh Khan) is smitten with Meghna (Manisha Koirala), but she leaves, and it's only during a second chance encounter that he realizes he may have feelings for her. She repeatedly rebuffs his flirtatious advances, but arrives at his doorstep just as he's preparing to marry Preeti (Preity Zinta). This time, Amar won't let her get away—not with his heart, and not with her nefarious plan.

BARADWAJ RANGAN: *Dil Se* was your fifteenth film. Had it become easier, by then, to handle failures like *Iruvar*?

MANI RATNAM: I started with my first four films not doing well. You become a veteran by the time you make your fifth film. An underperforming film will always hurt you. It will always bother you. But you have to move on. With *Iruvar*, I didn't realize how much I'd moved away from what I was doing before—in terms of narrative, style, everything. I just thought it was the next film. I didn't realize I was shifting gears. To me, it was just an extension. But when the result came in, there was no hiding from it. It was a call for me to sit back and think. I had probably taken one step too many. But it's a film I enjoyed making. I had no doubts that that was the direction in which I wanted to move. The question is how many people you can take along with you on that journey.

RANGAN: Does the failure of a film result in stocktaking—where you went wrong, things like that?

RATNAM: You don't consciously sit down and take stock. There's a residual feeling you get after a period of time, after some distance from the film. It takes two or three weeks for it to sink in, and then you have this crystallized opinion. That's all. Maybe sometimes you think 'this is the reason' or 'that is the reason'. It's like saying, 'I shouldn't have played that drop shot at 4-5.' That could be one of the reasons I lost, but it doesn't mean that if I didn't play that shot, I would have won the set and the match. You have to take the overall result. If you take the appreciation, you should also be able to take the criticism when they don't accept the film. But I should also see if this is what I want to do. Maybe I've not narrated it in a way that communicated to enough people, but if it's still where I want to go, I have to see how to go about it. If I like it, if I would have liked it had somebody else made this film, then all I have to do is to find a way to tell this story so that there are enough people who will listen to it and, hopefully, like it. I don't see myself as being too different from the audience.

RANGAN: So *Iruvar* did come close to what you set out to do.

RATNAM: I think *Iruvar* is my best film. I can see where it kind of slackens and I could have made it tighter, but that is in hindsight. If it had worked well at the box office, I could have gone more in that direction. Anyway, it is never too late.

RANGAN: Has that been a constant across all your films, that you pretty much end up with what you started out wanting to do? Or are there specific films where the gap between the concept and the end result is lesser than with others?

RATNAM: I don't know if you can really measure it. Honestly, I don't have a crystal-clear film in my head before I start the shoot. It's a myth to say that the whole film is in my head and that I'm trying to capture it. I'm trying to find it as I go along. It's like a mass, an abstract form. And with the actors, with the staging, with the way we shoot, with the way we edit, with the music, we are trying to get it to a concrete form. And you really can't judge your own film. You are so close to it that after a point, you just see pixels. You just have a very gut-level feeling that 'this is okay' or 'this is not okay' or 'it feels good' or 'maybe I could have shot it better'. It's more a sensation than a judgement. It's really difficult to like your own film because you see too many defects. You measure it in terms of what appealed to you about the subject before you started the film—and if you're able to hold on to it and get it across, then it's good. If you ask me, I'll say that I'm not happy with any film that I've done. And that's the absolutely honest answer.

RANGAN: To ask the same question a little differently, have you, before any film's release, felt something along the lines of 'Oh this has come out well . . . I'm reasonably happy'?

RATNAM: You feel that with almost every film because you work at it so hard. At no point of your career do you feel, 'now I know the craft and I can do it effortlessly'. It's never that. You struggle till you are happy with the product. You chisel it. You polish it as well as you can and it is put out. What is put out is a complete form, the overall thing which I've lost vision of. Seen that way, I'm quite happy with all the films; otherwise, I wouldn't have let them go out of my hands.

RANGAN: But surely there are things beyond your control (a performance not turning out the way you want; disruptions at the shooting spot) that result in compromises you're not happy about.

RATNAM: There are pluses and minuses. There are some things that turn out much better than what you originally conceived. There's some magic that happens which elevates whatever's on paper. And sometimes you struggle to get on film what is good on paper. Maybe it was not good enough on paper itself. You just assumed it was. You were not looking at it deeply. But when you have to actually put it up there, on stage, in front, with the actors, the flaws show. So you struggle to see how you can fill up those flaws. You can't hide them from yourself for too long. It's not that you can always get something extraordinary. You keep struggling each time. You keep pushing yourself, pushing the actors, pushing everybody around you to see that there's something extra that will come in to make it really special.

RANGAN: Can you recall a scene from *Dil Se* that transcended the page and became—as you call it—'extraordinary'?

RATNAM: There was the drama of the

topography. We took that risk of going past regional logic and staging scenes at Ladakh, though it was not a part of the story, just to get across the drama of the emotion and the background together. That enhanced all the sequences. There is a sequence where Meghna is 'lockjawed'. She is unable to close her mouth. To actually be able to make the actors understand that there could be something like that, and then have a moment between the two of them, through that, in the middle of a journey in a barren landscape—for those things to convert themselves into a scene is what makes it work. That's what lifts it from what was on paper.

RANGAN: How did *Dil Se* come about?

RATNAM: I'd written the script of *Alaipaayuthey*. I was supposed to do that after *Iruvar*. I met Shah Rukh [Khan]. I told him the story. We even spoke to Kajol. I was looking at a film about a man and a woman before and after marriage—and Shah Rukh and Kajol looked like people you could very easily do that film with. We'd seen the locations, the railway tracks, everything. But I still wasn't happy with the script. One thing hadn't fallen into place—the format, where the story starts the day the wife goes missing after getting into an accident. That was not there. It was just about this couple who were in love, who had a secret marriage, and about what happened afterwards. That portion was ready. But the beginning and the end weren't tied in.

RANGAN: You mean the back-and-forth-in-time structure wasn't there.

RATNAM: Yeah. It was linear. We were searching for something and it hadn't fallen into place. So we left it and moved on to *Dil Se*. Sometimes, that's the best solution. It was fifty years after Independence. There was a lot of celebration, a lot of noise, a lot of excitement. The papers were full of articles about what we've done in fifty years, all our achievements, and I felt that there were some things that could be looked at while we were gung-ho about all this, some problem areas which had not been tackled. That's how *Dil Se* came about. By the time I finished *Dil Se*, the *Alaipaayuthey* script fell into place.

RANGAN: You cast Manisha Koirala again, the first heroine you repeated after Revathy.

RATNAM: One reason was that this role was the exact opposite of what I had her do in *Bombay*. I'd worked with her, so I knew I could push her over to this side. It was not something she had done before and we needed somebody who could play this intense person on a mission.

RANGAN: I felt you cast her because she's from Nepal, and you wanted someone who looked like she was from the North-East. And Amar even refers to her small eyes: '*Chhoti chhoti aankhen . . .*'

RATNAM: That was also there. Casting is

'The film is treated like a classical love story, something like Laila–Majnu—it is doomed because of where the two characters come from and where they are headed.'

about getting somebody who'll deliver in the role and also physically fit the role, somebody who's available and right for it, who's the best among the lot for that particular role, and someone who is as keen about the film as you are. It should all, kind of fall into place. And then they should agree to the time and they should agree to the film and they should want to do something different and be willing to travel with you through all the troubled times during production.

RANGAN: Meghna is from the North-East. Amar is from the North. Preeti is from the South. They form a literal cartographic triangle, apart from the love triangle they are enmeshed in.

RATNAM: It was tough to pass Preity Zinta off as a Malayali, but still . . . It was the fiftieth year [of Independence] and we wanted to represent the length and breadth of the country.

RANGAN: And after *Roja* and *Bombay*, you're back in your pan-India mode, as opposed to your Chennai-mode of your early days.

RATNAM: I think that was a phase when I was interested in doing films that were not just personal stories—or they were personal stories against a macro backdrop. That's the age when those things matter. I probably felt I'd done the personal stories, the *Mouna Raagam*s, and what

Dil Se 185

fascinated me at that time was to see whether I could do a relationship story in this kind of a dramatic backdrop. It's still a relationship story. It's set against a larger canvas, that's all. So it's not pan-India as such. It's only because it is set in the North-east—that is where this could happen—that this became a Hindi film. Otherwise, it need not have been in Hindi.

RANGAN: But you would have made a Hindi film anyway, at this stage.

RATNAM: Yeah, it would have been *Alaipaayuthey*. We even had the title *Mast* registered for it. The romance that starts on suburban trains—all that is because it was set in Bombay. I was to shoot the entire thing during the monsoon in Bombay.

RANGAN: When we talked about *Thalapathy*, you mentioned that you weren't keen on doing Hindi films.

RATNAM: *Roja* and *Bombay* had done well in the north, so I was a little more favourable to the idea. I could do the film that I wanted and I could reach across to a wider audience.

RANGAN: This being your first film in Hindi, how did you tackle the language barrier?

RATNAM: You are dependent on others a lot more. I had this friend called Tigmanshu [Dhulia] on the sets right through. The dialogues were not the conventional Hindi dialogues. We were trying to make it sound like we would have done it in Tamil. The dialogues were written in Tamil [by Sujatha]. They went from Tamil to English and from English to Hindi. With Tigmanshu, the Hindi dialogues were in safe hands. You also learn to trust the actors. Shah Rukh was from Delhi, so his Hindi was good and he had a sense of what we were trying to do. He was fantastic to work with. He is with you all through. He'll do anything for the film. He'll do the most dangerous things. If you tell him he needs to be on a hill, he'll be there—he'll climb up and start doing his movements. You have to keep him in control.

RANGAN: Due to this dependence, did you feel less in control (than you would have on the sets of your Tamil films)?

RATNAM: That doesn't happen. The only problem was to keep Shah Rukh's enthusiasm under control. It's as difficult to do a Hindi film as it is to do a Tamil film. The language really didn't bother me, except that when you go to Ladakh, they give you tea which is pink in colour. That's the only other problem I remember.

RANGAN: In the early parts, Amar doesn't seem so much in love with Meghna as merely intrigued. At first, he's hit by the image of her face, that whole 'thunderbolt' aspect you used in *Bombay*. He flirts a bit, nothing happens . . .

RATNAM: And that's it. Amar himself calls it the shortest love story in the world. He accepts that she will be only a memory. It is only when she appears again that he gets drawn, he gets attracted. And then it develops over the period after the accident in Leh, in that landscape, when these two people are on a journey. Both are going on a different mission, and that mission gets sidelined by a third thing, by the accident, which leaves the two of them in a void where they can just be themselves. And that is when something connects. It's easier for him. He's ready to look at women. He's ready to fall in love. She's not. She's not ready to look. She's not ready to fall in love. And yet she gets drawn in.

RANGAN: Their attraction in that Leh segment is very clear. I'm talking about the portions before that, where he comes off as a stalker. He's obsessive. There's something about her that's gnawing at him. And the odd thing is, it's only in the two songs—*Dil se re* and *Satrangi*—that Meghna is wearing pretty, colourful, feminine clothes. Elsewhere, she's like a man—or rather, desexualized. So it's even more of a leap for him to fall for a girl whose face is pretty, but who is otherwise so 'unfeminine', so aloof. You can understand this exuberant Delhi boy falling for Preeti, who's equally exuberant.

RATNAM: You cannot come up with a commandment about who a Delhi boy can fall in love with and who he cannot. Why do you think that falling in love has to be only with the stereotypical other? With Amar, there's something that happened with a girl in a railway station, but it passed and went away and he comes to terms with it. He accepts it. But when it happens again, when he sees her again and has the same pangs, he wonders if it was meant to be. He was ready to forget about her for the rest of his life and it would have been perfectly fine, but she came up again and pushed him into a zone. You can try to explain it, but it's just the way it is. You wonder why, and then you reach out and it becomes an impulse that leads you, and somewhere there's something that works because of that impulse.

RANGAN: And that impulse leads him to a strange and obsessive place. At one point, vexed by her attitude, he doesn't say that he'll slap her but that he'll throttle her and take her life. ['*Galaa dabaakar jaan se maar daaloonga.*']

RATNAM: The more elusive something is, the more you want it. If she had been a character like Preeti, who is open, you know that it's an easier relationship to get into. Here, you know that the person is attracted to you, but still will not take the step. When I'm with her, I know that she's equally attracted. I don't have any proof but I know it inside. But still there seems to be something that's stopping her. That's that love story.

RANGAN: This is a question you get asked all the time, but what makes you so good with these relationships?

RATNAM: What about the other relationships? Why do you ignore all the non-romantic relationships that I have done? I really like the relationship between Shalini and her mother in *Alaipaayuthey*...

RANGAN: I agree. All your relationships are expressively delineated. But I'm talking about the romantic relationships in particular. There's a tang, a spice to the love you depict. That's not the case with most of the couples we see on screen, and we make love stories all the time.

RATNAM: I don't have an explanation. But Balachander used to flesh out man–woman relationships really well. I still remember his early films with Kamal Haasan...

RANGAN: Are you talking about *Manmadha Leelai*?

RATNAM: No, not *Manmadha Leelai*. I'm talking about *Avargal*, *Nizhal Nijamaagiradhu*... Even in *Aboorva Raagangal*, it's not an easy relationship.

RANGAN: No, I'm getting at something that I think you're trying to avoid answering. Those are tangled relationships, not simple boy-meets-girl love stories made refreshing by that tang, that spice.

RATNAM: That's the way it would be. If you take a [Vaikkom Muhammad] Basheer story and see the relationship between the couple, it will never be plain. If you invest in both the characters, they should be something—they can't just be plainly exchanging looks. There should be something worth dramatizing on paper and on film. That is what you search for. One character should see something exciting in the other to fall in love. If we are able to see that exciting element, the story becomes interesting.

RANGAN: There's a spiritual/existential undertone to most of the songs, even the outwardly jolly *Chaiyya chaiyya*.

RATNAM: This is one of the best albums I got. The songs were very, very special. Rahman was in a zone. We probably laboured a lot more over the *Bombay* songs than with this. *Dil se re* happened, and that night I was telling him about this seven-stages-of-love idea, and the next morning he had a tune. And it was not a simple tune. He was in a flow, and Gulzar was there. It was the kind of thing where you discover that three people work well together, complementing each other. The first song we recorded was *Chaiyya chaiyya*. That set the bar really high. From then on, we had the momentum.

With *Chaiyya chaiyya*, it was a concept we'd worked on much earlier—not in terms of the song, but in terms of the visuals on top of a train. PC [Sreeram] and I had scouted around for locations for a Telugu film we were supposed to do before *Geetanjali*, just like I was supposed to do *Alaipaayuthey* before *Dil Se*. The idea for this song on top of a moving train started there. That script never got made and we shifted to *Geetanjali*. Then when I did *Iruvar*, I tried a shot of Anandan on top of the train for the *Aayirathil naan oruvan* song, but I did not use the shot as it didn't feel right. It finally fell into place only when *Dil Se* happened, a capping of the love story up to that point. The song was like the finish of a prologue or a Chapter 1. The film is treated like a classical love story, something like Laila–Majnu—it is doomed because of where the two characters come from and where they are headed. The structure is very much in that mould, and therefore the songs had that sense. Somewhere it sets the tone for something that's unrequited. It's not an easy, flippant, happy love story. It's full of angst.

RANGAN: Even in *Raavan*, you begin *Behne de* as Beera descends from a cliff into the lake and begins to search for Raagini—it's a literal 'falling' in love. But like the love songs in *Dil Se*, there's a spiritual, philosophical, existential quality to the words that seem to make it more than just about love.

RATNAM: That's where Beera changes. Till then, he really didn't see this woman as

'I'd worked with her . . . It was not something she had done before and we needed somebody who could play this intense person on a mission.' Shah Rukh Khan and Manisha Koirala.

anything more than a captive. She was just somebody's wife and he just wanted to teach that man a lesson. Then he sees this woman as a person who's probably braver than him, who'd do something that he would be scared of doing. And he doesn't know if he should be angry with her. He's taken aback by her act. His world was under his control and he never thought that this would happen to him. And he comes down to earth—literally—trying to save the woman he was ready to kill. It is that big a transition, happening in a matter of seconds, and that is what starts the song. The content of the song is not necessarily only for this moment but for the entire trajectory through which he will travel. When he says *Usire poguthey* ['I am dying', in the Tamil version], it's not about what's happening to him just then, but what he will feel at the end of the film. We were trying to get a song that would go forward rather than just talk about that moment.

RANGAN: *Chaiyya chaiyya* came to be used in [Spike Lee's] *Inside Man*.

RATNAM: When we did *Alaipaayuthey*, we had a song at the beginning of the film, with the hero and his headphones. We shot it using a bit of a *Backstreet Boys* song, and we used the song while editing. We asked for permission to use that bit. *Alaipaayuthey* was with HMV. We went through them, as they had the rights for *Backstreet Boys*. The parent company quoted a fancy figure of one crore rupees. We said, 'Forget it!' We composed a new piece and it worked absolutely fine. Much later, they asked us permission to use *Chaiyya chaiyya*. Till then, none of them had ever paid anything to an Indian film unit. So we quoted exactly the same figure. The music company was ready to give it to them for nothing, but we said no. If they can charge us this much, then we'll charge them as much. And we got it.

RANGAN: Ah, a revenge against the evil 'West'. That's worthy of Manoj Kumar. How was it working with Gulzar, given your unfamiliarity with the language and the fact that his poetry is so literary and filled with wordplay?

RATNAM: *Dil Se* was the first time I was working with a lyric writer with Hindi as a base. I didn't understand the nuances of the lyrics he was writing, but I had to tell him what I wanted. Sometimes the brief used to be [the Tamil nationalist–poet] Bharatiyar's songs. I used to translate them and tell Gulzar that this was the kind of thing we were looking at. We also looked at being a little abstract, a little lateral, instead of trying to write directly for the situation. For example, the *Dil se re* song is literally a love story happening in a battlefield. In the midst of turmoil, there's a bond that's developing. The song tried to capture that. The lyrics had to have an abstract quality. Even *Satrangi* had a little bit of that Sufi quality where we looked at the various stages of love.

RANGAN: The only conventional song is the beautifully erotic *Jiya jale*, which is purely about this girl's feelings before marriage. Every other song works on multiple levels. The lyrics, the picturization in *Jiya jale* have an overtly sexual thrust that's startling in a film that's elsewhere quite 'desexual'.

RATNAM: And we thought we could get away with *Jiya jale* only because we put Malayalam smack into it, in the chorus; so at least in terms of the song, it broke away from the conventional form. In a conventional situation, if you put in one thing that's totally unconventional, then you get something new altogether. The Malayalam verse added the freshness. The situation is about a wedding, and the character of Preeti is not inhibited in any form. She's not shy about things. So it's completely liberating, and completely the opposite of his relationship with Meghna. Nothing is spoken there, but here everything is spoken, everything is open, everything is physical. That defines the person and the relationship. The contrast you talk about is really more of a contrast in the relationships than anything else.

RANGAN: There's another borderline erotic moment, in Leh, when Amar stumbles on Meghna bathing. He looks at her, and when she catches him looking, she returns his look and continues to bathe, unconcerned.

RATNAM: I remember that moment. The water had to be hot. When two people are travelling together, sharing experiences, sometimes it gets intimate in a very unconventional way, and those moments are what you try to capture. Sometimes, you write them and don't shoot them. There was quite a bit of that in *Raavan* too, moments which I think are beautiful and are unconventional because you're thrown in situations which are very unusual. Both of them, in this case, are going through a transition of sorts. It could go anywhere. It could just become a physical affair. It could become a lifelong thing. And neither of them is planning anything. He had something to do, and she had something else to do. So this comes in between. Both of them face it, become aware of it, and each reacts differently. One just lets her guard down for a minute, and the next morning she disappears. This bathing scene is the point of contact, really, though they're far apart in the scene.

RANGAN: It was also slightly surreal. The film, at this point, has detached itself from what-next plot mechanics and stopped to observe these two people, who seem to be trapped in some kind of timeless fever-dream.

RATNAM: And there's another moment— I'm not sure if it comes through. It's the one where she drinks water. It's just the way she drinks, with the water dripping over her. If the bathing scene is the contact point for her, this moment is the contact point for him. She's now become not just an idea that he flirts with, but somebody he wants now, someone he's totally committing to physically. This was the peak he was reaching.

RANGAN: That does come through. She catches him staring and says, '*Kabhi ladki nahin dekhi kya?* [Never seen a girl before?] *Dil Se* was your first tragedy after *Anjali*. In general, how important are happy endings to you, since you consider yourself a commercial film-maker?

RATNAM: I don't know if you start off saying you'll have a happy ending. The story leads you to it. With some films, you know how they are going to end. When I started *Mouna Raagam*, I knew that they would get back together, and we worked backwards. With *Nayakan*, we knew he was going to die. How he was going to die was the only question. But with some films, you don't know how they're going to end. *Dil Se* was one such. The idea of the film doesn't tell you the ending right away, and that is what makes you work backwards or go forward. But we knew that we were working in the mould of a classical love story, and they would never get together. She was steeped in one thing. He was someone from All India Radio, a representative, a voice of the common man. There was no other option, really, in this case. The characters are defined that way. If you want a positive ending, you shouldn't touch this subject—you should do *Alaipaayuthey*.

RANGAN: I feel that this post-*Iruvar* period is when you began nudging mainstream cinema into slightly edgy territory. You were no doubt, trying out different themes earlier. But now you began to get a little abstract, a little personal. Not everything was done with the audience in mind. For instance, you began breaking up songs—even in *Guru*, for all its mainstreamness, *Ae hairat-e-aashiqui* is split up into segments. In the earlier days, your songs would have played out in full.

RATNAM: Because that's the direction in which I wanted to go, and I tried to put these elements—like the songs—into formats that would move the narrative forward. Just because *Iruvar* was not received very well doesn't mean that everything about the film was not received very well. If you're confident enough that you can tell stories with slightly different tools, then you just go ahead. Sometimes, the most beautiful song is what gets lost, what can't be translated into visuals. *Ae ajnabee* is really wonderful. But it was conceived for a purpose, as a song played by him over the radio, and used like that. You wish you had not worried about its integration into the narrative and just shot it as a song. But no. Unfortunately, the overall film is more important than the individual elements.

RANGAN: But *Ae ajnabee* worked precisely because of the way it was staged. There's this on-again–off-again relationship between the two, and that's mirrored in

'Shah Rukh had a sense of what we were trying to do. He was fantastic to work with. He'll do the most dangerous things.'

her switching the radio on and off and on again when the song is playing. *Ae hairat-e-aashiqui*, on the other hand, is just a love song.

RATNAM: I know. But it is used like theme music and not as a full song, as there wasn't enough space in the film.

RANGAN: Are these experiments also because you don't want to get bored? One valid way of making films is to hit upon a workable formula and keep mining it for variations. Another is to always keep doing something different.

RATNAM: From the beginning, I've tried to push myself. From *Mouna Raagam*, when I shifted to *Nayakan*, the story was entirely different. *Mouna Raagam* was about an arranged marriage and I knew how it would fall into place. The beginning and the end were there in the very thought itself. With *Nayakan*, I just knew that this was the graph of this man, the rise of this man. I had no clue how to make a drama out of it. It was a totally unknown zone. That pushes you a lot more.

In fact, when I finished my first film, *Pallavi Anupallavi*, I thought, 'Now what will I do?' Whatever I knew, whatever I wanted to do, I put into that film. I wanted the actors to perform in a particular fashion and not do a few things that I disliked in the actors of the time. I wanted not to

'Casting is about getting somebody who'll deliver in the role and also physically fit the role, somebody who's available and as keen about the film as you are.'

shoot in a particular fashion, not make the actors dress in all kinds of colours. I tried to address everything that was annoying me about the films of that time. Now where would I go next? I thought I would be dried up by the time I came to my next film. And then you realize, when you are into the next script, that there is a new set of things that you discover within yourself, which you were not aware of. When you pick up something absolutely new, enter a territory you've not been to, you're left with more ideas flowing inside you. If you start at a place where you're saying, 'I don't know how I'm going to do this', that gets you going. That's the only thing that keeps you fertile.

RANGAN: Also, what is new or groundbreaking changes every ten years or so. One reason people from my generation are so in love with your early films is that they were so new, so different from what we were seeing, whereas people born in the 1990s wonder why there's all this fuss about *Mouna Raagam*. One final question about *Dil Se*. Did Meghna's comrade, the Mita Vashisht character, go through with the plan? She was the backup, after all.

RATNAM: If something had happened at the Republic Day parade, I am sure we would have heard of it.

13

'Our middle class is very capable of melodrama'

Alaipaayuthey (2000)

Karthik (Madhavan) falls in love with Shakti (Shalini). When their parents don't get along, they get married in secret and retreat to their respective homes. But when Shakti discovers that she may be asked to marry someone else, she comes out with the truth and moves into a new house with Karthik, only to find that living with someone is quite different from loving someone.

BARADWAJ RANGAN: A lot of your films are centred on the plight of the married woman. Is this just something that comes with the story? In the sense, does the story that interests you at that point just happen to feature a married woman? Or do you say something like 'Let's revisit Divya from *Mouna Raagam* and look at her from another angle'? Because *Alaipaayuthey* is very much a companion piece to *Mouna Raagam*, a look at a young, modern-day marriage.

MANI RATNAM: The only time I thought about revisiting a character was while making *Anjali*, especially while casting Revathy. I thought about what Divya's married life would be like ten years after *Mouna Raagam*. So at one point, we toyed with the idea of casting both Revathy and Mohan from that film. Mohan's dates didn't work out. But that's all. It was more a theoretical exercise than anything else. *Anjali* is a different film altogether. The issues are different. It's just that, in your mind, because you're using the same actor, Revathy, you think of this character as a Divya who has settled down. *Alaipaayuthey* may be a companion piece to *Mouna Raagam*, but *Mouna Raagam* dealt with the problem arising out of the arranged-marriage system, while *Alaipaayuthey* dealt with just the problem between two individuals. The stage on which both the films were mounted is marriage, but they dealt with two different issues.

RANGAN: Did you feel like doing something lighter after a decade of dealing with love in war zones like Kashmir, Bombay and the North-east? Does that sort of thing ever come into consideration while choosing subjects?

RATNAM: You just want your film to

'The mother–daughter relationship was really crucial to the film.' Shalini and Jayasudha.

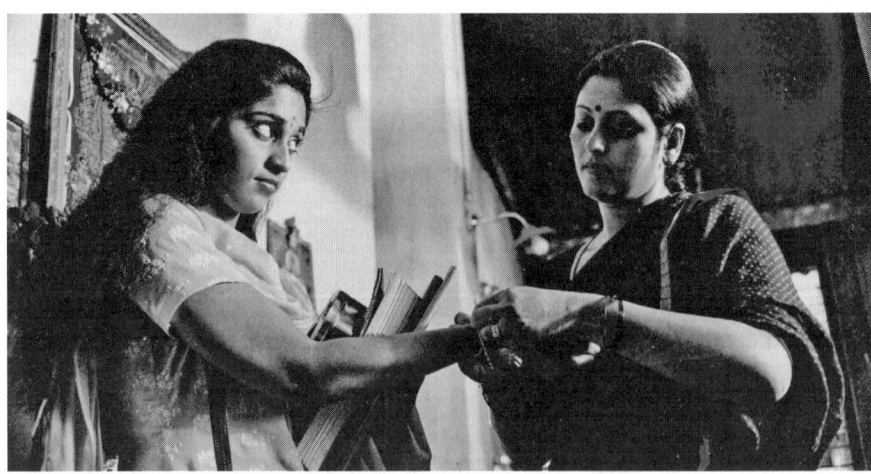

be different from your previous film. That's all. There should be something fresh about it for you. You are starting with a clean slate. Ideally, that's what I prefer. *Nayakan* is different from *Mouna Raagam*. *Agni Natchatiram* is different from *Nayakan*. It keeps me on my toes and makes it interesting. With *Alaipaayuthey*, I wanted to do a love story where most love stories ended. Okay, they meet, they fall in love, they get married. Then what happens the next morning? I always felt that there was a story there. What happens the next morning is a practical and sometimes harsh reality.

In any relationship, there's one phase where you don't take the other person for granted, and therefore you're at your best. Then, the moment the other person is within your grasp, you change without realizing it. You start taking them for granted. And sometimes the relationship re-forms in a different way. That was the theme *Alaipaayuthey* tried to deal with. This phase where the small differences creep up, I thought, is something that will connect and bring a smile to everybody who sees it, because we've all gone through it. And if you can get the characters to mirror today's characters, then you have a story you can relate to.

RANGAN: But this is ideal material for a Tamil film. Why would you consider making it in Hindi? I can understand *Dil Se*, for instance, making a case to be made in Hindi.

RATNAM: What interested me was that, in Hindi, this was the time the great romances were being made, all huge films. *Hum Aapke Hain Koun!*, *Dilwale Dulhaniya Le Jayenge*—those were the love stories. And I wanted to look at what happened afterwards. The idea was to go into their zone and take another page from that and try to make a story.

RANGAN: Once you decided to make the film in Tamil, were there any problems, any changes that had to be made?

RATNAM: The only problem I had was how to fix the end of the film, which in turn formed the beginning of the film.

RANGAN: The earlier version of your screenplay was a linear story—first love scene, second love scene and so forth, as opposed to starting with the present day, going back to the first love scene, returning to the present day . . .

RATNAM: And the ending wasn't there. The start-today-and-go-back comes because the end is like that, the fact that she gets into an accident and he realizes that he wants her to come back. That's the completion of that love story. The accident, that one day of him searching for her and realizing what she means to him, and her coming back—that was not there. One film had to happen in between before that could fall into place.

RANGAN: After a long time, you shared

screenwriting credit here—with R. Selvaraj. But usually, you write your screenplays yourself.

RATNAM: With the screenplay, to a large extent, it's better if it's close to you. The embellishing of the dialogue is where I really feel the need, where I like to collaborate—after the scenes and the flow have been conceived, and I know where I want the film to go. And then the actual conversation comes in. I worked with Selvaraj on Bharathiraja's *Tajmahal*. That's when I met him. He was someone I could bounce the script off, sit with and sort it out. But there's no fixed rule. Typically, I'll have a rough idea and collaborate with somebody and get a few thoughts. I did that with Sujatha. You just need somebody with whom you can work well and who adds another layer and who is on a similar wavelength, and yet adds new texture to the work.

From *Roja* onwards, Hasini [Suhasini] has written at least a couple of scenes in almost every film, though she hasn't been credited for all of them. In all the difficult scenes she has probably chipped in. She wrote 50 per cent of the scenes in the second half of *Roja*. I wrote the other 50 per cent. If you look closely, you can see the difference. Her scenes are more free-flowing, mine are more structured. Hers are more earthy and verbose, mine more cryptic. We work well together. Sometimes we work independently on scenes and then merge them together. Other times, like in the last courtroom scene of *Guru*, we write together. I use her help for the tough emotional scenes. In *Alaipaayuthey*, when Shalini returns to her house and sees her father dead, there's a big emotional scene between her and her mother. That was completely Hasini's.

RANGAN: Do you outline a script before beginning to fill out the scenes? Or do you proceed to complete a scene, then go on to the next one, and so on till you finish?

RATNAM: I don't follow any particular pattern because I haven't learnt screenwriting in any particular way. It's not as though I define Act 1, Act 2, Act 3. At first, I had no clue how people wrote scripts. When I began making films, we didn't have much literature on films, leave alone film writing. The only way to learn was by watching films. I also read a lot of screenplays and plays at the USIS—those were the only examples of writing that I could get hold of. But actually figuring out how writers do their job happened much later, when I met Sujatha Sir and I started meeting writers not of films but outside them. I've been talking to a few novelists because I've always wondered how they do it. And most of them say that they do not know where the story is going. They say that the story will take you to its destination.

It's the exact opposite, I think, when you write for the screen. With films, you should know the structure, the flow

'They felt trapped by the secret they were holding in their hearts. And that secret gets released. They can be open now.'

of the film. You have to know where it's going to start and how it's going to proceed before you get into the details. That's how I go about it. At first, I just outline the rough content of the scenes and the flow of the film, and then I begin to structure it. We should balance it out; otherwise it gets random and there's no rhythm to it. Most of the time, when you see a film, you know that it has been structured, that it has been crafted this way. I think a certain craft is required to write for the screen. You need to have a build-up. The flow is very important, and once you have the flow, you work out the details, scene by scene, and try to make sure that there's something alive in each scene. The expert screenwriter, of course, makes sure that you can't read his craft so easily. The structure and the lines are not visible and the film looks like a freely flowing work.

RANGAN: By novelists, do you mean writers like Ashokamitran? Speaking of whom, didn't any of his stories grab you by the throat and demand that you make a movie out of it? There are so many good stories by Tamil writers, and yet the first time we heard of you adapting a book was when *Lajjo* [based on Ismat Chughtai's short story] was announced.

RATNAM: I've not met Ashokamitran. I'd like to meet him someday. I think he is a master. World-class, I would say. I love his short stories. Hopefully, I will get to make one of them into a film someday. I wanted to make *Ponniyin Selvan*. The transition from literature to Tamil cinema has been really limited. There have been adaptations like [A.P. Nagarajan's] *Thillana Mohanambal*, but very few really.

RANGAN: And also, much later, Sujatha's *Karaiyellaam Shenbagapoo*...

RATNAM: But that's a thriller. It's a little easier to take such a story to the screen. It's tougher to take something a little more serious, to be able to actually get a hold of an Ashokamitran or a Thi. Janakiraman [story] and make it into a movie. I guess you should be able to do it. They do it in Malayalam all the time.

RANGAN: How do you work with screenwriters? I read an interview with Sujatha where he said he participated in all the screenplay discussions for *Roja*, but with *Dil Se*, you asked him to write a short story first, without thinking about its conversion into film.

RATNAM: I wanted him to write the opening episode of *Anjali*, till the child is born, as a short story. He was based in Bangalore at the time. I went to meet him, to see if he could write this opening sequence for me. I didn't want him to think of cinema, but just write it as a short story. He wrote a bit of it for me. But he was there and I was here and we couldn't carry it forward. By the time *Roja* happened, he had retired and come down to Chennai. He had the time and we could collaborate more easily. When working with people, my job is to get the best out of them. Sujatha is a writer. His strength is in short stories. He's written an amazing number of stories. So if he is able to develop characters and pull things together into a story, a form that he is very comfortable with, then I can get something out of his story to put into my screenplay. The *Dil Se* opening is very similar to *Anjali*, in its short-story approach.

Similarly, during the post-production of *Dil Se*, I got the idea for the start of *Alaipaayuthey*, wherein the wife goes missing. Then it's about his search, his reflecting about what had happened during this search, his finding her, and the end, where something has changed between yesterday and today. It's the perfect material for a short story that encompasses the main theme. I wanted Sujatha to write only this story, the present-day scenario—not the *Alaipaayuthey* screenplay, but the start and the end, which is really a short story about what happens in one day. Converting a story into film is something I've been doing for twenty years, so I'm not really scared of it.

RANGAN: Before Sujatha, did you use other writers?

RATNAM: For dialogues, sometimes, I've used others. *Pagal Nilavu* was written by a couple of writers.

RANGAN: I'm talking about *Mouna Raagam* onwards, when you stopped being a director for hire and started making the movies you really wanted to.

200   *Conversations with Mani Ratnam*

RATNAM: For *Mouna Raagam*, I asked a few writers. They refused. In *Nayakan*, Balakumaran wrote the dialogues. There was a Telugu writer, Rajashri, for *Geetanjali*. The dialogues were written in Tamil first, and he was someone who used to dub Tamil films into Telugu. And Pani Sir, who joined me at that time, helped me translate them. Wherever I can get help, I get help.

RANGAN: This is the first time you were working with someone who has become a long-term collaborator, Sreekar Prasad. What is your involvement with the editing process? Do you let the editor assemble a rough cut and then come in, or are you involved right from the selection of the takes?

RATNAM: I worked with Lenin for a long time. He was really amazing. He's not just doing the mechanical process of putting pieces of film together, he's also looking at the performances, at the magnifications, at the rhythm that adds something to the film, the flow that comes along with it. It's really an extension of screenplay-writing. And that is a very, very important part of the final output. I've always felt that someone better than me should be doing that job. If there is a cameraman, he should be better than me—then I can get something extra out of him, not just what I'd do. If I need someone to do exactly what I want him to do, I just need an assistant. Once you have an intelligent mind that is on the same page, the chances of having a synergetic effect are much higher. I can bring something and he can bring something, and we can put things together and reach a plane higher than the one we would have reached individually.

I've known Sreekar for a long time. I'd run into him at Prasad Labs—he had his editing suite there. I'd seen his work on Santosh Sivan's early films, seen the first copy with him, and he was there when I was looking for an editor for *Alaipaayuthey*. That was the time we really got to know each other. However much I've seen his work, it takes some time for him to understand me, for me to understand him, and *Alaipaayuthey* was where we found our footing. Nowadays, Sreekar does the assembling even as I'm shooting. Once I finish shooting, he has a rough cut ready, and then we start seeing how to take it further. In fact, these days, I bring him in at the script stage itself. He is aware of what I'm going to shoot, how the screenplay is progressing, and if there are any issues, he brings them to the table at that point of time. He's very much a part of the entire unit.

RANGAN: There's a young heroine in Shalini and a brand-new hero in Madhavan. Aren't the chances of getting an initial audience greater with an established pair?

RATNAM: I thought that this film need not be driven by established actors. We just needed actors who'd be right for the role,

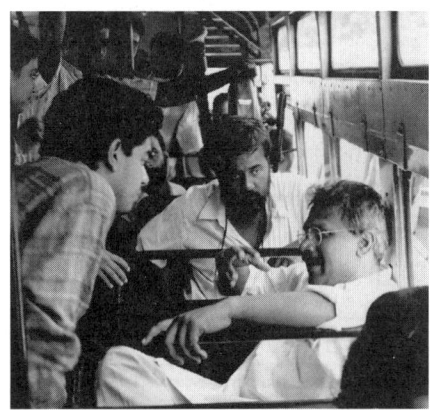

people you could identify with. Take *Ek Duuje Ke Liye*. Take *Bobby*. All these big love stories have worked with new people. It is a proven, established mainstream format. Don't ever doubt it.

RANGAN: The unfinished house that they move into looked like more than just an art director's conceit. It looked like a metaphor for the Madhavan–Shalini marriage, which is still in an 'unfinished' and early stage.

RATNAM: It is a metaphor. It was kind of something that was not completed, which was unfinished, which will hopefully become a home tomorrow, hopefully become a strong relationship. We used the house as a tool to tell the story. It was not necessarily a part of the screenplay. But that is what a director is paid to do. We saw at least ten buildings in the city before we found the right house.

RANGAN: Jayasudha was an extremely good fit as Shalini's mother. We hadn't seen her on screen for a while. I like the scene where Madhavan comes to Shalini's home looking for her. He's met by Jayasudha, who addresses him respectfully as '*neenga*' at first, but eventually, as her worry mounts, she drops this term of respect and addresses him as '*nee*'.

RATNAM: This was the first shot that Madhavan acted in. He was there with the unit for four or five days, when we didn't make him do anything, and then there was this emotional scene that he had to do.

There's an earthiness and dignity to Jayasudha, and she's such a good performer. The mother–daughter relationship was really crucial to the film. It was good to have two good actors doing these roles.

RANGAN: You used Vivek very unusually here, as Shalini's shy suitor. I can't remember if, at that point, he was already an established comedian.

RATNAM: I didn't want to make him just a comedian but a character, the kind Nagesh would have played some time back. I wanted to make him real, somebody you could relate to. I conceived a much bigger character, but I couldn't bring it all to screen, in terms of space and time. By the time we finished, he became a big comedian.

RANGAN: The funniest scene in the film, for me, doesn't involve Vivek. It's the one where Madhavan's mother is secretly giving him some money while the father is asleep nearby, next to a copy of the *Economic Times*.

'*In Hindi, this was the time the great romances were being made.* Hum Aapke Hain Koun!, Dilwale Dulhaniya Le Jayenge. *And I wanted to look at what happened afterwards.*'

RATNAM: He is that kind of person, a lawyer who probably has a small amount of money in the market and has to keep in touch with everything. He is a down-to-earth man who will not mince words. He's defined with certain characteristics and the *Economic Times* was part of that.

RANGAN: Madhavan's is an interesting character. He doesn't want to become a lawyer or an engineer—he's undecided. He's an atheist. When you write characters, do you first draft a backstory with all these traits? Or do the character and his traits evolve as you write the screenplay?

RATNAM: If it's an urban person and if the story is set in current times, you have a clear view of the character. It is very well-defined in your mind. You don't have to invest in an elaborate backstory about where he was born and so on. But in *Yuva*, for example, Lallan's character—Inba in the Tamil version—had a backstory about how he got married, where he came from, all that. It helps the actor get into the part, whereas here it's not very difficult to get into that kind of mindset.

RANGAN: Is it just for the actor, or for you as well?

RATNAM: When the character is far away from you, it's good to know where he comes from. It's not a formula. It's not a rule that you have to have a backstory. It just helps you understand the person better. If you already have a very strong hold of the character, this becomes a superfluous exercise.

RANGAN: There are a lot of light, cute incidents even after the marriage—'hello, *pondatti*', that kind of stuff. Most love stories have them in the 'before' stage.

RATNAM: That's because most love stories don't deal with the 'after' scenario. This is a young couple, married, living away from their families. There surely should be some chemistry, and since they are in private spaces, it becomes more vocal and open.

RANGAN: There are a lot of traditionally melodramatic constructions in this film. In the scene where Shalini receives a marriage proposal, she allows her mother to take her inside, undress her, change her into a sari (and yet never revealing her *thaali* [*mangalsutra*]), and only when she comes out does she say she's married. This delay brings into play the suspense about how she is going to handle this situation.

RATNAM: Sometimes, in a critical situation, when you have something to say, your mind says 'say it' a hundred times before you actually go ahead and say it. We don't just blurt out these things. For her to say to her mother and father that she's married, she needed to be pushed into a corner. If she had said it then and there, then it means that nobody mattered to her, that it was not a big step that she was taking. But it was. She tried to say it inside the room, to her mother, but the mother just didn't let her. She was hoping that something would happen that would make the problem disappear. Maybe the guy would say, 'No, this is not right for me.' And when she realizes that nothing is going to save her, that's when she has to take the plunge.

RANGAN: Another instance of melodrama arises from the fact that she does not keep in touch with even her sister, whom she's so close to. The parents, of course, don't want anything to do with her, but it's this sister who helped her get married in the first place.

RATNAM: There is no absolute reason for this. When a family splits, when it really cracks open, you may not have a fight with everyone, but it's still awkward. The sisters talked every day about whatever was happening, but once the split happens, it weighs you down and stops you from reaching out. You look at any separation—between brothers, between anyone else; the people who stay back on one side stick to that side, not because they personally have issues with the other side, but because that is the *dharmam*, that is the right thing to do. It's like the Pandavas and the Kauravas. After the split, you have to choose sides and stay on that side. Even if they remain in touch, it would be in a clandestine manner.

RANGAN: What about the melodrama of Shakti's father throwing her out of the

---

'We just needed actors who'd be right for the role, people you could identify with. Take Ek Duuje Ke Liye. Take Bobby. All these big love stories have worked with new people.'

house, tossing her suitcase out from the balcony?

RATNAM: I think our middle class is very capable of melodrama. They are not hesitant to be dramatic. I've seen it all around me. It kind of reflects their sense of right and wrong in a very strong fashion. The scene is dramatic and it is shot in a dramatic manner.

RANGAN: During the drinking session on the terrace, the house owner gives Madhavan some advice about roots and flowers and relationships. This made me wonder if *Alaipaayuthey* was conceived as a more serious film than the one that came out.

RATNAM: He is the kind of neighbour or landlord who thinks that he has to be next to you, holding your hand through anything that goes on. A drunken man has a philosophy for everything. You don't know if it's the alcohol talking or if it's a serious philosophy towards marriage and man-woman relationships. The scene is just meant as that. What looks superficial is actually deep, or maybe the other way round.

RANGAN: You have a couple of unusual songs here. *Pachai nirame* is based on colours.

RATNAM: That's an idea we touched upon in *Dil Se*—in *Satrangi re*, though we didn't really push it. The song talked of several shades of love. *Pachai nirame* is just a visual extension of the *Satrangi* thought. It stemmed out of that. You have to find ways in which to get the guy's emotion across. It could be a smile, a simple gesture, a performance, or it could be a song which conveys the same or a similar thing—the joy of having found somebody you like very much. A flourish in his mind is converted into a song. Instead of being a generalized song that meanders all over, the expression through colours gave it a certain identity, a focus, a language in which it could speak.

RANGAN: What about the *Kaadhal sadugudu* number, which occurs in 'reverse'?

RATNAM: These are two people who've gone against the grain, against parents, against society. They felt trapped by the secret they were holding in their hearts. And that secret gets released. They can be open now. They don't have to be scared about being seen together. There's a certain amount of liberation that comes with that kind of feeling and with physical intimacy. We needed that to be a little magical—a little mundane and also a little not mundane. And we were trying to do that kind of magic within a closed space, within a room in an unfinished apartment. We needed a tool, and this 'reverse' was the tool we used. It gives you a sense of poetry. It gives a sense

'In any relationship, there's one phase where you don't take the other person for granted. Then, the moment the other person is within your grasp, you change without realizing it.' Shalini and Madhavan.

of anti-gravity, a sense of liberation. It was an absolutely blind, new experience. The first time we tried a shot, we had to check it on Avid to see if the reverse lip-sync was working. Because it would be foolish if we did everything and the lip movements didn't match. There was somebody looking after just the reverse lip-sync—knowing the part of the song to be shot and whether the actors were mouthing that part correctly. It was such a strange experience. It was happening in reverse and we were shooting in high-speed, twice the speed. The song sounded like gibberish. It took a lot of effort on the part of Madhavan to learn the lyrics in reverse.

RANGAN: Am I right in saying that *Alaipaayuthey* is the first Tamil film that showcased the software boom?

RATNAM: It is not just a reflection of the software boom that was happening then, but something I had seen much earlier, in 1992 or 1993, when a group of people—three or four engineers—invited me to the opening of their small firm in T. Nagar. One of them was talking of a chip that would have a huge memory and hold so much information that it would change everything. It was a dream. I could see that generation happening—these guys who came out of colleges and didn't take up jobs and were dreaming. They could see what was going to happen and they were ready to go into it. It was really that that I carried forward into this film.

Alaipaayuthey 207

14

'An outsider's eye, a distant eye'

Kannathil Muthamittal (2002)

Thiruchelvan (Madhavan) reveals to his young daughter, Amudha (Keerthana), that she is adopted and that her mother—Shyama (Nandita Das)—hailed from Sri Lanka. A devastated Amudha begins to spurn the mother (Simran) who raised her, and longs to see the mother who abandoned her. The family arrives in strife-torn Sri Lanka, where the child's trauma is eclipsed by troubles of an entirely different kind.

BARADWAJ RANGAN: We've been talking about songs off and on in these discussions. What do you feel about songs in general? Every so often, you say that you want to do away with songs in your films.

MANI RATNAM: The song is a huge tool. It is a tremendous high if you use it correctly. So you don't want to leave it. But you don't want it to be something that plays in a pause mode—as if the narrative is paused—and ends at the same point of the narrative. If you take off with a song, with a flourish, you should land on a different note. And it should also give you the breathing space you require. Any kind of film requires some breathing space. I think a song is a much, much more creative type of breathing space than what they do in Hollywood, where they have these long shots of cars going over bridges with cameras on helicopters following them. There's nothing in those shots except breathing space. It fills time and lets something sink in.

I would rather use a song to do that as it gives me the chance to be a bit more innovative. You can tell a story in the song or let it contrast with something that is happening or let the lyrics play an important role. Several layers are possible, and that is what you keep exploring. And this is one place that frees you from the logic of drama. There is a certain grammar to the way drama is staged. But in a song, you can break that grammar. It can become abstract. It can give you the freedom to be stylized and get across what you want to say. I start every film, saying, 'I'm going to do it without songs' but end up doing it with songs. It's too hard to resist, especially if you are lucky to have Ilaiyaraaja or AR [Rahman] to compose for you.

RANGAN: In *Kannathil Muthamittal*, you use the song *Oru dheivam thandha poove* twice, both times with the child as the pivot. The male version is about the child and her father, the female version is about the child and her mother.

RATNAM: Using the same song in two different situations is something Indian movies have been doing forever. And actually, each version has only one *charanam* [post-interlude portion].

RANGAN: Yes, of course, there's always been a happy version and a sad version and all kinds of variants thereof. But I'm asking why *you* did it. This isn't a device you typically opt for, with the probable exception of *Thenpaandi cheemayile* in *Nayakan*.

RATNAM: The song here is a device which unites a relationship, defines a relationship. There's a child they've adopted who's become their own, and in the first instance of the song, the bond between the mother and the daughter is brought in. They are at conflict on a surface level. The child has a fight with her mother. The song kind of pacifies

Kannathil Muthamittal

'You reveal [something like this] very, very gently, starting when they are four or five.' Madhavan and Keerthana.

the rift between the two. The father is a little more lenient towards her, and in the second half of the film, she sees something disturbing—she sees a human bomb up close. She had just been speaking to this man a while earlier, and she sees him explode with a shattering blast. That shakes her up. She leans on the father when she sees her first harsh reality in a world that's a battlefield. A change occurs in that relationship, between the child and her father.

This song is used a second time as a definition for the same kind of relationship—of the child with a parent—but earlier it was a rift (with the mother) and now it's a revelation (with the father). He has opened up something for her, he has told her where she belongs, and he's brought her to see something that they normally could have avoided. He's showing her the darker side of the world and—somewhere—he's trying to console her in the dark. She has seen death for the first time. And he helps her prepare for the rest of their journey, the rest of her life. So it makes sense to hold on to the same song instead of composing a new tune for the second situation. If you had only music, without lyrics, then you would use the same theme music to bind together the two situations with the two parents. It's really just that. The song is just the theme that brings the child and a parent together.

210 *Conversations with Mani Ratnam*

RANGAN: These two songs are similar not just in tune but also in treatment. The mundane, earthbound relationships in the story are depicted at a surreal level. There's that visual of a clothesline on the beach.

RATNAM: In the song with the mother, it's a barren landscape in which a relationship with someone who's come from nowhere—the adopted child—blossoms. The visual concept we adopted was that of a vast space with a single, fixed vertical element in the frame, around which there were two moving objects (mother and daughter). The 'single elements' were the branch, the shipwreck, the fence that divides them, and the rooted quality of the backyard of a house with a clothesline in it. These are static, firm and alone—like a root. And against these single elements we set the dynamic image of the mother and child, ever moving, transient, intangibly bound together. And the song with the father takes it to the next level. There is God. There is closeness to death, closeness to eternity. And somewhere, there is a kind of purification. It's connected to Sri Lanka, to Buddhism, and that becomes the visual motif.

RANGAN: You work really hard on your songs.

RATNAM: Songs can become your trump cards or your pitfall. You have to find a way to make them interesting, riveting, inventive, something that can be taken back home even after the film is over. The dialogue scenes have some kind of drama that defines them. Songs don't have that drama. So you need to put in something else. It can't be just pieces of images, visuals. There should be a concept that unites it all. It could be a locked-in-a-room scenario that unites it all, like *Hum tum ek kamre mein band ho* in *Bobby*. It could be that the entire thing is shot on the seashore. It could be various colours that bind the song. But there should be some unifying factor. I start off very early. At some point during scripting, I'll start writing what I can do for each song. I keep putting in elements that I think of. With some of them, you don't know how to get what you want, but finally, it will come into shape.

RANGAN: What is the biggest challenge about filming a song? It's the one thing our cinema has that the rest of the world doesn't, except in one-offs.

RATNAM: I've always found songs very exciting and very scary. In my first film, *Pallavi Anupallavi*, we had a choreographer for the song, *O Premi*. It was Sundaram Master, Prabhu Deva's father. I've done a lot of films with him since then, but that was the first time we were working together. We got into a fight—a squabble—over the song. This song is about the guy inviting the girl to college, saying that there's a music function. She comes there and the open-air theatre is empty. It's just him and his friends pulling a fast one on her. That was the song. I wanted it to be realistic and still have the impact of a song, with a stage and lights and all that.

But a choreographer thinks only in terms of movements. I tried to make him do it realistically and not make it look like dance. He'd been doing songs for a long time and he couldn't understand what this new guy was saying. By the end, we got into an understanding, but we started off on a stand-offish note. And this struggle with each song hasn't changed from that time. It's almost like a mini-film. Sundaram Master and I used to call it an examination. Because it has to be a part of the story, you have to come up with something new—it can't be something you've done before, and it has to have some energy. The first day of shooting a song is really torturous. It takes a day into the song before we feel we've crossed a huge barrier.

RANGAN: The challenge is the newness, then, making every song look like nothing that came before it.

RATNAM: Sometimes you have an idea of how you want the song to be, but you don't know how to capture it that way—especially when you're experimenting a bit. We have this Holi song in *Nayakan*, *Andhi mazhai megam*. There have been so many Holi songs in Hindi films. You've grown up on them, and you just hate it after a while because they're all shot the same way. What we needed was a kind of celebration, so we came up with the idea of a Woodstock-ish song.

We had thirty dancers brought in, but we didn't want them to dance in any kind of choreographed form. When rain happens in a rock festival, people let go. We wanted to capture that. It's easy to say that this is what you want—but how do you get that on film? The first day is a struggle to evolve a strategy to get that. You don't know how to get there. And it is tougher to explain it to the choreographer. This process of discovery becomes the exercise on the first day. But once you land on a shooting strategy, you tend to relax and enjoy the process.

RANGAN: I never saw the Woodstock connection in that song.

RATNAM: You're not supposed to see it.

RANGAN: But it still came together on screen as a celebration. But in the *Kannathil Muthamittal* song, if the audience is to get the full sense of your intent, you're asking them to do a bit of deconstructing. Otherwise, it's just a mother and daughter running around on bizarre open-air sets.

RATNAM: The song will be remembered for the barrenness. It's like doing a love story in Ladakh. The contrast of visual and emotion is a very strong thing to have on film. That's what this song is doing. At the basic level, one is a song

'I feel very happy about the way we staged the action. You feel you're in the midst of it, you feel you're with them in the crossfire.'

about a mother and a daughter, and the other is a song about a father and a daughter. Over and above that, there is an underlying something that we feel is right for this point in the narrative, adding a few layers to make it what it is. I don't think everyone should literally know what each thing is and what you're trying to say. But it will make an impact. It will make sense. It will feel not like fragments, jumbled pieces thrown together, but like a single flow. It will connect, not consciously, but it will connect. It's like a modern-art painter using colours, which is more difficult to appreciate than a literal painting because it doesn't have the logic to bind it. It has only the colours, the way they fade out and fade in. But there's some form to it. A good painter makes it look smooth. The good paintings stand out because the abstraction is brought out amazingly. The song has to have that kind of quality.

RANGAN: How did *Kannathil Muthamittal* come about? I've heard a story involving an article from *Reader's Digest*.

RATNAM: I think it was in *Reader's Digest* too, but what I saw was in *Time*. It was a story about a child adopted from the Philippines and brought up in the US, and her parents bringing her back to the Philippines to see her birth mother. There was an emotion there that could be placed in this movie. I think Hasini was the one who read the article and showed it to me. That's how the germ of the idea came about. I told her to make it into a film. At that time, she was into television serials. She didn't want to get into films.

The idea kept gnawing at me and I told someone about the way I was seeing the film, with the Sri Lankan background. A child is brought up here and she becomes the vehicle through which you travel through that conflict. The (Sri Lankan) issue has been happening in our backyard for so long. You see various shades of it. You see the way people react changing so much, within Tamil Nadu. And this was a simple emotional story through which you could travel into that zone, through the eyes of a girl who's totally unaware—a girl who's from the mainland—and look at something that's happening so close to us. That was the attraction to convert that article into this film.

RANGAN: You looked at the story of the girl as a vehicle to look at Sri Lanka.

RATNAM: She becomes the viewpoint. So it's possible to see all the ravages around her, a society being torn apart—through the eyes of this nine-year-old girl.

RANGAN: I thought it was the other way round, that the conflict was a human-interest backdrop for the story of this little girl.

RATNAM: The conflict was the important thing. Otherwise, this story, by itself...

RANGAN: It's still an emotional story. And one with meaty relationships, which has always interested you.

RATNAM: I know. But it wouldn't have drawn me in. To me, the girl's story was just something to hang the Sri Lankan story on. It gave you a stage on which you could set this journey. What fascinated me was this journey. Otherwise, it was not what I wanted to do.

RANGAN: Apart from your general interest in the issue, did the conflict appeal to you because of the fresh dramatic possibilities? It's not been explored a lot on screen.

RATNAM: I think there was one other film around that time that dealt with a similar backdrop. But I'm not too worried about whether someone else is making a movie or not. If you think you can make it well, that is enough reason to do the film. The girl's perspective gave the conflict a very strong point of view. It wasn't the way we looked at it. It was slightly different—starting from the mainland, and then she goes closer, seeing it as it comes to her. The film is not seen through the eyes of somebody who's grown up there, who's lived through that, but somebody who's away and who's just now seeing the trauma of what's happening. The eye is, to a large

'The film uses [Keerthana] as the vehicle through which we travel, and her speaking to the camera becomes an extension of that.'

extent, an outsider's eye, a distant eye. I looked at the film as a journey through a battlefield.

RANGAN: Why not look at this journey, this conflict, through the eyes of the father? He's a writer—a polemical, fiery, poetic writer. You could have made a stronger statement through his eyes.

RATNAM: But that becomes a very strong single-person-centric view. You become the author, the writer, and you are taking definite judgemental calls on what is right, what is wrong, what should be accepted. You're trying to pass a one-motion judgement on something that's being going on for twenty years, twenty-five years, without any resolution. A writer would have a definite stance, and that single point of view becomes the only way to narrate the film. But this way, the audience experiences the journey from a neutral point of view, from the slightly lower angle of Amudha looking at this imposing horror, and experiencing the agony of it as she goes through it. It is not the lecture of a writer that the film is dealing with, but the emotional experience of witnessing a struggle.

RANGAN: And that's why you use the device of the girl narrating to the camera, because this is her subjective viewpoint and she is the one taking us through this story.

RATNAM: The film uses her as the vehicle by which we travel, and her speaking to the camera becomes an extension of that, showing us that she's this kind of person. So the early part of the film is shot with that kind of flow, keeping the camera very close to her. We are literally in her world and the way she sees things, at that kind of pace. The first song has all sorts of angles and circular movements, and it's shot with the kind of energy that a bright girl of that age would have. The sequences inside the house were all choreographed in that fashion, with the camera going in and out, in a single flow, with high energy. It's her energy that we tried to capture. Then something happens to her. She goes through a change and the journey starts.

RANGAN: You don't use this device throughout. She speaks to the audience while introducing her family, and then the events unfold without narration.

RATNAM: The narrator was just a device to get into her shoes. The film starts in Sri Lanka. And when we got into the girl's story, we needed a device that would drag the audience into this story. She's a Tamil writer's daughter. Her mother is a television newsreader. She has grown up in that environment. Her narration expresses that aspect of her background, and we use it as her bridge into the story. But after establishing her world, the story should hopefully gather momentum without this device. We should know what she thinks without her having to tell us about it. Unless it contributes something more, the device just becomes a gimmick.

RANGAN: Why, then, the reintroduction of this device when she's on the plane to Sri Lanka? She does a bit of narrating again.

RATNAM: Possibly because, considering where she started off, it's a moment that is very crucial. It's where her journey really begins. You don't have to write your diary every day. You write it when you feel like it. She has a notebook with her. She is writing notes and questions for her biological mother.

RANGAN: When you opt for a device like this—'Amudha's viewpoint'—how faithful or invested do you have to be? For instance, there's a later scene where her mother is on the phone with a sobbing son, and that's not entirely shown from Amudha's point of view.

RATNAM: The device is not a rigid constraint. It just gives you a direction, a path. It is not a rule. Even in the scene with the mother and son, it starts with Amudha. She is talking to her stepbrother and he says something nasty and she leaves and comes out, and we come away with her. She goes away, drifts away, hurt, and then she bumps into those girl-warriors. From one emotional situation, she lands into another world altogether, and comes back running. So we don't really take leave of her all that much in that space.

RANGAN: She realizes that even if home has its problems, the outside is so much worse. Is that why she needs the protection of that big yellow umbrella in a song? Okay, jokes apart, there was a rumour that the film was first titled *Manjal Kudai* [*Yellow Umbrella*]. She has an umbrella while leaving the church. The father holds a protective umbrella over his family at the end. Even a woman in the Sri Lankan park carries an umbrella. The umbrella is something of a motif.

RATNAM: It was a motif. There was a tentative title called *Kudai*—not *Manjal Kudai*. But the imagery would have been there anyway. It was a concept that conveyed a sense of shelter, a family or a country. You're talking about adopted kids, but it could also be an adopted land, an adopted immigrant—all become a part of it under one common roof, one common sky. The umbrella kind of represents various people under one cover.

RANGAN: So you just abandoned that title

'In the song with the mother, it's a barren landscape in which a relationship with someone who's come from nowhere—the adopted child—blossoms.'

and retained the visual motif. And the title you ended up with is reflected in the scenes with a kiss on the cheek.

RATNAM: You don't need a title to have a kiss on the cheek. It's about a child and the title comes out of a Bharathiyar song, a Kannamma song, *Chinnanjiru kiliye*. It's about a child clinging to a parent's neck, like a diamond necklace. The imagery, really, is from there.

RANGAN: The graph of the child is wonderful, grappling between fact (the mother next to her) and fantasy (a mother somewhere out there). On the one hand, she asks this mother not to cry, but on the bus in Sri Lanka, she says that this is not her 'real mother'—as if she wants to hurt this mother and make her cry. How much of this was your addition to the *Time* story?

RATNAM: The *Time* story was just a trigger, not our story. It was just a three- or four-page article. It was really an incident—this family trying to come and meet that woman, and the meeting with the woman. It was just the end, the last situation of the film. This film was an extrapolation, reimagining it in the Sri Lankan scenario. When you develop a character, their attitude and their nature will be present in all their scenes. The scene in the bus was like that. It came with Amudha and her mental framework.

RANGAN: In the scene where the parents find Amudha at the railway station after she runs away, she runs into her father's arms. One reason, of course, is that he is the more lenient parent. But she also seems to be getting a bit conflicted about this mother after knowing that there's another mother somewhere out there.

RATNAM: I think this happens in most parent–child relationships. When a child feels guilty about doing what she thinks is wrong, it is easier to go to the lenient parent, where she can hug him and it's forgotten, whereas with the mother, she knows that there's a little more work involved. She knows that she has done something she shouldn't have done. And she knows the mother too well, that she's not going to let it pass. Every kid knows which parent will not let things pass, so it's an automatic instinct to have one person on your side, to reach for that first, and then be ready for the battle which will go on for the next month, or two or three.

So this scene is about what happens logically within the family. It is not meant to draw too much attention to the child's confusion about mothers. The relationship between this mother and daughter has been like that right through—the stricter mother who's actually fonder of the daughter, and the father who's more ready with affection and then goes about his life. If you look at the relationship between husband and wife, he's the one who writes. He writes about social issues. But she's the one who has to push him to convert one of his writings—about this abandoned child—into action. She's the one who actually acts upon his thoughts. For him, the moment he theorizes about something and writes about it, he's found a solution to it. It's out of his system. Whereas she asks him, 'Is that all there is? Is it only about writing?' She's the doer in that family, converting what he preaches into action.

RANGAN: There's a nice bit of irony that Indira is the one who urges Thiruchelvan to adopt Amudha, and she marries him to facilitate this. And yet, she's the one, later, in danger of losing her status as mother.

RATNAM: But she is the one Amudha comes back to in the end. The bond there is a very strong one. And it's a micro-form of the bigger problem, isn't it? This is within a family, the turmoil that happens due to an 'outside child' who's come into the family. And similarly, a group of outsiders comes into a nation and there's all the turmoil that happens there. One is at the micro-level and the other is at the macro-level.

RANGAN: Aha! So you *do* think along sub-textual lines. It's just that you like

---

'When you read about those who go on a journey, the reports invariably talk about meeting people in forests, in camps within those forests.'

to brush it off when other people do the same with your work.

RATNAM: Hah!

RANGAN: The part about Indira instigating Thiruchelvan, that entire flashback, is easily one of the most wondrous passages of film you've done.

RATNAM: I think it gets highlighted because of where it is placed. If you take that piece out from the middle and start the film with it, it'll just be a platform to build a story. But because it comes in the middle of a dense story, at a different emotional plane altogether, in a different rhythm, it comes as a breath of fresh air.

RANGAN: That may be true the first time you see it, but that passage works just as well the twentieth time. I think it's more than just about the platform.

RATNAM: Okay, I'll take the compliment.

RANGAN: Did you have any particular reason for the child being nine when her father tells her about the adoption? I remember that the film got a lot of criticism about this aspect, especially from people working in the adoption circles.

RATNAM: And they were right. Ideally, you don't reveal something like this at one go. You reveal it very, very gently, starting when they are four or five. It's best that they know the truth from you instead of learning it from somewhere else. As a parent, it could be difficult, sometimes, to bring up this issue and break the news. Sometimes the kid will not listen. You might have told them, but it never really registers. In some form, they just block out the news. For the sake of the story, we had to compress a few things and put them into one scene, something that could have happened over two or three years. You reduce it to one moment that brings the drama out, and then you get on with the rest of the story. But yes, they advise you to tell the child as early as possible.

RANGAN: First, when Amudha is an infant, we see her birth mother outside the room with the cradle, through the bars of a window. And when Amudha grows up and runs away, her parents come to the same room and look out of the same window. Only this time, it's Amudha who's outside. It makes sense that we see the child exiled through the same window we saw her exiled birth mother earlier. Is it just the fact of shooting in the same room, or is there something else to this repeated image?

RATNAM: Do you want me to give you a cinematic answer or a very practical, honest answer?

RANGAN: Oh, anything. Preferably both.

RATNAM: Sometimes, you have to shoot

'When a child feels guilty about doing what she thinks is wrong, it is easier to go to the lenient parent, where she can hug him and it's forgotten, whereas with the mother, she knows that there's a little more work involved.'

bits and pieces at different locations and link them visually without anybody knowing that you have done that. The first shot of the window was taken in the set of the refugee-camp that we erected in Rameswaram. The second shot, of the child looking out at the sea, was filmed at Dhanushkoti. The room wasn't there. It was back in Rameswaram, where there was nothing outside the window. If the parents had looked outside, they wouldn't have seen anything but bushes and buses passing by, whereas we wanted them to see the child looking out across the sea, where she feels her mother is, her motherland is, her people are, where she belongs, not here but somewhere there. It was very important to link the two moments, the birth mother seeing the child and going away, and Amudha looking across the sea.

You can link the two in any way you want. We could have seen the girl through a doorway, for instance. But we felt that the window was the link that made sense. We needed to have that one image—through the window—to get that scene across completely. So we built a replica of the wall with the same window from Rameswaram, transported it to Dhanushkoti, near the sea, and shot it. There was this open space in which there was just this wall, and we shot the scene through that wall's window. Both the exteriors—the exterior shot of the Sri Lankan mother leaving the child and the one in the present, when the writer and his wife see their adopted child looking out at the sea—were shot close to each other on the Dhanushkoti beach. Making that wall with the window and carrying it with us was worth it as it could be amortized over two scenes.

RANGAN: Did you shoot any part of the film in Sri Lanka?

RATNAM: Not with actors. We had to pick up shots of the car on the road, some long shots. A day's work. The camera crew went and did it.

RANGAN: You don't usually shoot in foreign locations, do you? Even for songs. Unless your story itself is set, for instance, in Turkey, in the case of *Guru*.

RATNAM: There's no rule. *Guru* was shot there because that's where the story took us. I don't go to foreign countries to shoot songs and come back. As it is, songs stand out in a film. And to shoot in foreign locations with totally out-of-context things happening would make the song pop out even more. It draws too much attention to the song, to the fact that the song is an external element. I'd rather have it blended inside the story in the location the story takes place.

RANGAN: This is a very practical answer. I was hoping you'd give me a more patriotic reason, something like, 'Why should I go abroad when there are so many great locations right here in my own country?'

RATNAM: I don't think patriotism needs to be carried into the way you shoot songs. I am a very practical man.

RANGAN: The redness of that auto outside the church is striking. Coming from Chennai, we expect our autos to be yellow.

RATNAM: The auto is there to give the hint that they were following this family, that they didn't just come by later and conveniently meet up.

RANGAN: How easy or difficult was it to get into the mind of the Sri Lankan characters, like the old man, the caretaker of the temple, who refuses to join the mass exodus from his village? Suffering, of course, is universal, but how did you go about lending this suffering a specific Sri Lankan flavour?

RATNAM: None of these are cooked-up stories. Most of them are incidents that happened or could have happened, drawn from anecdotes in Sri Lankan literature and magazine articles, or from stories and poems about the troubles in Sri Lanka. They're practically snippets from real life. Even the poetry Thiruchelvan recites when he is being dragged away was not written by us. It is Sri Lankan Tamil poetry. These people are a cross section of normal human beings in Sri Lanka. The glimpses had to be as genuine as possible, not made-up and larger-than-life for the girl's sake. It had to be real and it had

222 *Conversations with Mani Ratnam*

'The first shot of the window was taken in the set of the refugee-camp that we erected in Rameswaram.'

to be hurting enough, impactful enough to show their agony, what they've been going through over the years in various parts of the country.

RANGAN: Did you always have Nandita Das in mind to play the Sri Lankan representative?

RATNAM: Yeah, she was the first one we asked for that role.

RANGAN: Thiruchelvan, on stage in Sri Lanka, says that a writer should be driven by the zeal that he should write the story better than anyone else can or will. ['*Naama ezhudha pora kadhayai vera yaaraavadhu innum sirappa ezhudhuvaangala-nu paakkanum.*'] Is that an extension of you, your film-making philosophy?

RATNAM: That is Sujatha's line. Not mine. That speech was completely written by him. Maybe he felt that way.

RANGAN: The walk-and-talk discussion between Madhavan and Prakash Raj is shot in the calm open, amidst grass swaying in the breeze. There is the practical reason, of course, that at the end of the talk, they have to run into the group of insurgents. Is there anything else?

RATNAM: When you read about those who

go on a journey, the reports invariably talk about meeting people in forests, in camps within those forests. These meetings don't happen in conventional places like a tea shop or a restaurant, but in places out of the common man's sight. The northern part is a more difficult terrain, and they were able to go on that journey only because they had a Sri Lankan along to take them in. Even when the scene was on paper, it was conceived like that, so that the next thing that happens doesn't come out of the blue. The background gives you the sense of a journey to the darker side.

RANGAN: Like a *Heart of Darkness* kind of scenario.

RATNAM: Yeah.

RANGAN: Thiruchelvan, for all the fire in his writing, seems at heart the kind of artist who experiences anguish more than anything else, at least at this point. You did say that his wife was the stronger person. The serenity of this scene suggests a man railing against fellow man while Nature watches calmly. And then he runs into the insurgents and he bursts into a Tamil poem to prove that he speaks their language. This is a hyper-realistic moment in a so-far understated narrative.

RATNAM: I think he's the kind of character who could slip into that mode. He was Tamil, he was a writer, and he was passionate about it. So instead of saying, 'I am a Tamilian' and logically trying to convince them, he uses poetry, which is a heightened form of emotion. The arrogance of him is in saying that I'm not just a Tamilian by birth but by mind, by thought, by consideration. I know as much or more about the issue than you do. I am a part of it in some form or the other. That's what poetry does. In four lines, it's able to capture something much more than what can be said by much lengthier prose or dialogue. It's the easiest way for him to say, 'I am one of you. I am your reflection on the other side.'

RANGAN: So in a sense, he's a descendent of Rishi in *Roja*, who responds to his captors with a 'Jai Hind!'

RATNAM: Rishi is a common man, like you and me. You or I could say something like that. But this is a heightened response and he's saying it at a much more elevated plane.

RANGAN: Are you saying that the emotion here is more elevated than in the case of Rishi?

RATNAM: There, it was just defiance. He's just defying the enemy. He could have just as easily uttered a swear word. Here, what the writer is trying to say is the opposite. He's not defying them. He's trying to say something that sinks into them so that they realize that he is like them.

'The Sri Lankan issue has been happening in our backyard for so long. You see various shades of it.'

RANGAN: In the elaborate action sequence at the end, Thiruchelvan is again a passive onlooker, protecting his wife and daughter more than anything else. Did you toy with the idea, if only for commercial considerations, that Madhavan should grab a gun at some point?

RATNAM: And what would he do? Who would he shoot? He probably would write a detailed description of the guns and where they were first made and under what circumstances gunpowder was invented, etc. He is a writer. I doubt that he has ever held a gun. This action sequence is not about war, saying that we are on one side and they are the enemy. It's about the people on the island. There are bullets coming from both sides and this ordinary man could be shot by either party. The people who are getting wounded are the people in between, who are in no way connected to the war. The crossfire they're caught in is what we're trying to show. You don't say that this is an elaborate action sequence with a hero and you have to milk it. It's not that. Just protecting his family is heroic enough. I feel very happy about the way we staged the action. The fact that you feel you're in the midst of it, you feel you're with them in the crossfire—that's the story at this point.

RANGAN: I was looking at this more from the viewpoint of, say, *Anjali*, where you told the story you wanted to, but also had your star-value hero—Prabhu—flex his muscles and give the audience the sight of a star doing starry things.

RATNAM: But even in *Anjali*, I didn't think of it in that sense. For me, Raghuvaran was still the hero of the film. If he had gotten caught in that situation, he would have done nothing. There's no way he would get into a fight and solve the whole problem. There was this person who was a convict, who had come out of prison and had a dark life, and he's the one in the fight. I didn't think that that was a big commercial sacrifice or that here I've matured beyond that.

RANGAN: I don't think that that was a commercial sacrifice either—just that it was done well in a way that gratified a certain expectation of the audience. The concept of an action scene is ingrained in us, and when we see it unfold through someone we identify with, like the hero, it resonates more.

RATNAM: Yeah. I know.

RANGAN: Despite the eventual turbulence—and even the existing turbulence—you begin the film with a very peaceful song, a song of hope, *Vellai pookkal*.

RATNAM: It's almost like saying that this is the way it should have been or it could have been, with a sense of peace, calm, a settled quality. This is what their life is

'Because the flashback comes in the middle of a dense story, at a different emotional plane altogether, at a different rhythm, it comes as a breath of fresh air.' Madhavan and Simran.

'The umbrella was a motif. It was a concept that conveyed a sense of shelter, as a family or as a country.' Nandita Das, Keerthana, Madhavan and Simran.

like till trouble comes to their homes. So it is both their past and their future. It is both what used to be and what could be (or what one hopes it would be). And if you're going into the troubles through the girl's eyes, that is when you want the unrest to be felt, not right at the beginning, before she enters the film. That's why we first show a marriage. It looks peaceful. But within that peace, there is this conflict that creeps into an ordinary, simple life.

RANGAN: You continue to play the song even when they're on the storm-tossed ship.

RATNAM: It's also an inner thing. The turmoil can be played in two ways. One is to play to the drama of the turmoil—the external thing. Another is to play up the hurt that runs deep inside. It's almost as calm as water, but it is still hurt. It is so deep that the ache of the parting just settles in like that. In a way, it is a counterpoint to peace. There is this tranquil thing, but it has a lot of hurt and agony beneath.

RANGAN: The lyrics also point to this being a song of hope—white flowers blooming and little children waking up.

RATNAM: It was conceived as a song of hope. The imagery of vellai pookkal [white flowers] itself gives a sense of peace. It's what starts the film and finishes the film. It's for the peace of yesterday and for the peace of tomorrow. It is what everyone wishes would happen.

15

'The railway station is a better place to get a sense of farewell'

Aayidha Ezhuthu/Yuva (2004)

Lallan/Inba (Abhishek Bachchan/Madhavan) is a goon hired to assassinate the local do-gooder Michael (Ajay Devgn/Suriya), and the attempt on a bridge is witnessed by Arjun (Vivek Oberoi/Siddharth), who finds that his self-centred plans of fleeing his problematic country for the conveniences of America isn't going to be as easy as he had imagined, and that the first sign of a good citizen is the willingness to get your hands dirty.

BARADWAJ RANGAN: Remakes are common in India. Directors have not only remade films by other directors, they've also remade their own films. But making two films in two languages at the same time is fairly unusual, the exceptions being films like *Chandralekha*.

MANI RATNAM: No, *Chandralekha* was dubbed, I think. Or maybe it was partially remade. But *Yuva* was not planned as a bilingual. It was planned, first, as a Hindi film and we shot about 70 per cent of it. We were shooting the climax, when we had this accident with Vivek Oberoi on the bridge. His leg was broken and he was laid up for a few months. We were toying with the option of a Tamil version. I'd talked to both Suriya and Madhavan, roughly saying that I was thinking of something like this. But I wasn't too sure I'd be able to go ahead and do it. But when this accident happened, there was a three- to four-month gap in the shooting schedule. I asked them whether they were interested. The story was about three people. It was in three sections. Each actor was required only for a limited number of days. So we could shoot the Tamil version in that gap, while Vivek was recovering, and then we completed the Hindi version.

RANGAN: Does the option to make a bilingual present itself because you can get more mileage out of the same script—twice the bang for the same buck, so to speak?

RATNAM: See, I don't think I'll ever do a remake. Once a film is over, I don't think I'll have the passion to make it again. But the thing is, if I did only the Hindi version, the gap between my Tamil films increases greatly, or if I did only Tamil, the gap between the Hindi films increases tremendously—unless they get dubbed, the way *Guru* was dubbed in Tamil. The trouble with dubbing is that after some time, it becomes clear that it's a dubbing. There are things which don't really stand up. So here was a possibility, of making a bilingual. I was hesitant. I was not too sure I'd be able to pull it off. But this accident with Vivek opened that door. That's how we jumped into it. If *Yuva* had gone as per schedule, I don't know if I'd have had the energy to do it all over again in Tamil.

RANGAN: But you said you'd talked to Suriya and Madhavan even earlier.

RATNAM: I didn't want to do the films simultaneously, the way I would end up shooting the two versions of *Raavan*. When I wrote the film, it was meant to be in Hindi. The film needs three young men, but I wasn't getting the cast I wanted. The casting of Abhishek and Vivek was done, but I didn't get the right person for the role that Ajay Devgn eventually played. So I thought I'd see if the casting would fall into place if I did a Tamil version. That's how I ended up talking to Suriya and Madhavan.

It's a city-based story. It could easily

be relevant here [in Chennai], because politics is such an integral part of student life here. People are conscious of it. And it's from here that my story really came up. Actually, the story of Suriya's track was something that had been in my mind for a long time. It's based on a real-life incident, and I was looking to make a film out of just that incident. Similarly, Madhavan's story could have easily been a film of its own. That's also a graph I'd worked out as a totally independent script. It's only when we came up with something that could connect all of them—with the possibility of looking at three different ways the youth of India could go—that it got compressed into one form.

RANGAN: So you just took those individual stories and connected them.

RATNAM: Yeah. One of them thinks he can change society. There is another who thinks you can use society for what it is. And there's a third person who is indifferent, who just doesn't care. We all operate, in some way, within these three moulds. Some of us are all three at different times, some of us exhibit two of these shades—but we have these streaks in us. So I tried to bring them all together and see what happens. I had two independent stories already chalked out, and the third one—Vivek's and Siddharth's story—was the story of any kid today, who thinks of going to the US. If there's a problem, he avoids that path and takes the next path. He thinks he's cool. He doesn't want to sweat it out.

RANGAN: He's a *'vellakaaranukku kooja thookara'* case [the white man's bootlicker], in other words. That's a really funny line.

RATNAM: That's Sujatha's.

RANGAN: Is there a cost benefit to making bilinguals?

RATNAM: Not really in this case. It's like making two completely individual films. The Hindi version was shot in Calcutta. The Tamil version in Chennai and Bombay. The film needed to be set someplace where politics and student movements go hand in hand. For *Yuva*, I thought it should be Delhi or Calcutta, two places where politics is a part of student life. It definitely couldn't be Bombay. Calcutta seemed more attractive because not many films have been shot there—and it had the most fantastic-looking bridge. The bridge was the central element in all the three stories.

RANGAN: There are bridges in *Roja* and *Raavan(an)* as well. Is this another visual motif you are drawn to, like rains and mirrors and trains?

RATNAM: I wish I could say that the bridge is a connecting device and that it links two viewpoints or characters, but in actuality—when you don't want to intellectualize everything—it is like a stage. It isolates the players and gives them a frame to perform in. Maybe it is a fantastic visual device on which to picturize a crucial action.

RANGAN: What portions of the Tamil version did you shoot in Bombay?

RATNAM: Just one week before the shoot, we realized that we were not getting the permissions to shoot freely in the location we wanted—the dockyard, the fishing harbour where Inba lives. So with very little time left, that entire portion had to be shot in Bombay. His house was created in Mukesh Mills, near the fishing harbour in Bombay. That's the strange thing about cinema. Something is supposed to happen in Chennai, but we end up shooting it in Bombay, because that's where we could simulate the look we wanted.

RANGAN: What about something like *Raavan(an)*, where you shot both versions in the same jungles? Is there a cost saving then?

RATNAM: There may be a bit of cost saving in that case. But even there, there are other things that go against it. The trouble you go through with two versions is a lot. Purely in economic terms, it might make sense if someone very efficient and quick does it. But if you're trying to make it work on all counts, pushing it to the edge and working with different sets of actors and trying to get different dimensions for the same situations, then it doesn't really work that way. Our structured union rates vary drastically if it's a bilingual. It shoots up your shooting cost and makes it absolutely unrealistic to venture into. If a film is based elaborately on one set, a huge set, then it kind of amortizes itself over two versions. But if you're going to shoot in real locations, then it doesn't make much sense.

RANGAN: There are a few differences between the Hindi and the Tamil versions that are quite intriguing, and I'd like to ask you about some of them. For instance, when Inba returns from jail and his wife prepares to leave with him, her mother says that her father will disown her if she leaves. And she pleads, '*Sabikkaadheenga ma.*' [Don't curse me.] Whereas in *Yuva*, she just hugs her mother and leaves. There's no dialogue. That casual colloquial colour is missing.

RATNAM: Tamil is the language I write in, so it is easy for me to put this emotion into words. In Hindi, if I'm not able to get the equivalent of those words with the writer, if it doesn't ring true, if it's too heavy a word, then I let it go. The same girl can react in different ways. One way of shutting up someone who is predicting bad things is to just show affection and go away. Rani is the kind of character who can do that very easily. She's the same person. To me, it's just two sides of the coin of dealing with a

Aayidha Ezhuthu/Yuva 231

SCENE 24   COLLEGE CANTEEN

Michael is explaining physics on the canteen table. He has a group of students who watch him with rapt attention.

        MICHAEL: அதுக்கு 50 வருஷம் இருக்கு super string theory அப்பா நான் உனக்கு உபதேசம் பண்றேன்.

He clears his table of tea cups and uses it as black board - He hands over his glass to Radhika who is standing close by and continues.

        M: **Universe**-ன் இருக்கும் அத்தனை Matter-ம் எங்கே இந்த பஞ்சபூதங்கள்ல தான் தாங்க - மண், தண்ணீர், ஆகாயம்.

Michael gives his friends a free lesson in the canteen in an early draft of the screenplay for Aayidha Ezhuthu.

person. I am quite happy with the way I could convert the 'sabikkaadheenga ma' into the hug. I think it is an imaginative equivalent.

RANGAN: You're saying that the bilingual aspect allowed you to indulge in both options. Because, when you're writing a screenplay and there are two options, you have to make a choice, whereas with a bilingual you can have it one way in Tamil and the other way in Hindi.

RATNAM: Even if you're doing the film in a single language and you want to do it one way, if the actor is not comfortable or if it doesn't ring true or come through convincingly, then you have to quickly come up with something else. You do it all the time. The emotion in what we're trying to say is the same in both. This emotion could be expressed through words, it could be expressed through action, or through a look. So it's not that I got this opportunity because I was doing two films. It's just that you may not have seen the other option had it been a single film. Here we see the other option too.

RANGAN: Here's a difference that doesn't involve dialogue. When Lallan [in *Yuva*] walks into his brother's house after the latter has been beaten up and is quivering in a corner, he's shocked. Whereas Inba [in *Aayidha Ezhuthu*] seems very matter-of-fact, even a little amused.

RATNAM: I don't know. I have to see it again. See, that is the first time he is getting into this business. He thought that his brother was this big shot, and now he sees that this brother is not invincible, that something like this can happen even to him. The brother is shocked, shaken, and Lallan/Inba actually steps into his shoes. This is the transition point for a character who has so far been running errands. He is taking the next step, which happens all the time with those kinds of characters. It is a transition, and we tried to do it that way in both languages. So if Madhavan comes through the way you say, then one of us, either Madhavan or me, must have had a bad day.

RANGAN: There are also tiny touches like the woman behind [the slimy politician] Bharathiraja—his wife presumably, who is always holding a tumbler of coffee. She's not there behind Om Puri's equivalent character.

RATNAM: I think that's an advantage of doing it the second time, after we'd finished it in Hindi. You get a chance to embellish some scenes. Bharathiraja brings an earthiness to the part, a very rustic feel, and so we could add something normal to his background.

RANGAN: It's a brilliant performance, really. It's so raw . . .

RATNAM: I thought so too. But I felt he was a bit unhappy with me and the role. I think he probably wanted a bigger launch or something like that. But it was wonderful to have him. I think he was playing a role after a very long time and took a bit of time to warm up, but after that he made the character alive. There was this earthiness to him and we could keep pushing it. We tried to do it with Om Puri too. Om's a very good actor and it's very easy to work with him. The fact that he's inhaling steam under a towel and giving instructions... Major decisions were made during minor domestic activities. We could do things like that. But with Bharathiraja, it was easier and more fun because of the Tamil ethos. There's this air of a rural man who's come here and made it big in the city. It was very easy to show that with him. Also, we have a common language—so it becomes easier. That's how all those additions happened.

RANGAN: Like that docile wife behind him.

RATNAM: We don't know if she's docile. We don't know what happens later.

RANGAN: The threat of rustication to Suriya is issued in the library, while Ajay receives his threat in front of a notice board.

RATNAM: One was shot in Calcutta, the other in Chennai. The thing that's nice about this is that the geographies are different. So it was not like we could do the same thing in another language. We had to recreate it at a place which would be visually interesting and which would make the scene work. It gave us the liberty to improvise and take it further.

RANGAN: Suriya's act of aggression is in blocking the water lorries on the bridge, but Ajay, in the equivalent scene, gets involved in a good, old-fashioned chase.

RATNAM: The episodes were drawn from what had happened in real life, so they would have influences that represent something that had happened in these cities at that point in time—this makes it look like they are rooted there. We tried to bring in whatever was local in Calcutta to fit into the Hindi film. Water lorries, of course, are an indispensable part of Tamil Nadu.

RANGAN: There's one scene that's strangely absent in the Hindi version—the wonderful bottle-breaking scene that shows that Michael and Inba are evenly matched. Due to the absence of this scene, we do not get the same sense with Michael and Lallan.

RATNAM: We had the same episode in Hindi too. We started shooting it—it was done here, in Chennai. But we ran into a personal problem. Ajay's child was unwell, I think. He had to go and we couldn't really complete the scene. So we just moved on.

RANGAN: I thought you had this scene in

(Above) The spectacular songs and dances of Thiruda Thiruda.

(Facing page and above) Thiruda Thiruda, *a film in constant movement.*

(Above and next page) The modern urban family in Anjali, *in thrall to science fiction and special effects.*

(Above and facing page) Thalapathy, *a story of relationships with mothers, wives, friends, foes.*

(Top) Thalapathy. *(Above)* Husband and wife in Kashmir, in Roja.
(Facing page) Troubled outdoors and tranquil indoors in Bombay.

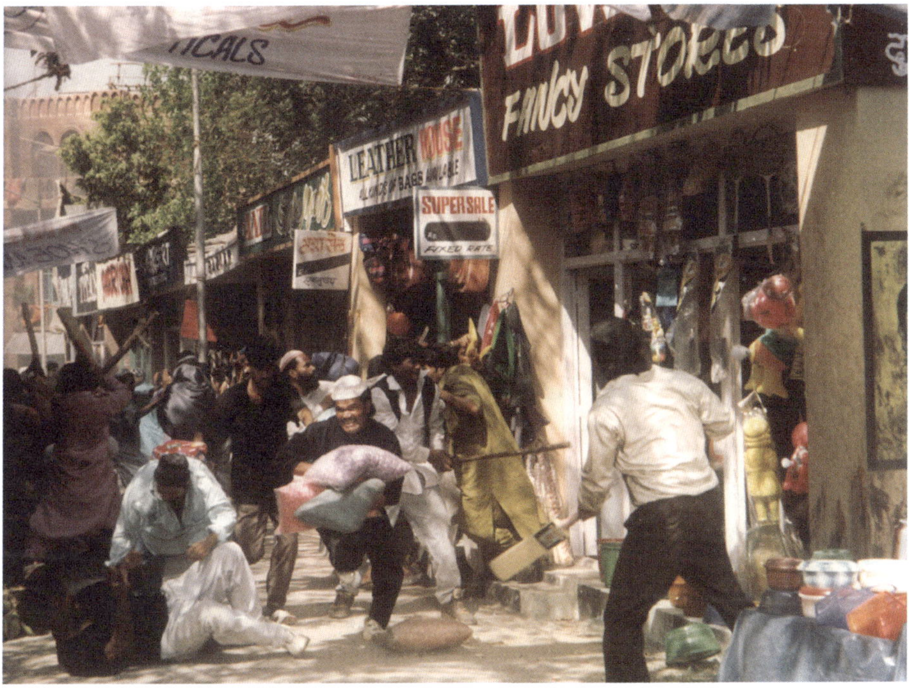
TICALS
LEATHER HOUSE
SUPER SALE
FIXED RATE
Fancy STORES

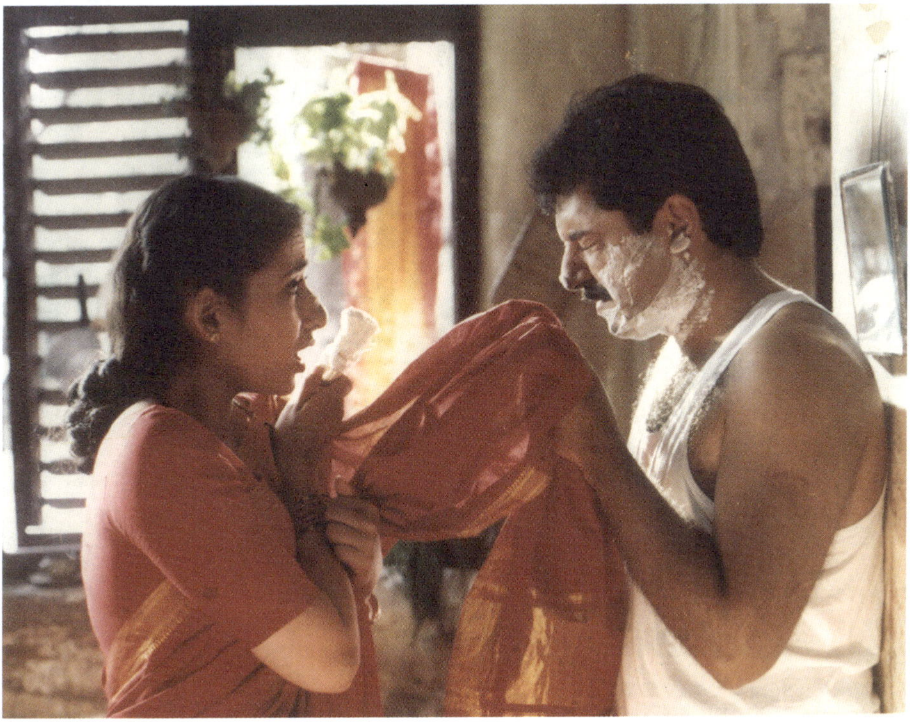

(Above) Two sides of the tragedy in Sri Lanka in Kannathil Muthamittal.
(Facing page) A child at home and in a strange land.

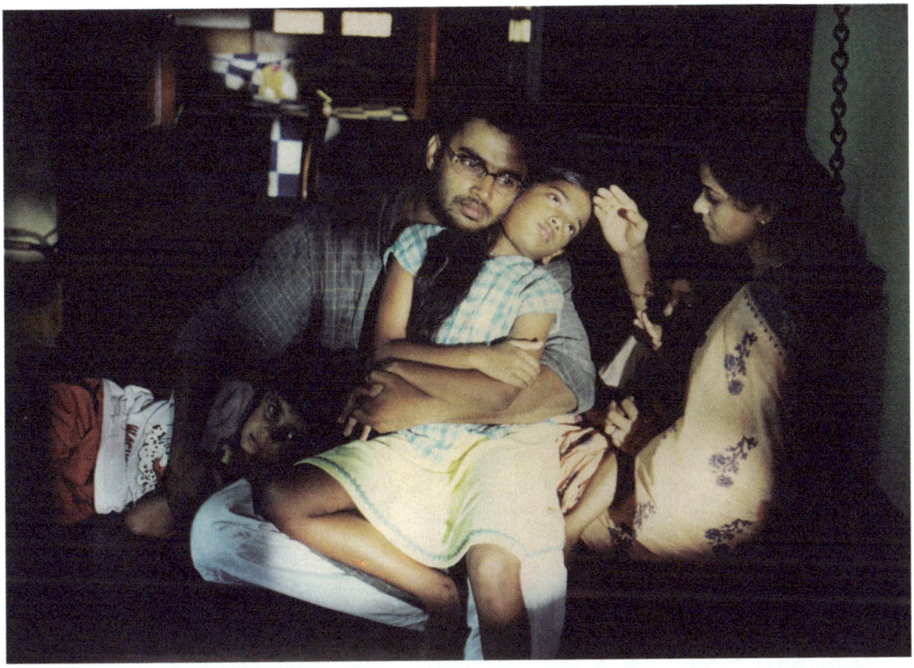

VILLAGER

VISIONARY

WINNER

A MANI RATNAM FILM

GURU

MUSIC A.R. RAHMAN LYRICS GULZAR CINEMATOGRAHY RAJIV MENON
ART DIRECTOR SAMIR CHANDA DIALOGUE VIJAY KRISHNA ACHARYA DIRECTION MANI RATNAM
PRODUCER MANI RATNAM / G. SRINIVASAN EDITING SREEKAR PRASAD
CHOREOGRAPHY SAROJ KHAN, BRINDA ACTION VIKRAM DHARMA AUDIOGRAPHY H. SRIDHAR

MADRAS TALKIES

www.guru-themovie.com   www.madrastalkies.com

SONY BMG
MUSIC ENTERTAINMENT

மெட்ராஸ் டாக்கீஸ்

A MANI RATNAM FILM

குரு

மணி ரத்னம் A.R. ரஹ்மான் வைரமுத்து

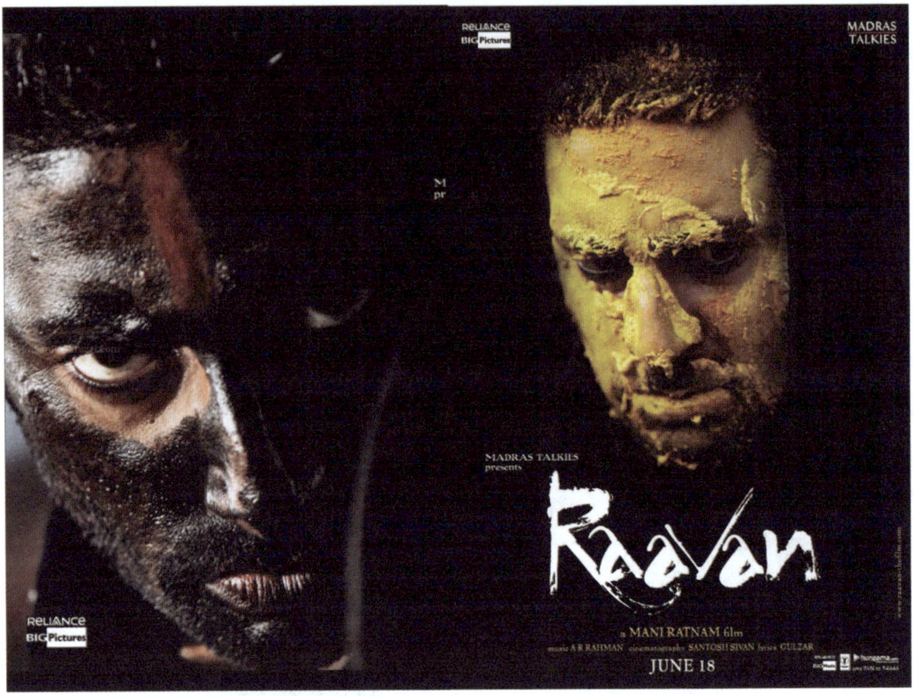
RELIANCE BIG Pictures
MADRAS TALKIES
MADRAS TALKIES presents
Raavan
a MANI RATNAM film
music A R RAHMAN cinematography SANTOSH SIVAN lyrics GULZAR
JUNE 18
RELIANCE BIG Pictures

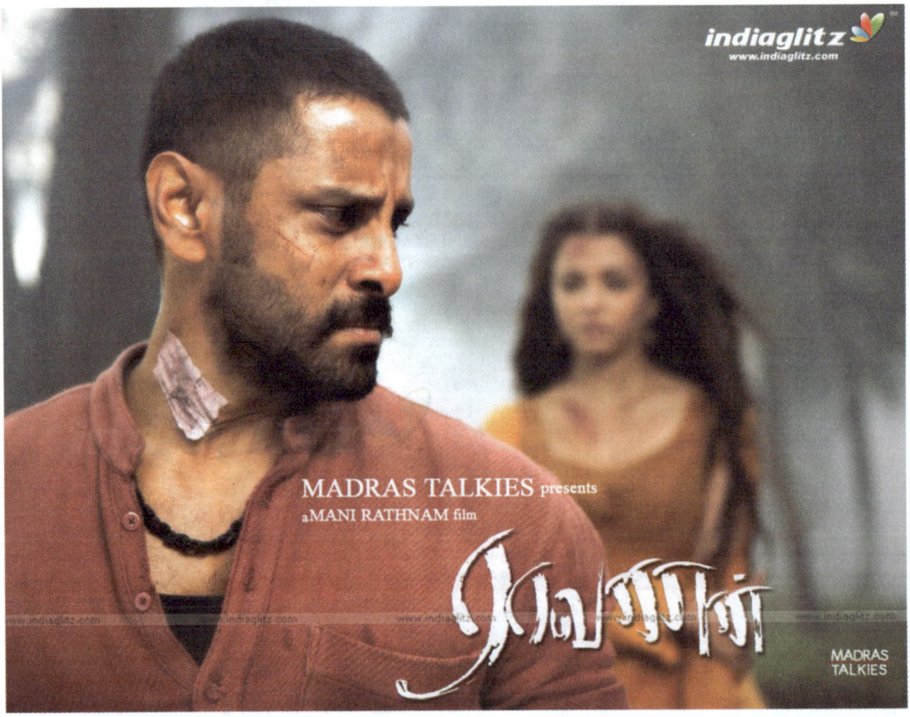
indiaglitz
www.indiaglitz.com
MADRAS TALKIES presents
a MANI RATHNAM film
ராவணன்
MADRAS TALKIES

(Above) Mani Ratnam directs Abhishek Bachchan in Raavan.
(Following page) Living by the gun in Yuva

Tamil because audiences here like displays of 'heroism' from their heroes.

RATNAM: They don't mind it in Hindi either.

RANGAN: That's my favourite scene of Madhavan in the movie. He really gets across this vibe of 'So okay, you beat me here, but I'm going to get you eventually.' Did you miss this scene in *Yuva*?

RATNAM: It's not the be-all and end-all. But it gives a flavour. It sets up two of your major characters against each other, directly. Also, we had finished Inba's story, and when we got to Michael's, it was good to have Inba make an appearance. This additional criss-crossing of characters makes the narrative more convincing.

RANGAN: Trisha and Siddharth have their farewell at a railway station (all the better for you to shoot your favourite trains), but Kareena goes to Vivek's house to say goodbye.

RATNAM: Ideally, the railway station is a better place to get a sense of farewell. The parting is very imminent. Whereas at home, it looks kind of static–it looks like they've enough time to change their minds. So it's easier to place the scene in a station. But getting permission from the railways and getting all the other things when you're doing a multi-track story becomes a logistical difficulty. So you tend to choose a different location. I can't remember why, but I think it's one of those reasons.

RANGAN: Siddharth steps away from the scene of Michael's accident because he's afraid that his passport will be confiscated. There's a wonderful dichotomy to this character at this instant, where he's just helped this man who was dying, but doesn't want that to affect his chances of going abroad. That's not there in *Yuva*.

RATNAM: I don't know why it's not there. Sometimes, it's because Hindi has a problem. In Tamil, we tend to speak briskly. We tend to finish scenes within controlled limits. In Hindi—I don't know if it's the language or the way it's spoken or both—the same scene plays out a little longer. And invariably, the rhythm of the film changes. The same film shot in Hindi ends up being about ten minutes longer. So it's a problem, sometimes. You have to make the Hindi version crisper by leaving out pieces rather than spoiling its rhythm by pushing it and deliberately making it pacy.

RANGAN: Are you saying that Hindi dialogues are usually longer compared to their Tamil equivalents?

RATNAM: You take any film that is being made from Tamil to Hindi or from Telugu to Hindi. It is always longer in Hindi. I think that the sentences are longer. Also, the way they say their lines and the pauses

Aayidha Ezhuthu/Yuva

they have, make it longer. I think Tamil is a language we tend to speak fast. Even in *Raavanan*, there are more dialogues than in its Hindi counterpart. But still the lengths of the two films are not all that different. With fewer dialogues in Hindi, we can still make it the same length as the Tamil version. But there's a definite difference.

RANGAN: In *Raavanan*, when the Sita character is kidnapped, someone from the enemy camp says specifically that she will pay for what's been done to their people. But in Hindi, the character just says that she will die (without the additional point about this being some sort of revenge). The Hindi version plays a little more abstractly—there's a little more mystery about the 'why'.

RATNAM: It's just the dialogues. The incident is so big—the woman has been kidnapped and is possibly going to be killed with a gun. Against that drama, this revelation is really a minor thing. We know that her husband is a cop and it's about something that he's done. That much is all that's going to be revealed.

RANGAN: So you didn't especially compress the lines in Hindi. Because you just said that the equivalent lines in Hindi usually come out longer.

RATNAM: It's not the length. It's just how it flows. Length is never a factor by which you decide things at the writing stage. That consideration comes later, predominantly at the editing table, where you might have to make it sharper.

RANGAN: Given the choice between making the films 'crisp' and making them the way you want them made—even if the latter means a few extra minutes—what would you choose?

RATNAM: I think the way I want to make the film includes the crispness. It's like a tennis racquet. It should have a certain tension. That tension cannot be sacrificed. The whole film works because of the details and the tension built into it. I can't just leave the tension a little slack to pack in more information. The idea is not just to share information; the idea is to tell a story in a particular framework.

RANGAN: And I guess not everyone who sees these two films is going to be doing this sort of frame-to-frame comparison.

RATNAM: But even if he does, it's fine. We never said they were the same film.

RANGAN: The last comparison. You end the Tamil version with the chant of '*Ini oru vidhi seyvom*', a clarion call for a new order. That's not there in *Yuva*.

RATNAM: Maybe they don't have the concept of *Ini oru vidhi seyvom*. The advantage of doing a film in a language

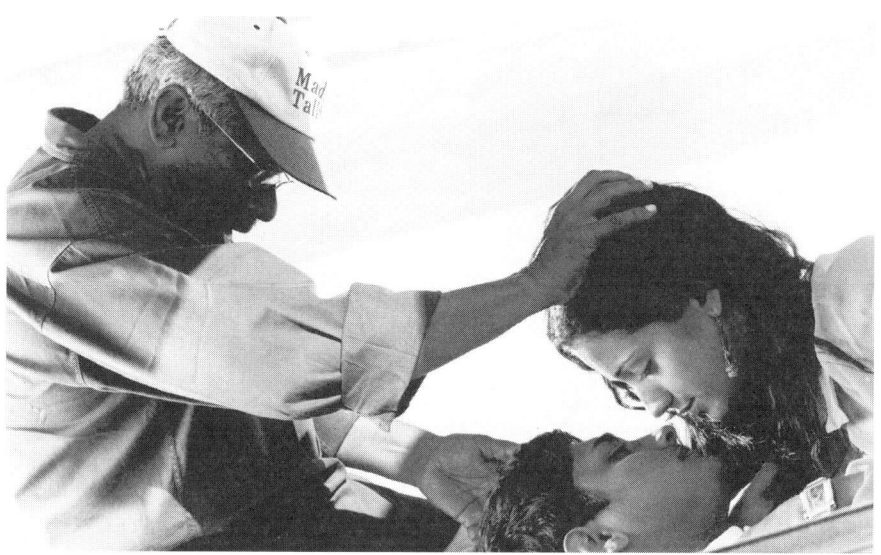

'No relationship is sacrosanct, and no one wants to be tied down to or bogged down by the system—especially when it comes to having a last hurrah.'

you are so familiar with is that you can use all the other forms of the language. Even in *Raavanan*, there is more poetry than in its Hindi version. In Hindi, they tend to tell you that it will look false, that it will look forced and deliberate to have something like that, whereas with Tamil, we know that that's not true. We know that the language has been around for so long that poetry gets into prose very easily without sticking out or going against the grain of the rest of the film. We could have looked for something similar in Hindi, but if it's not in the nature of the language to accommodate poetry along with prose, then you don't want to force it just because you're doing it in Tamil.

RANGAN: Who are 'they'?

RATNAM: The writer, the lyric writer, everybody.

RANGAN: Like you did with *Dil Se*, did you write this film in Tamil and English, and then have it translated into Hindi?

RATNAM: I wrote it in Tamil and English. Anurag Kashyap was the writer on *Yuva*. He came here. We sat down. He wrote a draft and he made whatever changes we wanted to make. I don't like to spoon-feed, really. As a rule, I don't want a word-for-word translation. I want it to be reinvented. I invariably gave him the gist and I always had a backup of what I had written for the Tamil version. If there was something that came out nicely in Hindi, I took that and inserted it in the Tamil version, and whatever I thought I'd lost from the Tamil version, I tried to make him bring that into the Hindi draft. We went back and forth a bit and got it right.

RANGAN: What do you think about the interval concept in Indian cinema?

RATNAM: I think it's fantastic. I love it.

RANGAN: A lot of film-makers complain about it.

RATNAM: I know. I know. We are so West-oriented that we think anything we do is bad. I think it's beautiful to have that structure if you're going to have a film that's two-and-a-half hours long. It's good to have a pause. It's good to gather your thoughts about what's happened, then come back and get on with the story. Our films have songs. They are long. If you have a ninety-minute film, then you don't need an interval. The structure has to be decided accordingly. You can't take this and that, and compare, really, in the same sense. They have grown up on Act 1, 2 and 3. That is their definition of screenwriting. It's like saying Indian classical music should have western structuring. It's not necessary.

RANGAN: Of all your films, I feel that this is the one where you struggled with the interval. You have the stories of two men before the interval. Afterwards, you have the last man's story, and, finally, the unification and culmination of these three stories. The culmination felt rushed.

RATNAM: Maybe. If the first-half–second-half structure has benefited you for so long, sometimes it has to give you trouble. There will be some stories that are not so easily amenable to a first-half–second-half structure. Then you have to see how to get around it. When you do it, you think you've cracked it. But if at the end of it you come and tell me that it is unbalanced, then maybe it's not been cracked correctly. It could have been done better.

RANGAN: What did you feel personally about this particular interval point?

RATNAM: It is a tricky narrative because it has these three stories and, in addition, the story of all of them coming together—so it has four parts. The interval was an issue. You try your best. I remember several versions of the script where we placed the interval at different points, and then we kind of landed on one which I thought was the best way to go about it.

RANGAN: What are the pros and cons of using live sound in India?

RATNAM: I think that's the way we should be going. The magic of the ambience

'Om's a very good actor. The fact that he's inhaling steam under a towel and giving instructions . . . Major decisions were made during minor domestic activities.'

adds something to the performance. The kind of layer we get from the atmosphere around the performance is so real that whatever we do, we cannot recreate it when we are clinically dubbing the lines. But unfortunately, with regional languages, not everyone speaks the language well. So we tend to use other voices. And when we try to mix the live sound with the dubbed voice (if you are just dubbing the voices of one or two characters), matching the two takes too much effort. In a dubbing theatre, you have the mic right next to your face and it's a different quality of sound altogether. The dubbed track becomes clinical and crisp and too clean. It stands out, whereas with live sound, you tend to mic it with the ambience there. It has a certain quality to it. *Aayidha Ezhuthu* was not an easy film for live sound. It was completely set on roads and not much in a controlled environment. But we had a very good sound engineer, Bob Taylor, and we kind of enjoyed the experience.

RANGAN: The reason I ask is that *Aayidha Ezhuthu* and *Yuva* were your first films with live sound . . .

RATNAM: That's right.

RANGAN: And there are some portions where you can detect a muffled quality to the voices, which has always been a problem with Indian films that use live sound—due to the noisy studios or whatever.

RATNAM: I don't think that that's the problem. I think we're too used to listening to dubbed voices that are recorded in the studio, without any of the real 'live' sounds alongside. The two of us are talking here, in this room, and there's an A/C machine running right now and there are birds outside. We can simulate these sounds, but the fact that our voices merge along with these sounds is what makes this conversation really alive, makes it irreplaceable. Dubbing makes it too clean and then we add the sounds of the A/C and the birds and the mush. Even that is okay. The problem comes when we have portions of a film in live sound and some other portions as a dubbed track—then it kind of jars. That is when you say some portions sound muffled because you are getting used to the clinical sound. If you have a predominantly live track, you won't hear the noise, which is how it is in a western film. When everything is merged, you don't notice it. It's only when something is too crisp that you tend to think of the other sound as noise.

RANGAN: In the scene where Janakaraj and Suriya are at the station, waiting for Esha's train to arrive, you get a sense of the dialogue, but probably not every word. Is this deliberate sound design to mirror the chaos in a station or is it a case of the 'live' ambience overpowering the dialogue?

RATNAM: As far as possible, you want your dialogues to be clear. You don't make an effort to make them unclear. I don't want the audience straining to listen to what the characters are saying. But at the same time, I don't want to spoon-feed them. I don't want to have subtitles running under the scene every time. You try to hit whatever is real, but predominantly audible. That is the balance you try to achieve. Sometimes you err on one side or the other, but you basically want it to be clear. That's your benchmark.

RANGAN: So you go for clarity over reality.

RATNAM: Every film-maker in the world will go for it unless it is built into the scene that the character doesn't hear something properly. You cannot cut away the ambience totally to bring out dialogue that's 100 per cent clear, but you try to hit a kind of balance. Even in the West, in the crowd scenes, they have people speaking but in hushed tones. The attempt is that the ear should catch what the eye catches. If you are able to focus on the main characters, the ear should also be able to focus on them. Even if you use live sound, that's what you do.

RANGAN: When we spoke about *Roja*, you said that you began with the capture of Wasim Khan to give the audience an inkling that this is where the narrative is headed. Is that the same reason you begin this story with the scene on the bridge,

'I'm fascinated with all three characters . . . If you take Siddharth/Vivek's character, he's so much like any of us. In the name of being chilled out, we avoid all problems.' Vivek Oberoi and Kareena Kapoor.

which is where all the three narratives will finally converge?

RATNAM: This is a very structure-driven script, a *Rashomon* kind of thing. The real narrative thread is the structure, the fact that there is one particular incident with three people involved. One is the cause, one is the effect, and one is the witness. And we go back to each one of them to see how they came to this point, and then we see the conclusion. So, logically, we have to have the converging point, and then go back individually to A, B and C. That was the narrative predetermined by the structure. That is how it was in the script.

RANGAN: The characters are coded through specific colours—red for Lallan/Inba, green for the Michaels, and blue for the Arjuns.

RATNAM: There were three stories and yet they were part of the same theme—three people from three walks of life. It was possible to treat each story in a different shade depending on where they were born and what they were made of. One was in browns and reds—basically someone who is really at the lower end of the social spectrum and with a certain amount of violence built into him. Ajay's track (as well as Suriya's track) is in green because they represent somebody who looks at the future, at ways of taking us into the future. And the other—the one in blue—is somebody who is cool, laid-back and chilled out, very today, not affected by anything. That is what we tried to represent. In fact, for a short while, I was even contemplating calling the film *Traffic Signal*. That was the working title we had, as there were three different colours.

The story allowed for a clear demarcation between the way each character's story was shot and cut. There were different kinds of lensing, different kinds of editing patterns used. The way Abhishek's and Madhavan's scenes are shot is kind of jerky, with a lot of hand-helds, and the way these scenes are cut is within the same axis—we just go closer and closer. We use concentric frames that go deeper and deeper. It's a cut that's not conventional. We get a glimpse of him and yet we don't have it. He's kind of elusive. Whereas with Ajay and Suriya, the scenes are more or less smooth. The shots are longer. There's no jerky cutting. The Vivek and Siddharth portion is really modern. It's a little psychedelic in the way it's shot, with fast frames and flares. It's a little more kinetic than the other segments. It's not classical. Rarely do you pick a subject that gives you a structure that lets you experiment with three different styles and merge them together. This was an opportunity to do a three-in-one kind of film.

RANGAN: There are scenes where we see the predominant colour of one character, but somewhere in the background there's also the colour associated with another character. The colours seem to come together like how the characters will eventually come together.

RATNAM: If you try to take this colour coding to the extreme, it will start standing out and interfering with the narrative. What you look at is the tone with which you're telling the story. You don't cut off everything else, but you try to steer it towards a particular tone. And in that, there will be leaks from other colours, which is good. Sometimes, it is these leaks that really make the primary colour stand out. You have some contrast. If you want the warm tones to come out, the blue has to be in the background. That's when the warm tone really feels correct.

RANGAN: So if there's a bit of blue behind the red, it's to emphasize the red rather than to hint at the character in blue.

RATNAM: Yeah.

RANGAN: In *Iruvar*, we discussed the possibility that you felt more for Anandan than Thamizhchelvan. Here, I walked away with the feeling that you liked Lallan/Inba more than the other two.

RATNAM: Actually, I'm fascinated with all three characters. Each of their stories could have been a full-fledged film. If you take Siddharth/Vivek's character, for example, he's so much like any of us. In the name of being chilled out, we avoid all problems. We don't want to face them. We want to float. We have a name for it and we wear it on our sleeves and go about our lives—till something is forced down our throat and we realize that beneath this exterior, inside each of us, there is still this normal guy. There is enough in that character to be able to study it in detail. Similarly, with Suriya's character, all of us are in the same place but a few are willing to look beyond. They have a vision, the conviction that they can change things. They are willing to take that step. They have the quality of a leader, the quality that makes people follow them. They have ideas and are able to convert their strength in one field—say, academics—into something that is practical. The merging of the intellectual with the practical world is amazing if you actually end up doing it. In that sense, all three were fascinating people.

RANGAN: Lallan/Inba is like a kid at the beginning, sulking when he loses in kabaddi. From there, he evolves into a very heartless man, killing his brother and abandoning his wife. In comparison, the other two characters are more straightforward. They don't undergo this dramatic a transition.

RATNAM: I think Lallan/Inba comes from a background that is drastic, compared to the other two guys who have the basics all sorted out for them. Their exercise is really more on an intellectual level, on an ideological plane, whereas Lallan/Inba is in survival mode. The path that he has to travel is very rough, harsh and drastic. We've left one segment of society far behind, or far below. So his issues and his growth are much more melodramatic than yours and mine. The reason for him doing something and not doing something cannot be understood at the same pitch as the reason for your doing something or my not doing something. And for him to rise beyond that and move to the next step is the transition the film is trying to trace.

RANGAN: I wasn't talking about the melodramatic aspect of his transformation so much as the choices he makes. He loves his wife so much and you think he cannot live without her, and then at the end, she doesn't figure in his calculations at all.

RATNAM: He has extreme reactions. His anger is extreme. His love is extreme. He is extremely passionate. When push comes to shove, he's willing to kill his brother, which you and I may never be able to do, and he is willing to let go of this woman who matters the most. His only driving force is his ambition. It is also about survival. If survival was possible any other way, then he'd love his woman, he'd care for his brother and repay him—but when survival itself is a question, then the other considerations seem to fade away.

RANGAN: Why does Inba bother to return the gun at the end? Why couldn't he just have left with his wife?

RATNAM: If he is trying to get out of a

certain way of living, returning the gun is his resignation letter. It represents his wanting to come clean and lead a straight life. The gun has always been an issue between him and his wife. The moment she found the gun, she knew that he was on the wrong path and that he was more dangerous than ever before. So giving it back is probably his way of reassuring her. He cannot just take it and go with her. Also, if you are reluctant to do something but are doing it for somebody else, you tend to push it and stretch it and live on the wild side a little longer. If he was going just because he had to go, he would probably have dumped the gun in a gutter and run away. But if he was going because of his wife, there would have been a tendency to cling on to his old life a little more.

RANGAN: This is Mani Ratnam BA, BL. You have this amazing ability to argue your way out of every corner.

RATNAM: Hah! Was I in a corner?

RANGAN: The *Dol dol* song is a burst of energy when it appears, the perfect anthem for Lallan/Inba. And its melancholic version—just the theme—is used superbly when he kills his brother. Did you ask Rahman for a song (that was later used as theme music) or for theme music (that was later converted to a song)?

RATNAM: We were shooting, and I'd gone to Rahman's studio in the evening. I told him I was looking for something that would define Lallan's character—a high-energy piece with which I could get his rhythm. I actually asked Rahman to give me a track, any rough scratch, for me to shoot with. When I landed up for the shooting the next morning, he'd sent this new rap track that he'd recorded the previous night. It was amazing, both the track and the speed at which it arrived.

RANGAN: Right from *Mouna Raagam* and *Agni Natchatiram*, you've shown urban youngsters making use of public transport—buses, trains, autos. And they do so here too. In the post-liberalization India of today, if you're twenty-five and somewhat well-off, you have a bike or a car. When you write these characters, are you still living in an idealized India of your youth—or even mine?

RATNAM: I don't think so. I see kids growing up in my family. I think they use public transport. If they want to do something they want you to have no clue about, then they have no qualms about getting into any kind of transport and getting away. When my brother's girls—teenagers—want to go somewhere, like Mayajaal [theatre], they take a bus and come back by bus. I'd be surprised. I'd ask them if they wanted me to send the driver. But they'd say no, and they'd manage by auto or bus. They don't want you to keep tabs on every movement they make. They want a little bit of independence and they find a way. They learn to exist between two

'Lallan has extreme reactions. His anger is extreme. His love is extreme. He is extremely passionate.' Rani Mukerji and Abhishek Bachchan.

worlds. And I think that's what's nice about India. However middle class or upper-middle class you are, there is this earthiness still left in the normal person. Maybe the degree has come down. But I think it still remains.

RANGAN: I love the casual lack of 'traditional Indian values' in Trisha and Kareena—engaged to one man and not having qualms about fooling around with another. Do you think you were able to get away with this because it was just one segment of the movie? I'm not sure that this kind of slippery-morals character would have worked across a whole film, that too as a heroine (from the audience-acceptance point of view).

RATNAM: Let me put it this way. I find it real. And I think that if it's real, it should work. I think that's the way a lot of youngsters are today, effortlessly so, and I think that a lot of people will identify with this. No relationship is sacrosanct, and no one wants to be tied down to or bogged down by the system—especially when it comes to having a last hurrah. There's nothing that excludes these characters from being in a full-fledged film. That's how you break the rules. Instead of being afraid of what the audience will or won't accept, if you show them something that's real and if you make them understand that, then they will accept it.

16

'The swing has a floating quality to it, like a dream'

Guru (2007)

Gurukant Desai (Abhishek Bachchan) returns from Turkey with plans of operating his own business, with capital raised from a hasty marriage to Sujata (Aishwarya Rai). Husband and wife leave for Bombay, where he finds himself stymied by the establishment. He realizes that a few rules need to be broken, even if that will invite the displeasure of his morally upright mentor, the newspaper publisher Manik Dasgupta (Mithun Chakraborty).

BARADWAJ RANGAN: Was this the first Indian film to be premiered at Toronto? It's a very Indian story. Perhaps it deserved a premiere in India.

MANI RATNAM: I have no idea. I'm really not much of a premiere person. We've grown up with Tamil films, where a premiere was never an issue. For us, releasing the film is the big issue. The red carpet is not the most important thing. But in Hindi, that's what they want to do, and the Toronto premiere did help *Guru*'s reception in North America. A big premiere gives you a chance to market the film, to take it across to the press. So you do it. It is your baby. You'll have to do anything that will help market the film.

Toronto was not my idea. These things are out of my purview. My job finishes at the point we get the prints the way we want. I'm not worried where it is premiered. That's just part of the marketing exercise. The people handling the overseas distribution took a call about where it should be premiered. Toronto turned out to be a very good idea because there are a lot of Indians there. Not too many films are premiered there, and this was done in a really big fashion. The turnout was really, really huge. And it was so close to New York that there was enough press coverage. The North American launch was covered very well. It was a good decision finally.

RANGAN: In many ways, *Guru* is a latter-day parallel to *Nayakan*—two people from small towns go to big, bad Bombay and battle the establishment through means not entirely legal. While writing *Guru*, were you aware of these similarities?

RATNAM: No. You're tracing a biopic kind of story...

RANGAN: And again, both films are biopics.

RATNAM: That's the only thing that binds the films together. I didn't really think that they were similar. If I'd thought of it that way, it would have taken away the enthusiasm about the project.

RANGAN: But Hitchcock made several films about a wrongly accused man on the run...

RATNAM: Hitchcock was a master. He could afford to do it. But unless I feel that it is something new, an area I haven't been to before, something that is happening in India in front of me, a transition that I can capture, it doesn't excite me. If you feel that it is a variation on what you've done, then the project starts with a dampener. It's like making a movie with a template.

RANGAN: I don't see it that way. If you treat four plot points like four dots, you could travel through them in a straight line, or you could weave in and out. We talked about this while discussing *Mouna*

Raagam, which is somewhat similar, story-wise, to *Nenjathai Killadhey*. As long as the journey is different, I don't think the similarity of plot points matters.

RATNAM: I know. Maybe. But it's all right to feel this at the end of the film, not at the beginning. If you start by thinking that *Guru* is a counter to *Nayakan*, then it doesn't get you much. It doesn't help you to be open to things.

RANGAN: So, in principle, if you start working on a film and after, say, four scenes it sounds similar to an earlier film, then you drop it.

RATNAM: Ideally, I should not even get to four scenes. Today, I met somebody at the gym. He said, 'Can I ask you a question?' I said, 'Yes'. He said, 'When will you make another film like *Mouna Raagam*?'

RANGAN: Did you kill him?

RATNAM: I told him, 'I hope never.'

RANGAN: Maybe he was asking, in a way, what I asked you a little earlier, about film-makers returning to certain storylines and situations and characters which may be encoded in their system. For instance, you could say that *Unaru* was your first 'angry-young-man' movie. Mohanlal's 'I-want-to-change-the-world' character is later found in Michael in *Aayidha Ezhuthu*/*Yuva*. It also has the trade unions from *Guru*, the unemployed youth from *Agni Natchatiram*.

RATNAM: I think all critics like to find films that they can bunch into one category and put under one chapter. You are trying to do exactly that. The character in *Unaru* was not really like that. He's an innocent guy, who comes into this city looking for a job and then gets caught up in these unions which are controlled by a few sleazy lawyers. He joins them and then slowly realizes what they are about, and then he rebels. I don't know where the connection to *Guru* or *Agni* comes in.

RANGAN: It's not that you're doing exactly the same thing over and over—just that there are echoes of earlier work in the later films. For instance, the class dynamics in the scene in *Thalapathy* where Mammooty, on behalf of Rajinikanth, asks Shobana's father for her hand in marriage harks back to the scene in *Pagal Nilavu* where Sathyaraj, on behalf of Murali, asks Revathy's brother for her hand in marriage. Even in *Guru*, you could say that there's a bit of the Lallan character from *Yuva*, someone from the wrong side of the tracks trying to make his way through an unsympathetic world.

RATNAM: I thought of *Guru* during *Yuva*, when I was thinking about the way we were emerging as a nation. When I was in school, Lal Bahadur Shastri had said that if every individual abstained from

'This scene in Guru *is out of a bhoomi pooja I saw in Keezhakarai. It's an image I was actually moved by.'*

eating one meal a week—Tuesday nights, I think—there would be that much more food available for the poor. This was the India that I grew up in, talking of abstinence, talking of doing something for the rest of your countrymen. It was a very important thing. And from that time, we have come to a stage where it's no longer an issue to say, 'I am more important. I'll take care of myself. The rest will automatically take care of itself.' And not in a negative way, but really saying, 'If I do well, then everything else will start doing well.' That transition in these thirty years is quite alarming. There are some people who still stand there, with the old stance, and there are some people way up in front, bending rules and doing anything with the thought that the results justify the means. I think we are still in the process of transition. A drastic change is happening in front of our eyes. I was trying to capture that.

RANGAN: And you felt that the Ambani story captured this transition.

RATNAM: I think that it represented one end of the spectrum. That story in itself is not the film. I couldn't have done it unless I had this peg of a newspaperman (Mithun Chakraborty) who is old-school, who believes in right and wrong. To me, that contrast is what makes it work. If I have to tell the Ambani story and I don't have this fulcrum, then it's just hanging in the air. It is this newspaperman who helps me tell the story, though I think it is subtle in the film. It brings out the contrast that this is where we were and this is where we are going, and the film takes these two statements across.

RANGAN: I think that did come across, because instead of a hero and a villain, we have the conflict between Old India (Mithun, whose newspaper, like India, is 'Independent' and New India (Abhishek). My favourite scene with Mithun is the one where he learns that Guru has been paralysed, and he has to take a decision about printing an article against him. To sympathize with New India, or crush it when the opportunity becomes available—that is the question before him. He's really fantastic here.

RATNAM: It's like taking a step against your own son. There is a conflict between what you stand for versus what you are bonded to, and one wins over the other. You take the step but it makes you sad. That is probably when he decides to go to the hospital to see Guru. It kind of puts him at a crossroads.

RANGAN: You begin the film in black and white, in the present, but then you switch periodically to black and white only to show the newspaper headlines.

RATNAM: All the newspaper portions that convert themselves into words and not into pictures—the accusations, the 'black-marking' of Guru, registering what the press can do by pegging somebody—were stylized in black and white. The black and white, by itself, is not significant. The fact is that a newspaper prints words. These newspaper statements are being made about him, and these words are like driving a nail into somebody's character, like a *chhaapa* [stamp]. Unlike today, where it's the television medium that dominates with its colour images, it was what was printed in black and white that mattered then.

RANGAN: In the black-and-white beginning, the protagonist alludes to his past with a mention of his father ['*Mera bapu kehta tha...*'] and then you cut away to a flashback. What does that one split second of Guru give you here, as opposed to beginning directly with the flashback?

RATNAM: When you are trying to trace one person's life, when the film isn't about a plot but a journey, it's good to know that after the journey, you've come back full circle. So it's better to mark the point at which you start, so that when you land back at the same place there is a sense of completion. It is more a device through which you can take off and land back.

RANGAN: You're basically hinting at where he is at the end.

RATNAM: Yeah. Structurally, this ties the film up together.

'He got exposed to a big setup in Turkey, and somewhere a dream took birth, and then he felt that he should be as big as that.'

RANGAN: This sort of thing, was it there in the screenplay? ('Scene 1: Begin with shot of Guru's final speech?') Or did it happen after shooting, while putting the film together?

RATNAM: Sometimes, it's in the screenplay. Sometimes, it evolves. You think at first that what's on paper is the right way, but as you work, you keep finding better opportunities and better ways of doing things.

RANGAN: It's also the fact that he refers to his *sapna* [dream], and the whole film thereafter is the realization of this dream.

RATNAM: Yeah.

RANGAN: I felt that there was another 'I-have-a-dream' moment when Guru alights from the train when he returns to India. The sun is rising—a new dawn for him, and for his country after Independence.

RATNAM: There was nothing symbolic there. It was just cold, logical timeline. Sujata escapes in the night. She tries to slip away when the early-morning train passes by. That morning shot with the sun was part of this flow of events, that's all.

RANGAN: Even though she's seen only at the beginning, Jhumpa—the Mallika Sherawat character—casts a shadow over the film. During the conversation in the hospital between Guru and Manoj Joshi's character, we realize that she was a huge part of their lives in Turkey.

RATNAM: We shot more of her than what ended up in the film. She was a slightly bigger character in the script. She was central to their lives in Turkey. She may have been the first woman they met who was different, who was ambitious—there possibly is a story with Manoj there. But when you're trying to get your film in as tight as possible, when you're doing a biopic kind of film, you have to give things up. This kind of decision to leave out a bit from the story or a character happens with every film. Sometimes you have to lose a few portions in order to make the other portions work better. Besides, if two people go back twenty-five years, thirty years, there are going to be things that they recall, especially in a moment of crisis or a moment very close to death. Things that were irrelevant. Things that bring laughter even at a very critical stage. So even if we didn't have her in the script, they could still share their memories of her. That's the only reason this part of the dialogue in the hospital is still left in the film, because it is very true of what happens in critical times.

RANGAN: I guess it's just like you couldn't show everything about Velu Nayakan's life in his biopic. I'm watching *Nayakan* again after watching all your films in a cycle, and it's fascinating to see your signature elements creeping into place—like the prelude with the little boy, the pre-titles sequence.

RATNAM: Actually, there's a prelude in *Pallavi Anupallavi* too. It is about Lakshmi coming back and finding her husband in bed with another woman, and that breaks the relationship.

RANGAN: We are introduced to Mallika Sherawat in *Mayya mayya*, and barely five minutes later, we are introduced to Aishwarya Rai through *Barso re*. Two fully picturized songs in quick succession. Songs, usually, are spaced out a lot more.

RATNAM: One is a prologue, almost, which winds up the pre-title portion. It portrays the Turkey part of Guru's life in a nutshell. It's not just his business activities—one, two, three, four—but his life, his attitude that the song tries to compress. A song is a very good way to get this time-transition done. Then we have the titles, after which they come back to India and we start with another character altogether. The entire tone is different. The look of the film changes. There are rains. It's a completely different spirit of joy, a contrast to the ambition that was there in Turkey. This girl is looking for freedom. It's two different kinds of people coming together. If you're confident of your screenplay, your narrative, I don't think you have to metrically position the songs. If

252 *Conversations with Mani Ratnam*

'The swing has a seamless, floating quality to it, like a dream. It brings across the vision with which the film starts and ends.'

there's an emotional motivation, then the first song registers as one chunk of narrative and the next song comes in as another.

RANGAN: If you had two songs in the background while 'narrative' events unfolded on screen, we wouldn't notice them being so close—but both these songs are explosions of choreography. To have two dance-heavy pieces barely minutes apart . . .

RATNAM: Did they intrude when you saw the film? They didn't intrude for me, so I left it at that. If you're going to have songs, it's better to have them with all their energy. A song is not just something you tick off, something you just add to make it, say, five songs in the film and fill the album. A song is a strong narrative device, and you're looking to use the energy that the song brings with it. It is not a compulsion that is thrust on you, but a special card that you hold in your hand. In a very short time, you get what Sujata stands for in the film. It tells her entire story—till she meets Gurukant Desai—in one form, in an absolutely complete manner. It says that Sujata is independent, free-spirited, determined, and that she had a boyfriend she was planning to elope with, but the boyfriend deserted her and she was stranded, not knowing if she should go back or forward. All this is in a nice, peppy song. To me, this way of using a song is much more effective.

Guru 253

That's what I like doing, instead of having the song unfold in the background, as if you're very apologetic about it.

RANGAN: In *Raavan*, too, there are two songs that come in quick succession, *Thok de killi* and *Kata kata*.

RATNAM: I think you watch films with a stopwatch. Anyway, when you work for so long on a script, you try to make sure that two successive songs are spaced out well and are not on top of each other, because this affects both songs, and results in pacing problems. But sometimes when you put the film together, you're surprised that the two songs come so close to each other—there are hardly two scenes between them—and still don't hinder the narration or look wrong. When I saw it on paper, I was not too sure. But it worked, so it's okay.

RANGAN: How did that scene of Guru's little girls singing *Jaage hain* by the bedside come about? The song is more like a theme. Was this rendition of the song a part of the screenplay, or was it like *Shauq hai*, a song that wasn't originally planned, but created as part of the background score and later used in the film?

RATNAM: A few months before shooting that scene, Charuhasan, my father-in-law, met with an accident in Paris. He was close to eighty, and he fell down the stairs in a restaurant. His bones were broken, he had a head injury—he was found in a pool of blood. He was admitted to a hospital nearby. Hasini had to go there (from here). She was with him for ten days. He couldn't remember anything. He didn't know who she was. He was hearing only French all around. They told her that unless she kept speaking to him, he might not get back his memory. Her elder sister came, and Charu didn't recognize her either. When Hasini came back, she told me about her experience. It was a process. She would sit next to him and sing Carnatic songs that she grew up with, in a hospital in Paris, and he would join her in the singing, and it was that kind of thing that brought him back to the present. Music was the first thing that came back to him and then slowly everything else followed. That was what I was trying to recreate.

So I was looking for a song that would be relevant in the Hindi milieu. If it was Tamil, we could have easily used one of the popular traditional songs. I worked with the writer Vijay Acharya and with Gulzar saab and realized that maybe we should record something new, not try to use something that already existed. Hospital permissions were difficult to get. We found a place, where we were going to shoot in a day or so. The previous day I called Rahman and told him about the scene. I told him that I wanted a song. He had done *Jaage hain* as a piece of background score, as a theme. (He had composed this element when he composed the other songs.) Then

'He didn't expect their relationship to be this good, and she—after being jilted—didn't at all expect to find somebody with whom she'd gel so well.'

we got Gulzar saab to write the lyrics then and there. We recorded it the day before the shoot. These kids, the twins who were acting as the daughters, came in the morning, and till afternoon, the only thing they had to do was learn the song. They were from Bangalore, I think. We just managed to scrape through the shoot.

RANGAN: That's a great story. The only issue I had was that this was a grown-up's song, an anthem, and it was odd to hear it from the mouths of kids. But I guess that's a level of reality films easily cross.

RATNAM: If the kids were to sing *Alaipaayuthey kanna*, would that mean they understood it? Music goes beyond that. You sing what you have learnt. The character does not have to come up with a song, compose a tune then and there, and sing it. Right in the beginning, when we composed it as a theme, it was conceived as a lullaby that Guru's father would have sung to him. And that is possibly what Guru sang to put his kids to sleep. So it's a song that they've heard before, which has been sung to them all their lives, and they're just using it now to try to connect with their father.

RANGAN: And after this song plays out, you cut to a very quiet, very brief shot of waves lapping by the Gateway of India. You yank the movie out of the story for a second, for an atmospheric shot, and then return.

RATNAM: The music was soaring towards the end. It was exploding into another zone. We needed it to die down. So we used the sound of the waves as a pause. It's really the music that drove us to get a bigger shot before returning to the story. It was the moment where the film was stepping into the final act. The pause kind of underlines it.

RANGAN: How would you explain a somewhat similar 'breathing space' in— let's say—*Raavan*? Beera's sister narrates what happened at the police station, and the next morning her lifeless body is pulled up from a well. And instead of cutting directly to Beera at the well, you show a sequence of events. He's woken up. The sun streams in. There's a wordless communication of tragedy. And then he runs through alleys before reaching the well.

RATNAM: The previous scene has her breaking down—it's an emotional peak. If we had jumped to another emotional peak right away, it would have affected the second peak. So we reach an emotional peak, and then we back off a bit, and then build it a little bit, and then show the second peak. When we have two peaks next to each other, it helps to have a valley between them. It's all there on paper. You're most aware of these things at the writing stage. When you write, when you see the way the film flows, you're looking at the film as a whole, almost like you're seeing a full cut. So you're aware of these things and we build them into the narrative. When you shoot, you're well inside the product. When you edit, again you're outside, and you can fine-tune the product.

RANGAN: I like the quietly poetic visual during the bhoomi puja for the factory, where Guru stands alone with the blueprints in the rain. There's an abstract quality to his feeling here, more than just the happiness of finally achieving his dream.

RATNAM: Very long back, when I was doing *Pagal Nilavu*, I'd gone with the producer to Keezhakarai for a marriage— just to see what Keezhakarai looked like. I had the feeling it would be an input, for me, for *Pagal Nilavu*. And there, along with the marriage, there was a bhoomi puja. They were putting up a hospital. This scene in *Guru* is more or less out of that. The fact that the puja was taking place on the ground and they were sitting there—it's an image I was actually moved by. This was Guru's first big step, literally his foundation, a very crucial moment in his path. The scene could have easily moved from the open tract of land to a shot of the blueprints and then to the real building, but that would have been very prosaic. The same thing can be said in a different fashion. The fact is that this big dream of an empire is in his mind, and if the film is able to show that it is in the mind, it works to a larger extent. It's one of the big advantages of cinema.

RANGAN: At what point does Guru decide that he wants to get into the clothing business? Because to Sujata's father he says he's going to import merchandise from Turkey.

RATNAM: There's possibly a process through which he comes to the clothing business. You can explain this process. You can fill up that gap on screen very easily. But it's not necessary. But yes, the fact remains that he wasn't born with the vision of getting into clothing. Sometimes, there are people who are five years old who decide they want to be actors. This is not like that. He got exposed to a big set-up in Turkey, and somewhere along the way a dream took birth, and then he felt that he should be as big as that. Even when he was getting married, he was not too sure that this [the clothing business] was what he was going to do. He was going to the city with a new wife and a lot of ambition, and he was going to see what opened up there. He is ready to get into anything, any opportunity that opens up. He could have gotten into the spare parts business and gotten into automobiles, for all you know. He was just looking for something. A door opened and he walked in and made the best out of it.

RANGAN: Guru has an interesting relationship with the necktie. First, in Turkey, he resists a job where he has to wear a tie. Then, as his stature rises in India, he has to adopt the tie as an accessory of his growth. He grows into the very 'suit' he was trying to avoid working under earlier.

RATNAM: It's a shade of his character. It's not consciously thrust into the film. He looks like the kind of person who is an outsider, who was not 'born with a suit'. But he had to get used to it, even though he'd rather sit on the floor and eat. He's basically a person who's moved upwards in terms of spirit, but in terms of actual preference he's still earthy.

RANGAN: In the meeting between Guru and the politician, you shoot the latter from the back. We never see his face. Was this to avoid real-life comparisons?

RATNAM: Sometimes, it could be X and not a specific person. The politician is not the point. The point for me is only Gurukant Desai. Who he's speaking to is just a chair, just a person in a position of power. I remember a Balachander film, *Iru Kodugal*, where the heroine goes to meet the chief minister. The camera is focused on the chair. The chair is moving slightly, from side to side, and we only hear the voice of the CM. It's a device that's been used. It was done this way so that attention is not drawn to who the authority was, but to what was being dealt with.

'By having Vidya, we get some colour. She's Mithun's legacy, somebody else who will carry the torch forward.'

RANGAN: Sujata is a little older than Guru. Is it because—in the India of that era—marrying an older woman (whether for money or any other reason) was taboo? Did you want to show him as a rule-breaker even in his personal life?

RATNAM: It's more the fact that such a thing doesn't stop him from going ahead. It very quickly defines his character, saying that that was not an issue. I don't think it was that big an issue in the India of that time. If you look at it, because the Partition was happening and Independence had just been gained, people were a lot more progressive. There were a lot of progressive things happening in our society at that time. There were so many people who married outside their communities, their caste, their languages. And then we went back to being very conventional.

RANGAN: Sujata's former lover is an impotent communist. It helps you underline the fact that she, like her country, would be drawn to capitalism, which Guru represents.

RATNAM: And that's where we were going. We were firmly rooted to the left of centre at that point of time—Nehru's time. We were strongly leaning towards the left. And look where we have ended up.

RANGAN: You sound unhappy about this.

258 *Conversations with Mani Ratnam*

RATNAM: It's a fact. It's not a choice about you being happy or unhappy. We've left a lot of things behind and we've gone ahead in one fashion, thinking that this is the way to go.

RANGAN: After the marriage, you cut to the scene of Guru boarding the train. I thought you may have wanted a private moment between the couple, considering the opportunistic circumstances through which the union came about.

RATNAM: Like I said earlier, when you're trying to capture an entire life, you have to capture it without being hurried and you also have to move in chunks. You can't have a lot of moments and rush through each one of them. It is better to choose the right ones and linger on them. What we needed to show is how they bond together, and that was enough. Ten years back, maybe, I'd have shot a scene to show what happens between them after the marriage and before they board the train. In fact, there's still a reference to such a scene, when she asks—on the platform—if he won't take her with him, and he says, 'You were the one who said you wouldn't come.' And she says, 'You could have asked me again.' The scene this refers to is the scene that's not there in the film, where he asks her to come and she says she won't. Those elements were there earlier. It was written. But if we can convey that within this scene, if we can get it across in one simple emotional moment, then it seems enough, instead of dwelling on the same thing in both scenes.

RANGAN: Also, there are always people around—in the train where they first meet, at her home, even now at the station. That's why I asked if you considered a private moment between them.

RATNAM: But that comes about when she's there on the swing—the swing he buys for her in their Bombay chawl. That swing becomes their private world, a private moment that is carried through to the end. That is when they share a dream. That is when the real bonding takes place.

RANGAN: The swing is important to their relationship. She's sitting on one when he comes to ask for her hand. There's one in the small apartment in Bombay. He has his heart attack on a swing. It's some sort of symbol.

RATNAM: It's a very Gujarati thing, too. When he brings it to her, it's as if he's brought his home, his roots along with him. The swing has a seamless, floating quality to it, like a dream. It's not firmly rooted. It brings across the vision with which the film starts and ends. There is ambition. There are dreams that can float.

RANGAN: *Tere bina* begins when Abhishek and Aishwarya part, but you picturize the song as a choreographed celebration, intercut with a few mood moments of him and her alone, pining. A sad situation, in the conventional (or perhaps clichéd) sense, would demand a sad song, with the hero and heroine being sad.

RATNAM: You have love songs in each and every one of our films, coming back to back, so you have to keep reinventing things for the song to be alive, for it to make sense, for it to be unique in your film, and for it to help this particular story (not anything else). The way the love story is developed is that it's a marriage of convenience. It's only later that they start striking a rapport, and this break comes after they have formed a bond. The first emotional ripple in their life together is this parting. It's their first conflict, and there are different ways of interpreting it. We have to break convention, break away from saying what has already been said in the plot through the elaborately staged scene of their split. This is just a small emotional break and a reunion, and that is bridged by the fact that the two of them have otherwise had a nice relationship.

He didn't expect their relationship to be this good, and she—after being jilted—didn't at all expect to find somebody with whom she'd gel so well. The song, therefore, is what is inside them, what could have been or what should be. Instead of just narrating the loneliness of the parting, it also shares the fact that this relationship has come out of nowhere, and that it has been really beautiful. And it builds a reason for the two of them to come back to each other. There's no need, after this, to state why her anger went away, or show that she heard that he's hurt and that's why she took him back. You don't need that logic. You can go purely with the emotion that's brought out through the song. It's a man and a woman, and they've been living together and they really care for each other and he's come back. That's enough for her. The music conveys this very, very easily, so you don't have to rationalize their reunion.

RANGAN: In the scene by the mirror when his wife is pregnant, Guru lets his big belly hang out loose and she jokes that there are all these people inside it, all his shareholders. In an amusing sense, here, he's a literal 'father', who's 'birthed' a generation of rich Indians, but later, in the climax, he literally compares himself to the Father of the Nation. Where were you going with this?

RATNAM: That was a moment between husband and wife. We had taken a lot of effort to make sure that Abhishek had a big paunch by that time. So by showing it off, we were just milking that effort. We were moving from the younger days and a younger relationship to a slightly more settled, middle-aged one. And even in the end, I was not comparing him to the Father of the Nation. I am not doing the comparison—he is. He's just making a logical point, nothing more. If you and

'He looks like the kind of person who is an outsider, who was not born with a suit.'

I have a conversation and you want to make a point, then you make the point as effectively as you can. If you're smart enough, you will pick similes that are effective. And he is a smart guy.

RANGAN: Your inevitable 'rain scene' in this film takes shape when the 'family' of shareholders turns against Guru. Is there a reason you stage this in an open ground?

RATNAM: It's basically using the elements to convey a particular emotion. Those kinds of meetings do take place in open grounds. There are too many shareholders to be put inside a controlled space.

RANGAN: But an earlier scene with the shareholders was staged in a shamiana.

RATNAM: The first meeting too was in this same open-air stadium. We built a shamiana on the other side. But when the crowd becomes larger and larger, it invariably fills up the whole stadium. And the rain adds a dramatic impact to the turnaround that is happening, suggesting a downpour that pushes him to another side of the spectrum.

RANGAN: After this 'turnaround', as you put it, he goes to his old house and dejectedly asks his wife what he looks like to her. She says he resembles her husband.

RATNAM: That's the first time he is possibly doubting himself. That's the first time he's been accused, fingers have been pointed, and for a man who's been so confident, there's the first element of doubt. I'm sure he's had doubts before, but this is the first time he openly admits them, the first time he's voicing them. And there's somebody trying to tell him that it doesn't matter, that he's still the same person. She says it in such a way that it becomes a personal statement more than anything else.

RANGAN: Then he has a stroke and ends up in hospital. Why are film-makers so fond of the 'stretcher shot', where someone is wheeled into the operating room, the camera racing alongside the stretcher as loved ones walk along with worried faces?

RATNAM: Because you know the scene can't be too long—it has to finish within the length of the corridor. And there's an energy to it, a speed to it. It's a crisis and you're walking into the crisis, you're wheeling into the crisis.

RANGAN: The little girl who grows up to be Vidya Balan is: (a) a human-interest character who softens the story, which is otherwise about Guru's brashness; (b) she's the story's crippled conscience; and (c) she's in a wheelchair, with multiple sclerosis, a representative of an old India that was not as robust as the New India. And despite her loyalty to her grandfather's Old India, she looks longingly at Guru, the embodiment of the shiny New India. Was she essentially a symbol when you wrote her?

RATNAM: As I told you, the story took shape only when I hit upon Mithun-da's character. That became my anchor, my counterpoint to the blind ambition in Guru's story. He was still rooted in the old school, the Old India. Without that, I wouldn't have done the film. That is what makes the story for me. While we are detailing the rise of this young India, the Old India has to be defined. Mithun's background had to be defined. And that's where she comes in, as a force that's, in a way, dented but not dead. It is alive. It has got a mind, a view. There are people who still believe in idealism, who still feel that there's nothing wrong in feeling the way we felt those days instead of being blindly West-oriented. By having Vidya, we get some colour. It's not just a single character (Mithun's) hanging around on its own. She's his legacy, somebody else who will carry the torch forward.

RANGAN: She does something funny at one point. She uses very specific numbers when referring to the number of days she has left to live—first she says something like three days, and then, when Madhavan proposes, she says 429 days.

RATNAM: She's saying that her days are numbered. That is all. It's just a fancy way of saying it. She probably has a fetish for numbers. Some people have that kind of habit, where they're being specific but not in terms of the exact thing. They exaggerate to a decimal

'I couldn't have done this film unless I had this peg of a newspaperman who is old-school, who believes in right and wrong.' Mithun Chakraborty.

point. It's more to get across the point that it could be as finite as that.

RANGAN: Her final scenes are intercut with the climactic courtroom scenes.

RATNAM: That's just to wrap up her story.

RANGAN: What about the other Old India—to an extent—the character played by Arya Babbar? He breaks off his relationship with Guru because of an ego issue (not being consulted about their company going public), but there also seems to be some conflict between his old values and Guru's new values.

RATNAM: He was a friend who helped Guru, whose money helped Guru do what he wanted to do, but he is not willing to get on board and go at the speed at which Guru is going. So he had to drop out. He had no choice. He's not able to run as fast as Guru, climb the stairs as fast as Guru, and Guru doesn't look like he's going to stop for someone to catch up. He's going to reach the top first, not wait for someone to join him in the race and then go together. What upsets Arya is the fact that, for Guru, their relationship is not as important as reaching the top.

RANGAN: The moment Jignesh and Guru race up the stairs of that wonderful old structure—did you have the scene set in such a location in the script? Or did you write it as a standard dialogue scene (set, say, in a room) and then, when you saw the location, decide that the elevation would add a dimension to this interaction?

RATNAM: It was there in the script, the fact that they compete to reach the top. It was written on this very table before we went to the location. And maybe it was a bigger scene when it was first written. You tend to write a lot more when you're conceiving the characters, to get a structure. So even for Guru's childhood, we had on paper—though we didn't shoot them—scenes where he would do that run. He would sell these things on top of the hill, outside the temple. It was a motif that was there right through. It came very early into the script. And the spirit of it still remains in that scene, and that's why we looked for some place where he could do such a run.

RANGAN: There are some scenes where it looks like you've tried to capture Guru's energy by employing handheld camerawork. But when Mithun is attacked in his car, later, there's again a handheld camera. I'm guessing the choice wasn't based on a character so much as the situation. From a cinematographic sense, what were you and Rajiv Menon trying to do?

RATNAM: We were trying to tell a story.

RANGAN: Very funny. But you know what I'm asking.

RATNAM: Right from the time Guru is in the commodities market, before the titles, before *Mayya mayya*, he's getting into this world of doing something other than being an employee. He's getting into this world where there is a business, there is risk, there is growth, there is a chance. That's where the handheld camera first comes in, trying to get into the space of this adrenalin rush. And from then on, it's used wherever we felt there was a rush, wherever there was an extraordinary element that needed to be expressed at a different level compared to the rest of the film.

For example, the confrontation on the street between Guru and his brother-in-law is a point at which everything is at stake for him. There is an element of what Guru stands for, the fact that he wouldn't hesitate to do a few things; and then he comes out and accepts it, saying that that's just the way it is. It kind of breaks and somewhere cements his relationship with Sujata further. This moment was not in his normal graph. It was an extraordinary moment in his life. Similarly, in Mithun's relationship with him, the fact that there was an attack, the fact that it took a violent turn, was a moment which pushed that relationship to the next level. These are the elements we were trying to underline with a handheld camera.

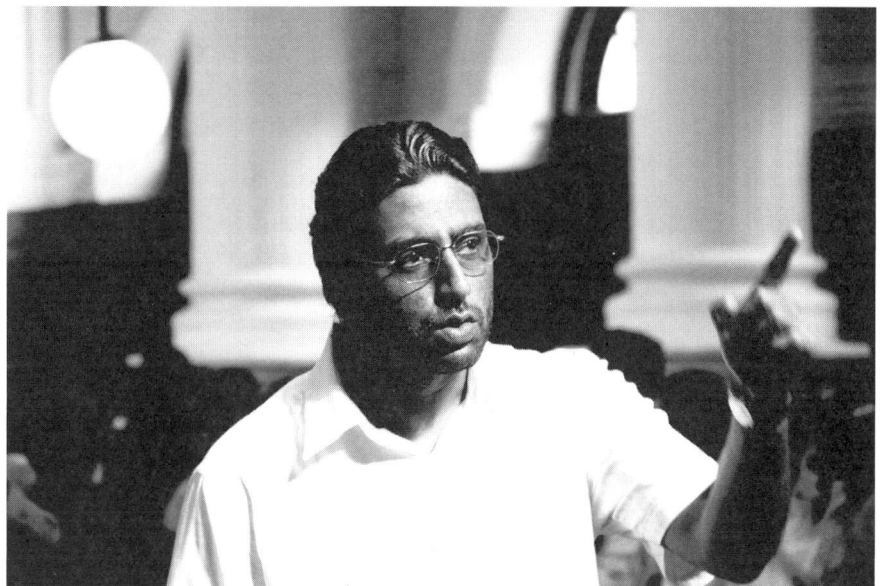

'If I'd thought Guru *was similar to* Nayakan, *it would have taken away the enthusiasm about the project.'*

RANGAN: The courtroom scenes at the end are stylized—energized, rather—with ramped-up shots and strobes and whatnots. It's a head-scrambling circus.

RATNAM: It's also war—a battle between Old India and young India that's trying to break the shell and come out, rattling its way up with its own rationalizations and logic.

RANGAN: Roshan Seth is associated so closely with Nehru, the part he played in *Gandhi*. It's amusing to see him cast in (and carrying that association over into) a film about the breakdown of Nehruvian socialism.

RATNAM: He's a terrific actor. That's why we cast him. He's played a lot of roles other than Nehru. We needed somebody really good because he comes for a very short time and he has to come in with authority and convey what he has to convey. We were lucky that we got somebody who could deliver that.

RANGAN: In the final scene, you have Guru addressing an empty stadium, and as the camera circles around him, we see that there are people and it's a full house. It's quite a dramatic transition, as opposed to starting the scene with a full house.

RATNAM: The way I thought of it was that he possibly would have come there before everything had been set up, seen it,

'He's going to reach the top first, not wait for someone to join him in the race and then go together.'

---

gone back and returned for the function in the evening. The film starts with this scene and ends with it. It is almost the same image as him running up the stairs and reaching the top and looking at the world below. Here, too, he sees the whole world in front of him, calling out to him. It's just that it doesn't have a cut, so it looks seamless—we have the facilities to do this now. It's a nicer way to narrate the story.

RANGAN: So, in a sense, the audience is initially in his head, and then it becomes a reality in front of him.

RATNAM: Yeah.

RANGAN: The title sequence has an interesting flip-book effect.

RATNAM: Didn't you like it?

RANGAN: I found it visually interesting, but I couldn't quite tie it to the film.

RATNAM: It's about texture. In the film, there's an old-fashioned printing press on one side. And on the other side, there's this newly formed polyester king. So the titles tried to blend these elements. It's textured paper. It's newer material, newer technology, set against an old-fashioned typeset kind of situation. It's really the new and the old, in that sense.

17

'In the epic, we gloss over the harsh side of Ram'

Raavan/Raavanan (2010)

Beera/Veera (Abhishek Bachchan/Vikram) kidnaps Raagini (Aishwarya Rai Bachchan) in order to avenge himself on her husband, the police officer Dev (Vikram/Prithviraj). He plans to kill her, but is astounded by her feistiness and fortitude, and he finds himself increasingly drawn to her. She discovers, too, that he's not entirely the brute he appears, but her husband, baying for blood, doesn't share her sympathies.

BARADWAJ RANGAN: From one *nallavana-kettavana* character, you moved to another: from *Guru* to *Raavan*. Did the film come about because you wanted to look at the mythological monster in a sympathetic light?

MANI RATNAM: I think Raavan is a dramatic character. The Tamil version of the Ramayana—the *Kamba Ramayanam*—makes him even more dramatic, even more spectacular. If you look at folk arts like Kathakali, it is always Raavan's story that's performed. It is a tradition to narrate the story of the doomed person. It's quite amazing to think that there was a guy with ten heads. Where did that come from? How could somebody imagine this? What did they mean by it? Is it about multiple personalities? He's a Shiva *bhakt* and he's also the most evil person. It's like these facets are there next to each other, rubbing against each other. It's a character you'd really like to explore.

He's abducted this woman—out of anger, out of whatever. Apart from the conventional Stockholm syndrome—the modern-day answer to this kind of relationship—I wanted to know what happened between them in those years. This is all I was trying to capture in the film. Two people from two different worlds moving from Point A to Point B—did their equation change during this process in that period of time? Did they start off with an assumption about each other and refuse to move away from that assumption? And if it changed, did it change slowly? And did they acknowledge the change only when it passed? To me, these were fascinating questions, worth exploring, worth attempting in a modern-day set-up.

RANGAN: You said that you saw *Thalapathy* not so much as the Mahabharata, but as the story of a single character, Karna. I thought you might have wanted to do the same with the Ramayana, with the single character of Raavan.

RATNAM: Not the single character, but the relationship between the two. I was not trying to understand only Raavan as a character. I was trying to see what happened between the captive and the captor in that period of time.

RANGAN: And in that process, you were also deconstructing Ram, who is no longer the completely noble and good hero from the epic, but a flaws-and-all human being.

RATNAM: And somebody who's set himself a goal and is achieving it. In his way, he is absolutely right.

RANGAN: That's his dharma.

RATNAM: Yeah.

RANGAN: There are times when Ram appears crueller than Raavan—as when he tortures the man who's just had his hand chopped off. He may be just doing his duty, trying to find Sita, but you can't

'She is not demure, quiet—she's a fiery person. She will not cave in so easily.'

help thinking that this is not what Ram would do.

RATNAM: Can we stick to calling the characters Dev and Beera and Raagini, please? Only they are under my control. I have no say over Ram or Raavan or Sita. So Dev, in this situation you talk about, has to extract information. He has to find what the others don't see. The others look at the man with sympathy. But he realizes that there's more to it, the fact that Beera and his group have done this—cut a hand off, and left this man to be found. There's a message being passed on and Dev wants more information. He will try to extract as much as he can from the man in order to move forward. He's a cop through and through. He will not let something pass by on humanitarian grounds alone.

RANGAN: In the epic, when Rama and Lakshmana kill the demons harassing the sages, we don't care, because those demons are evil and deserve to die. But here, the way Dev tortures this armless man—or when he kills the Vibhishan character who's come to broker peace—you do seem to paint him in crueller colours.

RATNAM: I think he's a simple, strong cop who has no qualms about getting his work done. The reason he's so successful is that he's so focused. Even in the epic, think of how Ram killed Vaali through deception. He was willing to hide, to strike from under the cover of trees. He did this because he was focused on killing somebody he thought needed to be killed. So that's really a parallel. It's about where you stand, where you take a call about what's right and wrong.

RANGAN: In contrast, the Raavan character comes across as a principled warrior in the classical sense. On the bridge, he doesn't use his gun on an unarmed Dev. He throws it away and fights with his hands.

RATNAM: I didn't see it like that. Beera is arrogant. He's someone who's always been with tribals and brutes, and he's used to outsiders coming and powering their way through. He thinks it's not fair. If you want an equal argument about an issue that you've been battling over, you have to play on an equal plane. And maybe he'd made up his mind long ago, without realizing it, that he will not kill Dev, that he will let Dev stay alive for Raagini.

RANGAN: He's not trying to get Raagini for himself?

RATNAM: Not unless she wants it. He came to her and asked her. He told her that he was envious of Dev. That is the way he was trying to get her, by winning her over, not through force. He doesn't want to get her by getting rid of her husband.

RANGAN: So, again, it seems to me that Dev, the Ram equivalent here, is crueller than in the epic, and Beera kinder.

RATNAM: If we look at it this way, then probably yes. In the epic, we gloss over the harsh side of Ram, as we are looking at the story from his point of view.

RANGAN: Did the name Raagini come about because it goes with Raavan?

RATNAM: No, it was a different name in the first draft. We just wanted a name for her that went well with her role as someone into classical music and dance.

RANGAN: I ask this because I wondered if, at any point, you saw this film as some sort of a love triangle.

RATNAM: No.

RANGAN: There's no point where she's torn between Dev and Beera? I got the feeling that things were not quite all okay between husband and wife. In the Tamil version, for instance, isn't there a bit of sarcasm in Prithviraj's voice when he calls his wife *'naatiya peroli'* [great dancer]?

RATNAM: Whoever said that there is no fun and sarcasm between husbands and wives? You are seeing it that way because you're seeing only glimpses of their relationship. If you extrapolate that statement, he's probably saying it indulgently, and it has possibly the same shade as Arvind Swamy calling his wife *'pattikaadu'* [villager] in *Roja*. These are just terms of endearment between two people from two different worlds. He's a cop and she's an artist. With Arvind, you

270 *Conversations with Mani Ratnam*

went through the full scene. Here it was a glimpse, a flash of memory.

RANGAN: Even at the end, we're left with the impression of a woman crying out to a lover who has been cold-bloodedly murdered by her husband. Before falling to his death, he marks her with his blood and she whispers his name in a tragic–romantic manner.

RATNAM: I think she just moves from thinking that this man, Beera, is a beast, an animal, to realizing that there is another point of view; that they have an issue that needs to be solved; that what you judge from one side of the line need not necessarily be true. It's just that transition. And at the end, it's just one call, that's all—the first and the last time she's ever called him by name. It's a half-broken whisper that comes out when she knows he is falling to his death.

RANGAN: In an earlier scene, there's a certain deliberateness when Dev goes up to the tribals and holds out his wife's picture to ask if they've seen her. He pauses before revealing Beera's picture, which is just behind her photo. Looking at the spatial relationship among the three characters, you feel that Beera's come between the husband and wife.

RATNAM: When you're not communicating verbally, the order in which you show the photos becomes important. He's watching their reactions, to know if there's a change when Beera is revealed. So he shows the wife's picture. There's no reaction. When he shows the one right behind it, the photograph of Beera, there is a visible reaction. That's when he knows he's on the right track, somewhere close to where Beera and Raagini are.

RANGAN: Even the scene where Beera and Raagini talk in front of the broken statue of Vishnu suggests some sort of triangle, with changing equations. It's just that one person is in the background, strong and all-seeing and silent.

RATNAM: A lot of forests have these historical ruins. The statue of Vishnu is modelled after one of the pieces from the forest. This is to give the sense that as they travel deeper and deeper into the jungle, they get into this zone where they are surrounded only by Nature and maybe the presence of God. It isolates their life, for that moment, from the rest of the world.

RANGAN: So you don't see that Vishnu statue as Dev, namely Ram.

RATNAM: No, that's just Vishnu—*perumal*, an idol, and in her eyes a god.

RANGAN: This is when we hear the first strains of *Jaa ud jaa re*. In Hindi we hear the words, the lyrics. But in Tamil, it's an instrumental version.

RATNAM: That song was composed for

the end credits. And then we used it in a couple of places in the film. The Tamil lyrics, *Naan varuven* [I will return] sound very literal. In Hindi, the lyrics are a little more abstract. They don't go against the grain of the flow of the scene, whereas the Tamil lyrics underline it. The tone of the lyrics makes you decide whether you want to use the words or not. If it is abstract enough, then it just becomes a layer, but if the lyrics are specific, it clashes with the narration. In such cases, just the score does the job better.

RANGAN: Had you been mulling over this story for a while?

RATNAM: I think all scripts remain with you for a while.

RANGAN: And then you make the film when the time is right.

RATNAM: It's not that time suddenly rings a bell. At any point, you are looking at two or three ideas, and you pick the one that you keep going back to again and again. You make what excites you at that point of time.

RANGAN: Did this become a bilingual for the same reason as *Aayidha Ezhuthu* and *Yuva*? You said, there, that you'd planned a Hindi film and made a Tamil version to decrease the gap between your Tamil films.

RATNAM: Actually, I started it as a Tamil film. The first person I told the idea to was Aishwarya, when we were shooting the *Barso re* song. I thought she had the perfect face for Sita. I told her that I wanted to do a Tamil film after *Guru*, and that this is what I was interested in. After I finished *Guru*, I was working on a couple of things before I decided to do *Raavan*. I'm not sure at which point of time it became a bilingual, but it became one somewhere along the line.

RANGAN: In *Yuva* and *Aayidha Ezhuthu* the actors were different, the locations were different. You shot one film and then moved to the other. But here, with (mostly) the same actors in both versions, did you shoot the Hindi and Tamil versions of the scenes back to back?

RATNAM: In the initial schedule, we did one full scene in Hindi and then the same scene in Tamil and so on. I thought this would give the actors time and space to do the scene comfortably. Then I realized that I was as important as the actors. I had to make sure that I got my shots right. Setting up shots in a forest is a very elaborate process. So after a while, once they all got into their characters, we used a mix of two approaches. For some scenes, like the one in front of the Vishnu statue, the Hindi version was shot separately and the Tamil separately. But others, like the one where Beera and Raagini climb back up the cliff after her jump, required a bigger set-up.

'In a way, he's a rakshas. He's not a clean, good-looking hero. There is a beast in him.'

RANGAN: The name of the village, Laal Maati [Red Earth], suggests that Beera and gang were Naxals/Maoists.

RATNAM: That wasn't the reason for the name. It just sounded right, that's all.

RANGAN: When you began casting, did you already know you wanted Vikram to play hero in one version and villain in the other?

RATNAM: Yeah. It was an experiment and at a high cost because what suffers most is the film-making. We had to wait for him to finish Beera and then be comfortable enough to get into Dev. It was a very elaborate exercise which pushed the logistics into a lot of issues, in terms of hairstyle, looks ...

RANGAN: That is why I wondered how you managed to shoot one scene in Hindi, then another in Tamil.

RATNAM: But there are very few scenes with both Beera and Dev together. We did practically everything with Beera, and then shot the Dev scenes.

RANGAN: The film begins with a series of events that occur on the way to capturing Raagini. And you open the movie like *The Fountainhead*, almost—a near-naked hero at the edge of a cliff and a lake far below him. It's an abstract image, a private moment far away from the events he's unleashed elsewhere.

RATNAM: Originally, the format of the film was slightly different. The early portions were about establishing the characters—that Beera is kind of dominant in this village, and into this village comes a man, a policeman who's been transferred here because he's been too rigid, too straight. So he's been sent to this forest. He comes with a newly married wife, he settles down, and so on. It was a more linear narration that I wrote when I was ready to start the shoot. And this was the first sequence that I'd conceived. When you think of opening the film, you think of how to get the character in. You know what you want to say. You know that he is Raavan. How do you bring that across? How do you narrate it? You have to find a way that's away from the clichés. So the idea was to show a man in his everyday process, which begins with his jump from the cliff, and you show bits of violence happening in three different places. You show this man swimming through all that. Without having to say much, you could understand that this man caused those bits of violence.

RANGAN: Even in the linear version, this was the opening sequence?

RATNAM: Yes. He jumps. There are three acts of violence. And it concludes with him coming out of the water and running into somebody there, possibly thanking him for what he's done. Instead of showing the act—what he's actually done—I wanted to show how he handles the person who comes and thanks him.

RANGAN: The three acts of violence in the linear version of the film, then, were not linked to the kidnap of Raagini, as in the non-linear version.

RATNAM: Yes. That was in the pre-Dev days. In the original version, the kidnap of Raagini was the interval point.

RANGAN: That's a really different movie from the *Raavan* that got made.

RATNAM: That was more linear, in a more conventional form, easier to follow. But somewhere down the line, I thought I'd done that kind of storytelling too many times. What interested me in *Bombay* was the child getting caught in a riot, and I built a huge backstory that lasted the entire first half and got into what I wanted to do only in the second half. *Roja* was about a girl fighting for her husband who's been kidnapped, and again I built a huge first half that's entertaining and only then got into her struggle. I thought it was time for me to concentrate only on what really fascinates me and not try to have a backstory which would conveniently put it on an easy-to-follow platform. I thought we were ready to move to the next form of narration. I'm very happy that that's the way the film turned out.

RANGAN: In the psychedelic opening and closing credits sequences, you show Beera's many faces with many different looks—one with spectacles, one with an exaggeratedly clownish smile and so on—all coming together. Some of these faces are not in the movie.

RATNAM: If he was Raavan, if he had ten heads, if he was a complex person, then he existed in a jumble of colours. And the credits came over a song that was throbbing with energy. We wanted the graphics to be as effective as if we'd shot the faces with a camera. We wanted the same energy. We'd done a few sequences that are not there in the film, with the ten heads inside him as ten different characters, as voices that are speaking to him.

RANGAN: But that's still there in a few scenes, like the one where he's debating whether or not to kill his captive.

RATNAM: But there are just hints in the film now. We don't have the length and breadth of it all. We'd planned and shot a more specific interpretation of these ten heads. All the heads were specific. There was Beera as an intellectual, with spectacles, Beera as a woman, Beera as a warrior ... And each Beera would speak in a particular fashion. Those images are the ones we used for the titles.

RANGAN: Was this [the ten specific heads] in the earlier version of the film you just talked about?

RATNAM: It was there till the final cut. We were playing the character as a wild man who has voices inside his head, asking questions and giving answers and making decisions. We tried to capture this—for the actor and for ourselves—by conceiving those characters and thinking of what they would say, how they would behave. Sometimes, there were lines written for all the heads. We read out those lines and removed the counter answers from the other heads and just had him perform like it was all there—so when you first see him, it's like he's talking to himself. Then you realize that he's talking to those other heads, that there are voices inside his head. Then you see a watery image of those voices, and then you see those heads specifically, that he's battling with them. It was conceived like that. But when we cut the film and put it together, we felt that it was not necessary. That layer of having the voices inside was enough to convey what we were trying to convey. We didn't want to get literal about the ten heads.

RANGAN: In the flashback with his sister's wedding, Beera comes across as a very normal human being. At that time, was he already this ten-faces–ten-personalities creature?

RATNAM: Even in those circumstances, he was normal with normal people. That was his 'normal head'. But if he faced a confrontation, he would become someone else. So there was his sane face and then his insane face.

RANGAN: There's a tiny moment—just one shot really—where the sister speaks in sign language to her father just before she's married off. There's no other reference to sign language in the film.

RATNAM: That's just something we planned and, apart from this one shot, didn't make its way into the final film.

RANGAN: Both Abhishek and Vikram have pockmarks on their faces. Like the hunchback of *Richard III*, the Shakespeare play, these marks are an external manifestation of internal beastliness.

RATNAM: In a way, he's a rakshas. He's not a clean, good-looking hero. There is a beast in him. There is a roughness to him. There is a hurt, a wound that's generations old, which he has been carrying since his birth. So the marks from these wounds are what he's wearing on his face. It is not just Abhishek Bachchan, but Beera who we have to see.

RANGAN: Abhishek was criticized for his performance, Vikram not so much.

RATNAM: I wanted them to perform with that kind of intensity, to break a few shackles and not be constrained by having to deliver a restrained performance. It's not very easy for someone to stand on top of a hill with a woman and act mad—unless he has a reason to act mad. To be very honest, I'm actually very happy with Abhishek's performance in the film. Till today, I don't understand why he got so much flak for it. Maybe over years, people will realize that it's an intelligent performance. I think he's really done a brilliant job. It's probably his best performance. I'm very happy with it.

But if so many people were not happy about it, then it's not just his mistake, it's also my mistake. As far as I was concerned, I was trying to get Vikram and Abhishek to play the part in their own way, in the sense that I worked with them independently and tried to get the best out of each of them. I wanted them to interpret the character the way it came to them, instead of making them both conform to some prototype, one specific model. Essentially, the two performances are the same. It's just that the physicality is different. I played on that physicality because they're built very differently, and they convert themselves into a beast in a very different manner altogether. It's just two different ways of presenting a character—one is very easily acceptable, one not so much.

RANGAN: Was the 'psychobabble'—the *bak-bak-bak*, the *jhik-jhik-jhik*—improvized by Vikram and Abhishek?

RATNAM: No. It was on paper. To get there took an effort. To get to the character, we had to conceive these ten heads, with each one of them speaking, and it was out of that, that we got everything else. One of those characters—one 'head'—would go into clown-mode, saying *bak-bak-bak* and things like that. We interpreted the other nine heads and their specific ways and we tried to put all of them into one final person.

'The song was a balance between the dance and action choreographers and the actors. If we pushed it too much towards dance, it looked false, and if it went too much towards action, it looked very normal.'

RANGAN: The Hanuman character tells us that this is not going to be a straightforward retelling of the epic. Early on, when he intercepts Dev, there's a hint that he could actually be working for Beera.

RATNAM: I was not trying to question and doubt things that were there in the epic. I was saying that if you brought them into the present context, into these circumstances, this is what each one might do. I'm sure that if you look at the circumstances in which Hanuman joined Ram in the epic, it was not a very straightforward course. Till Vaali is killed, he is with Sugreeva and he is somebody from some other side. He meets Ram and only then gets devoted to him. There must have been a transition. He can't be somebody who just comes and falls at Ram's feet.

RANGAN: But you could still question it. After all, just like Kamban and others reimagined the Ramayana in their own ways, this could be the way Mani Ratnam looks at the epic.

RATNAM: But I wasn't trying to look at the Ramayana. I was only trying to tell the story between Beera and Raagini. That's all. And in this, we catch glimpses of those other characters you could draw parallels to.

RANGAN: The only character that's literally rendered is Hanuman. He speaks in verses like the *chaleesa*. He leaps about and he's shown with a blade of grass on his back, like the Sanjeevini herb.

RATNAM: We did this because he's a fun character. When you grow up listening to the Ramayana, the first character you get hooked on to is Hanuman. He's got an energy which brings a smile to your face. He's a very specific character, and we thought that one character in the film could take that colour.

RANGAN: And yet, unlike the Hanuman of the epic, here he voices the misgivings in his master's mind. And in the interrogation scene in the tent, for instance, he's practically sowing doubts in Dev's mind.

RATNAM: In the conventional form, the entire thing is seen through Ram. Therefore, the journey is completely about what is in his mind. The problems he's facing, his angst, his anxiety—everything is clearly depicted. Here, the story is predominantly seen through Raavan. So we have very small windows through which we can make updates on where we stand as far as Ram/Dev is concerned and bring out what he's going through. We needed somebody to bounce these thoughts off, to give us these updates in a very natural fashion, just enough to know what's there. Through his interactions with Hanuman, we are making clearer what's in Ram's mind.

RANGAN: And what about what's in Raavan's mind? When Raavan/Beera fails to kill

'In the West, paintings have always been a huge source of inspiration for visuals. Our art is abstract and more tribal-like.'

Raagini as planned, for instance, he shoots bullets into the river.

RATNAM: I look at it as the trauma he's going through. He was supposed to kill her, but instead, he rescued her and brought her back. He doesn't know what's happening to him. He knows that some change is happening, and by firing shots into the water, he's firing shots at his reflection, at himself. He is also firing a shot for Dev, telling him where Raagini is. It's a call for Dev to come and finish the war before things change any further.

RANGAN: And then there's a look at Sita/Raagini's mind, in that sort of dream scene by the edge of the lake. There is a change of scenery to depict her inner state.

RATNAM: We're trying to get into the mind of a captive, somebody who's been tied up and kept in a claustrophobic area, screaming for freedom, screaming for help. With the rest of them, she puts on a brave front. She doesn't want to cave in. She wants to fight till the end. But inside her is this cry, this desire to be taken away, to be protected and cared for. And this scene is her call to her husband, in a setting that's completely opposite to the one she's trapped in—not somewhere claustrophobic but an open place, which is actually pretty Zen-like and calm and quiet and almost monochromic in nature.

RANGAN: Are you the kind of film-maker who researches older films and old paintings for the look of a film, to see how people are lit and things like that? It's a very common practice in the West.

RATNAM: We talk about it. The references are invariably in our minds. There's one very funny thing that's always happened between PC [Sreeram] and me. Whenever we sit and talk before beginning a film, there are some films that we say are 'cool'. There's Kubrick's film *Barry Lyndon*, which neither of us has seen, and yet it's been a major reference. We've possibly just seen stills and we know what the feel is. Till today, I have not seen *Barry Lyndon*. I probably don't want to see it, because I'm still stuck with my image of it—that keeps it fresh. Yeah, I'll see it someday. But it's like that. It's more a feel and a kind of understanding [with the cinematographer], and invariably it's a connection with a specific school or tone that we're looking for. But I'm sure—in every case, anywhere in the world—that these references are just a starting point.

RANGAN: I asked this because this is a movie set in a jungle, and I wondered if you researched other such films, or even photographs or paintings of jungles.

RATNAM: Not really. In the West, paintings have always been a huge source of inspiration for visuals. It's very easy to look at a painting from a particular period to get a feel of that period. Whereas here, for a period film, we'll invariably get caught up in the Ravi Varma school, which has been done to death. Our paintings are very different. Whether it's Mughal or Tanjore, our art is abstract and more tribal-like. It's more two-dimensional in style, without depth. It's more an interpretation of what is being shown. So those cannot really be an inspiration or a starting point for the look of a film. We still look towards western painting. Vermeer and Rembrandt become an easier source to refer to, but only for specific kinds of things. I collect photographs. I collect moods, feels. I have those as references.

RANGAN: So you have some sort of scrapbooks that help you communicate what you have in mind to your technical collaborators?

RATNAM: Yeah. For something like *Bombay*, we had an entire album of images of riots and things like that. And most of what we shot of the riots was a recreation of those specific photographs, because we wanted it to look like the riots that had really happened. In something like *Raavan*, there were forests we looked at, the various ways in which they could be shot. We had a folder of jungle photographs.

RANGAN: Were there any jungle-photography clichés that you set out to avoid?

RATNAM: Nothing. We were not too worried about what was done before us—only about getting our story right. We were trying to take the story farther away from civilization as we went along. As the film progresses, as Beera becomes more

'As they travel deeper and deeper into the jungle, they get into this zone where they are surrounded only by Nature and maybe the presence of God.'

and more human, we get to the heart of Nature, the heart of the jungle. There's an untouched quality to the area. It no longer has transportation or other things that have come and polluted the place. We just aimed for a little more saturation, a quality where you feel you can touch it. Almost as if you are capturing the purer emotion that Beera has inside him.

RANGAN: There's a great visual where Dev burns cigarette holes into the heads of his wife's kidnappers in the newspaper photograph. On some level, he's literally creating the visual of the mythical Raavan around his wife, a man with a number of heads.

RATNAM: Yes, the photo is really about one woman caught among ten different heads. And the cigarette holes are a deliberate attempt to show what he wishes to do with each one of those heads, so that he can get her back. I think somewhere along the line for him, the focus changes. It's not just about his wife any more, but Beera. His focus changes from a rescue mission for a woman who is kidnapped to a revenge mission against the man for having kidnapped her. It goes beyond her, to that man. In that scene in the tent where he flips the back-to-back photographs of Beera and Raagini, he's more obsessed with Beera as he rotates the photograph. Beera's face keeps coming back, again and again, to haunt him. His obsession with Beera is getting merged with his obsession for Raagini. That is his path. In the beginning, he is travelling through the forest with a clarity of purpose, and in the end, he almost reaches this state where what he started towards and what he's seeking now are completely different.

RANGAN: And that's why, after the bridge collapses and he reaches his wife but bays for Beera, she asks if he came for her or for Beera. But a little before that, just before Beera's attack on Dev's camp, there's a shot of the hero lying in bed. In the Hindi version, his head is at the bottom half of the frame, in Tamil, it's on top. It's probably nothing, but I'm curious about this change of camera set-ups for a single throwaway shot.

RATNAM: We do whatever's needed to make the actor more comfortable. The shot is basically about Dev sensing that something is not right. It's just an instinct, a protective instinct that each one has. We shot them on two different days, and probably set up the camera differently. When you're doing the same scene with two different actors, we work it out with one actor, till the scene falls into place, and we work out the scene again with the other actor. You can't just ask him to show up and do it the same way. He may come up with something else that feels right for the scene, and you try to capture that. It's only when you see the two versions together that you see the difference.

RANGAN: What is that rousing chant we hear in the action sequence that follows?

RATNAM: It's a bit of centuries-old poetry in Tamil called *Kalingathu Parani*. It describes war. [Journalist and film maker] Nasreen Munni Kabir, who was doing this book on Rahman, was there when we were doing the background score. Vairamuthu was also there. She talked about poetry and translations, and Rahman asked Vairamuthu to recite something to show her what Tamil poetry sounds like. So Vairamuthu narrated this poem. The sound of it was so militaristic that after they left, I asked Rahman if we could use this, and he said yes. We called Vairamuthu on the phone and asked which portions of the poem would be relevant for us, to connote war and what would happen during preparations for war. We got hold of a copy of *Kalingathu Parani*, marked those portions and recorded them that night. That was quite a session. We were trying to experiment, do something that makes this contemporary sequence related, in some subliminal way, to an epic.

RANGAN: Did you find an equivalent for the Hindi version?

RATNAM: No. We had to ask Gulzar saab to write something in accordance with the rhythm of the Tamil poem.

RANGAN: The colours in the film are very specific, especially on Raagini. At the end, after Dev rescues her, she's in white. That's, of course, to symbolize her purity. Is there a reason she's in yellow at the point of the kidnap?

RATNAM: The clothes should reveal a certain

outward quality about the person. She is not demure, quiet—she's a fiery person. She will not cave in so easily. She will not give in without a fight. She is interested in the arts. She is into classical music and dance, and therefore her tones and colours would be very Indian, very ethnic. But she's still modern. She's today's woman. That's what we tried to capture. We didn't deliberately try for specific colours. She hardly has two or three clothing changes throughout the film. But yes, the white is very intentional, very specific. At the end of her ordeal, we wanted her to come out clean and pure, like the original Sita.

RANGAN: The movie ends with the end of Beera. Just like you jettisoned a private scene between the just-married leads in *Guru*, you don't show a moment of reconciliation between Dev and Raagini. Didn't you feel you needed one? Because as things stand, she's feeling betrayed at being used to track down the villain, and we never see what happens to the couple afterwards. At the end of the film, she realizes that her husband is not as 'good/kind' as she thought he was, just as the villain isn't as 'bad/cruel' as she thought. Again, your favourite *nallavana-kettavana* conundrum . . .

RATNAM: Dev is a cop. He's used to pushing people around—for reactions, for confessions—and that's exactly how he's dealing with his wife. He's not looking at her as his wife, but as a possible source through which he can finish the job he came for. It's not that he actually doubts her or does not love her. It's just that he thinks his job is more important, that he has to do that too. He thinks, 'You're mine. That is a given. Now I want this guy.' That is his mental framework. And she gets that. So hopefully, they're back to normal at the end. Hopefully, she'll get it completely. And I think that any relationship works that way. You're pushed to an extreme, and then you realize what this relationship means to you.

RANGAN: Just like *Guru* brings to mind *Nayakan*, there are moments here reminiscent of *Roja*, especially the part where Dev discovers where his kidnapped wife was kept bound and there's a segue to a song, like with *Kaadhal rojave*. Even the reunion of husband and wife in both films happens around a bridge.

RATNAM: There are bound to be similarities because it's such a dramatic moment in both films. The kidnap forms the real point at which the films take off. But in terms of comparison, it's not just the gender of the kidnapped person that's different—the entire milieu is different. This had something that was so rooted in the epic, whereas that was rooted in the present. The two films are in completely different planes altogether.

RANGAN: After the bridge falls, Raagini is found tied to a tree at the edge of the waterfall. This seems to be another link to the epic, where Sita was kept under a tree in Ashokavanam. But we don't see her being moved from Beera's camp to this strange spot.

RATNAM: Consider her graph. They had her gagged and tied at the beginning, when they kidnapped her. Then the gag came off and the 'tied' quality alone remained for a while, till they knew that she came back even after he let her go. After the *Ranjha Ranjha* song, he disappears. She could have escaped if she wanted to. And in the second half of the film, she's not tied up. She moves freely among them. There has been a transition—which has not been underlined, but will be there if you look for it. Only in the end, when Beera gets into the fight on the bridge, he binds her to the tree, probably to draw this man back to her or to make sure that she doesn't get lost. In a way, he binds her to what's destined for her.

RANGAN: And there's the repetition of an image. Just like her arc (with Beera) begins and ends with being bound, it also begins and ends with her being blindfolded.

RATNAM: Yes. In a way, he's sending her back the way she came, the way he brought her.

RANGAN: Let's talk about the other elements that are repeated. The fact of Raagini being kidnapped while on the riverboat seemed to me a parallel to Beera's sister dying in water—a sort of poetically justified revenge.

RATNAM: If we'd wanted to say that, we would have said it a little better. I don't know how—but that was not the intention. In the earlier script, in the first

---

'Apart from the conventional Stockholm syndrome—the modern-day answer to this kind of relationship—I wanted to know what happened between them in those years.'

half, there was a sequence that showed why she was there on the boat. There is a scene between her and her husband at the dining table, the day she gets abducted. They have their first tiff. He's still flirting with her, then he goes away, and she sees this boat from her kitchen. We picked a house on the river bank so that we could shoot that scene. She looks at this boat on the river, in golden light, almost like the golden deer that draws Sita in the epic. She knows that it's a time when the risk to her security is high and she shouldn't be stepping out—yet she steps out. And the next cut is to her on the boat. If we had all the time in the world, we could have told the story this way. I thought that the main point was not the plot, but the clash of two different kinds of people.

RANGAN: Another repeated element is the percussive score that opens the film. We hear it again when Beera raids the tent, at interval point. It provides a kind of bookending symmetry, opening and closing the first half on an action high.

RATNAM: Yes, it's a bookend. Sometimes, a piece of music becomes a kind of a theme. AR composes it and gives it to you. You bring it to the Avid and you place it at a few different places. Sometimes, he's capable of using it at a different place that I wouldn't have thought of. We kind of try to tell a story together.

RANGAN: The song *Ranjha Ranjha* is also repeated. When I first saw the film, I'd only heard the regular version of the song. This 'psycho' version took me by surprise, along with its stylized picturization.

RATNAM: We composed the song in its melodic form and then we had to see how to convert it to this rustic form. Even while shooting it, it's not as if we had a very clear idea of how to get what we were after. When we started working on it, it was something like stage choreography. That didn't work even at the composing stage. I had enough crewmates asking me not to do the song as it was coming just before the interval and it wouldn't register. It was slightly overboard and what we wanted wasn't coming through. So, with the action choreographer, we converted it into a simplistic action scene about a girl trying to get away and somebody trying to block her. And that action was stylized with the dance choreographer.

The song was a balance between these two choreographers and the actors. If we pushed it too much towards dance, it looked false, and if it went too much towards action, it looked very normal. We wanted a certain amount of fluidity, a certain amount of poetry in the movement, and when you have two different schools of choreography—dance and action—happening at the same time, it's bound to be stylized. If we are looking at a song between the beast and the beauty, it has to be stylized. There is a prohibited zone beyond which the attraction never moves forward. But there's still a kind of magnetism, which exists along an edge of violence. Even on paper, it was looked at as a very stylized scene, and the song took a lot of effort. We could have shot the song the normal way, but this extra bit of magnetism between the two may not have happened if we didn't have the action and the music going together.

RANGAN: And yet there are moments that work purely as dance choreography. When she kicks the stone from under his feet, she's literally making him 'lose his balance'. *Ranjha Ranjha* is then repeated in the flashback with Beera's sister.

RATNAM: The very thing about *Ranjha Ranjha* is that it's a somewhat generic song. The stylized version was the mainstay. That's the reason the song was composed. But we used the original form, the more melodic form, as the other love song. It's used more as a background score, really.

RANGAN: Another moment that works as a literal translation from image to intent is when Beera, on the spinning coracle, sees Raagini dressed up like one of them. His 'head is spinning' at the sight of her.

RATNAM: That's the moment for him when he's fully started seeing her as a woman, not as somebody's wife. He's not a very sophisticated person, so his approach is somewhat direct, abrupt, when he asks her to stay back. When he wanted to kill her and she jumped—that was the first moment he noticed her as a person, as Raagini, and not as bait. And then, there was this *Ranjha Ranjha* moment. She tried to escape, and there was a distinct physical attraction. From the way she speaks and what she says, he finds that she's not what he thought she was. And that is what attracts him. That was the second moment of transition for him.

And after that, when he is on the *parisal* [coracle] with the kids, going round and round, he sees her and he thinks that if she had been a part of them, maybe she's the person for him. His mind changes after that stylized song. He cannot deny any more—whether through one head or ten heads—that he's really drawn to this woman. So with all the children around him shouting, in his own rustic and naive manner, he really thinks that if all was well with the world, she would be his. It's that turnaround that's happening here.

The spinning coracle was not on paper. It was the second day's shoot, and the first scene that Aishwarya was doing in the film. Abhishek had done just one scene earlier, the one where he's sitting by the waterfall while his brother is eating. We had not planned to shoot the scene with a coracle. When we went there and saw that serene location, I asked them if they could get me a parisal. It was not available there and they had to bring it overnight from Salem. We wanted to keep the scene alive, with the children and the noise—he says something that is very serious, but he says it with absolute innocence. He is a violent brute, but when it comes to this emotion, there is simplicity and honesty in him.

RANGAN: When she attempts to escape

'I was trying to see what happened between the captive and the captor in that period of time.'

and there's that choreographed moment, that's when the erotic element comes in.

RATNAM: Yes, that's when it turns physical.

RANGAN: And finally, when she dresses up like one of them, that's when he fully falls for her, body and soul.

RATNAM: Yes. That completes the arc.

RANGAN: When you work so closely on scripts, when you know the tricks and the apparatus and how scenes are constructed, is the magic of cinema destroyed? Are you still able to sit down and enjoy films like the proverbial member of the audience?

RATNAM: If the film holds you, you don't notice anything else. You're just like the guy next to you, watching the film. That is what you look for in a film—that it draws you in and you do nothing but be a part of the audience. If the film doesn't hold you, then you tend to look at other things. You tend to look at where the cuts are. You start noticing the angles and the rhythms with which the scene is constructed. When the film is really magical, you don't notice anything else. In some cases, a film could be magical and really poetic, and in such a case, you take in the film like any other viewer, but you also see a master at work. And maybe you'll see the film again and again to really understand what he's done. The high you derive out of watching a good film is tremendous.

18

'I wanted to do a film about a guru and his shishya'

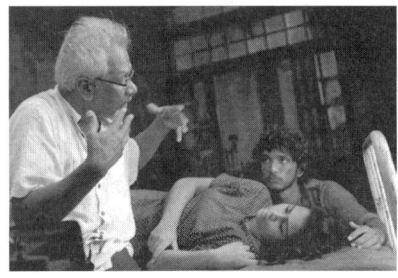

Kadal (2013)

An orphaned villager named Thomas (Gautham Kartik) is mentored by Father Sam (Arvind Swamy), the local priest. But when Bergmans (Arjun), a spawn of Satan and a long-time enemy of Sam, connives to send the priest to jail, Thomas switches sides and turns evil—until he comes under the influence of an angel named Beatrice (Thulasi).

'Sometimes a song is so seductive when it is composed that there is no way you can let it go, but it just won't go with a narrative of this sort.'

BARADWAJ RANGAN: My first thought when I saw *Kadal* was that it's quite a departure for you, with all this explicit religiosity—like the Madonna and Child imagery when we first see Thomas. But later, I realized that this was just an extension of your interest in retelling epics. You have toyed with modernized versions of the Ramayana, the Mahabharata, the Satyavan–Savitri story, and this is your update of a biblical good-versus-evil tale.

MANI RATNAM: Ha. There you go again. You like to pin a film or a maker into broad categories, and fit him tightly there. It is either the nallavana–kettavana slot or it is the modernized mythology slot. I suppose I'll have to accept whatever slot you fit me into. I may not be a religious person at all, but that doesn't mean that I don't understand people who believe in religion. And here, this backdrop brings with it a lot of specific imagery, which helps me connote things without dialogue. The visual symbols bring across the story of the characters, without falling into clichés. If you want to show a man going and joining a seminary, you can just plant a big cross and show his feet walking towards it, and get across, in one frame, the content of the first section of the film: he is going on that path, towards God. It's easy to communicate this because Christianity, like any religion or culture that has stood for so long, has such a large history and

Kadal 289

culture and imagery associated with it. Similarly, if you're doing a film on the Chola period, you'll find enough imagery to help you convey things easily.

RANGAN: But in another sense, the film is definitely a departure. From *Raavan(an)* onwards, you've changed the way you narrate stories. *Raavan(an)* and *Kadal* are very compressed films. Here, as the film opens, we learn that Sam is the son of the owner of 'Anthony factory', that he's renounced his riches, that he's here to find peace (which was missing at home), and around the fifth minute, you've already set up a conflict between Sam and Bergmans. It's like boarding an express train . . .

RATNAM: Regarding the narrative, I'm conscious of this change that you are talking about. It happened after *Guru*, while writing *Raavan(an)*. I found that I didn't want to show this police officer, Dev, coming to this town controlled by Beera, taking charge, etc. . . . It's the way I'm tending to tell stories. It's the way I'm tending to like films. Earlier, if you take *Roja*, the story is really about a couple going to Srinagar and the husband getting kidnapped. But this happens only at midpoint because I had to set up the characters and their relationship, and build things up. That is what I was doing. But after some time, if you keep doing only that, it bores you. The structure is safe but predictable. After all these years, you think you can jump directly to where you want to go—which is what happened with *Raavan(an)*. I was interested in the relationship between Beera and Raagini, so I went there directly instead of building their backstories and having a lot of character exposition. If you spend a lot of time on the build-up, then what you want to deal with gets shortened. It was the same with *Kadal*, where we had so much content, so many visuals we had to deal with. My story is that of Thomas, and the beginning with Sam is a kind of prologue—and a prologue has to necessarily be short.

RANGAN: You've had prologues earlier too—in *Anjali*, for instance, where we see a single event in the arc of the family whose story we will continue to see. It's a fairly linear progression. But here, the prologue sets up *two* aspects of the story. One, the background of Sam (in relation to Bergmans). Two, the death of Thomas's mother, and the relationship with Chetty, his father. That's what I meant by compression. The earlier Mani Ratnam would have had just the prologue with the young Thomas, and introduced Sam in the scene where he enters the fishing village.

RATNAM: If you take the case of *Roja*, the prologue is about the militant Wasim Khan who gets caught. And then we tell the story of this girl Roja in a village, and the impact of the prologue comes back only at the midpoint, when Rishi is kidnapped. So it is possible to be linear or tangential, and still have it tied up. But you're right. There are two prologues here. We did try various versions to avoid this. But the problem is: when you bring Bergmans into the story (without the Sam–Bergmans prologue), somewhere around three-fourths of the first half, you're starting a new story. You see him, and then you have to go back into his story. It's very tacky, a bit clumsy. I tried it a couple of times, but it just wasn't smooth enough. I wanted something simple and straightforward, which would flow very easily. As it is, this is not a simple, linear story. There are more than two tracks. So I have the Sam–Bergmans conflict right at the top. Then I proceed to Thomas's story, and then, when the time comes, we can lean back on Sam's past without breaking the flow with a flashback or some such thing.

RANGAN: Some amount of compression was already there in your song picturizations. We've spoken about how a significant 'story development' occurs within the space of *Uyire* and *Ranjha Ranjha*—in *Bombay* and *Raavan(an)* respectively. A similar thing happens with the two iterations of the *Magudi* number in *Kadal*. The first time, we see Thomas's transformation from a helpless child to a delinquent. And the second time, you compress all of Thomas's misdeeds into this song, so much so that if someone walked out and came back as the song ended, they wouldn't know Thomas had turned into such a bad man. Had you fleshed out Thomas's 'evil phase' through scenes instead, do you think the audience would have had more of an emotional connect with his transformation?

RATNAM: This was the first time I was working with a story from someone else (Jeyamohan). The arc that you mention, where the boy grows up, had been brilliantly written. *Kadal* was written, first, as a novel, and not in the screenplay format—and every development could have become a scene. But, for the film, all we needed was to show that Thomas has become evil, because there is so much more to say. The song is about the seductive pull of the evil side. The female voice in the song represents the Evil that is seducing him, like a siren—though Rahman was very hesitant to call it an evil song. But if I'd thought that scenes, instead of a song, would have helped with the emotional connect, then I would have done it that way. I could have had incidents—one, two, three, four ... But you think the audience will get it without your going on and on about it. That's what I believed.

I think the disconnect was more on an overall plane. The first half is very linear. Except for the prologue, once Thomas's life starts, it's his story—how he meets Sam, how he meets Beatrice, how Bergmans comes back into Sam's life and creates a problem, and what that does to Thomas, who's now lost in the middle, between Sam and Bergmans, between the right path and the wrong path. In the second half, we bring in another angle—an angel, who represents hope for his redemption.

Kadal 291

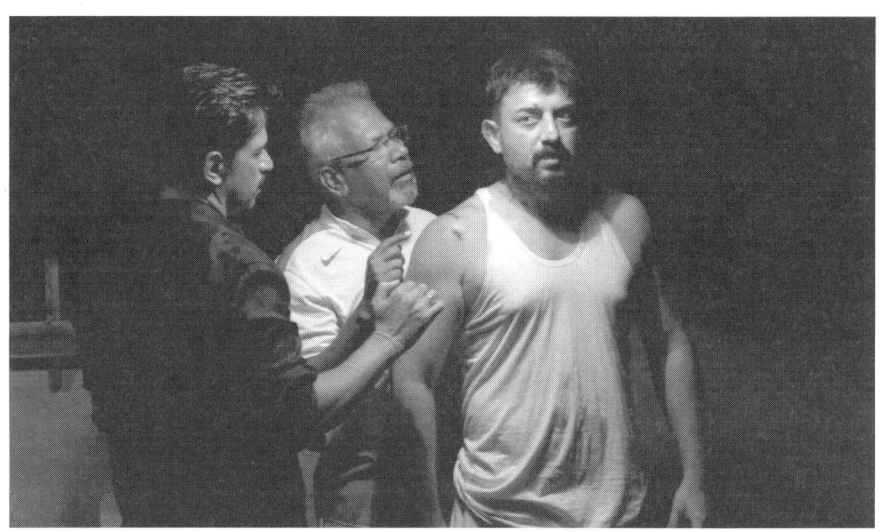

'In his own way, Bergmans is trying to be Satan. That's his path—but he's not Satan. He fails just like Sam.' Mani Ratnam directs Arjun (in dark shirt) and Arvind Swamy.

Now, there's a third path, the path of love—and I think that this track, possibly, was not sound. Maybe, if you start with a linear narration, you can't suddenly switch to a multi-track narration. I feel that arc didn't come out well—the fact that there are these three paths in front of him. These three options weren't balanced well. Maybe all the three angles should have been present right at the beginning, and the story should have been written around that. That is what I would review not the lack of emotional connect because of showing something in a song versus showing it through scenes.

RANGAN: Even in this aspect you just mention, *Kadal* resembles *Raavan(an)*—there too, we had a villain who's gradually transformed through an almost otherworldly presence in his life.

RATNAM: Another thing common to these films is that they both didn't work . . .

RANGAN: A delicate question, but one that may be important in light of your recent films. You lost your brother, some time ago, when he fell into a gorge while trekking. Both your films that came after this tragedy—*Raavan(an)* and *Kadal*—involved a man falling from a height. *Raavan(an)* opened with this image. And in *Kadal*, it's there in the scene in the church's bell tower that results in Sam being charged with murder. Have you thought about this?

RATNAM: I don't think it was [something] conscious when I wrote it in, but when I shot it, I realized the parallels. But I'm not able to draw a direct connection. It's in there somewhere and I ask myself, 'What are you trying to do? Are you trying to exorcise what happened?' But I don't think it's that. That image was there in the way we saw the character. There was probably nothing else.

RANGAN: The last aspect of compression I want to ask you about is the dialogue, which is in a dialect that's rooted in the milieu and therefore somewhat hard to get (unless you're from the area). For instance, the name Thomas is pronounced Thommaa. That bridge is crossed easily enough. But sometimes, in the scenes that are tightly packed with information, you have songs over the dialogue. Of course, it's not necessary to be able to listen to and understand every line in a film, but do you think things like Bergmans's revelation of murdering his boss and marrying the wife, for instance, would have been better served had they been singled out in songless scenes?

RATNAM: You can't keep underlining these things. The lines have to be part of the flow. They can't be said deliberately and slowly, with translations and notes—once in Tamil and once in English, like in the old Tamil films. We decided to use a dialect which is close to the reality of the place—the fishing villages around Nagercoil—because we thought that, after *Paruthiveeran* or any of the Madurai films, we've reached a stage where we can do that in Tamil cinema. These films don't make an extra effort so that someone like you in the city can understand what they are saying. This is liberating. It gives your film a flavour that is unique. We took a lot of effort to remain true to the rhythms of speech of the place. When you're going from the city to capture that way of life, you have to be extra careful—so we had people from there to make sure the actors were speaking their lines the right way. If this has somehow resulted in the lines not being easily comprehended, then that's a problem. That was not the intention, which was only to make the dialogues as real and authentic as possible.

It doesn't matter if you don't know that Thommaa is really Thomas. Forget Thomas. You don't have to make the correlation that Thommaa is equal to Thomas. To the villagers, he's Thommaa. That's all that matters. And if you miss a few words here and there, it doesn't matter. If you go to such a place and interact with the people, you are bound to miss a few words. I feel that the overall narrative is more important than a few specific points. And if you were able to get that across on film, whether in the lyrics or in the dialogue (or using both), I thought it would be fine. Maybe it was a step or two more than we wanted, because I've heard this complaint from quite a few people. In trying to be authentic, we may have crossed the line. But I don't know if only people in the city didn't understand or if it was the same everywhere.

RANGAN: You've spoken a bit about what may not have worked in the film. What, in your view, worked?

RATNAM: With every film, regardless of the overall picture, there are several individual moments you are happy about. *Kadal* may not have been a hit, but I'm really happy that I achieved a lot of things I set out to do. It's satisfying just to get into a theme of this sort and make the film as impactful as possible. It's set in a different world from the one I come from. It's a different theme from what I am used to. It's good to jump into unknown territory. It pushes you into doing something different. You have to find newer ways of surviving instead of doing things you have always done. As to what worked specifically for me ... invariably when you're shooting, what affects you is the performance. There were quite a few roles in the film where it was difficult to find the correct pitch. It was good to see Arvind Swamy back, playing his scenes on a genuine note—that makes you happy. It was good to see how Arjun responded when pushed into a new territory. We would do three or four takes in a conventional way, to get him into the zone, and then I'd push him to do something wild and completely opposite to whatever he'd done. It wasn't what I had planned or what he had planned. And we invariably retained the wild takes. This made Bergmans look like the character, and not Arjun.

The various versions of Thomas came out well. The youngest boy, Nitish, was very, very good. He would create such a racket; continuity would go for a toss. In the shot at his mother's burial where he is crying and running, he's actually running to his real mother, who was on the set. He doesn't want any more shooting. I'd tell him very nicely that we needed to do it one more time, and he'd say, 'Don't you know any words other than "one more"?'

But you could really hold a close-up on him. When he comes to his father's house, his eyes, his expressions, were so magical. *Chithirai nila* is a theme for this boy as he grows up. It's a lullaby that's not being sung by the mother. The odds are stacked totally against him. But there's still a tomorrow. There's still hope.

For the slightly older Thomas, we tested quite a few boys and then we found Saravanan. We had to go through a few iterations to break down his mannerisms, but once he came to the location and began to move around with the local kids, he got into it. With Gautham, the moment Karthik brought him to my office, I felt that he was Thomas. He was the right age. He was tall. He didn't have the chocolate-boy looks. His face had some character. He went through an acting workshop. The first scene we shot with him was the baptism scene, so we pushed him right into the deep end. He is a very good talent. The girl was more difficult to cast, so for every new audition, Gautham would have to come in and do the same scene. There must have been about twenty-five tests. And then we found Thulasi. We had to push back the shooting a couple of months to make sure she lost weight and got some training. I think she's very spontaneous. She has a spark. She doesn't play it wrong. She doesn't 'act'. She plays herself. It was a difficult role and I was very happy with her work.

RANGAN: As with your other epics, you have the to-do list that the story demands and you also have to incorporate a set of symbols/parallels derived from the background. What comes first? For instance, Thomas's mother (named Mary) is a prostitute. Is this an allusion to the Madonna/Whore dichotomy, or was it just about showing what a wretched background the boy was from?

RATNAM: Her profession needed to be something realistic, and also give a shade to the character. If that can also hint at the themes you've taken up, it's a bonus. But it should not jump out at you. What is important is how Thomas is born. The mother was a prostitute, she was handicapped, she suffered and she brought him up, and she died. She was a marginalized person. The Madonna/Whore aspect comes across subtly. But if you leave the main story and try for this symbolism, then that becomes a problem.

RANGAN: In your earlier adaptations of epics, you had specific modern-day equivalents for each character. But *Kadal* appears a little more diffuse in terms of this one-to-one mapping. In an early scene in the seminary, there's a sense of Sam being Jesus, with his 'twelve apostles' around him. But during the commotion around the botched baptism, Thomas is referred to as the Son of God.

RATNAM: Sam has flaws. The film begins with the episode where he is so self-righteous that he gets Bergmans caught. And he stays that way till the end, when he sees his pupil forgive the man whom he cannot bring himself to forgive. He's just an ordinary man who's striving for something big. Despite his earnestness, he's struggling to get to the right path, the path of Jesus—he's not Jesus. And in his own way, Bergmans is trying to be Satan. That's his path—but he's not Satan. He fails just like Sam, because he's not able to kill his child.

RANGAN: Following the path of evil appears as difficult for Bergmans as following the path of good is for Sam. When on the boat with Bea, he says Satan is testing him, whether he can kill her.

RATNAM: What we were trying to say is that a man who tries to become a devil fails, whereas a man who is trying to follow God may be able to get there. However much Bergmans or Thomas try to follow Satan, there's still a part of God inside, and that will never let them cross the line.

RANGAN: How do you explain really evil people then?

RATNAM: They may be evil in general ways, but in some specific way there will be some goodness in them. Even if you don't want to label that goodness as 'God', there will be some caring, some love—for somebody, something. Bergmans is more flawed a devil than Sam is a flawed man of God.

RANGAN: So your favourite dilemma of *nallavana–kettavana* is sort of doubled here, with both Sam and Bergmans ending up with shades of grey. Did you see the film as a parable with archetypes, or as a naturalistic story with characters?

RATNAM: The base is a parable, with strongly defined roles for each character. But when you embellish the character, you try to make it as real as possible. The mould is very archetypal, but the polish is naturalistic. Sam isn't just a father in the priestly sense. He's another kind of father when he complains about Thomas needing a haircut. We had to make him a little unconventional. If people don't come into the church for prayers, he is willing to go to them with a tape recorder. That sort of thing helps to make him not just a typically pious person, but a real person—somebody who can think out of the box. He can't just be in church always, praying and giving sermons. That's what makes him believable as a character, and connects him emotionally to the audience. They should be able to believe that there is such a person.

RANGAN: You don't show him giving sermons at all. The first time we see villagers thronging the church is when Thomas begs to be baptized. Even later, there is no scene showing the villagers flocking back to Sam. We see a handful of them helping him build the statue of Jesus, and then, at the end, we see them gathered around Sam as he sings

Anbin vaasale and takes that statue to church.

RATNAM: The final reconciliation happens over time. We're not saying that he's back in his frock, that he's back as a priest. It's not that. In the song, he's in a kurta. But by running the ashram for underprivileged kids (which we don't show in the final cut), he becomes a part of the village again. Once people know what you are doing is right, they accept you again. There were scenes shot with the villagers coming back to him, but the song seemed an easier way to show this. Even in the song, Sam is walking with the kids from his ashram. So he is still in the process of being accepted by the adults—but it's happening.

About the sermon, again, we shot one such scene. Arvind [Swamy] had to learn every aspect of delivering a sermon. But when you put in something this conventional, it doesn't get you anywhere. It seemed like a cliché. It's more interesting to show Sam going to the villagers with a tape recorder. The purpose of showing a sermon would be to show that he's brought about a change in the village. The same fact comes through as, say, a work in progress, when he takes the boy to the sea for the first time. You see people wishing him. You see that he is now integrated into the village.

RANGAN: Why doesn't Bergmans kill Sam when he has the chance? He knows that Sam, after catching him with a woman,

'She's not judgemental. She's as pure as a child. She is all the things that Thomas is not . . .'

will squeal on him, and that he will be evicted. Why does he opt to let Sam go, with the promise of making him 'fall into sin' instead?

RATNAM: He's tempted to kill Sam right then. He is angry, and there will be an attempt to kill Sam. I mean, in fights, you lunge for your opponent's throat. But then you stop yourself at some point. That's what happens with Bergmans. Maybe he cannot cross over to the other side so easily. It can't be that simple to kill for the first time, however much you hate someone. The rest is just talk. That's when this idea may have struck him. It's not as though he's completely planned everything, in that instant. From there he moves on, starts surviving, finds a path in the opposite direction from Sam and becomes a big shot—and then when he gets a chance, he looks for revenge.

RANGAN: That explains the fact that Bergmans doesn't immediately follow up on his threat to Sam when he leaves the seminary: '*Ippadhaan namma aattaam aarambichirukku.*' [Our game has just begun.] We expect him to hatch a plan and systematically extract revenge, and he does seem to have kept track of Sam's whereabouts (he knows that Sam is now Father Sam)—but when he meets Sam again, it's by accident. There's a sense of something greater at work here than just one man's thirst for vengeance. It's as if destiny conspired to bring Sam down.

RATNAM: Bergmans has certainly kept track of Sam. He tells Sam, in the jail, that he had thought of him every day. He's one of those people who cannot forget or forgive. But his life takes him to another path for a while. And it's destiny—or whatever you want to call it—that brings them back together, and this opens a door for Bergmans, who may not have otherwise taken the effort, despite his threat at the seminary. When you do a prologue, you want to end it with a hook that will keep the audience interested, with the promise that this story is not over. That's what that line ['*Ippadhaan . . .*'] is, an indication that something is definitely going to happen between Sam and Bergmans. But you needn't take that line literally. It could also be that the guy who's going away defeated is having the last word, saying, 'I'm going to come for you.' He could have said it in different words. He chooses these words because there was a chess game between Sam and Bergmans in the original, fuller form of the screenplay, in the seminary portion. The reference to the game came from there, but the line didn't seem wrong even when the chess game wasn't shot.

RANGAN: What do the contact lenses add to the character of Bergmans?

RATNAM: We wanted an Arjun who looks a little different from the Arjun we've seen earlier, because the character is so different from anything he's done. And we also made Thulasi wear the same kind of lenses so that we can see that they are biologically connected, but not in an obvious way.

RANGAN: Why did the village need to be so extremely godless, without a single believer? Why not have at least a couple of churchgoers?

RATNAM: That's just hair-splitting. If Sam comes to a village where everyone is God-fearing and goes to church, he has no role there. So this gives him something to do. Secondly, even though this is his first post, his superiors at the seminary have sent him to a tough terrain, like an outpost, so that he can learn to reach out to the people and bring them into the fold. So the godlessness of this village helped the narrative on both counts. And in that village, Sam finds this boy, who represents 'everyone'. He is able to mentor him and bring him up in a certain way—and in that process, he starts growing into what he's been trying to become.

RANGAN: What is the period of the story? It's not recent, we know, because of the model of the tape recorder and the rotary dial phone.

RATNAM: The first thing we decided was that the story would take place before the tsunami, which changed the entire coast. It was such a major thing that it would become a part of the film, part of the cause-and-effect of events. And we didn't want that additional external element.

So we set the film in the late 1990s. On paper, we had specific dates for when Thomas was five years old, when Sam came to the village and so on—and that helped us with the props. I could have put these dates on screen, but then I'd have to keep giving updates, and this sort of film doesn't need to be so metric.

There's a story behind the tape recorder. What was written originally was the part where the boy breaks down. Sam asks him to speak into the tape recorder, and he swears into the machine and runs away. He does this a second time, a third time, and the fourth time he breaks down. That is how the scene was written. It was actually the premise of a short story by Jeyamohan. We thought it could be an icebreaker for the relationship between Sam and the boy. Once we decided this, we had to incorporate the tape recorder into the earlier portions of the screenplay—so that it doesn't suddenly make an appearance only in this scene. So we had Sam take the tape recorder out to the people and record their prayers. And the tape recorder was the kind that was being used in that time period.

RANGAN: Did Jeyamohan bring this story to you?

RATNAM: It started with a basic concept that I told him. While working on *Ponniyin Selvan*, we kept discussing other ideas. I told him I wanted to do a film about a guru and his shishya, the relationship between a mentor and his pupil. Then he worked on it, set this up in a fishing village. The story could have been set in a small town anywhere. But he thought that it was possible to show a much more violent world near the sea. And the fact that a lot of these coastal villages are Christian settlements automatically led us to this backdrop. He developed the story and kept sending in chapters as and when he finished them. It was in the novelistic form, with a lot of backstories—so we had to leave out a lot. That was a learning curve on this film, of doing an adaptation from a large novel. I should have waited for the novel to be completed before developing it into a screenplay. Maybe then the third angle (of Beatrice) would have been a little more sorted out.

RANGAN: A novel has space for characters like Chetty, whose death in Thomas's arms is an important contributor to the boy's change of heart. But do you think the film could have achieved this through other means, without this third father figure in Thomas's life? I guess I'm asking what Chetty meant to you and if sacrificing his arc would have left you with more time to flesh out what you feel are the film's problem areas.

RATNAM: This film isn't just about plot. It's about a larger picture. Chetty roots the film in a particular time and place. He grounds the world around Sam. He establishes the fact, very firmly, that we are in this fishing village. That's what makes the film real and set in today's times, and not just a parable that is timeless. And once we have that background, we can think of ways to make Sam less of an archetype. If you take Chetty out, the characters hang in the air, without a firm footing. It becomes too clean. It shouldn't look as if Sam has just walked into a set. Even in the case of Thomas, it is Chetty who makes him believable. Thomas is defined by this relationship with Chetty that is not acknowledged, not confirmed—but it's still there, on both sides. He is not able to dismiss the boy completely. There is some doubt in his mind, whereas there's no doubt in Thomas's mind. Also, we are not really getting into the lives of fishermen, their ups and downs, so Chetty gives us a glimpse into what their life is like. Behind his brusque exterior, there's this guy who cares about giving this dead woman a proper burial. The fact that he is a normal human being with a very rough exterior of a fisherman is what we wanted. And his arc is completed when, in a strange way, his death occurs in his son's arms.

RANGAN: When Bergmans kills Chetty, he talks of putting the blame on a 'foreign power' that been killing our fishermen. Is this also something that roots the story?

RATNAM: Yeah, and also an attempt to show what is happening at present. It's talked about. It's feared. It reflects the life of the fishermen today. It's not making a political statement on the issue. It just tells you what is happening around us, and how somebody can use that as a cover.

RANGAN: Was there a symmetry playing in your mind (or Jeyamohan's) when you had Sam's eviction from church come about by a woman (just like Bergmans's eviction from church came about by a woman)?

RATNAM: Yes, the intent was to mirror the earlier scene—though we tried to make sure that it didn't look like the same thing. We were constantly aware that it looked too much like revenge by the same card.

RANGAN: So what really is the deal with Sam? What's his backstory? We want more than just teasing glimpses of his rich background—like the golden cradle that was made when he was born.

RATNAM: Oh, it's a great story. But it's a very big story. I can't say it in a few lines. Maybe, Jeyamohan will write it as a novel someday.

RANGAN: Despite Sam's devotion to the church, it doesn't come across as a very nice institution. We see its officials accepting Bergmans's handouts, which he calls 'Satan's money'. And later, after Thomas becomes a dangerous big shot, they allow his mother to be buried in the church's cemetery, something they refused to do at the beginning of the film.

RATNAM: There's a bit there that we weren't able to get into the film. When the bishop takes that cheque, he says that he wouldn't ask for money from Bergmans even if he was dying and penniless. But he needed money for the 5000 children in the orphanage he runs. This is to show that an evil man will find ways to muddy up any institution. But even without this background, I think this is true of any institution—it could be an educational institution, a hospital or an NGO. It wasn't an indictment of a particular institution. Money and success are able to buy things. That's the way we are. That's the way society is. If a pauper becomes rich and comes back to his village, he will be treated royally.

RANGAN: But what about the way Bergmans is expelled or the way Sam is summarily denounced in some sort of a kangaroo court? Even Thomas's confession and absolution occurs through Beatrice, who is someone *outside* the church. And the statue of Jesus that Sam builds is outside, too, as if to suggest that he is creating his own path after being cast out by the church.

RATNAM: I disagree with all your points. When Bergmans is expelled, we see the rector, the bishop. He's offered a chance to accept his mistake, but he's not willing to change. It was not a decision taken by the church but by him. In the case of Sam, the people *will* do that. It is not about questioning the institution but questioning

'How you treat a frame is very important. Each element should count for something.'

the people. If they think that somebody they trusted has sinned, they will not stop to reason things out. They will burst out in anger. But the fact remains that he is taken away by cops. He's taken to court, he's put into jail. That has nothing to do with the church.

This bit is based on a priest in Kerala. He was found guilty of murder, and imprisoned, and then, several years later, they found he was innocent. The scene is about what can realistically happen to an ordinary guy who becomes a priest. When someone smears muck on him, the people around are ready to believe the muck. They get violent. The bishop is there in that scene, trying to control the crowd, and when Sam is accused by Celina, that puts the last nail in the coffin.

Sam's statue is outside only because it's still being made. Whatever his reason for doing this, he's not making a statement. It's a way of culminating his story. He's creating a form of God in a place that was godless. Despite the problems he faced, he still goes ahead and does it—and in that process, Thomas and Beatrice are able to find hope, along with the villagers, who are with him now building the statue. This completes their arc too, from non-believers to believers. Sam's mission, if not complete, has at least started.

Coming to Thomas's confession, he is growing up. He has gone on the path of good, and he has gone on the path of evil. And in that path, he's found somebody. The confession is not treated as a 'confession' in the Christian sense, but just as a way he finds hope. And tomorrow, Thomas may end up a churchgoer. But it doesn't have to be the four walls of the church that shows you the light. It could also be a person. It could be Sam. It could be Beatrice. It's just that a perfectly innocent person is as much a representation of Christ as anybody else.

RANGAN: Is this innocence the reason you showed Beatrice—the 'angel' who saves Thomas—to be a childlike character? She's fleeing a hospital when we first see her.

RATNAM: 'Angelic' describes the way we shot her, with the white clothes, but the way we looked at her was as one who really doesn't know what is right, what is wrong, who would reach out without discrimination and help everybody. There are no intellectual barriers. She's not judgemental. She's as pure as a child. She is all the things that Thomas is not, and has never seen. He has seen only bitterness and—after shutting out her childhood trauma—she has seen only love.

She has a problem. She needs care and protection. That's why she's first seen in the hospital—to hint that she's not completely okay, and also to tie up her arc, at the hospital in the end. It would have been much easier to make her more angel-like. But later when we reveal that she's had a problem from childhood, it helps to hint at it with the hospital scene. To a large extent, the character is moulded on Dostoevsky's idiot, who has been in a sanatorium as he enters the story. Bea is, similarly, a pure soul who is too good for this world. But we had to make her someone we could relate to, someone we could identify with, and we did that by making her gifted in some things—like nursing—but shutting out other things. As a nurse, her life is about love and service, the opposite of Bergmans's. He is a man who lives only for himself and who denies any bonding with anyone. That his offspring is such a person provides a stark contrast.

RANGAN: Why does Beatrice, who's normally in [angelic] white, wear those vividly coloured clothes only in the *Moongil thottam* song?

RATNAM: The song is not treated as something happening in real time. It's more a representation of the emotional bond between Thomas and Beatrice. The woman inside her is coming out, blossoming. Hence those colours.

RANGAN: Did you consider developing this love track? What's there right now isn't about two people being in love so much as one showing the other the *path* of love.

RATNAM: There was one more sequence that we had shot. There was conflict and a reunion that underlined the love story a little more. But the size of the film prevented you from going off on one track in too much detail.

RANGAN: Celina too is referred to as an

angel. Bergmans calls her the *devadhai* [angel] who brought down a *devadhoothan* [messenger of God]. And when she testifies against Sam, we see her face bathed in an almost ethereal glow.

RATNAM: When we'd gone location scouting, we went to this church where there was a small statue on which light fell exactly the same way. We'd taken a still of that. And even as we were looking at that statue, we thought that this is how Celina should be lit when she lies in church and yet regrets it at the same time. This is something we decided on even before the church was built for the film. She's seeking to be forgiven, which is what the film talks about, and the light on her face represents the hope that comes and touches her. She's saying something that goes against everything inside her, and even at the worst moment of betrayal, her inner soul is bright, touched by the hope of redemption.

About her being referred to as a devadhai, the point was more about the devadhoothan. It's the kind of thing that Satan would pompously say. It's about the pomp of the language, and the fact that he still thinks that Sam is a devadhoothan and he's taking him on.

RANGAN: What happens with Celina after this scene? We learn from Bergmans that she's been dispatched to heaven. But she spoke of him as the one good man in her life, and there seemed to be something between them.

RATNAM: That's just her innocence. It says more about her than him. The fact that she's found someone who doesn't ill-treat her probably makes her romanticize him. He's the kind of guy who uses people. It's not as if he was extra kind to her. He needed a place to hide at some point, and he found her house, and during that time he did tell her that he'd marry her. But just because a man tells a woman he'll marry her, he doesn't become a great guy—and it doesn't mean he's going to. He will be good and he will be bad. That is the way Satan operates. There's a charming side to him, something very seductive and endearing. That is the only way he can remain evil. And he kills her because she's served her purpose and is no longer useful. Besides, he only tells Sam that he killed Celina. We don't know if he's lying or telling the truth.

RANGAN: Was *Nenjukkulle* originally meant to be picturized on Celina? There were tweets to this effect.

RATNAM: Yeah, we tried using the song during the part Bergmans was recovering from his wounds. Celina comes in and sees him, and his recovery was shown in the song. But it didn't work there. This happens all the time while making movies. You try something. It doesn't work. You try something else. Maybe I should have strict non-disclosure agreements next time.

RANGAN: The music videos, though terrific in isolation, threw me out of the film. *Elay* *keechan* is your first 'hero introduction' song since the one in *Geetanjali*, almost twenty-five years ago, and the fun-filled high-energy choreography is a bit of a shock after the intense first half-hour of narration. And speaking of *Geetanjali*, while I was able to accept an *O Priya Priya* without qualms—after all, that is not a *raja–rani* film, and the casually clothed hero and heroine suddenly morph into some kind of historical era—*Adiye* feels odd in *Kadal's* milieu. The picturization has the same kind of stylization; yet that feels organic, this doesn't.

RATNAM: As I said earlier, if you use songs, you should use them without apology. I don't like songs where the couple is walking, holding hands and eating ice cream. *Elay keechan* begins with the boy going into the sea and being able to stand on the catamaran. In very little time, it conveys the fact that he has become a fisherman. He has found a life. He has forged a bonding with the sea. The song is a celebration of this. I didn't look at this as a 'hero-introduction' song. In *Geetanjali*, that's the first time we see the hero. Here, the hero has already been seen as a child and as a young boy, and now we're just seeing him as a grown-up.

I resort to choreography only when I really need it, because dance is an extreme form of expression. And here I felt I could use choreography. It provides a high. The film is one thing, and the songs are another. It's a two-way street. The film defines what kind of song you want and where you want it. But once the song comes alive and becomes an entity of its own, you have to accept the fact that it has its own demands. If you have a song of a certain nature, you have to see how best to serve that song too. When the rhythm is strong and the music has so much excitement, you feel you can knock the ball out of the park with choreography. Had the song been composed in a more conventional tune, what is accepted as a fisherfolk tune, maybe you wouldn't have felt this way. Maybe it's the fact that this is another genre of music—maybe that's what's jumping out. But I have no issues with the song. I like the fact that we are going against the grain with the music, exploring the mood through an entirely different form. Experimenting with that kind of music is what Rahman has been doing for so many films. And I am very happy with that. Yes, the intensity of the preceding portions does probably play a part in how you saw the song, but I still feel that if the music had made it sound like a *Chemmeen* kind of song, you would have accepted it a little easier.

Adiye is a different thing altogether. Sometimes a song is so seductive when it is composed that there is no way you can let it go, but it just won't go with a narrative of this sort. This has happened more than once in my career—with *Raasathi* in *Thiruda Thiruda*, for instance. It does stick out. You do try to get it as right as possible, but it is still a leap of faith, and you hope that you have given enough 'clues' all along for the song to sail in and out of the narrative at that point. *Geetanjali* is not so raw and rooted, and also with that film, right from the beginning, we are tuned to a song-filled narrative. It's a platform we are used to, whereas here this cinematic element sticks out, however true you try to make it. You can't go into a song on an emotional link alone. You have to link it a little more. Maybe *Adiye*, with its blues and gospel influences, is too sophisticated in style to be in this kind of a film. But if I had to redo the film, I would still have the song and maybe reconsider the picturization.

RANGAN: *Kadal* is a serious film, an allegorical drama, but along the way—and especially after the music release—that angle got hijacked by the hype that this was a love story between Karthik's son and Radha's daughter. How much control do you exert over the marketing of your films?

RATNAM: I normally have complete control over the marketing. But you can't have control over speculation. The way we designed the trailer for the film was to break the impression that it's just a love story between star children. The casting was not planned that way when we started off. It just happened. At first, we had Gautham and Samantha, but when she fell ill we had to find another person. We could cast Thulasi only halfway through the shoot. We didn't want to begin marketing the movie by saying, 'No, no, no, this is not a love story.' But with the trailer and the subsequent build-up, I thought we could give the impression that the film is different from that. Also, you have the confidence that even if the audience comes in expecting a love story, if the film is good and powerful and it works, then it will hold them. The fact that it didn't is the only reason we are discussing this now.

I would have built up the film correctly, but the big storm around *Viswaroopam*'s release took attention away from us completely. It took away our preparation time. With all the controversy around that film, this got lost, and it probably got slotted as just a love story. We didn't have the space and the time to establish the kind of film that this was. And at some level, I was aware that we might face this kind of problem because the same thing had happened with *Kannathil Muthamittal*. The fact that it had Madhavan and Simran and that title [*A Peck on the Cheek*], people got the impression that it was a love story, though I thought that the early images of the children, one on top of the other, would take away this impression. So with *Kadal*, I knew that more inputs were needed to get across the content of the film, and that's why—for the first time—our trailer was quite explicit. It talked of the conflict between Bergmans and Sam, and there was hardly anything about the love story. And that is the way we would have gone about the marketing efforts and the campaign, had we had those twenty-five days leading up to the release. Without negating the love story

'He was the right age. He was tall. He didn't have the chocolate-boy looks.'

---

angle, we would have made the audience ready for a certain kind of film. And that didn't happen, which is why *Kadal* still came out being perceived in a certain way, and not the way we intended.

RANGAN: When I saw the film, the censor's certificate said it was around 160 minutes, but the film that played was about twenty minutes shorter.

RATNAM: The trouble is that we have to get the film censored early so that overseas prints can be sent out in time. The censoring was done even as we were checking the film and taking a call on the length. What was censored was the fuller version, while we wanted to make the film more compact. And by that time, some of the overseas prints had been sent.

RANGAN: Do you feel the film should have been longer?

RATNAM: No. I don't like long films. I like them tighter. It's just that this film had too much story, too much plot. There is the story between Bergmans and Sam that is happening right through the film. There is the story between Thomas and Sam—again, right till the end. There is also a story that is not developed much, between Bergmans and Thomas. And there is the track with Bea. That is what made the film interesting, different, and also difficult. It's not a simple story. It's not a *Mouna Raagam*, which is a straight-line story. Sometimes I wish we'd reduced the amount of plot and just focused on the characters. Plot is the thing that consumes time. You have to say what happened to this and to that and you have to tie everything up. That takes time, and that takes away from the characters and their growth.

RANGAN: Do you think this is because the film was adapted from a sprawling novel?

RATNAM: No, but so many big novels have been adapted to screen all these years, and I should also be able to do it. If I haven't been able to do it, then there's a flaw somewhere. A novel presents a problem because there is the desire to bring in all the elements in it, to have a multiple-track story without the audience realizing that it's a multiple-track story. Like I said, I'm happy with most of the film except the Bea track, which I wasn't able to crack correctly.

RANGAN: Finally, let's talk about the way you saw the sea and its moods in this film.

RATNAM: When your title is *Kadal*, you know you're going to have to shoot the sea in a certain way and use it to tell your story. As the film is set against the sea, each sequence is helped by the way the sea looks. Sam sees the sea as peaceful, when he meditates on the shore. The sea is romantic and colourful in the *Moongil thottam* song, which is the love track between Thomas and Bea. And it is violent in the climactic battle between good and evil, turning everything upside down. The sequence was a monster, a combination of [cyclone] Nilam's footage and CGI work. You don't get a chance every day to use your backdrop, the sea, as a vital tool in staging the action. But you cannot let it get monotonous, and with someone like Rajiv [Menon], it becomes easier. All my cameramen have been more than cameramen. They're my bouncing boards for the script. It's important to have a cinematographer who's as involved with the project as you are. This is a film that begins with a woman's leg being broken. The images have to be harsh. You cannot romanticize things. But they still have to be images that we would like to see. You can be very raw and real and still be aesthetically and compositionally very strong. That's where Rajiv is very good. He got a palette that wasn't glossy but also wasn't crude for the sake of rawness. He was able to evoke that raw feeling without it being ugly.

RANGAN: When you say 'aesthetic', are you saying that's the kind of image you'd like to see, as a viewer? One of the charges thrown at you sometimes is that, with all the impeccable imagery, your films look like ad films.

RATNAM: The fact that you are trying to convert life into two-dimensional images contained in a rectangle automatically brings you into the realm of art. Therefore, how you treat a frame is very important. Each element should count for something. It should have some definition of depth and tonal balance. It should have a compositional value. You cannot get away from it. Even those who make crude frames are making it crude for a purpose. But it's easy to convey harshness on screen by shooting the frames crudely, just like a handheld camera automatically conveys more tension than a static shot. But take Kurosawa's *Ran*. It's filled with war sequences. It's hard, it's real, but still, not a single frame is crude. You can't get grittier than the opening war sequence of *Saving Private Ryan*, but it's still stunningly shot.

For me it's important to have the frames composed very well, to be able to narrate the story through the way the artistes are positioned for the camera, among other things. I'm not worried if people say my films are like ad films. If they do say so, they don't know either features or commercials. In the first place, we take a lot of effort to make sure they don't look like ads. A person who appreciates the kind of film that's made crudely just to get across the point that it's about crude people lacks film knowledge and the ability to appreciate art. You can't say that it's effective writing only if it's scribbled. I work with people who are very good in their fields so that we create something that looks real and, at the same time, can stand up to anything that's being created anywhere else. I am not looking at just the films made here. Every film that you see, every film that you appreciate is something you aspire to compete with.

Filmography and Awards

Pallavi Anupallavi • 1983 • *Kannada* • *140 minutes*

CREDITS • **Story, Screenplay and Direction** Mani Ratnam • **Produced by** S. Krishnamurthy • **Dialogue and Lyrics** R.N. Jayagopal • **Cinematography** Balu Mahendra • **Music** Ilaiyaraaja • **Art** Thotta Tharrani • **Editing** B. Lenin • **Audiography** V. Govindasamy, M. Gothandapani • **Recording and Re-recording** S.P. Ramanathan and Pandurangan. **CAST** • Anil Kapoor – Vijay • Lakshmi – Anu • Kiran Vairale – Madhu

AWARD Karnataka State Award • *Best Filmography*

Unaru (Arise) • 1984 • *Malayalam* • *150 minutes*

CREDITS • **Direction** Mani Ratnam • **Produced by** N.G. John • **Written by** T. Damodaran • **Cinematography** Ramachandra Babu • **Music** Ilaiyaraaja • **Editor** B. Lenin. **CAST** • Mohanlal – Balan • Sukumaran • Ratheesh – Peter • Sabitha Anand • Balan K. Nair • Unni Mary • Ashokan

AWARD Karnataka State Award • *Best Filmography*

Pagal Nilavu (The Morning Moon) • 1985 • *Tamil* • *145 minutes*

CREDITS • **Written and Directed by** Mani Ratnam • **Produced by** G. Thyagarajan • **Cinematography** Ramachandra Babu • **Music** Ilaiyaraaja • **Editor** B. Lenin. **CAST** • Murali – Selvam • Revathi – Jyothi • Sathyaraj – Devarajan • Sarath Babu – Robert Manohar

Idhayakoyil (Temple of the Heart) • 1985 • *Tamil* • *160 minutes*

CREDITS • **Direction** Mani Ratnam • **Produced by** Kovai Thambi • **Written by** R. Selvaraj • **Dialogue and Screenplay** M.G. Vallabhan • **Cinematography** Rajaraajan • **Music** Ilaiyaraaja • **Editing** B. Lenin and V.T. Vijayan • **Art** C. Devadas • **Lyrics** Pavalar Varadharasan, Ilaiyaraaja, Vaali, Muthulingham, Na. Kamarasan, Vairamuthu, Mu. Mehta • **Stills** K.V. Mani • **Choreography** Sundaram. **CAST** • Mohan – Shankar • Radha – Suriya • Ambika – Gauri

Mouna Raagam (Silent Symphony) • 1986 • *Tamil* • *145 minutes*

CREDITS • **Story, Screenplay, Dialogues and Direction** Mani Ratnam • **Produced by** G. Venkateswaran • **Cinematography** P.C. Sreeram • **Music** Ilaiyaraaja • **Editing** B. Lenin and V.T. Vijayan • **Lyrics** Vaali • **Recording and Re-recording** S.P. Ramanathan, S. Babu • **Dialogue Recording** Duraisamy • **Make-up** Sundaramurthy • **Costumes** Raju, Rajendran, Nayem • **Art** Thotta Tharrani • **Choreography** Sundaram • **Action** Super Subburayan. **CAST** • Mohan – Chandrakumar • Revathi – Divya • Karthik – Manohar • V.K. Ramasamy – Chandrakumar's boss • Kanchana – Lawyer • Ra. Sankaran – Divya's Father • Vani – Divya's Mother • Bhaskar – Divya's brother • Kalaiselvi – Divya's sister • Baby Sonia – Divya's sister

AWARD National Award • *Best Regional Film*

FESTIVALS • Indian Panorama, 1987, New Delhi • Mani Ratnam's Love Films, National Film Theatre, 2002, London • A Retrospective of Mani Ratnam's Films, Calcutta Film Festival, 2002

Nayakan (The Hero) · 1987 · Tamil · 135 minutes

CREDITS · **Story, Screenplay and Direction** Mani Ratnam · **Dialogues** Balakumaran · **Cinematography** P.C. Sreeram · **Music** Ilaiyaraaja · **Editing** B. Lenin and V.T. Vijayan · **Art** Thotta Tharrani · **Choreography** Sundaram · **Action** Super Subburayan · **Recording and Re-recording** S.P. Ramanathan · **Lyrics** Pulamaipithan, Ilaiyaraaja and Pandurangan. **CAST** · Kamal Haasan – Shaktivel | Velu Nayakan · Saranya Ponvannan – Neela · Janakaraj – Selvam · Tinnu Anand – Ajit Kelkar · Delhi Ganesh – Iyer · Nizhalgal Ravi – Surya · Karthika – Charumati · Nasser – Assistant Commissioner | Charu's husband · Kitty – Shaktivelu's father · M.V. Vasudeva Rao – Hussain Bai | Vaapa · Tara – Shyla · R.N. Sudarshanas – Reddy brothers · R.N. Jayagopal – Reddy brothers

AWARDS National Awards · *Best Actor* Kamal Haasan · *Best Cinematographer* P.C. Sreeram · *Best Art Director* Thotta Tharrani

FESTIVALS · Indian Panorama, 1988, New Delhi · Moscow Film Festival · A Retrospective of Mani Ratnam's Films, Calcutta Film Festival, 2002 · Nominated for the Oscars from India in the category Best Foreign Language Film

Agni Natchatiram (Clash) · 1988 · Tamil · 155 minutes

CREDITS · **Story, Screenplay and Direction** Mani Ratnam · **Produced by** G. Venkateswaran · **Cinematography** P.C. Sreeram · **Music** Ilaiyaraaja · **Art** Thotta Tharrani **Editing** B. Lenin and V.T. Vijayan · **Lyrics** Vaali **Choreography** Sundaram. **CAST** · Karthik – Ashok · Prabhu – Gautam · Vijayakumar – Vishwanath · Amala – Anjali · Nirosha – Anitha · Tara – Mallika · Jayachitra – Ashok's mother · Sumithra – Gautham's mother · Janakaraj – Lakshmipathi · S.N. Lakshmi – Vishwanath's mother

FESTIVAL · Indian Panorama (Mainstream section), 1989, New Delhi

Geetanjali · 1989 · Telugu · 150 minutes

CREDITS · **Story, Screenplay and Direction** Mani Ratnam · **Produced by** C.L. Narasa Reddy · **Dialogues** Rajasri · **Cinematography** P.C. Sreeram · **Music** Ilaiyaraaja · **Art** Thotta Tharrani · **Lyrics** Vetury Sundararamamurthy · **Choreography** Sundaram · **Editing** B. Lenin and V.T. Vijayan. **CAST** · Nagarjuna Akkineni – Prakash · Girija – Geethanjali · Vijayakumar – Geethanjali's Father · Radhabai – Geethanjali's Grandmother · Sumitra – Prakash's Mother · Aruna Mucherla – Doctor · Chandramohan Showkar Janaki – Chancellor · Suthi Velu – Ooty House caretaker · Vijayachander – Prakash's Father

AWARDS National Award · *Best Picture Providing Wholesome Entertainment* | Andhra Pradesh State · Nandi Award

FESTIVALS · Indian Panorama, 1990, New Delhi · Mani Ratnam's Love Films, National Film Theatre, 2002, London

Anjali · 1990 · Tamil · 155 minutes

CREDITS · **Story, Screenplay, Dialogues and Direction** Mani Ratnam · **Produced by** G. Venkateswaran · **Cinematography** Madhu Ambat · **Music** Ilaiyaraaja · **Art** Thotta Tharrani · **Editing** B. Lenin and V.T. Vijayan · **Lyrics** Vaali · **Action** Super Subburayan · **Choreography** Sundaram. **CAST** · Raghuvaran – Shekhar · Revathi – Chitra · Master Tarun – Arjun · Baby Shruti – Anu · Baby Shamili – Anjali · Prabhu – Ex-convict (cameo appearance) · V.K. Ramaswamy – Neighbour

AWARDS National Awards · *Best Regional Film* · *Best Child Artist* Baby Shamili · *Best Audiography* Pandu Rangan

FESTIVALS · Indian Panorama, 1991, New Delhi · Days of Indian Culture, Russia,1996 · Mani Ratnam's Love Films, National Film Theatre, 2002, London · A Retrospective of Mani Ratnam's Films, Kino Xenix Zurich, 2002, Switzerland · Nominated for the Oscars from India in the category Best Foreign Language Film

Thalapathy (Lieutenant) · 1991 · Tamil · 152 mins

CREDITS · Story, Screenplay, Dialogues and Direction Mani Ratnam · **Produced by** G. Venkateswaran · **Cinematography** Santosh Sivan · **Music** Ilaiyaraaja · **Art** Thotta Tharrani · **Editing** Suresh Urs · **Costumes** K. Raju and Mahi · **Lyrics** Vaali · **Choreography** Sundaram and Prabhu · **Action** Super Subburayan · **Song Recordists** Satish Gupta and Yogesh · **Background Score Recordist** N. Pandurangan · **Dialogue Recording and Pre-mix** V.S. Murthy, A.S. Lakshminarayan and R. Ravichandran. **CAST** · Rajinikanth – Surya · Mammootty – Devaraj · Shobana – Subbulaxmi · Arvind Swamy – Arjun · Srividya Kalyani – Surya's Mother · Bhanupriya – Padma · Amrish Puri – Kalivardhan · Jai Sankar – Arjun's Father · Geetha – Devaraj's Wife · Charuhasan – Subbulaxmi's Father · Manoj K. Jayan – Manoharan · Nagesh – Panthulu

Roja · 1992 · Tamil · 137 minutes

CREDITS · Story, Screenplay and Direction Mani Ratnam · **Produced by** Rajam Balachander and Pushpa Kandaswamy · **Executive Producer** V. Natarajan · **Dialogues** Sujatha · **Cinematography** Santosh Sivan · **Music** A.R. Rahman · **Art** Thotta Tharrani · **Editing** Suresh Urs · **Lyrics** Vairamuthu · **Audiography** V.S. Murthy, A.S. Lakshmi and R. Ravichandran · **Action Horseman** Babu. **CAST** · Arvind Swamy – Rishi Kumar · Madhoo – Roja · Pankaj Kapur – Liaqat · Nasser – Colonel Rayappa · Shiva Rindani – Liaquat's follower · Janakaraj – Chajoo Maharaj

AWARDS National Awards · *Best Film on National Integration* · *Best Music Director* A.R. Rahman · *Best Lyricist* Vairamuthu | V. Shantaram Award · *Best Director*, 1985 | Tamil Nadu State Award · *Best Picture* · *Best Director* · *Best Music Director* A.R. Rahman · *Best Actor* Arvind Swamy

FESTIVALS · A Retrospective of Mani Ratnam's Films, Calcutta Film Festival, 2002

Thiruda Thiruda (Thief Thief) · 1993 · Tamil · 154 minutes

CREDITS · Screenplay and Direction Mani Ratnam · **Story** Mani Ratnam and Ramgopal Varma · **Produced by** S. Sriram · **Dialogue** Sujatha and Suhasini Maniratnam · **Cinematography** P.C. Sreeram · **Music** A.R. Rahman · **Art** Thotta Tharrani · **Lyrics** Vairamuthu · **Action** Super Subburayan · **Editing** Suresh Urs · **Choreography** Sundaram, Rajusundaram and Prabhu Deva · **Song and Background Recording** H. Sridhar and S. Sivakumar · **Dialogue Recording and Mixing** V.S. Murthy, A.S. Lakshmi and R. Ravichandran. **CAST** · Prashanth – Azhagu · Anand – Kadir · Heera Rajgopal – Rajathi · Anu Agrawal – Chandralekha 'Lekha' · S.P. Balasubrahmanyam – CBI Inspector Lakshminarayanan · Salim Ghouse – Ticket Teller Vikram · Shanmuga Sundharam – Panchayat Head · Malaysia Vasudevan – Inspector · S.S. Chandran – Lorry Driver · Madan Bob – CBI Officer · Ajay Ratnam – Ashok · Thalaivasal Vijay – CBI Officer

AWARDS National Awards · *Best Choreography* Raju Sundaram · *Best Sound Effects* Sethu

FESTIVALS · University of California, Los Angeles · A Retrospective of Mani Ratnam's Films, Calcutta Film Festival, 2002

Filmography and Awards 313

Bombay · 1995 · Tamil · 130 minutes

CREDITS · Story, Screenplay, Dialogue and Direction Mani Ratnam · **Producer** S. Sriram · **Cinematography** Rajiv Menon · **Music** A.R. Rahman · **Art** Thotta Tharrani · **Lyrics** Vairamuthu · **Editing** Suresh Urs · **Song and Background Recording** H. Sridhar and S. Sivakumar · **Dialogue Recording and Mixing** V.S. Murthy and A.S. Lakshmi · **Choreography** Raju Sundaram and Prabhu Deva · **Action** Ravi Dewan. **CAST** · Arvind Swamy – Shekhar Narayanan Pillai · Manisha Koirala – Shaila Bano · Prakash Raj – Kumar · Nasser – Narayanan Pillai · Kitty – Basheer · Tinnu Anand – Sakthi Samaj Head · Master Harsha – Kabir Narayan · Master Hriday – Kamal Basheer

AWARDS National Award · *Best Film on National Integration* · *Best Editor* Suresh Urs | Filmfare Awards, 1996 · *Best Director* Mani Ratnam | Screen Videocon Award · *Best Director Award* Mani Ratnam | Cinema Express, 18th Annual Awards, 1995, Chennai · *Best Picture* · *Best Director* Mani Ratnam · *Best Actor (Special Award)* Arvind Swamy · *Best Actress (Special Award)* Manisha Koirala · *Best Playback Female Singer* K.S. Chitra · *Best Lyrics Writer* Vairamuthu | Edinburgh International Film Festival, Scotland · *Gala Award* | Jerusalem International Film Festival · *Special Mention, Wim Van Leer in Spirit of Freedom Award*

FESTIVALS · Cannes International Film Festival, 1996 · Rotterdam International Film Festival · Hawaii International Film Festival · Edinburgh Film Festival · Indomania Festival, Paris · Toronto International Film Festival · Dublin Film Festival · Augsburg Weltbild, Germany · Jerusalem International Festival · Los Angeles (Asian Pacific Film & Video Festival) · Philadelphia Festival of World Cinema, 1996 · Göteberg International Film Festival, Sweden · Filmfest DC, Washington D.C. · National Film Theatre, London · Royal Tropical Institute, Amsterdam · Cinematica Portuguese, Lisbon · Bangkok International Film Festival · Espoo Cine Film Festival, Finland · Circulo de Bellas Artes, Madrid · Festival of the South, Copenhagen · Oslo Film Festival, 2002 · A Retrospective of Mani Ratnam's Films, Calcutta Film Festival, 2002

Iruvar (The Duo) · 1997 · Tamil · 163 minutes

CREDITS · Screenplay and Direction Mani Ratnam · **Produced by** Mani Ratnam and G. Srinivasan · **Dialogue** Suhasini · **Cinematography** Santosh Sivan · **Music** A.R. Rahman · **Art** Samir Chanda · **Lyrics** Vairamuthu · **Choreography** Raghuram, Saroj Khan, Farah Khan and Brinda · **Action** B. Thyagarajan · **Costumes** Bhanu Athaiya, Priya Balu, Vani Ganapathy, Sai · **Make-up** Sundaramurthy and Vikram Gaekwad · **Editing** Suresh Urs · **Audio Design** V.S. Murthy and A.S. Lakshminarayan · **Song and Background Score Recording** H. Sridhar and S. Sivakumar · **DTS Mix** H. Sridhar. **CAST** · Mohanlal – Anand (Anandan) · Prakash Raj – Thamizhchelvan · Aishwarya Rai Bachchan – Pushpa | Kalpana · Gautami – Ramani · Tabu – Selvam's Lover · Revathy – Selvam's Wife · Nasser – Anna Durai (the party leader) · Ravi – Ramani's Manager · Madhoo – Special appearance as Madhubala Narumugaiye · Rajesh – Party Functionary · Delhi Ganesh – Anandan's Helper · Sunder Rajan – Police Commissioner

AWARDS National Award · *Best Supporting Actor* Prakash Raj · *Best Cinematographer* Santosh Sivan | Belgrade Auteur Film Festival, 1997 · *Best Film*

FESTIVALS · Toronto International Film Festival, 1997 · Stockholm International Film Festival, 1997 · University of California, Los Angeles · San Francisco Film Festival · Edmonton Film Festival · Cleveland Film Festival · Newport Festival · Hong Kong International Film Festival · Filmfest DC, Washington DC · Philadelphia Film Festival · Midnight Sun Film Festival, Finland · Durban International Film Festival · Asian American International Film Festival, New York · Indian Summer Retrospective, Locarno Film Festival · Busan International Film Festival · A Retrospective of Mani Ratnam's Films, Calcutta Film Festival, 2002

Dil Se (From the Heart) · 1998 · Hindi · 162 minutes

CREDITS · **Story, Screenplay and Direction** Mani Ratnam · **Executive Producers** Shekhar Kapur, Ramgopal Varma and Mani Ratnam · **Dialogue** Sujatha and Tigmanshu Dhulia · **Cinematography** Santosh Sivan · **Music** A.R. Rahman · **Art** Samir Chanda · **Editing** Suresh Urs · **Lyrics** Gulzar · **Choreography** Farah Khan · **Action** Allan Amin · **Audiography** H. Sridhar. **CAST** · Shah Rukh Khan – Amarkanth Varma · Manisha Koirala – Meghna · Preity Zinta – Preeti Nair · Raghuvir Yadav – Shukla · Sabyasachi Chakraborty – Terrorist group Leader · Piyush Mishra – Group Member · Krishnakant – Group Member · Aditya Srivastava – Group Member · Ken Philip – Group Member · Sanjay Mishra – Group Member · Mita Vasisht – Mita (female terrorist) · Malaika Arora – Dancer on train

AWARDS National Awards · *Best Cinematographer* Santosh Sivan · *Best Audiographer* H. Sridhar | Berlin International Film Festival · *Best Asian Film*

FESTIVALS · Tokyo International Film Festival · Festival of Auteur Films, Belgrade · Filmfest DC, Washington D.C. · Days of Delhi Festival, Moscow · Love and Anarchy, Helsinki Film Festival, 2002 · A Retrospective of Mani Ratnam's Films, Calcutta Film Festival, 2002

Alaipaayuthey (Waves) · 2000 · Tamil · 135 minutes

CREDITS · **Screenplay and Direction** Mani Ratnam · **Produced by** G. Srinivasan · **Story** R. Selvaraj and Mani Ratnam · **Cinematography** P.C. Sreeram · **Music** A.R. Rahman · **Editing** A. Sreekar Prasad · **Art** Raghavan · **Lyrics** Vairamuthu · **Mono Mix** V.S.Murthy and A.S. Lakshminarayan · **Audiography** A.S. Lakshminarayan · **DTS Mix** H. Sridhar · **Choreography** Farah Khan. **CAST** · R. Madhavan – Karthik · Shalini – Shakti · Swarnamalya – Poorni · V. Natarajan – Karthik's Father · K.P.A.C. Lalitha – Karthik's Mother · Ravi Prakash – Shakti's Father · Jayasudha – Shakti's Mother · Vivek – Shakti's Cousin · Sukumari – Shakti's Aunty · Alagam Perumal – House Owner · Arvind Swamy – Guest Appearance · Khushboo – Guest Appearance

AWARDS National Awards · *Best Cinematographer* Santosh Sivan · *Best Audiographer* H. Sridhar

FESTIVALS · Cinemaya Film Festival, 2000, New Delhi · Busan International Film festival, 2000 · Calcutta Film Festival, 2000 · Birmingham Film and Television Festival, 2000 · Institute of Contemporary Arts, London, 2000 · Tokyo Filmex-2000 · Berlin International Film Festival · Festival of South India Latitudes Villetie, Paris · Nantucket Film Festival · The World Film Festival, Quebec, Montreal · Danish Film Festival · St. Louis International Film Festival, 2000 · Session on Indian Cinema, Galway Film Fleadh, 2002 · A Retrospective of Mani Ratnam's Films, Kino Xenix Zurich, 2002 · Vancouver International Film Festival, 2002 · Mani Ratnam's Love Films, National Film Theatre, 2002, London · A Retrospective of Mani Ratnam's Films, Calcutta Film Festival, 2002

Kannathil Muthamittal (A Peck on the Cheek) · 2002 · Tamil · 136 minutes

CREDITS · **Story, Screenplay and Direction** Mani Ratnam · **Produced by** Mani Ratnam and G. Srinivasan · **Dialogues** Sujatha · **Cinematography** Ravi K. Chandran · **Music** A.R. Rahman · **Lyrics** Vairamuthu · **Art** Sabu Cyril · **Editing** A. Sreekar Prasad · **Choreography** Brinda · **Audiography** A.S. Lakshminarayan · **DTS Mix** H. Sridhar · **Action** 'Vikram' Dharma. **CAST** · R. Madhavan – Thiruchelvan · Simran – Indra · Prakash Raj – Dr Herold Vikramsinghe · Nandita Das – Shyama · J.D. Chakravarthi – Dhileepan · P.S. Keerthana – Amudha · Delhi Kumar – Ganesan · Pasupathy – Terrorist · Bala Singh – Shyama's Father · Master Suraj – Vinayan · Master Kethan – Akhilan

AWARDS Cinema Express Awards, 2003 • *Best Film* • *Best Director - Special Jury Award* • *Best Choreographer* Brinda • *Best Stunt Director* Vikram Dharma • *Best Child Artiste* Baby Keerthana • *Best Actress* Simran | Indian Film Festival of Los Angeles, 2003, Los Angeles • *Best Film of the Festival* | Jerusalem International Film Festival, 2003, Israel • *In the Spirit of Freedom Award in Memory of Wim Van Leer* | Filmfare Awards, 2003 • *Best Director* • *Best Cinematographer* Ravi K. Chandran • *Best Actress* Simran | 50th National Fim Award, New Delhi, 2003 • *Best Regional Feature Film* • *Best Music Director* A.R. Rahman • *Best Lyricist* Vairamuthu • *Best Audiographer* A.S. Lakshmi Narayan • *Best Editor* Sreekar Prasad • *Best Child Actor* Baby Keerthana | Eighth Annual Zimbabwe International Film festival • *Award for The Best Picture*

FESTIVALS • Indian Panorama, 2002, New Delhi • Cinemaya Festival, 2002, New Delhi • Inside India: Bollywood and Beyond, Walker Art Centre, Minneapolis, 2003

Yuva (Youth) • 2004 • Hindi • 169 minutes
Aayidha Ezhuthu (Three Dots) • 2004 • Tamil • 159 minutes

CREDITS *Yuva* • **Screenplay and Direction** Mani Ratnam • **Produced by** Mani Ratnam and G. Srinivasan • **Dialogue** Anurag Kashyap • **Cinematography** Ravi K. Chandran • **Music** A.R. Rahman • **Editing** A. Sreekar Prasad • **Art** Sabu Cyril • **Lyrics** Mehboob • **Sync Sound Recordist** Robert Taylor • **Sound Design** A.S. Lakshminarayan • **DTS Mix** H. Sridhar • **Choreography** Brinda • **Action** 'Vikram' Dharma

CAST *Yuva* • Ajay Devgn – Michael Mukherjee • Abhishek Bachchan – Lallan Singh • Rani Mukerji – Sashi Biswas • Vivek Oberoi – Arjun Balachandran • Kareena Kapoor – Mira • Esha Deol – Radhika • Om Puri – Prosonjit Bhattacharya • Sonu Soo

CREDITS *Aayidha Ezhuthu* • **Screenplay and Direction** Mani Ratnam • **Produced by** Mani Ratnam and G. Srinivasan • **Dialogues** Sujatha • **Cinematography** Ravi K. Chandran • **Music** A.R. Rahman • **Editing** A. Sreekar Prasad • **Art** Sabu Cyril • **Lyrics** Vairamuthu • **Sync Sound Recordist** Robert Taylor • **Sound Design** A.S. Lakshminarayan • **DTS Mix** H. Sridhar • **Choreography** Brinda • **Action** 'Vikram' Dharma

CAST *Aayidha Ezhuthu* • R. Madhavan – Inbasekar • Suriya – Michael Vasanth • Siddharth – Arjun Balakrishnan • Meera Jasmine – Sasi • Esha Deol – Gitanjali • Trisha Krishnan – Mira • Janakaraj – Esha's Uncle • Bharathiraja – Selva Nayagam • Sriman – Dillid • Gopal Singh • Anant Nag – Arjun's Father • Vijay Raaz – Lallan's Friend • Abhinav Kashyap – Trilok

FESTIVALS • Venice Film Festival (Venice Mostra) • Busan International Film Festival • Bangkok International Film Festival • Palm Springs International Film Festival • Natfilm Festival, Denmark

Guru • 2006 • Hindi • 159 minutes

CREDITS • **Screenplay and Direction** Mani Ratnam • **Produced by** Mani Ratnam and G. Srinivasan • **Dialogues** Vijay Krishna Acharya • **Cinematography** Rajiv Menon • **Music** A.R. Rahman • **Editing** A. Sreekar Prasad • **Production Design** Samir Chanda • **Lyrics** Gulzar • **Choreography** Saroj Khan and Brinda • **Costumes** Sai, Ameira Punwani, Nikhaar Dhawan, Anu Parthasarathy and Aparna Shah • **Audiography** H. Sridhar.

CAST • Mithun Chakraborty – Manikdas Gupta • Abhishek Bachchan – Gurukant Desai • Aishwarya Rai Bachchan – Sujata • R. Madhavan – Shyam Saxena • Vidya Balan – Meenakshi Gupta • Roshan Seth – Thapar • Mallika Sherawat – Jhumpa

FESTIVALS • Cannes International Film Festival • Ibiza Intenational Film Festival • Busan International Film Festival • Turks and Caicos International Film Festival • India Splendour, Los Angeles • Cairo International Film Festival • Rome International Film Festival • Stuttgart Film Festival

Raavanan · 2010 · *Tamil* · *137 minutes*
Raavan · 2010 · *Hindi* · *138 minutes*

CREDITS Raavanan · **Screenplay and Direction** Mani Ratnam · **Produced by** Mani Ratnam and Sharada Trilok · **Dialogue** Suhasini Maniratnam · **Cinematography** Santosh Sivan and V. Manikandan · **Music** A.R. Rahman · **Production Design** Samir Chanda · **Editing** Sreekar Prasad · **Lyrics** Vairamuthu · **Costumes** Sai and Sabyasachi Mukherjee · **Choreography** Ganesh Acharya, Brinda, Shobana and Astad Deboo · **Action** Shyam Kaushal and Peter Heinz · **Audiography** Tapas Nayak

CAST Raavanan · Vikram – Veera · Aishwarya Rai Bachchan – Ragini · Prithviraj – Dev · Karthik – Gyanaprakasam · Prabhu – Singarasu · Priyamani – Vennila · John Vijay – DSP Hemant · Munna – Sakkarai · Vaiyapuri – Rasathi · Ranjitha – Annam · Varsha – Poonkodi · Ashwanth Tilak – Velan · Alagamperumal – Photographer · Saravana Subbiah – Ranjith

FESTIVALS Raavanan · Venice Film Festival (Venice Mostra) · Busan International Film Festival · Montreal International Festival of New Cinema · Mahindra Indo-American Arts Council Film · 21st Stockholm International Film Festival · South Asian International Film Festival, New York

CREDITS Raavan · **Screenplay and Direction** Mani Ratnam · **Produced by** Mani Ratnam and Sharada Trilok · **Dialogue** Vijay Krishna Acharya · **Cinematography** Santosh Sivan and V. Manikandan · **Music** A.R. Rahman · **Production Design** Samir Chanda · **Editing** Sreekar Prasad · **Lyrics** Gulzar · **Costumes** Sai and Sabyasachi Mukherjee · **Choreography** Ganesh Acharya, Brinda, Shobana and Astad Deboo · **Action** Shyam Kaushal and Peter Heinz · **Audiography** Tapas Nayak

CAST Raavan · Abhishek Bachchan – Beera · Aishwarya Rai Bachchan – Ragini · Vikram – Dev · Govinda – Sanjeevani · Ravi Kisan – Mangal · Priyamani – Jamunia · Nikhil Dwivedi – Hemant · Ajay Gehi – Hariya · Pankaj Tripathi – Gulabia

AWARD Raavan APSARA Award · *Best Audiography*

FESTIVALS Raavan · Venice Film Festival (Venice Mostra) · Busan International Film Festival · Tokyo Film Festival · Mostra de Valencia Film Festival, Spain · Sitges Film Festival, Spain

Kadal (The Sea) · 2013 · *Tamil* · *160 minutes*

CREDITS · **Direction** Mani Ratnam · **Screenplay** Mani Ratnam and Jeyamohan · **Produced by** Manohar Prasad and Mani Ratnam · **Story and Dialogue** Jeyamohan · **Cinematography** Rajiv Menon · **Music** A.R. Rahman · **Editing** A. Sreekar Prasad · **Art Direction** Shashidhara Adapa · **Lyrics** Vairamuthu and Karky · **Choreography** Brinda · **Costumes** Eka Lakhani and Sai · **Audiography** Tapas Nayak · **Action** Kanal Kannan and Kecha Khamphakdee. **CAST** Arjun – Bergmans · Arvind Swamy – Father Sam Fernando · Gautham Kartik – Thomas · Thulasi – Beatrice · Lakshmi Manchu – Celina · Ponvannan – Chetty · Kalairani – Mother Superior · Master Nithish – Thomas (5 years) · Master Saravanan – Thomas (10 years)

Acknowledgements

Thanks, first, to Mani Ratnam. For the movies. For the time. For these conversations.

Thanks, next, to Sushila Ravindranath. For meeting that software guy in Chicago. For telling him there was no money in writing. For those years at the *New Indian Express*. For now.

Thanks to Sandhya Sridhar for publishing my first film review in the *Economic Times—Madras Plus*. For the ones that followed.

Thanks to Kamini Mahadevan for telling me I had a book in me. For stoically bearing with all the books I felt I didn't have in me. For the aubergines. For this book.

Thanks to Aditya Sinha for the extended time off. For not making me swipe a card at the threshold of the *New Indian Express*. For understanding that a writer's gotta do what he's gotta do. For the tequila.

Thanks to N. Radhakrishnan and *Man's World* for allowing me to dip into what I wrote all those years ago.

Thanks to Pani Sir and Barani for the pictures. For the patience.

Thanks to L. Suresh, Milind Rau and Sivakumar Ananthasubramanian for reading. For responding. For the company along the journey.

Thanks to Sunil Laxman for being editor-in-law. For all the opinions, none held back.

Thanks to Manoj and Vinod for all those review clippings when I was all those states away, wrenched for the first time from Tamil cinema. For feeding the madness that has never quite abated.

Thanks to my blog readers for making me accountable. For discussing. For sneering. For arguing. For reassuring me that I don't dispatch my words into a vacuum.

Thanks, last but not least, to my friends and family for tolerating my numerous neuroses. I love you all.

Copyright Acknowledgements

Black and white pictures

pp. 5, 19 and 21, courtesy Mahendran; p. 6, courtesy Bharathiraja; pp. 9, 11 and 13, courtesy Venus Pictures; p. 16, courtesy Geo Films; p. 22, courtesy I.V. Sasi; pp. 25 and 26, courtesy Sathya Jyothi Films; pp. 30, 32, 33, 35, 37, 39, 41, 43, 45, 47, 50, 55, 61, 65, 67, 69, 71, 72, 73, 75, 76, 79, 88, 89, 91, 93, 95, 99, 101, 103, 105, 107, 108, 109, 113, 114 and 116, courtesy Sujatha Productions (G.V. Films); p. 49, courtesy Thotta Tharrani; pp. 80, 83, 85 and 87, courtesy Bhagyalakshmi Enterprises; pp. 119, 121, 122, 125, 128, 129, 131, 133 and 134, courtesy Kavithalayaa Productions. All other pictures courtesy Madras Talkies.

Colour pictures

pp. 1, 2, 3, 4, 5, 6, 7, 12, 13, 14, 15 and 16 (above), courtesy G.V. Films; pp. 8, 9, 10, 11, 17, 18, 19, 20, 21, 22, 23, 24, 288, 289, 292, 297, 302 and 307, courtesy Madras Talkies; p. 16 (below), courtesy Kavithalayaa Productions

Index

16 Vayadhinile, 7, 10, 68

Aalayam, 125, 136
Aayidha Ezhuthu, 33, 74, 159, 162, 228, 232–33, 239, 248, 272
Aboorva Ragangal, 77, 79, 123, 188
Acharya, Vijay, 254
Agarwal, Anu, 135, 148
Agni Natchatiram, 24, 28, 34, 44–45, 57, 67–70, 72–77, 81–82, 84, 88, 98, 112, 118, 120, 197, 244, 248
Alaipaayuthey, 11, 86, 88, 118, 150, 184, 186, 188–89, 192, 195–98, 200–01, 206–07
Amala, 45
Amaradeepam, 2
Amaran, Gangai, 97
Ambareesh, 6
Ambat, Madhu, 98–99
Ambika, 29
An Evening in Paris, 171
Anand, 135
Anand, Tinnu, 63
Ananda Pictures, 20
Anjali, 84, 90, 92–100, 102, 107, 117, 125, 170, 192, 196, 200, 226, 290
Apna Desh, 2
Arjun, 294, 298
Ashokamitran, 199–200
Athaiya, Bhanu, 171
Avargal, 188
Azhagan, 124
Babbar, Arya, 263
Babu, Ramachandra, 23
Babu, Sharath, 24–25
Bachchan, Abhishek, 64, 228–29, 242, 246, 250, 259–60, 267, 276–77
Balachander, K., 4, 7, 9, 25, 28, 54, 77, 112, 123–125, 136, 186, 257
Balachander, S., 5
Balaji, Suresh, 174
Balakumaran, 201
Balan, Vidya, 262
Balasubrahmanyam, S.P., 135
Bandit Queen, 136
Bangarutha Ghani, 5
Banu, Saira, 171
Bapu, 17
Barry Lyndon, 280
Basheer, Vaikkom Muhammad, 186
Benegal, Shyam, 104
Bhanupriya, 114, 116
Bharathan, 120
Bharathiraja, 7, 9, 31, 42, 149, 198, 233
Bharati–Vasu, 7
Bhattacharya, Aditya, 113
Bobby, 203, 211
Bombay, 35, 41–42, 68, 85–86, 106, 127, 139, 144–46, 148, 150, 153–55, 158–60, 162–64, 167, 174, 184–86, 188, 275, 280, 291
Brando, Marlon, 47

Chakraborti, Mithun, 246, 249–50, 262, 264
Chanda, Samir, 171
Chandralekha, 229
Charuhasan, 9, 254
Chatriyan, 136
Chemmeen, 305
Chugtai, Ismat, 199

Damodaran, 23

Das, Nandita, 208, 223
Dasaratham, 125
Dayavan, 54, 118
de Niro, Robert, 47
Deva, Prabhu, 211
Devgn, Ajay, 228–29, 234, 241–42
Devi Films, 10
Dhulia, Tigmanshu, 186
Dil Se, 32, 56, 136, 138, 147, 172, 179–84, 189–92, 194, 197, 200, 206, 237
Dilwale Dulhaniya Le Jayenge, 197
Do Aankhen Barah Haath, 69
Dostoevsky, 303

Eenadu, 22–23
Ek Duuje Ke Liye, 112, 203

GV Films, 10
Gaayam, 136
Gandhi, 265
Ganesan, Sivaji, 3, 92, 165
Ganesh, Delhi, 46
Gauthami, 161
Geetanjali, 11, 22, 29, 69, 74, 80–82, 84, 86, 88, 90–91, 93–94, 107, 109, 112–13, 118, 147, 189, 201, 305–306
Ghouse, Salim, 135
Girija, 80
Gopalan, Lalitha, 85
Goundamani, 28
Gulzar, 188, 190, 254–55, 282
Guru, 42, 64, 86, 138, 192, 198, 222, 229, 246–48, 268, 283, 290

Haasan, Kamal, 8, 15, 44–48, 50–55, 63–64, 70, 72, 92, 106, 123, 136, 147, 186
Hum Aapke Hain Koun!, 197

Ibrahim, E.M., 33
Idhayakoyil, 1, 28–29, 31, 90
Ilaiyaraaja, 14–17, 23, 29, 40, 52–54, 70, 76, 82, 97, 116, 132, 142, 209
India Talkies, 136
Iniyengilum, 22–23

Inside Man, 190
Iru Kodugal, 257
Iruvar, 58, 86–87, 120, 136, 161–67, 171–72, 175–78, 180, 182, 189, 192, 242
Iyer, Kalpana, 174

Janakaraj, 46, 48, 51, 240
Janaki, S., 97
Janakiraman, Thi., 200
Jandhyala, 81
Jayachitra, 52
Jayasudha, 52, 203
Jeyamohan, 291, 299, 301
John, N.G., 22
Joshi, Manoj, 252

Kabir, Nasreen Munni, 282
Kadal, 289–91, 293–95, 305–08
Kajol, 184
Kakki Chattai, 82
Kalakendra, 9
Kalyana Parisu, 2
Kalyug, 104
Kanchana, 52
Kannathil Muthamittal, 55–56, 84, 90, 94, 124, 150, 208–09, 212–14, 306
Kannu, Raj, 10
Kapoor, Anil, 9, 11, 17–18, 24
Kapoor, Kareena, 235, 245
Kapur, Pankaj, 35, 134
Kapur, Shekhar, 136
Karaiyellaam Shenbagapoo, 200
Karthik, 24, 31–33, 36, 40, 67, 73, 75–76, 88
Karthika, 43, 63–65
Kashyap, Anurag, 237
Keerthana, 208
Khan, Feroz, 54, 118
Khan, Shah Rukh, 181, 184, 186
Kher, Anupam, 118
Khushboo, 148
Kieślowski, Krzysztof, 178
Kitty, 125, 158
Koirala, Manisha, 144, 147–52, 174, 181, 184
Kokila, 18

Kovaithambi, 29
Krishnamurthy, Kalki, 113
Krishnamurthy, Raja, 8
Krishnamurthy, 'Venus', 2, 17
Kshana Kshanam, 136
Kubrick, Stanley, 280
Kumar, Ashok, 15
Kumar, Manoj, 190
Kumar, Sharath, 125
Kurosawa, Akira, 87, 113, 309

Lajjo, 199
Lakshmi, 6, 11, 17, 252
Lakshminarayan, A.S., 74
Lawrence of Arabia, 126
Laxman, V.S., 20
Lean, David, 126
Lee, Spike, 190
Lenin, 14–15, 23, 201
Leone, Sergio, 47

Madhavan, 555, 64–65, 88, 150, 195, 201, 203–04, 206, 208, 223, 225, 228–30, 233, 235, 242, 306
Madhubala, 119, 124, 133, 148
Madras Talkies, 136
Mahabharata, 66, 104, 107, 109–110, 268, 289
Mahendra, Balu, 13–16, 18–19
Mahendran, 7, 9, 12, 17, 32
Mahesh, 148
Malgudi Days, 17
Mammootty, 103, 107, 248
Manmadha Leelai, 188
Mann Vaasanai, 31
Mehmood, 35
Mehta, Harshad, 138, 140
Menon, Rajiv, 147–48, 174, 264, 308
Mohan, 31, 34, 38, 96, 120, 196
Mohanlal, 161, 174, 176, 248
Moondram Pirai, 50–51
Motherland Pictures, 29
Motwane, Vikramaditya, 3
Mouna Raagam, 10–11, 20, 22, 28–29, 31–34, 36, 42, 44, 51–52, 68–69, 72, 75, 88, 118, 120, 138, 147–48, 170, 185, 192–94, 196–97, 200–01, 244, 247–48, 307
Mudaliar, Varadaraja, 44, 59, 118
Muktha Films, 51
Mullum Malarum, 12, 14, 68, 108
Murali, 24, 248
My Dear Kuttichathan, 98
Nag, Anant, 31
Nag, Shankar, 148
Nagarajan, A.P., 200
Nagarjuna, 80–81, 88
Nagesh, 3, 203
Nair, M.T. Vasudevan, 147, 164
Narayanan, A.L., 26
Nasser, 43, 64, 158
Nayakan, 24, 26, 34, 40, 42–48, 50–53, 56–60, 62–63, 66, 68–70, 72, 75, 77, 81, 85, 88, 90, 92–93, 104, 106, 112, 118, 138, 146–47, 155, 158, 168, 192–93, 197, 201, 209, 212, 247–48, 252, 283
Nenjathai Killadhey, 17, 32–33, 248
Nirosha, 76
Nizhal Nijamaagiradhu, 188
Nizhalgal, 9, 63
Novak, Kim, 174

Oberoi, Vivek, 160, 203, 228–30, 235, 242
Oru Thalai Raagam, 33

Padayottam, 112
Pagal Nilavu, 1, 24, 27–29, 31, 34, 42, 72, 82, 200, 248, 256
Pagla Kahin Ka, 44
Pallavi Anupallavi, 1, 6–8, 10–12, 15, 18, 20–24, 27–28, 31, 37–38, 44, 54, 148, 193, 211, 252
Panneer Pushpangal, 7
Pani, 81, 94, 201
Panthulu, B.R., 5
Parasakthi, 123
Paruthiveeran, 293
Pathak, Supriya, 31
Pattanathil Bootham, 2
Ponniyin Selvan, 199, 299
Prabhu, 24, 45, 67, 98, 226
Prakash, R.C., 42
Prakash, Kutty, 7

Prasad, Sreekar, 201
Prasad Labs, 201
Prashanth, 135
Prithviraj, 267, 270
Punnoose, Jijo, 112
Puri, Om, 233–34
Raakh, 113
Raavan[an], 55–56, 60, 62–63, 66, 85, 88, 110, 128, 153–54, 189, 191, 229–31, 236–37, 254, 256, 267–68, 275, 280, 290-91, 293
Radha, 1, 29
Radhika, 25
Raghuvaran, 64, 89, 96, 226
Rahman, A.R., 40–41, 132, 141–43, 147, 154, 168, 188, 209, 244, 254, 282, 285, 291, 305
Rai, Aishwarya, 151, 161, 174, 146, 252, 259, 267, 272
Raj, Prakash, 55, 161, 173, 223
Rajaparvai, 15
Rajashri, 201
Rajgopal, Heera, 135
Rajinikanth, 65, 103, 106–09, 111, 114, 117, 248
Ramachandran, M.G., 164–65, 168
Raman, 5
Ramani, Roja, 6
Ramayana, 268, 278, 289
Ran, 309
Rao, Singeetham Srinivasa, 15
Rashomon, 241
Ratnam, Mani,
  and art, 280
  and art direction, 171
  and Hindi, 233, 235–37
  and his own films, 182–83, 286–87
  and intervals, 238
  and Sri Lanka, 211–216, 218, 221–23
  and trains, 172–74
  comedy tracks, 28
  communal issues, 156–57
  decision to make films, 6
    parents' reaction, 8
  film and politics, 162–67, 176
  first film, 16–20

Hatari, 3
Jungle Cat, 3
learning the ropes, 20–22
locations, 54, 188
myths about, 56–57
on censorship, 145–47, 178
on good and evil, 66
on stereotypes, 187
on style, 77, 79
posters, 37
purpose of films, 158–59
reading up on film-making, 15
shifting gears, 180
shooting dance sequences, 27
shooting techniques, 112, 168, 274
studies, 4–5, 7
thoughts, 38, 56, 180–81, 211–15, 258–59
use of music, 53, 81–84, 141–43, 209, 211–12, 253, 256
watching films, 2–4
with actors, 102, 150–51, 182
working with children, 91–93, 97, 100
working with Suhasini, 198–99
writing screenplays, 152–53
Rathnam, S.G., 2
Revathy, 24–25, 31, 38, 89, 99, 161, 184, 196, 248
Roja, 34, 42, 56, 68, 72–74, 88, 112, 119–20, 124–34, 136, 138, 141–42, 147, 154–56, 160, 185–86, 198, 200, 224, 230, 240, 270, 275, 283, 290

Saathiya, 118
Sadma, 50
Sagara Sangamam, 46
Sankar, Udaya, 6
Saranya, 48, 50–52
Sasi, I.V., 22
Sathya, 47
Sathyaraj, 24, 26, 42, 248
Saving Private Ryan, 309
Selvakumar, Peter, 14
Selvaraj, R., 198
Seth, Roshan, 265

Shalini, 188, 195, 198, 201, 203–04
Shamili, 89, 99–100
Shankar, Gowri, 10
Shankar, Ravi, 5–6, 17
Shantaram, V., 69
Shashi, Mudra, 147
Sherawat, Mallika, 251–52
Shivanand, 18
Shobana, 103, 111, 248
Sholay, 73
Siddharth, 228, 230, 235, 242
Simran, 208, 306
Sivan, Santosh, 132, 174, 201
Sreeram, P.C., 7, 10, 15, 31, 36, 40, 45, 57, 74–75, 98–99, 120, 140, 188, 280
Sridevi, 50
Srinath, 6
Srinath, Rohit, 17–18
Srinivasan, 'Muktha', 44
Sriram, 136
Srividya, 103
Subhash, K., 136
Suhasini, 17, 198, 214
Sujatha 121, 186, 198, 200, 223, 230
Sujatha Productions, 10, 136
Sumithra, 52
Sundaram, 211–12
Suraj, 2
Suresh, 7
Suriya, 228–30, 234, 240–43
Swamy, Arvind, 888, 103, 114, 119–22, 133, 144, 152, 156, 270, 294, 297

Tabu, 161, 173–74
Tagore, Sharmila, 171
Tajmahal, 198
Taylor, Bob, 239
Thalapathy, 26, 68, 74, 82, 88, 103, 106, 110, 112–114, 116, 118, 126, 132, 155, 167, 186, 248, 268
Tharrani, Thotta, 14–15, 36, 54, 58, 171
The Great Escape, 131
Thevar Magan, 120
Thillana Mohanambal, 200

Thiruda Thiruda, 69, 72, 102, 117, 135–36, 138, 140–41, 147–48, 160–62, 305
Thulasi, 295, 298, 306
Thyagarajan, 'Sathya Jyothi', 23
Tik Tik Tik, 42
Trisha, 235, 245

Udaan, 3
Udhiri Pookkal, 7, 10, 15
Ulagam Suttrum Vaaliban, 164
Umapathy, 67
Unaru, 1, 22, 27, 33, 147, 248
Uthamaputhiran, 2

Vaaname Illai, 124
Vairale, Kiran, 11, 17–18, 148
Vairamuthu, 143, 282
Vamsa Vriksham, 17
Vansh, 118
Varma, Ram Gopal, 73, 118, 120, 123, 129, 136, 153
Varumayin Niram Sivappu, 54
Veerappan, 28
Venkateswaran, G., 9–10, 106–07
Venus Studios, 2, 15, 99
Vertigo, 174
Vijay, John, 176
Vijayakumar, 67, 118
Vikram, 136
Vishnuvardhan, 6
Viswaroopam, 306

Yuva, 33, 74, 88, 159, 162, 204, 228–31, 233, 235–37, 239, 248, 272

Zinta, Preity, 181, 185